CORPORATIONS

CORPORATIONS
Second Edition

ROBERT W. HAMILTON
University of Texas School of Law

BLACK LETTER SERIES

WEST PUBLISHING CO.
ST. PAUL, MINN.
1986

COPYRIGHT © 1982 By WEST PUBLISHING CO.
COPYRIGHT © 1986 By WEST PUBLISHING CO.
      50 West Kellogg Boulevard
      P.O. Box 64526
      St. Paul, Minnesota 55164–0526

Library of Congress Cataloging-in-Publication Data

Hamilton, Robert W., 1931–
    Corporations.

    (Black letter series)
    1. Corporation law—United States—Outlines, syllabi, etc. I. Title. II. Series.

KF1414.3.H348 1986   346.73'066   86–13127

ISBN 0–314–99069–0   347.30666

    3rd Reprint—1989

PUBLISHER'S PREFACE

This "Black Letter" is designed to help a law student recognize and understand the basic principles of law covered in a law school course. It can be used both as a study aid when preparing for the course and as a review of the subject matter when studying for an examination.

Experienced law school teachers who are recognized national authorities on the subject covered write each "Black Letter."

The law has been succinctly stated by the author of this "Black Letter." In addition, the exceptions to the rules are stated in the text. The rules and exceptions have purposely been condensed to facilitate quick review and easy recollection. For an in-depth study of a point of law, citations to major student texts are given.

If the subject covered by this text is a code or code related course, the code section or rule is set forth and discussed wherever applicable.

FORMAT

The format of this "Black Letter" has been specially designed for review. First, it is recommended that the entire text be studied, and supplemented, if deemed necessary, by the use of the student texts cited. In addition, a number of other features are included to help you understand the subject matter and prepare for your examination. They are:

Capsule Summary: This is a study outline at the beginning of the book which can be used as a quick review of the subject both before and after studying the main body of the text. The headings in the capsule summary follow the main outline of the "Black Letter."

Analysis: This feature, at the beginning of each section, is designed to give a quick summary of a particular section to help you recall the subject matter and to help you determine which areas need the most extensive review.

Examples: This feature is designed to illustrate, through fact situations, the law just stated. This, we believe, should help you analytically approach a question on the examination.

Short Questions and Answers: This feature is designed to help you spot and recognize issues in the examination. We feel that issue recognition is a major ingredient in successfully writing an examination.

Essay Questions and Sample Answers: This feature is designed to familiarize you with the primary type of question asked on an examination. In addition to the exam questions for each area of the subject covered, there is a complete law school examination near the end of the book. This is provided so you can practice writing a complete examination prior to taking the final examination in this course.

Glossary: This feature is designed to refamiliarize you with the meaning of a particular legal term. We believe that the recognition of words of art used in an examination helps you to better analyze the question. In addition, when writing an examination you should know the precise definition of a word of art you intend to use.

We believe that the materials in this "Black Letter" will facilitate your study of a law school course and assure success in writing examinations not only for the course but for the bar examination. We wish you success.

The Publisher

SUMMARY OF CONTENTS

TABLE OF CONTENTS

CAPSULE SUMMARY

I. CORPORATION LAW IN GENERAL

A. "CORPORATION" DEFINED

A corporation is a type of legal institution or concept that defines relationships among people. Several different theories have been proposed to describe these relationships.

1. Entity Theory

A corporation can be most readily envisioned as an artificial, fictitious entity created for the purpose of conducting a business. In this view, the basic elements of a corporation are:

    a.   The artificial entity has the power to conduct its business entirely in its own name.

    b.   The artificial entity is formed by a grant of authority by a government agency.

    c.   The artificial entity must be generally recognized as such by the creating state, the Federal Government, and private citizens who deal with the corporation.

    d.   The artificial entity in a fundamental sense is a fiction. Courts may refuse to follow the artificial entity analysis to its logical

1

conclusions, if it leads to fraudulent or significantly unfair consequences, frustration of clearly defined statutory policies, or other undesirable results.

2. Concession Theory
A second theory of corporateness is that a corporation is a "grant" or "concession" from the state. The theory is based on the role of the state in the formation of the corporation.

3. Contract Theory
A third theory of corporateness is that the charter of a corporation represents a contract (a) between the state and the corporation, or (b) between the corporation and its shareholders, or (c) among the shareholders themselves. This theory is likely to surface in the current context in disputes between different classes of shareholders, or in disputes in which one class of shareholders claims that the class is being discriminated against in some way.

4. Nexus of Contractual Relationships
A fourth theory of corporateness is a "nexus of contracts." This theory, utilized by economists for analytic purposes, rejects the notion that the shareholders are the ultimate owners of the corporation and treats them instead as contractual providers of capital in anticipation of receiving a desired return. A corporation can therefore be analyzed as a "nexus of contracts."

B. CONSTITUTIONAL INCIDENTS OF THE CORPORATE "PERSONALITY"
A corporation is entitled to some but not all of the constitutional protections available to individual persons. For example, a corporation is not a citizen of a state or of the United States for purposes of the privileges and immunities clause, but a corporation has rights of free speech which may not be restricted as such by state statute. A corporation also does not have a privilege against self incrimination, but is protected against deprivations of property without due process of law and is entitled to the constitutional right of equal protection of the law.

C. SOURCES OF LAW
The law of corporations is derived from several sources.

1. State Incorporation Statutes
Every state has a general incorporation statute. Two sources of statutes have been particularly influential in modernizing and liberalizing the state statutes.

a. The Model Business Corporation Act prepared and maintained by the Committee on Corporate Laws of the Section on Corporation Banking, and Business Law of the American Bar Association; and

b. The Delaware General Corporation Law.

2. State Common Law Principles
Most common law principles are interstitial in nature in the law of corporations. They supply supplementary principles when the statutes are silent or they construe statutory provisions.

3. Federal Statutes
A significant portion of the law applicable to publicly held corporations is federal in origin, based on the Securities Exchange Act of 1934 and the Securities Act of 1933, and rules promulgated thereunder.

4. Federal Common Law
A general federal jurisprudence of corporations does not exist, and federal law applied to corporations is more or less firmly grounded in the securities acts and regulations.

D. FUNCTIONAL CLASSIFICATION OF CORPORATIONS
The basic distinction underlying much of the law of corporations is between the closely held corporation and the publicly held corporation.

1. Definition of a Closely Held Corporation
A closely held corporation is a corporation with most of the following attributes:

a. It has a few shareholders, all or most of whom are usually active in the management of the business;

b. There is no public market for its shares;

c. Its shares are subject to one or more restrictions on transfer; and

d. It has never registered a public distribution of shares under the federal or state securities acts.

2. Definition of a Publicly Held Corporation
A publicly held corporation is a corporation with most of the following attributes:

a. Some of its shares are held by members of the general public and the overall number of shareholders is usually large;

b. There is a public market for its shares which may be on a securities exchange or among brokers "over the counter;"

c. The corporation is subject to reporting and disclosure requirements under the securities acts;

d. It has made a distribution of shares to members of the general public that has been registered under the Securities Act of 1933.

3. **Theoretical Significance of the Distinction Between Closely Held and Publicly Held Corporations**
The most important distinctions between closely held and publicly held corporations are the number of shareholders and the marketability of their shares.

a. The presence or absence of a public market for the corporation's shares is a most important difference between the two types of corporations. Because of the nonexistence of a market for shares in the closely held corporation, a minority shareholder may be "locked in" to an unsalable asset. In contrast, in a publicly held corporation a dissatisfied shareholder can always sell his or her shares on the public market.

b. A second major difference is that in a closely held corporation, most of the shareholders are likely to be employed by or earn their livelihood through the corporation's business while in a publicly held corporation, most of the shareholders are not connected with management and have only a limited say in the policies adopted by the corporation.

c. A third difference is that the presence of public shareholders unconnected with the business of a publicly held corporation is thought to present a strong case for governmental regulation of internal aspects of a public corporation's affairs.

II. FORMATION OF CORPORATIONS

A. SELECTION OF STATE OF INCORPORATION
The first question that must be resolved in forming a corporation is what state should be the state of incorporation.

1. **Local or Closely Held Businesses**
For such businesses, the choice of the state of incorporation usually comes down to the state in which business is principally conducted or a state with a "liberal" statute, such as Delaware.

2. Interstate or National Business

For such businesses, incorporation in any one of several states is usually feasible. Most large publicly held corporations are interstate or national in character and may incorporate in any one of the 50 states. Many such businesses incorporate in a "liberal" jurisdiction, usually Delaware, for the following reasons:

a. A "liberal" statute is designed to simplify the problems faced by management in conducting business under that statute;

b. There are a large number of judicial decisions in Delaware construing the statute so that uncertainties are minimized;

c. There is a sophisticated judiciary and bar in Delaware familiar with corporation problems and corporation laws; and

d. There is a "climate" favorable to corporations and business in Delaware that may be reflected in prompt amendments to the statute if unsuspected problems arise.

e. The Delaware judicial system has been accused in the past of favoring management in its decisions. Recent Delaware cases do not uniformly support this accusation.

B. VARIATIONS IN STATUTORY REQUIREMENTS AND NOMENCLATURE

1. Statutory Requirements

To form a corporation, it is essential to comply with the specific statutory requirements of the state chosen for the state of incorporation.

a. There is a surprising degree of uniformity and consistency in most modern statutes.

b. Most states simply require a filing with a state official and nothing more. Some states, such as Delaware, also require a local filing in the county in which the registered office is located. Other states, such as Arizona, also require a public advertisement in a newspaper of general circulation of the fact of incorporation.

c. Variations among the states may exist with respect to filing fees, franchise taxes, stock issuance or transfer taxes, and similar items.

2. Nomenclature

The Revised Model Business Corporation Act nomenclature is followed in most states. In this nomenclature, the document filed with the secretary of state is called "articles of incorporation" and acceptance of the filing is evidenced by the issuance of a fee receipt. Many states require the secretary of state also to issue a formal document called a "certificate of incorporation" to evidence the acceptance of the filing.

C.   DOCUMENTS FILED IN THE OFFICE OF THE SECRETARY OF STATE

The basic filing requirement is that articles of incorporation which conform to statutory requirements must be filed with the Secretary of State and be accompanied by the appropriate filing fee.

1.   Procedure Under Older Statutes

Under most older state statutes, duplicate originals or an original and a copy of the articles of incorporation, must be filed.

   a.   "Duplicate originals" means that both copies must be manually executed with original notarial seals and the like.

   b.   If the articles conform to the statute, the Office of the Secretary of State attaches the certificate of incorporation to the copy or duplicate original and returns both documents to the incorporators or their representative.

   c.   A receipt for the filing fee is also usually attached.

2.   Procedure Under Newer Statutes

To reduce the problems of handling many pieces of paper, some states authorize the filing of only a single original executed copy of the articles; the incorporators receive only a receipt for the filing fee as the sole evidence of incorporation.

3.   Procedure Under the Revised Model Business Corporation Act

The RMBCA eliminates requirements that documents be verified or acknowledged; the executing officer must simply designate the capacity in which he signs. One exact or conformed copy of the executed document must be filed with the document; the secretary of state attaches the fee receipt or acknowledgement of receipt to the copy and returns it to the filing party.

D.   INCORPORATORS

Articles of incorporation are executed by one or more persons called "incorporators."

1.   Modern Relaxation of Requirements

Since the role of incorporators is a formal one without significant responsibilities, duties, or liabilities, virtually all states have simplified the requirements.

a.   Only a single incorporator is required. There are usually no age or residency requirements.

b.   Requirements of oaths, verifications and seals have been eliminated in the RMBCA and the statutes of some states.

c.   Incorporators execute the articles of incorporation and receive back the certificate of incorporation. They generally serve no other function.

d.   In some states, the incorporators meet to complete the formation of the corporation. Under the RMBCA the meeting of incorporators is an optional method of completing the formation of the corporation.

2. Dummy Incorporators
Since incorporators have no substantive responsibilities in most states, the practice is widespread of using a "dummy" incorporator, i.e. a person unconnected with the future business who is willing to allow his or her name to be used as an incorporator.

E. CONTENT OF THE ARTICLES OF INCORPORATION

1. Mandatory Requirements
a.   State statutes generally require the following *minimum* information to appear in every articles of incorporation:

1)   The name of the corporation;

2)   Its duration;

3)   Its purpose or purposes;

4)   The securities it is authorized to issue;

5)   The name of its registered agent and the address of its registered office;

6)   The names and addresses of its initial board of directors;

7)   The name and address of the incorporator or incorporators.

b.   Most corporations elect the duration to be "perpetual" and their purposes to be "the conduct of any lawful business."

c.   The RMBCA provides that every corporation automatically has a "perpetual" duration and a purpose to "conduct any lawful business" unless a narrower duration or purposes clause is inserted.

2.   Discretionary Provisions

State statutes usually provide that certain additional provisions may be included in the articles of incorporation at the election of the corporation.

a.   Some state statutes provide that corporations may elect to eliminate or modify specified rules of fundamental corporate governance by specific provision in the articles of incorporation.

b.   Many other discretionary provisions may be placed either in the articles or the bylaws.

c.   State statutes generally make it unnecessary for corporations to include any provisions relating to corporate powers. References to specific powers may be helpful where the state statute is silent or unclear on whether corporations generally possess the specific power.

F.   THE CORPORATE NAME

A corporate name must usually (i) contain a reference to the corporate nature of the entity, (ii) not be the same or deceptively similar to a name already in use or reserved for use, and (iii) not imply that a corporation is engaged in a business in which corporations may not lawfully engage. The Revised Model Business Corporation Act substitutes the test of "distinguishable upon the records of the Secretary of State" for the "same or deceptively similar" test.

1.   Name Uniqueness

The requirement that each corporation have a unique name is primarily to avoid confusion in such matters as sending tax notices and naming defendants in law suits or to prevent unfair competition. Statutes prohibiting the use of "deceptively similar" names may involve an unfair competition standard as well as name confusion.

2.   Reservation of Name

An available name may be "reserved" for a limited period of time (usually 120 days) for a small fee. The reservation of a name permits the preparation of corporate documents, ordering of stationery, etc., with the assurance that the proposed name will be available if the articles are filed within the period the name is reserved.

3.   Registration of Name

Many states allow a foreign corporation not transacting business in the state to register its name with the Secretary of State to assure that no local business will obtain the right to use its name. Registration of a name thus protects the foreign corporation's good will reflected in its name and its option to later expand its operations into the state under its current name.

4. Use of Assumed Name by Foreign Corporation

Corporations generally may adopt assumed names. Also, a foreign corporation that has not previously registered its name may discover that its own name is not available when it seeks to qualify to transact business in a new state. In this situation, the statutes of many states require the foreign corporation to qualify to transact business under an assumed name in the new state and file an assumed name certificate with the Secretary of State.

G. PERIOD OF DURATION

Modern statutes authorize the corporation to have "perpetual" existence. It is almost never desirable to create a corporation with a shorter period of existence because to do so creates the risk that the corporate existence may expire without renewal with uncertain rights and liabilities of participants thereafter.

H. PURPOSES

Most modern statutes authorize very general purposes clauses, e.g. "The purpose of the corporation is to engage in any lawful business."

1. History of Purposes Clauses

The nature of purposes clauses has evolved over a long period of time, reflecting varying attitudes of mistrust toward the corporation. They were formerly of much greater importance than they are today.

    a.   In the earliest period all corporations were formed by special legislative enactment. In effect, each purposes clause was separately negotiated.

    b.   In the nineteenth and early twentieth centuries, under the earliest general incorporation statutes, corporations could only be formed for a single limited and specific purpose.

    c.   State statutes were modernized to permit corporations to include any number of specific purposes clauses. Many corporations adopted the practice of including tens or even hundreds of specific purposes clauses routinely in every articles of incorporation. This practice quickly eliminated any significance the purposes clauses might have.

        d.   The modern practice of allowing corporations to have general purposes is a logical simplification of the practice of using multiple purposes clauses.

        e.   Today, there is little or no reason to have a purposes clause at all, and doctrines based on limited purposes clauses, such as ultra vires or implied purposes, have little modern relevance.

    2.   **Limited Purposes Clause as a Planning Device**
        A limited purposes clause may be used today as a planning device or as a protection for investors.

I. SECURITIES
The securities a corporation is authorized to issue must be described in the articles of incorporation.

J. INITIAL CAPITALIZATION
Some states require that a corporation have a minimum amount of capitalization before it may commence business. One thousand dollars is the most common amount.

    1.   **Current Trend**
        The modern trend is to eliminate such requirements because they are arbitrary and do not provide any meaningful protection to creditors.

    2.   **Failure to Meet Minimum Capital Requirements**
        Directors are usually made personally liable if business is commenced without the required minimum capital.

        a.   This liability is usually limited to the difference between minimum required capitalization and the amount of capital actually contributed.

        b.   A few state statutes have been construed to impose unlimited liability on directors for all debts incurred before the minimum capitalization was paid in.

K. REGISTERED OFFICE AND REGISTERED AGENT
The registered office and registered agent at that office must be specified in the articles of incorporation. They serve the purposes of providing a location where the corporation may be found and a person on whom process may be served.

L. CORPORATE POWERS
Every state statute lists general powers that every corporation possesses. It is unnecessary and undesirable to list some or all of these powers in the articles

of incorporation. The Revised Model Business Corporation Act provides in addition to a list of general powers, that every corporation "has the same powers as an individual to do all things necessary or convenient to carry out its business and affairs."

1. **General Powers**

The general powers possessed by corporations under most modern statutes include:

   a.   To sue and be sued;

   b.   To have a corporate seal;

   c.   To purchase, receive, lend, sell, invest, convey and mortgage personal and real property;

   d.   To make contracts, borrow and lend money, and guarantee the indebtedness of third persons;

   e.   To conduct its business within or without the state;

   f.   To elect or appoint officers or agents, define their duties, fix their compensation, and provide pension, profit sharing, and stock option plans;

   g.   To make charitable, scientific or education contributions or donations for the public welfare;

   h.   To be a partner or manager of a partnership or other venture;

   i.   To make and alter bylaws for the administration and regulation of its internal affairs.

2. **Acts in Excess of Powers**

If a corporation does an act which it does not have power to do, it is usually considered to be acting ultra vires.

3. **Partial Enumeration of Powers**

The danger of a partial enumeration of statutory powers in the articles is that a negative inference may be drawn that the inclusion of some enumerated powers implies the exclusion of unenumerated ones.

M.   ULTRA VIRES

"Ultra vires" means beyond the scope of the powers of a corporation. It is used to describe acts that exceed either the stated purposes or powers of the corporation.

1. **The Common Law Ultra Vires Doctrine**
   The early common law view was that an ultra vires transaction was void since the corporation simply lacked the power to enter into the transaction. Over time this view softened, but the common law doctrine often led to unfair or unpredictable consequences.

2. **Current Trends**
   Four factors have greatly reduced the importance of the ultra vires doctrine:

   a. The use of multiple purposes clauses or general purposes clauses.

   b. The broadening of the general statutory powers of corporations.

   c. The power of a corporation to amend its articles of incorporation in order to broaden its purposes after an ultra vires issue was raised.

   d. Statutes treating the subject of ultra vires.

3. **Statutory Treatment of the Ultra Vires Doctrine**
   Modern statutes sharply limit the ultra vires principle. Under these statutes, ultra vires may be raised only:

   a. In a suit by a shareholder against the corporation to enjoin an ultra vires act, if all affected parties are present in the litigation and the court finds that it is equitable to enjoin the ultra vires act;

   b. In a proceeding by the corporation against incumbent or former officers or directors of the corporation;

   c. In a proceeding by the state attorney general to dissolve the corporation or enjoin the ultra vires act.

4. **Modern Areas of Ultra Vires Concern**
   Ultra vires issues may continue to arise in some states on the question whether or not the corporation has power to enter into the following acts:

   a. Making charitable or political contributions;

   b. Granting employee fringe benefits;

   c. Entering into partnerships;

   d. Acquiring shares of other corporations;

   e. Guaranteeing indebtedness of others; and

   f. Making loans to officers or directors.

N.   COMPLETION OF THE FORMATION OF THE CORPORATION
The filing of articles of incorporation is only the first step in forming a corporation.

1.   Additional Steps
Lawyers are expected to take additional steps to complete the formation of the corporation, including:

a.   Prepare bylaws;

b.   Prepare minutes of the various organizational meetings, including waivers of notices or consents to action without formal meetings;

c.   Obtain share certificates and make sure they are properly prepared and issued;

d.   Prepare shareholders' agreement, if any;

e.   Generally oversee the preparation and execution of the various forms, certificates and other documents;

f.   Obtain taxpayer identification numbers;

g.   Open a bank account for the corporation.

2.   Consequences of Failure to Complete Formation
The consequences of a partial formation of a corporation usually arise in the context of a suit against the officers, directors, or shareholders to hold them liable for an obligation incurred in the name of the corporation. A number of cases hold that no such personal liability is created so long as articles of incorporation were filed. If personal liability is imposed despite the filing of articles of incorporation, the result is likely to be analyzed as a case involving:

a.   Promoters' liability;

b.   Piercing the corporate veil; or

c.   The failure to comply with a mandatory condition subsequent.

Personal liability is usually (but not invariably) imposed if no articles of incorporation were filed.

III. PREINCORPORATION TRANSACTIONS

A.   PROMOTERS
"Promoters" are persons who assist in putting together a new business. These individuals serve important social and economic functions.

1.   **Basic Function of Promoters**
     In promoting a new venture, promoters:

     a.   Arrange for the necessary business assets and personnel so that the new business may function effectively.

     b.   Obtain the necessary capital to finance the venture.

     c.   Complete the formation of the corporation.

2.   **Location of Discussion of Promoters in this Outline**
     Part III, B of the outline deals exclusively with problems of contracts entered into by promoters in arranging for the necessary business assets and personnel so that the business may function. Part IV discusses the problems of raising capital. Part III, C discusses the fiduciary duties of promoters.

B.   PROMOTERS CONTRACTS
Promoters may enter into contracts on behalf of the venture being promoted either before or after articles of incorporation have been filed. Most problems are created by preincorporation contracts. The legal consequences of these contracts will vary depending in part on the form of the contract itself.

1.   **Contracts Entered in the Name of a Corporation "To be Formed"**
     A contract of this type shows on its face that the corporation has not yet been formed. A typical form of execution is "ABC Corporation, a corporation to be formed."

     a.   Such a contract can be analyzed in several different ways.

           1)   The most common analysis is that the promoter is personally liable on the contract and will remain severally liable with the corporation if it is subsequently formed and adopts the contract. Under certain circumstances the promoter may be entitled to indemnification from the corporation.

           2)   A second possible analysis is that the promoter is personally liable only until the corporation is formed and adopts the contract. This is an example of a "novation."

           3)   A third possible analysis is that no one is liable on the contract until the corporation is formed and adopts it.

           4)   A final possible analysis is that the promoter is not personally liable on the contract but has agreed to use his best efforts to cause the corporation to be formed and to adopt the contract.

The promoter may be liable on his promise if no steps are taken to form the corporation even though he is not liable on the contract itself.

b.   The test of which of these four alternatives is the appropriate one in a specific case depends on the "intention" of the parties. Most cases find the promoter personally liable on one theory or another.

2.   Contracts Entered Into in the Corporate Name

These cases differ from the preceding cases in that the contract is entered into in the corporate name and one or both parties erroneously believe the corporation has been formed.

a.   The common law developed concepts of corporations *de facto* and corporations *de jure*. The finding of the existence of either a *de jure* or a *de facto* corporation absolved the promoter of liability. However, the state could attack a *de facto* corporation.

1)   A corporation *de jure* had sufficiently complied with the incorporation requirements so that a corporation was legally in existence for all purposes. Compliance with all *mandatory* statutory requirements gave rise to a *de jure* corporation; failure to comply with less important *directory* requirements did not affect the *de jure* status.

2)   A corporation *de facto* is a corporation that is partially but defectively or incompletely formed. These corporations are immune from attack by everyone but the State.

(i)   The traditional test of *de facto* existence is threefold:

(A)   There is a valid statute under which the corporation might incorporate;

(B)   There has been a "good faith" or "colorable" attempt to comply with the statute; and

(C)   There has been actual use of the corporate privilege.

(ii)   Modern statutes often substitute a more objective test for the common law *de facto/de jure* distinction. Several state statutes provide that individuals who act as a corporation without authority to do so (before the issuance of the certificate of incorporation) should be liable as partners.

(A) Some courts have found the issuance of the certificate of incorporation to be the "bright line" and have found personal liability on all precertificate obligations.

(B) Some courts have held passive investors not personally liable on transactions entered into before the certificate of incorporation is issued.

(C) In some states the argument may be made that the common law concept of the *de facto* corporation may continue to exist because the statute contains provisions making the issuance of the certificate of incorporation conclusive of the existence of the corporation but does not refer to persons "who assume to act" as corporations.

(iii) The Revised Model Business Corporation Act provides that "all persons purporting to act as or on behalf of a corporation, knowing there was no incorporation under this act," are jointly and severally liable for liabilities incurred.

b. Some cases have applied a concept of "corporation by estoppel" that appears to be potentially independent of modern statutes and the common law *de facto* corporation concept.

1) The concept of "corporation by estoppel" is actually "reverse estoppel" because the person representing the existence of a corporation is permitted to escape liability while the person who relied on the representation is being estopped from disputing the representation.

2) Only persons who honestly but erroneously believe that articles have been filed should be able to take advantage of the corporation by estoppel concept since the concept, if carried to its logical conclusion, would permit shareholders to obtain the benefits of limited liability simply by consistently representing the corporation's existence.

3) The doctrine of corporation by estoppel is usually applied when a defendant seeks to avoid liability on the theory that the plaintiff is not a lawful corporate entity.

c. Unpredictability of result and irreconcilable precedents often result in this area of the law of corporations.

1) Under the common sense approach there should be unlimited personal liability for all obligations entered into in the corporate name before the corporation was formed.

2) Some courts have accepted the argument that where third persons deal on a corporate basis with an apparent corporation, they receive a "windfall" if they may subsequently hold other persons liable. These courts have refused to impose personal liability even in circumstances where no steps toward incorporation have been taken.

3.   Liability of Corporation on Promoter's Contracts
A corporation is not automatically liable on promoters' contracts; the newly formed corporation may accept or reject all preincorporation contracts.

a.   An acceptance of a preincorporation contract by a corporation is an "adoption" of that contract.

b.   This rule allows subsequent investors in some cases to review promoters' contracts and reject those that seem improvident.

c.   Adoption may be express or implied. A recovery in quasi contract will normally be available where benefits are received even though the contract is not adopted.

d.   Mere existence of the corporation does not constitute an "adoption" of a contract relating to services leading to the formation of the corporation.

4.   Relationship Between Promoter's Liability and Corporate Adoption
Corporate adoption of a contract will generally release the promoter from further liability only if the parties agree that a novation will occur.

a.   Williston's position is that a novation is almost always contemplated.

b.   Under this "complete novation" theory, promoters may form "shell corporations" solely to escape personal liability even after it is clear that the promotion will fail.

C.   PROMOTER'S FIDUCIARY DUTIES
Copromoters of a venture owe fiduciary duties to each other, to the corporation, and to subsequent financial interests in the venture.

1. **The Corporation as the Beneficiary**
   After the corporation is formed it may obtain from the promoter any benefits or rights the promoter obtained on its behalf.

2. **Copromoters as the Beneficiary**
   Any benefits or rights one promoter obtained must be shared with the co-promoters.

3. **Subsequent Investors as the Beneficiary**
   The major issue relating to promoters' fiduciary duties is the extent to which subsequent shareholders or investors may be protected by such duties.

   a. Two rules have been established. The "Massachusetts Rule" allows the corporation to attack an earlier transaction if the subsequent sale to public investors was contemplated when the earlier transaction was entered into. The "Federal Rule" will not allow the corporation to attack the earlier transaction if all the shareholders at the time consented to the transaction.

   b. The "Massachusetts Rule" has been more popular than the "Federal Rule."

   c. The real issue in this type of case is the lack of full disclosure about the promoters' transaction.

   d. Many cases of this nature have arisen in the modern era as "disclosure" or "securities fraud" cases rather than as "promoters fraud" cases.

4. **Creditors as the Beneficiary**
   Some cases have applied fiduciary concepts to protect creditors against unfair or fraudulent transactions by promoters.

D.   AGREEMENTS TO FORM CORPORATIONS
A preincorporation agreement to create a corporation is enforceable in the same ways as any other contract. The preincorporation agreement or contract will normally not survive the formation of the corporation unless specific and precise provisions to that effect are included.

E.   PREINCORPORATION SUBSCRIPTIONS
A preincorporation subscription is a promise by a person to purchase a specific number of shares of a corporation at a specific price after the corporation is formed. Under modern statutes these promises are irrevocable for a stated period even if they are not supported by consideration. Statutes also require subscribers to be uniformly treated after the corporation is formed.

IV.   PIERCING THE CORPORATE VEIL

The phrase "piercing the corporate veil" (PCV) is a metaphor to describe the cases in which a court refuses to recognize the separate existence of a corporation.

A.   TRADITIONAL TESTS

The traditional tests for PCV are to "prevent fraud" or to "achieve equity." Other courts have applied a concept of "shareholder domination" or "alter ego" as the basis for PCV.

1.   One Person Corporations

One or two person corporations are treated no differently than other corporations in PCV cases.

2.   Motive

The separate corporate existence may be recognized even though the corporation was formed solely to avoid unlimited liability.

3.   Brother-Sister Corporations

The separate existence of related corporations, i. e., corporations with common shareholders, may be ignored so that the two corporations are treated as a single entity.

4.   Inactive Shareholders

Active shareholders may be held liable for corporate debts on a PCV theory while inactive shareholders may be found not to be liable.

5.   Estoppel Against Shareholders

PCV is generally only available against the corporation itself or its shareholders and may not be used affirmatively by them.

B.   INDIVIDUAL SHAREHOLDER LIABILITY FOR CORPORATE DEBTS

1.   Consensual Transactions

In most cases involving *contract* claims the third person should not be able to PCV and hold the shareholders personally liable because he has voluntarily dealt with the corporation and "assumed the risk." PCV may apply in consensual cases, however, where the corporation is being used in an inequitable way.

2.   Nonconsensual Transactions

In most cases involving nonconsensual transactions (usually torts) courts are more willing to accept PCV arguments because there is no element of voluntary dealing. To recognize the separate existence of a nominally capitalized corporation in such a case may result in an unacceptable shift of the risk of loss.

3. Failure to Follow Corporate Formalities
The failure to follow corporate formalities is often a significant factor in PCV cases and will often result in the imposition of individual liability.

4. Artificial Division of a Single Business Entity
An important factor in many PCV cases is whether a single business is artificially divided into several different corporations to reduce exposure of assets to liability. Usually the entire entity will be held responsible for the debts of the business.

C. PARENT CORPORATION'S LIABILITY FOR OBLIGATIONS OF SUBSIDIARY CORPORATIONS
Courts are more likely to PCV when the shareholder is itself a corporation than when the shareholder is an individual.

1. Confusion of Affairs
Parent liability for the subsidiary's debts usually arises from a failure to maintain a clear separation between parent and subsidiary affairs. Conduct such as mixing assets; mixing business affairs; referring to the subsidiary as a "department" or "division" of the parent, etc., may lead to parental liability.

2. Permissible Activities
If practices similar to those described in the previous paragraph are avoided, a PCV argument should be rejected even though one corporation owns all the shares of the corporation; the corporations have common officers or directors; and the corporations file a consolidated tax return or report their earnings to their shareholders on a consolidated basis.

3. Conclusion
The willingness to PCV in the parent-subsidiary relationship appears to be based on the view that it is less serious to hold an additional corporate entity liable than it is to hold an individual shareholder liable.

D. USE OF THE SEPARATE CORPORATE EXISTENCE TO DEFEAT PUBLIC POLICY
The flexibility of the corporate fiction often permits it to be used in a way that arguably tends to defeat or undercut statutory policies.

1. General Principle
The issue in such cases revolves around the strength and purpose of the state public policy rather than the degree or extent of formation or method of operation of the corporation.

2. **Qualification of Shareholder for Employee Benefits**
    A corporation may be used to qualify a person for public benefits available to employees which that person would not be entitled to if he or she conducted business in his or her own name. The validity of this practice depends on an evaluation of the policies underlying the grant of benefits.

3. **Other Policy Issues**
    A PCV analysis may be used to determine other issues, such as whether a parent corporation is bound by a subsidiary's union contract.

E. **PIERCING THE CORPORATE VEIL IN TAXATION CASES**
    The Government has broad power to ignore or restructure fictional transactions which have as their sole purpose the avoidance or minimization of taxes.

1. **Recognition of Corporation in General**
    The separate corporate existence of a corporation will generally be recognized for tax purposes if it is carrying on a bona fide business and is not merely a device to avoid taxes.

2. **Estoppel Against Taxpayer**
    The taxpayer is generally bound by his selection of the corporate form of business and cannot argue that the separate existence of the corporation should be ignored.

F. **PIERCING THE CORPORATE VEIL IN BANKRUPTCY**
    Courts have considerable flexibility in dealing with corporations and shareholders for the purpose of preserving the rights of creditors.

1. **Piercing the Corporate Veil**
    The court may ignore the separate corporate existence and hold the shareholders liable for all corporate obligations.

2. **Reclassification of Transaction**
    The court may refuse to recognize or may reclassify or change the form of a transaction between shareholder and corporation where it is equitable or reasonable to do so.

3. **Subordination**
    The court may subordinate claims of shareholders to claims of other creditors where the claim of the shareholder is in some sense inequitable. This power is viewed as inherent in the bankruptcy jurisdiction of federal courts and is now codified in the bankruptcy statute.

V. FINANCING THE CORPORATION

A.   IN GENERAL
There are four likely sources of capital for a corporation.

1.   **Equity Capital**
Capital contributed by shareholders in exchange for shares of stock is usually referred to as "equity capital."

2.   **Loans From Shareholders**
Capital loaned by the shareholders to the corporation may be substituted for equity capital in whole or in part.

3.   **Loans From Third Persons**
Capital loaned by third persons to the corporation is usually referred to as "debt financing" and should be distinguished from loans by shareholders because of the significantly different economic and legal consequences of such loans.

4.   **Internally Generated Funds**
Capital internally generated from the corporation's business through the retention of earnings, creation of reserves, sales of appreciated assets and the like is a final source of funds needed by a corporation.

B.   THE ISSUANCE OF "COMMON SHARES"; AN INTRODUCTION TO PAR VALUE
Under the Revised Model Business Corporation Act the articles of incorporation must set forth the number of shares the corporation is authorized to issue. If the corporation is authorized to issue more than one class of shares, the number of shares of each class, and a distinguishing designation for each class, must also be set forth.

1.   **The Trend Toward the Elimination of Mandatory Par Value**
The Revised Model Business Corporation Act has eliminated the concept of par value and the current trend is toward the elimination of this concept in state statutes.

2.   **The Concept of "Common Shares"**
The rights of common shares need not be described in the articles of incorporation since they have the two basic rights of common shares: (1) entitlement to vote, and (2) entitlement to the net assets of the corporation when distributions are made or upon dissolution.

3. Authorized and Issued Shares

It is customary to authorize additional shares over what is planned to be issued at the outset in the event additional capital is needed at a later date.

4. Par Value as the Pricing Floor

Where par value shares are involved, the one basic rule is that such shares should never be issued for less than par value. It has become customary to use "low par" or "nominal par" value shares rather than "high par" value shares.

5. Par Value and the Capital Accounts

Under most corporation statutes, the aggregate of the par values of issued shares constitutes the "stated capital" of the corporation and any excess received for the issuance of shares over stated capital is "capital surplus."

6. No Par Value Shares

In most states "no par" shares are permitted which may be issued for any consideration specified by the directors; there is no minimum price for no par shares.

7. Ineligible Consideration for Shares

Many state statutes prohibit shares from being issued for promissory notes or promises of future services.

8. Watered Stock

"Watered stock" is a generic term used to describe the issuance of shares below par value or, in some situations, shares issued for a price below the price set by the directors for the issuance of no par value shares, or shares issued in whole or in part for ineligible consideration.

C. ISSUANCE OF MORE THAN A SINGLE CLASS OF SHARES

Common shares are the residual ownership interests in the corporation. Other classes of shares with limited or preferred rights may also be created. The Revised Model Business Corporation Act does not use the terms "common shares" and "preferred shares" but these terms are widely used in practice and in many state statutes.

1. Preferred Shares

Most preferred shares have dividend and liquidation preferences, i.e. the preferred shares are entitled to a payment of a specified amount before the common shares are entitled to anything.

2.   Classified Common Stock

Common stock may be issued in classes with variations in rights from class to class. Classes of common shares are often used as planning devices in closely held corporations.

3.   Preferred Issued in Series

Many state statutes authorize the creation by the board of directors of "series" of preferred shares, the financial or other terms of which may vary from series to series.

4.   Equivalence of Shares Within a Class or Series

All shares of a class or series must have identical preference, limitations and relative rights with those of other shares of the same series or class. This requirement is a matter of controversy in "poison pill" preferred stock that have rights that vary in connection with changes in external circumstances.

D.   THE USE OF DEBT IN THE INITIAL CAPITALIZATION OF THE CORPORATION

Typical debt securities are bonds, debentures, and notes.

1.   Bonds, Debentures, and Notes Described

Bonds and debentures are usually long-term negotiable unconditional written obligations to pay to bearer a specific amount at a future date. A bond is a secured debt while a debenture is unsecured. A note is a short-term negotiable instrument payable to the order of a specific person representing an unconditional promise to pay that may be secured or unsecured.

2.   Debt Instruments Compared With Preferred Stock

Bonds or debentures differ from preferred stock from a legal standpoint in such respects as interest; maturity; and rights of foreclosure.

3.   Advantages of Providing a Portion of the Initial Capital in the Form of Debt

There are both tax and nontax advantages for shareholders to lend a portion of the initial capital to the corporation. Interest on a debt is deductible by the corporation while dividends are not. A repayment of debt may be a tax-free return of capital rather than a taxable dividend.

4.   Third Party Debt

Loans from third persons to the corporation do not provide the tax or planning benefits of loans from the original investors; however, such loans may provide the advantage of leverage.

5. **Debt/Equity Ratio**

The ratio between a corporation's equity capital and its long term debt is often called the corporation's debt/equity ratio.

E. **APPLICATION OF THE FEDERAL AND STATE SECURITIES ACTS**

The possible impact of Federal and state securities acts must always be considered when raising capital.

1. **General Description of Purpose**

These statutes are designed to protect the public investor from fraudulent or misrepresented promotions or sales of securities. The goal is usually full disclosure of all relevant facts about the securities being sold.

2. **Cost of Registration**

The registration process, particularly at the federal level, is so expensive as to be impractical for most small and medium-sized public offerings.

3. **Exemptions from Registration**

Attention must be focused on the availability of exemptions for a particular offer. The principal exemptions under the Securities Act of 1933 are the following: Rules 504, 505 and 506; Section 4(2); Section 4(6); Section 3(b); and Section 3(a)(11).

4. **Restrictions on Transfer of Unregistered Securities**

Since the availability of several exemptions is dependent on the ultimate investors having certain knowledge or sophistication, or being residents of specific states, SEC regulations and accepted corporate practice require restrictions on transfer to be imposed on securities sold pursuant to an exemption.

5. **Control Persons and Secondary Distributions**

A secondary distribution is a public distribution of unregistered shares by a person other than the issuer—either an "underwriter" or a "control person." Secondary distributions must be registered unless an exemption is available.

6. **What is a Security?**

Securities acts define "security" broadly. A "security" has been judicially defined as any contract, transaction or scheme whereby a person invests money in a common enterprise and is led to expect profits solely from the efforts of others.

7. **State Blue Sky Laws**

The provisions of state "blue sky" statutes often parallel the federal securities act but many do not. Some state statutes do not adopt the "full disclosure" philosophy of the federal act but permit distributions to be registered and sold in the state only if their terms are "fair, just, and equitable." The private offering and other exemptions in state statutes are often more numerical and objective than the corresponding exemptions in the federal act. Generally, the registration requirements of the state statutes are in addition to the requirements of the federal securities act.

F. ISSUANCE OF SHARES BY A GOING CONCERN

Shares issued by a going concern create unique problems because the new shares will have an effect on outstanding shareholders.

1. Preemptive Rights

The principal common law protection for existing shareholders is the doctrine of "preemptive rights," which gives outstanding shareholders the right to subscribe and pay for their proportionate part of any new issue of securities by the corporation at the price established by the board of directors. Under modern statutes preemptive rights are discretionary and may be eliminated by provision in the articles of incorporation.

2. Fiduciary Restrictions on the Oppressive Issuance of Shares

Where preemptive rights are inapplicable or have been eliminated, the power of controlling shareholders to issue new shares may be limited by the fiduciary duties they owe to minority shareholders.

3. Securities Acts Applicable

The federal and state securities acts are applicable to shares issued by going concerns.

G. DIVIDENDS AND DISTRIBUTIONS

A "dividend" is a payment out of current or past earnings; other distributions, to the extent permitted, may be called "capital distributions," "distributions in partial liquidation," or by other names that indicate that they are distributions of capital, not distributions of earnings.

1. Dividend Policies in Publicly Held Corporations

Publicly held corporations generally adopt stable dividend policies that permit regular periodic distributions even though corporate income fluctuates.

2. Dividend Policies in a Closely Held Corporation

In a closely held corporation, the dividend policy generally adopted is "no dividends," because the payment of dividends is likely to carry a higher tax cost than the payment of the same amount in the form of salaries, rents or other payments that are deductible by the corporation.

3. **Legal Requirements for Dividend and Distributions**
    The tests for corporate distributions may differ depending on whether the state retains par value concepts, or whether it has eliminated par value and the related concepts of "stated capital" and "capital surplus". The Revised Model Business Corporation Act imposes two tests to determine whether a distribution may be lawfully made: (1) an "equity insolvency" test, and (2) a "balance sheet" test, i.e. the requirement that after the distribution assets must exceed liabilities plus the preferential amounts due any class or classes of preferred shares.

    State statutes that retain par value concepts usually permit dividends to be paid only out of "earned surplus", but they usually also permit non-dividend distributions out of capital surplus or other surplus accounts.

4. **Contractual Restrictions on Dividends and Distributions**
    Because state statutes provide few restrictions on distributions and therefore little or no protection for creditors, creditors usually impose contractual restrictions on dividends and distributions in loan agreements.

H. **REDEMPTIONS AND REPURCHASES OF OUTSTANDING SHARES**
    A redemption or repurchase by a corporation of some of its outstanding shares has the same economic effect as a dividend or distribution to the shareholders whose shares are redeemed or purchased.

1. **Reasons for Redemptions in Publicly Held Corporation**
    Share redemptions or repurchases may occur in publicly held corporations for several reasons: e. g., to provide shares for employee share purchase plans or for the acquisition of other businesses.

2. **Reasons for Redemptions in Closely Held Corporations**
    Redemptions in closely held corporations are usually designed to permit a shareholder to withdraw from the corporation and liquidate his investment.

3. **Status of Reacquired Shares**
    Reacquired shares under most early statutes were classed as "treasury shares." The Revised Model Business Corporation Act eliminates the concept of treasury shares. Reacquired shares under this Act have the status of authorized but unissued shares.

4. **Redemptions at Option of Corporation**
    Corporations may issue preferred shares that are redeemable at the option of the corporation. In many states common shares may not be made redeemable at all or may be redeemable only if there exists another class of common shares that is not redeemable.

5.   Illegal Dividends or Redemptions
Generally, assenting directors are liable for an illegal dividend or distribution; shareholders who receive such a distribution are generally liable to repay it only if they knew it was unlawful when they received it.

I.   SHARE DIVIDENDS AND SHARE SPLITS
Unlike cash or property dividends, a share dividend or share split does not dissipate corporate assets.

1.   Definitions
Share dividends differ from share splits primarily in accounting treatment. In a share split, the par value of each old share is divided among the new shares while in a share dividend the par value of each share is unchanged and the stated capital of the corporation is increased by the number of shares issued as a dividend. The Revised Model Business Corporation Act refers only to "share dividends".

2.   Effect on Market Prices
The market price of new shares after a stock split is often somewhat greater than the price of the old shares. A share dividend rarely has a noticeable effect on market prices.

3.   Treatment of Share Dividends and Splits
Litigation has arisen over the proper classification of such distributions as principal or as income for trust or fiduciary administration purposes. In most of these situations, the intention of the creator of the interest, if clearly expressed, will control.

VI.   THE STATUTORY SCHEME OF MANAGEMENT AND CONTROL

A.   THE STATUTORY SCHEME IN GENERAL

1.   Shareholders
Shareholders have only limited power of management and control. Their control is exercised through the power to select or remove directors.

2.   Directors
Directors have general powers of management and control. In large, publicly held corporations, they oversee the management rather than actually managing.

3. **Officers**
Officers generally carry out directors' decisions rather than make policy decisions though officers may be delegated decision-making authority and have some inherent power.

B. ATTEMPTS TO VARY THE STATUTORY SCHEME

1. **Common Law Approach**
The common law treats shareholders agreements which restrict the discretion of directors to be against public policy and unenforceable.

2. **Relaxation of Common Law Rule by Courts**
Courts relaxed the strict common law rule where only "slight impingements" were involved that injured no one. Courts were more willing to uphold arrangements that interfered with the discretion of directors where all the shareholders agreed, but not even unanimous agreement would validate a major impingement on the statutory schemes.

3. **Relaxation of Common Law Rule by Statute**
A number of states have adopted statutes that permit a close corporation to dispense with the board of directors entirely and have the business and affairs managed directly by the shareholders. Others permit restrictions on the discretion of directors to be included in articles of incorporation; these provisions may not be restricted to closely held corporations.

4. **Orders and Directions of Majority Shareholders**
Directors need not follow orders or directions of majority shareholders. The shareholders only recourse is to elect more compliant directors.

At common law directors could be removed only for cause. Under most modern statutes directors may be removed without cause, thereby simplifying the problem faced by majority shareholders if directors refuse to follow their wishes.

The justification for providing this degree of directoral independence is that directors have fiduciary duties to the corporation and should have freedom to act to meet their duties.

5. **Delegation of Duties**
Directors may not delegate all their duties of management to third parties. However, reasonable delegation, which includes a power to review the performance of the manager, has been upheld.

6. **Directors' Voting Agreements**
Directors may not commit themselves in advance to vote by consensus or in the way a shareholder or other person directs.

7. Testamentary Directions
Directions in wills that shares owned by the estate shall be voted to elect specific persons as officers of the corporation have been held invalid.

Even a direction to testamentary trustees that they elect themselves as directors may give rise to potentially serious conflicts of interest.

C. THE STATUTORY SCHEME AS AN IDEALIZED MODEL
The statutory scheme does not reflect the reality of management in either the large publicly held nor the small closely held corporation. It may, however, approximate reality in "in between" corporations.

1. In the Publicly Held Corporation
In large, publicly held corporations, the professional management establishes business policy; directors may be selected by management or by the incumbent board with their selection ratified by the shareholders. Even the CEO may be selected by management rather than the board.

2. In the Closely Held Corporation
In the closely held corporation, the owners of the business usually serve as shareholders, directors, and officers. The business may be run completely informally.

VII. SHAREHOLDERS' MEETINGS, VOTING AND CONTROL ARRANGEMENTS

A. SHAREHOLDERS' MEETINGS

1. In General
Shareholders are required to hold annual meetings each year to elect directors and deal with other appropriate matters. All meetings other than the annual meeting are special meetings.

2. Statement of Purpose of Meeting
The principal difference between annual and special meetings is that the notice of a special meeting must set forth the purposes of the meeting and the meeting is limited to the stated purposes. The notice of an annual meeting need not specify any purpose.

3. Notice
Notice is required by statutes but may be waived either before or after the meeting. Attendance at a meeting may constitute a waiver.

4. Quorum Requirements

A quorum is typically a majority but many states authorize the quorum to be reduced either without limitation or to a specified fraction. The Revised Model Business Corporation Act permits the quorum requirement to be reduced without limitation.

5. Voting

In most states, the general rule is that a majority of votes at a meeting at which a quorum is present is necessary to adopt a measure. The Revised Model Business Corporation Act adjusts this requirement so that an action is approved if the affirmative votes exceed the negative votes; this eliminates the negative effect of abstentions. The Revised Model Business Corporation Act also establishes a plurality vote requirement for the election of directors in order to take into account the possibility of three or more factions competing for directorships.

6. Supermajority Quorum and Voting Requirements

Statutes generally allow the quorum and vote requirements to be increased up to and including unanimity.

7. Action Without a Meeting

Most states permit shareholders to act by unanimous written consent without a meeting. A few states allow a majority of the shareholders to act by written consent, binding the corporation.

8. Multiple or Fractional Votes

The traditional rule is one vote per share but an increasing number of states now authorize shares with multiple or fractional votes per share.

All but a small handful of states authorize nonvoting shares even if they are otherwise one vote per share states.

9. Fiduciary Duties

Directors may be tempted to manipulate the rules with respect to meetings for their own purposes. Earlier cases hold that such manipulation is proper, but more recent cases hold that such manipulation may constitute a violation of fiduciary duties.

B. ELIGIBILITY TO VOTE

Eligibility to vote is based on "record ownership" on the "record date."

1. The Concept of Record Ownership

Shares are always issued in the name of some person, known as the record owner. The corporation treats that person as the owner of shares.

A person who acquires shares without having them recorded in his name is known as the "beneficial owner." The beneficial owner, as against the record owner, may exercise rights of ownership, is entitled to vote and to dividends, and may compel the record owner to endorse the certificates so that the beneficial owner can become the record owner.

2. The Concept of Record Date

Eligibility to vote at a meeting is determined by the record ownership on a date set by the board called the "record date." A person acquiring shares after the record date may not himself vote the shares but can compel the record owner to execute a proxy so that he may vote the shares.

3. Voting List

Many state statutes require a corporate officer to prepare an accurate list of shareholders entitled to vote and have it available for inspection at or for a brief period before the meeting.

4. Miscellaneous Voting Rules

Generally only record owners may vote; exceptions are made in many state statutes for executors, administrators and receivers by court appointment. Other fiduciaries, such as trustees, must have their shares registered in their names as trustees if they wish to be able to vote.

5. Inspectors of Election

Voting disputes are resolved by inspectors of elections who may have discretionary authority to resolve such disputes based on the corporate records.

C. CUMULATIVE VOTING

Cumulative voting allows a shareholder to "bunch" all the votes he may cast in an election for directors on one or more candidates.

1. Straight Voting

Straight voting allows a shareholder to vote only the number of shares he owns for each candidate. In straight voting, a majority of the shares will elect all directors and a minority can never elect a single director.

2. Mechanics of Cumulative Voting

In cumulative voting a shareholder with 100 shares and three places to be filled may give one candidate 300 votes or divide his votes among more than one candidate as he desires.

3.   **Advantages and Disadvantages of Cumulative Voting**
Cumulative voting allows large minority shareholders to obtain representation on the board. It may also increase factionalism or partisanship on the board.

4.   **Minimization of Effect of Cumulative Voting**
The effect of cumulative voting may be eliminated or minimized by several devices: elimination of the privilege entirely (in most states), reduction of the number of positions to be filled at a single meeting (e. g., staggering of board), removal of a minority director, or "working around" such a director.

D.   PROXY VOTING
A proxy is a grant of authority to another to vote.

1.   **Prevalence**
Voting by proxy is almost universal in large publicly held corporations and is often used in other corporations where an individual shareholder will not be present in person at a meeting.

2.   **Formal Requirements**
Proxy appointments must be in writing and are usually valid for only 11 months. Under the Revised Model Business Corporation Act a proxy appointment is valid for whatever period is specified in the appointment form.

3.   **Revocability**
Proxy appointments are usually revocable even if stated to be irrevocable. A revocable proxy is revoked by any inconsistent act by the granter, such as granting a later proxy to a different person.

A proxy appointment is irrevocable only if it is "coupled with an interest" which usually requires a property or financial investment in the shares or in the corporation itself.

E.   SHAREHOLDER VOTING AGREEMENTS

1.   **Scope**
Shareholder voting (or "pooling") agreements are valid so long as they deal only with matters within the authority of shareholders.

2.   **Formal Requirements**
No special formal requirements are made applicable to pooling agreements in most states.

3.   Determination of How Pooled Shares Should be Voted
Voting of pooled shares may be specified in the pooling agreement or
may be determined by agreement from time to time with arbitration or
similar resolution of dispute provisions applicable in the event of a failure
to agree.

4.   Enforcement of Pooling Agreements
In many states, specific enforcement or irrevocable proxy provisions make
it clear how pooling agreements should be enforced. In the absence of
such provisions, one court simply disqualified noncomplying pooled shares
from being voted, a solution that in some situations may defeat the
essential purpose of the agreement.

F.   VOTING TRUSTS
Voting trusts are formal devices by which shares are transferred to voting
trustees on the records of the corporation but the beneficial owners retain all
the incidents of ownership other than the power to vote.

1.   Common Law Attitude
The common law was hostile to voting trusts, an attitude largely changed
by statute.

2.   Statutory Requirements
Most statutes require copies of the voting trust agreement to be filed
with the corporate records and limit the duration of the voting trust to
ten years. Failure to comply with such requirements makes the trust
unenforceable.

An arrangement that has the economic or legal effects of a voting trust
must meet these statutory requirements if it is to be enforceable.

3.   Uses of Voting Trusts
Voting trusts may be used for a variety of purposes, e. g., preservation
of control, assuring stability of management, or protecting interests of
corporate creditors.

4.   Voting Trusts in Publicly Held Corporations
Voting trusts are often thought to be incompatible with corporate
democracy in publicly held corporations, and securities exchanges may
refuse to list securities if a voting trust exists with respect to such
shares.

5.   Powers of Trustees
Some decisions have imposed equitable limitations on the power of
trustees to make fundamental changes in the corporation or the rights of
the shares without the consent of the beneficial owners.

G.   CLASSES OF SHARES AS A VOTING DEVICE
Voting power may be allocated as desired by creating special classes of shares with specified voting rights. Court decisions have broadly validated such devices which are essential planning tools in many corporations.

H.   SHARE TRANSFER RESTRICTIONS
Share transfer restrictions are contractual in nature. Their validity is based on contract principles, including a prohibition against unreasonable restraints on alienation.

1.   Use in Closely Held Corporations
In closely held corporations, share transfer restrictions are used to assure each shareholder that he will have a voice in who his coshareholders are. They may also be used to resolve internal disputes, to guarantee valuation and liquidity for estates of deceased stockholders, and to assure availability of the subchapter S election.

2.   Use in Publicly Held Corporations
The principal use of share transfer restrictions in publicly held corporations is to assure that exemptions from securities registration remain available. Shares that are subject to restrictions on transfer for this reason are called "restricted securities" and may be sold publicly only to the extent permitted by rule 144.

3.   Miscellaneous Uses
Share transfer restrictions may also be used in miscellaneous situations, such as professional corporations, where restraints on who may be shareholders exist.

4.   Legal Requirements with Respect to Share Transfer Restrictions
The common law view was that share transfer restrictions should be strictly construed since they are restraints on alienation. This view has gradually changed.

5.   To Whom Option or Buy-Sell Restrictions Should Run
Restrictions may run to the corporation, to the other shareholders, or to both *in seriatim*. The choice is one of administrative convenience, who has the necessary funds, and so forth.

6.   Establishment of Price in Option or Buy-Sell Arrangements
In closely held corporations, the price at which shares are to be bought or sold may be established in the agreement itself, by reference to book value, or by negotiation or arbitration. The lack of a market for closely held shares complicates this process.

VIII. DIRECTORS

A.   NUMBER

Today, most states permit a board of directors to consist of one or more directors. Historically, three directors were required and some states retain this requirement. Some states allow boards of one or two directors only where there are one or two shareholders.

B.   MEETINGS, QUORUMS AND RELATED MATTERS

   1.   Notice

   Unlike shareholders' meetings, directors' meetings may occur without notice or with only such notice as provided by the bylaws. The Revised Model Business Corporation Act requires that special meetings be called upon two days' notice unless a longer or shorter notice is required or permitted by the bylaws.

   2.   Quorum

   A quorum consists of a majority of the board of directors unless a higher percentage is provided by the bylaws. Exception is provided to fill vacancies on the board. The Revised Model Business Corporation Act also permits the quorum requirement to be reduced to one-third of the directors.

C.   COMPENSATION

Directors traditionally serve without compensation but, increasingly, publicly held corporations are providing substantial compensation for outside directors.

D.   RESIGNATION OF DIRECTORS

The Revised Model Business Corporation Act permits resignation either immediately or at a future date. Most state statutes do not expressly cover the resignation of directors. In the case of a resignation at a future date, the director may participate in decisions before that date, including the selection of his successor.

E.   FILLING OF VACANCIES

Vacancies may be filled by either the board of directors or the shareholders.

F.   HOLDOVER DIRECTORS

Directors hold office until their successors are qualified. As a result, directors in office upon a deadlock of shareholders will remain in office indefinitely.

G.   REQUIREMENT THAT DECISIONS BE MADE AT MEETINGS

The common law rule permitted directors to act only at meetings.

   1.   Rationale

   The rationale was to provide, for the protection of minority shareholders, the benefits of mutual interchange and discussion.

2. Implications

The meeting principle leads to rules prohibiting directors voting by proxy and requiring strict adherence to notice and quorum principles.

3. Modern Status of the Rule

While the rigidity of the common law rule has been relaxed by statute in areas such as action by informal written consent and telephonic meetings, and by application of principles of estoppel and waiver, the rule maintains some force even in the modern world.

H. DIRECTORS' DISSENT TO ACTIONS

Directors are deemed to have assented to action taken at a meeting at which they are present unless their dissent is duly noted.

1. Avoidance of Liability by Filing Dissent

To avoid liability, a dissenting director must make sure that his dissent is noted in the corporate records or file a written notice of his dissent shortly after the meeting.

2. Avoidance of Liability by Reliance on Opinion of Others

Statutes of many states limit the liability of directors if they rely in good faith on the opinions of accountants or others.

3. Resignation

A director who resigns because of his objection to a transaction must nevertheless file the required written dissent.

4. Objection to Notice Defects

A director waives objection to defects in a notice of meeting if he or she participates in the meeting.

I. COMMITTEES OF THE BOARD OF DIRECTORS

Committees of the Board are authorized by state statutes.

1. Committees Under the Revised Model Business Corporation Act

The Revised Model Business Corporation Act authorizes the creation of committees of the board of directors to exercise functions of the board of directors subject to certain limitations on the matters that may be resolved by a committee.

2. Executive Committee

An executive committee may make routine business decisions between board meetings.

3. **Audit Committee**
Audit committees are becoming increasingly popular in publicly held companies. Composed entirely of non-management directors, audit committees provide a variety of audit-related functions to the corporation.

4. **Nominating Committees**
A nominating committee composed primarily of non-management directors provides criteria for directors' nominees and may review and recommend board candidates.

5. **Compensation Committees**
A compensation committee composed entirely of non-management directors provides review of management and directoral compensation.

6. **Public Policy Committees**
A public policy committee considers non-business related activities of the corporation, such as policies with respect to charitable contributions. The newest of the committees of the board, its use is gradually growing in publicly held corporations.

IX. OFFICERS

A. **CORPORATE OFFICERS AND THE SOURCES OF THEIR AUTHORITY**
The traditional corporate officers are a president, a treasurer, and a secretary. One or more vice presidents or assistant officers may also be provided for. The Revised Model Business Corporation Act does not require any designated officers except an officer performing the functions usually associated with the office of secretary.

1. **Authority of Officers in General**
Officers have limited inherent authority to bind the corporation. Express authority is usually found in the bylaws or in specific resolutions of the board of directors.

2. **Inherent Authority of Corporate Officers**
Each designated officer may have limited inherent authority to bind the corporation based on the title of his or her position and the description of that position in the bylaws.

B. **NONSTATUTORY OFFICERS**
Bylaw provisions, or a board of directors by resolution, may create nonstatutory offices and provide appropriate authority for the holders of such offices.

C.   DETERMINATION OF OFFICERS' AUTHORITY
Persons dealing with a corporate officer must satisfy themselves of the officer's authority.

1.   Oral Representations by Officer
As is generally true in agency law, a representation by an agent as to the scope of his or her agency is not binding on the principal.

2.   Reliance on Officer's Title
Since corporate officers have only limited inherent authority, reliance on an officer's title is unlikely to provide assurance that the act is authorized.

3.   Reliance on Certified Resolution
Obtaining a resolution of the board of directors certified by the secretary of the corporation is the traditional method of assurance that the corporation is bound by the officer's action. It makes no difference whether or not the resolution was actually authorized by the board of directors since the corporation is bound by the secretary's certificate unless the third person knows that the resolution is not accurate.

D.   INHERENT AUTHORITY OF THE PRESIDENT

1.   Traditional View
The traditional view is that a corporate president has limited authority to bind the corporation to routine business transactions.

2.   Current Trend
The general trend is to broaden the authority of the President so that it more closely conforms to the general understanding of the public as to the authority of that office.

E.   APPARENT AND IMPLIED AUTHORITY OF OFFICERS
Various common law concepts—implied authority, apparent authority, ratification, estoppel and unjust enrichment—may be used to bind the corporation to acts by its officers in specific situations.

F.   FIDUCIARY DUTIES OF OFFICERS
Corporate officers owe fiduciary duties to the corporation that are analogous to the duties of a corporate director.

G.   OFFICERS' LIABILITY ON CORPORATE OBLIGATIONS
Corporate officers are presumably not liable on corporate obligations in which they participate as agents except in the following circumstances:

1. **Express Guarantee**
    Such a guarantee may have to be in writing under the statute of frauds.

2. **Confusion of Roles**
    An officer may not clearly delineate that he is acting as an agent and may therefore become personally liable under agency or estoppel principles.

3. **Statutory Liability**
    A few statutes provide for officer liability for certain types of corporate obligations. The most important is the provision of the Internal Revenue Code that imposes personal liability on officers who are required to collect employee withholding taxes. The Revised Model Business Corporation Act imposes a duty of care on officers analogous to the duty of care imposed on directors.

H. **CORPORATE "NOTICE" OR "KNOWLEDGE"**

1. **General Rule**
    General principles of agency law determine when the knowledge of an officer is attributed to the corporation.

2. **Agent Acting Adversely to Principal**
    An officers' knowledge may be imputed to the corporation in some circumstances even though he is acting adversely to the corporation.

3. **Corporate Criminal Responsibility**
    Generally, a corporation may be held criminally responsible for conduct imputed to it in the same way as any other principal.

I. **TENURE OF OFFICERS AND AGENTS**
    Officers and agents generally serve at the will of the electing or appointing authority.

1. **Employment Contracts in General**
    While election or appointment does not create a contractual right, officers or agents may be given an employment contract. Such a contract gives rise to a claim for breach in the event of a premature termination of the relationship. An employment contract may extend beyond the term of the office.

2. **Lifetime Employment Contracts**
    Claims that a person was given a lifetime employment contract are not favored. Such a claim, usually based on parol testimony, is viewed as being inherently improbable.

3. **Discharge for Cause**

   Officers or agents with employment contracts may always be discharged for cause. It is unnecessary to consider the issue of "cause" in contracts at will.

4. **Compensation Patterns**

   Compensation of officers or agents may be based on earnings or the market performance of the corporation's shares. Officers or agents may also be compensated in shares or in options to purchase shares. They may also receive various kinds of indirect or deferred compensation.

X. MANAGEMENT OF THE CLOSELY HELD CORPORATION

A. **CHARACTERISTICS OF A CLOSELY HELD CORPORATION**

   The basic characteristics of a "close" or "closely held" corporation are as follows:

1. **Lack of Market for Minority Shares**

   Because minority shares do not carry with them a right to control or participate in management, and there is no guaranteed financial return, minority shares are apt to be unsalable because there are few or no interested purchasers.

2. **Shareholder Participation in Management**

   Management of a closely held corporation is usually associated with the principal shareholders or all the shareholders.

3. **Dividend Policy**

   For tax reasons, participants usually prefer that no dividends be paid and that earnings be distributed in the form of compensation, interest, or rent.

4. **Informality of Management**

   Business is usually conducted without formal meetings or voting.

5. **No Compulsory Dissolution**

   Unlike a partnership, a minority shareholder has no right to dissolve a close corporation. Under special statutes such a right may be provided by agreement.

6. **Freezeouts and Squeezeouts**

   The foregoing factors permit majority shareholders to exclude minority interests from any participation or benefit in the corporation.

7.   Fiduciary Duties Between Shareholders
The traditional view was that no fiduciary duty existed between shareholders. However, since 1965 several cases have imposed such a duty.

B.   CONTROL DEVICES IN CLOSELY HELD CORPORATIONS

1.   Traditional Control Techniques
Close corporation planning may entail the use of devices such as classes of shares, pooling agreements and voting trusts.

2.   High Quorum and Voting Requirements
Minority control devices may sometimes be effected by increasing quorum and voting requirements so as to give minority interests an effective veto over corporate actions.

C.   DISSENSION AND DEADLOCK WITHIN THE CLOSE CORPORATION

1.   Dissension
Dissension may occur without a deadlock if there is majority control. Usually the minority is in a weak position and may use dissension as a negotiating technique.

2.   Deadlock
Deadlock arises where there are two factions with equal voting power or there is a minority with veto power. In the event of a deadlock, persons in control when the deadlock occurs usually remain in control indefinitely since elections of successors are deadlocked.

D.   REMEDIES FOR DEADLOCKS
Deadlocks may sometimes be negotiated out but advance planning is preferable. A buy-out arrangement, compulsory dissolution or compulsory arbitration may be provided by agreement. In the absence of agreement, statutes provide involuntary remedies: dissolution, the appointment of a receiver, or a custodian; the appointment of provisional directors, mandatory arbitration or mandatory buy-out agreements. The most important of these is involuntary dissolution based on failure to resolve a deadlock within a specified period of time.

E.   SPECIAL MANAGEMENT PROBLEMS IN THE CLOSE CORPORATION
The primary management concerns in the closely held corporation are convenience, flexibility, and simplicity.

1.   Consequences of Failing to Follow Formalities
Close corporations often conduct affairs informally. Such informality may sometimes lead to personal liability for corporate obligations on a "piercing the corporate veil" theory.

2.   **Consequences of Failing to Follow Statutory Norms**
     Reasonable control arrangements may be held unenforceable if they do
     not conform with traditional corporate statutory norms.

**F.   JUDICIAL RECOGNITION OF THE SPECIAL PROBLEMS OF THE CLOSE
       CORPORATION**
     Since 1965 several judicial decisions have accepted the argument that strict
     requirements of complying with the statutory norms should be relaxed for the
     closely held corporation, and that it should be treated more like a partnership.

G.   SPECIAL CLOSE CORPORATION STATUTES
     Some states have adopted special statutes designed to provide necessary
     flexibility for close corporations that elect to adopt the statutes. Among other
     things, these statutes allow close corporations to dispense with boards of
     directors, to apply partnership management principles to the corporation, and to
     elect simplified dissolution procedures.

     Experience with these statutes indicate that they may not be widely used.

XI.   MANAGEMENT IN THE PUBLICLY HELD CORPORATION

A.   CONTROL OF THE PUBLICLY HELD CORPORATION
     The large publicly held corporation bears little relationship to the theoretical
     structure of state business corporation acts.

1.   **Limited Role of Small Shareholders**
     The number of voting shares in the large publicly held corporation is so
     large that the votes of any single shareholder are largely irrelevant on
     any issue.

2.   **Who Selects the Directors**
     The directors are selected by the determination of who should be put
     forth by management as candidates. Shareholders ratify this selection by
     their vote.

3.   **Who Runs the Business**
     Professional management, not the board of directors, runs the business.
     The full-time professional management runs the business while directors
     serve a much more limited role.

4.   **Who Selects the Management**
     Incumbent management usually selects their successors, though directors
     and major shareholders may also have an important voice.

B.   THE ROLE OF SHAREHOLDERS IN THE PUBLIC CORPORATION

1.   Pro-management Bias

Shareholders tend to have a pro-management bias because dissatisfied shareholders normally sell their shares rather than "fight city hall." Also, management largely shapes the information distributed to shareholders.

2.   Limitations on Management Control

There are several sources of external pressure, e.g. large shareholders, members of the financial community, the "market for control", and shareholder litigation to test the validity of management conduct, that limit management power and provide incentives to maximize the welfare of shareholders.

3.   The Role of Institutional Investors

The size of shareholdings of institutional investors has increased steadily until now they approach a majority in many corporations. With this growth has come increased recognition of their potential power over management. However, such investors prefer to view themselves as passive investors rather than potential controllers.

4.   Nominee Registration

Institutional investors use nominees as record holders to simplify transfer. The use of nominees may also tend to obscure the extent of institutional shareholdings.

5.   Street Name Registration

Speculators planning to resell shares promptly will usually not register securities in their own names and, for simplicity, will not take delivery of their securities. Such securities are usually registered in the names of Wall Street firms, endorsed in blank, and transferred between brokerage firms by physical delivery of certificates. Such registration is usually called street name registration.

The number of shares in street name at any one time may be 20 or 30 per cent of the outstanding shares.

XII. PROXY REGULATION

Most proxy regulation is federal in origin based on section 14 of the Securities Exchange Act of 1934.

A.   CORPORATIONS SUBJECT TO FEDERAL PROXY REGULATION

The corporations subject to federal proxy regulation are the corporations that must register under Section 12: (1) corporations with securities registered on an exchange and (2) corporations with five hundred shareholders of record of a single class and more than three million dollars of assets.

B.   TERMINATION OF REGISTRATION

Once registered, a corporation remains subject to the 1934 Act requirements until (1) the number of shareholders of the class is reduced below 300 or (2) assets are reduced below $3,000,000 and the number of shareholders of the class is reduced below 500.

C.   CONSTITUTIONAL BASIS FOR FEDERAL REGULATION OF PROXIES

The Securities Exchange Act of 1934 requirements are based on the regulation of interstate commerce and the use of the mails.

D.   PROXY STATEMENTS AND ANNUAL REPORTS

SEC proxy regulations require annual proxy statements and annual reports containing specified information. These reports are an important channel of communication to shareholders.

1.   Disclosure Documents

SEC regulations require disclosure of basic information in *annual reports* and *proxy statements*.

2.   Form of Proxy Documents

SEC regulations prevent undated or post-dated proxies, require shareholders to be given voting options on the selection of directors and other issues, and so forth.

3.   Presolicitation Review

The SEC reviews proxy documents on a 10-day review process that does not involve in-depth analysis.

The SEC does not pass upon the accuracy or adequacy of the disclosure in this review.

4.   What is a Solicitation?

The concepts of "proxy" and "solicitation" are broadly construed to favor regulation in close cases.

5.   Exempt Proxy Solicitations

SEC has promulgated exemptions for solicitations that do not require the protection of the act, e.g. those involving less than ten persons.

6.   Corporations That Do Not Solicit Proxies

Corporations usually must solicit proxies in order to assure the presence of a quorum. Some corporations do not solicit proxies because a few blocks of shares may constitute a quorum. Section 14(f) of the Securities

Exchange Act, however requires such corporations to distribute the same information they would have to distribute if they did solicit proxies.

7. **Problems Created by Street Name and Nominee Holdings**

These registration practices create problems for the disclosure system. Brokers and dealers are obligated to "pass through" the voting decision to the beneficial owners, and give them copies of the disclosure documents. The SEC also requires brokers and dealers to provide issuers with the names of beneficial owners (who do not object to the disclosure) to permit direct communication. These devices apparently work reasonably efficiently. The Revised Model Business Corporation Act proposes an alternative device that permits the corporations to establish procedures to treat beneficial owners of shares as traditional record holders.

E.   SHAREHOLDER PROPOSALS

Rule 14a–8 of the SEC regulations requires corporations to include certain shareholder proposals in proxy statements so that the proposals may be voted upon by the shareholders.

1. **Number of Proposals**

A shareholder may submit not more than two proposals for any proxy solicitation. Moreover, repetitive proposals are limited, depending on the support obtained from shareholders on the previous solicitation.

2. **Proposals That May be Omitted**

Rule 14a–8 contains over a dozen carefully described exclusions. In addition, the SEC has developed a "common law" of shareholders proposals that flesh out and apply these exclusions.

3. **Practical Importance of Shareholder Proposal Requirement**

While most shareholder proposals are defeated, the device may serve a useful communication link with management.

F.   FALSE AND MISLEADING STATEMENTS IN PROXY SOLICITATIONS

Rule 14a–9 forbids false or misleading statements in proxy solicitations. Both affirmative misstatements and omissions are covered.

1. **Private Cause of Action**

The United States Supreme Court held in *J. I. Case v. Borak* that private causes of action exist for violations of rule 14a–9.

2. **Nature of Post-*Borak* Litigation**

Since *Borak,* the Supreme Court has decided two cases that have shaped rule 14a–9 litigation. Under these cases, successful plaintiffs may have their attorneys fees paid; however, the definition of a "material" misrepresentation has been tightened to make summary judgments on the pleadings less likely.

3. Remedies in Rule 14a–9 Cases

Where a substantial transaction has been approved on the basis of a proxy statement containing material misrepresentations, courts have had difficulty devising a reasonable remedy.

XIII. PROXY FIGHTS, TENDER OFFERS AND OTHER STRUGGLES FOR CONTROL

A. PRINCIPAL FORMS OF CONTESTS FOR CONTROL

Contests for control may take a variety of forms: proxy fights, cash tender offers, exchange offers, "bear hug" transactions, unconventional tender offers, and "palace coups."

B. PROXY CONTESTS

A proxy contest is simply an election campaign to persuade shareholders to vote out incumbent management.

1. Management Advantages

Management has the advantages of the natural pro-management bias of shareholders plus access to the corporate treasury for reimbursement of expenses.

2. Insurgent Tactics

Insurgents purchase an equity position in the corporation, obtain a shareholders list and mount a campaign for proxies which may involve individual contact with shareholders.

3. Corporations Subject to Proxy Contests

Proxy fights are not feasible for very large corporations. Small or medium size corporations with older management, weak earnings records, and poor shareholder relations are typical proxy fight candidates. However, in recent takeover attempts against very large corporations proxy fights have sometimes been used as part of the aggressor's strategy.

4. Regulation of Proxy Contests

Proxy contests are regulated by the SEC which broadly imposes a "truth in campaigning" requirement.

5. Who Pays the Cost of Proxy Contests?

The corporation may be charged with reasonable management expenses in a policy dispute. Successful insurgents may also have the corporation pay their expenses if approved by the shareholders. The corporation thus may end up paying both sides.

6. Defensive Tactics
Modern courts have intervened to prevent management from using its power to set meeting dates or places as weapons to defeat insurgent proxy contests. A reasonable business purpose may have to be demonstrated for such changes.

C. TENDER OFFERS AND OTHER TAKEOVER DEVICES

1. The Williams Act
Regulation of cash tender offers is provided by the Williams Act which requires disclosure of accurate information in connection with tender offers, provides "rules of fair play" in tender offers, and imposes a prohibition against the use of false, misleading or incomplete information. The Supreme Court has held that a defeated contestant for control has no private cause of action for damages for violations of this prohibition.

2. State Antitakeover Statutes
In *Edgar v. Mite Corp.*, 457 U.S. 624, 102 S.Ct. 2629 (1982) the Supreme Court held that the Illinois Business Take-Over statute was inconsistent with portions of the Williams Act and unreasonably interfered with interstate commerce. As a result it is probable that all state tender offer statutes are unenforceable. Following *Mite* several states have adopted more sophisticated statutes; the validity of such statutes has not yet been resolved.

3. Sophisticated Defensive Tactics
As experience with unwanted tender offers has increased, the sophistication of defensive techniques has also increased.

4. Role of Arbitragers
Arbitragers often have major influence on the success of tender offers by purchasing shares on the open market and tendering them at a profit.

5. Exchange Offers
An exchange offer differs from a cash tender offer in that securities of the aggressor, rather than cash, are offered to the target's shareholders.

6. Miscellaneous Takeover Techniques
As sophisticated defensive tactics have developed, more emphasis has been placed on unconventional takeover techniques, such as limited offers to institutional investors.

7.   Economic Analysis of Cash Takeover Bids
A great deal of interest and controversy surrounds attempts to analyze the benefits and cost of modern takeover activity.

D.   INTERNAL STRUGGLES FOR CONTROL
Internal struggles for control are rarely litigated. They provide power struggles within the corporate framework rather than takeover techniques from outside the corporation.

XIV.   FIDUCIARY DUTIES OF DIRECTORS, OFFICERS AND SHAREHOLDERS

Duties to the corporation and to other interests within the corporation are primarily a matter of state law but the federal securities laws also impose some duties of a fiduciary character.

A.   DUTIES IN GENERAL
Duties to the corporation and to other interests within the corporation to some extent depend on the nature of the relationship between the office involved and the corporation.

1.   Directors
Directors owe broad duties to the corporation. The relationship is *sui generis*. Directors are not trustees but do owe both a degree of care and a high degree of fidelity and loyalty. They are also not employees and need not spend their full time on corporate affairs. Directors generally owe duties to the corporation as a whole rather than to individual shareholders or classes of shareholders.

2.   Officers and Agents
Most officers and agents are full time employees expected to give their full time and attention to corporate affairs. Depending on their responsibilities, they may owe essentially the same fiduciary duties as directors.

3.   Shareholders
Shareholders have no management responsibility and their duties to the corporation are limited. Some courts have held, however, that shareholders in a closely held corporation may owe duties to other shareholders similar to the duties one partner owes to other partners.

B.   DUTY OF CARE

1.   General Tests
The duty of care is a duty of minimum skill and attention. Mistaken judgments made in good faith cannot be attacked with the benefit of hindsight under the business judgment rule.

2.   Failure to Direct
Few cases involve liability for a total failure to direct even though such failure is a breach of the duty of care. Problems of causation explain this attitude in part as does a reluctance to impose often crushing liabilities for relatively minor omissions.

3.   Knowing Authorization of Wrongful Act
Liability has sometimes been imposed for authorization of wrongful acts, but even here there is a reluctance to impose liability that may be extremely large for decisions that were intended to benefit the corporation.

4.   Dismissal of Litigation
Committees of disinterested directors have been formed in recent years to recommend that in their business judgment specific derivative litigation should not be pursued. Some courts have accepted this application of the business judgment rules; Delaware, however, has required the court to exercise an independent business judgment on the dismissal in all "demand unnecessary" cases.

5.   Duties in Connection with Tender Offers
When faced with an adverse takeover attempt, management may usually oppose the attempt consistent with the business judgment rule. If, however, a decision to sell the business has been made, the management must thereafter seek to obtain the best possible price for the benefit of the shareholders.

C.   SELF–DEALING

1.   Definition
Self-dealing transactions are direct or indirect transactions between the corporation and director. The Revised Model Business Corporation Act defines a "conflict of interest transaction" to be a "transaction in which a director of a corporation has a direct or indirect interest".

2.   The Danger of Self-Dealing Transactions
The danger of self-dealing transactions is that the director may favor his personal interests to the corporation's interest.

3. **The Modern Test for Self-Dealing Transactions in Absence of Statute**
    Fairness is the standard usually applied to test modern self-dealing
    transactions. Some weight may be given to ratification or approval of the
    transaction by disinterested directors or shareholders, but transactions
    involving fraud, oppression, overreaching or waste inherently cannot be
    ratified.

4. **Statutory Tests for Self-Dealing Transactions**
    The Revised Model Business Corporation Act and most state statutes that
    address the issue of self dealing transactions purport to exonerate self-
    dealing transactions from a rule of automatic voidability if the transaction
    is approved by disinterested directors, by the shareholders, or if the
    transaction is fair. Provisions of these statutes, however, vary widely and
    courts have sometimes construed them as basically involving a test of
    fairness.

5. **Ratification by Shareholders**
    Ratification by shareholders will validate some self-dealing transactions.
    In this vote, the interested party may vote his shares in favor of the
    transaction. The Revised Model Business Corporation Act does not permit
    interested shares to vote. In any event, transactions involving fraud,
    oppression, overreaching or waste inherently cannot be ratified.

6. **Remedies**
    Rescission is normally the sole remedy for a corporation setting aside a
    voidable transaction.

7. **Indirect Transactions**
    Self-dealing transactions involving corporations with a common director are
    usually judged solely on a fairness test, though the active participation of
    the interested director may make the transaction voidable without regard
    to fairness.

8. **Exoneratory Provisions for Self-Dealing Transactions in Articles of
    Incorporation**
    Provisions in articles of incorporation that attempt to validate self-dealing
    transactions are given limited effect; they may permit the interested
    director to be counted toward a quorum and may free self-dealing
    transactions from adverse inferences.

D. **EXECUTIVE COMPENSATION AS A SPECIAL CASE**
    Establishment of compensation of officers and senior employees often involve
    elements of self-dealing, either because the officer involved is also a director,
    because of the likelihood of "mutual backscratching" of members of a group
    setting each other's salary, or because of considerations of friendship and
    mutual respect.

1. **Test for Excessive Compensation**
    In publicly held corporations, courts review executive compensation on the basis of whether it is so large as to constitute spoilation or waste.

2. **Tests Under Internal Revenue Code**
    In closely held corporations, compensation is often part of tax minimization schemes. Such compensation is reviewed on a simple reasonableness test and unreasonable compensation is considered a dividend.

3. **Need for Benefit to the Corporation**
    Some compensation plans have been attacked on the ground they are not supported by consideration. To avoid this argument it is necessary for the plan to involve some benefit to the corporation which can be used to support the compensation plan.

4. **Compensation Based on Stock Performance**
    Compensation plans involving stock purchase plans, stock option plans, phantom stock plans, and stock appreciation rights all provide for compensation based on stock price performance. These arrangements have generally been upheld.

E. CORPORATE OPPORTUNITIES

1. **General Test**
    A director who personally takes advantage of a corporate opportunity may have to account to the corporation for his profits. The test for this doctrine is basically one of reasonable business ethics.

2. **When Is an Opportunity a "Corporate Opportunity?"**
    The modern test usually applied is a "line of business" test coupled with basic fairness. Some states have adopted a pure fairness test; others have relied primarily on a "line of business" standard. An earlier test, now largely rejected as too narrow, is that the corporation have an "interest or expectancy" in the opportunity.

3. **Factors Considered in Evaluating Whether an Opportunity is a Corporate Opportunity**
    The courts consider various factors to determine whether an opportunity is a corporate opportunity. For example, the courts consider whether the opportunity was offered to the corporation or to the director as an agent of the corporation.

4. **Rejection of Corporate Opportunity**
    Directors may take advantage of a corporate opportunity if the corporation determines that it does not want to take advantage of the

opportunity. Such a corporate decision is a type of self-dealing transaction.

If the corporation lacks the financial ability to take advantage of the opportunity, it is not a corporate opportunity. This rule, however, must be cautiously applied; while a director need not lend money to the corporation to assist it to take advantage of the opportunity, he may not hide behind the financial inability argument and do nothing to assist the corporation. The proposed ALI Corporate Governance Project does not recognize this ground as an independent basis for a director to take personal advantage of an opportunity.

5. Director's Competition With the Corporation

Since directors are not full time employees they may compete with their corporations so long as they do so openly and do not use trade secrets or engage in unfair competition.

F. DUTIES IN CONNECTION WITH FREEZE OUT MERGERS

The statutory right of dissent and appraisal is normally available to minority shareholders in freeze-out mergers. The validity of freeze-out mergers is based on tests of full disclosure and entire fairness; compliance with statutory formalities is not sufficient.

G. MISCELLANEOUS TRANSACTIONS SUBJECT TO FAIRNESS TEST

Fairness is the criteria for testing a variety of transactions that arguably have the effect of injuring minority shareholders. These duties may be imposed on majority shareholders or on the directors named or elected by the majority shareholders.

H. RELATIONSHIP OF "FAIRNESS" AND "BUSINESS JUDGMENT" RULES

Many transactions arguably should be evaluated under either the business judgment or fairness test; in general, the fairness test should be applied when the majority is obtaining an advantage that is not available to the minority and the business judgment test should be applied to transactions that affect the corporation only or affect the shareholders proportionately.

I. STATE STATUTORY LIABILITIES

State statutes impose personal liability on directors for certain transactions.

1. Acts for Which Liability is Imposed

The acts for which personal liability is imposed typically involve failure to comply with the financial provisions of the statute.

2. **Directors Who Are Liable**
Joint and several liability is usually imposed on all directors present at the meeting at which the transaction is authorized unless a dissent is formally noted in the corporate records.

3. **Defenses**
State statutes may provide for defenses usually based on good faith reliance on the opinions or reports of corporate officials.

4. **Practical Importance of Statutory Liability**
There are very few reported cases involving these statutory liabilities.

XV. DUTIES RELATING TO THE PURCHASE OR SALE OF SHARES

Duties relating to the purchase and sale of shares arise either under state law or under the Federal Securities Exchange Act of 1934, particularly rule 10b–5 and section 16(b).

A. TRANSACTIONS IN SHARES BY AN OFFICER OR DIRECTOR ON THE BASIS OF INSIDE INFORMATION

1. **State Law**
The common law originally applied no special rules for sales of shares by insiders. Gradually, however, three principles developed: fraud or misrepresentation, special facts (which is an expansion of fraud), and fiduciary duty (adopted only in Kansas). New York has adopted a special rule based on the idea that inside information is a corporate asset and gains therefrom belong to the corporation.

2. **Federal Law Relating to Insider Trading**
Rule 10b–5 is a broad antifraud provision under which most of the modern law of insider trading has developed. See XV, D.

B. PURCHASE AT A DISCOUNT OF CLAIMS AGAINST THE CORPORATION
If the corporation is solvent, claims may be purchased by an officer or director at a discount unless they constitute corporate opportunities. If the corporation is insolvent when the claims are purchased, the purchase is improper since the officers or directors should try to liquidate outstanding claims as inexpensively as possible.

C. PURCHASE OR SALE OF SHARES IN COMPETITION WITH THE CORPORATION
Purchases or sales of shares in competition with the corporation are usually usurpations of corporate opportunities.

D. PURCHASE OR SALE OF SHARES BY A CORPORATION IN A STRUGGLE FOR CONTROL

1. Questionable Transactions
Whenever the assets of a corporation are committed to purchase shares, or the corporation decides to issue additional shares, in the context of a struggle for control, the transaction involves a possible misuse of corporate position by the incumbents and is questionable.

2. Applicable Test
The state law test usually applied to such a transaction is whether the transaction is reasonable and whether it serves a proper business purpose.

3. Application of Federal Law
If the transaction is fully disclosed, attacks on such transactions under rule 10b–5 seem foreclosed by the Supreme Court holding in *Santa Fe Industries v. Green* that deception is an essential ingredient for a rule 10b–5 suit. Some such transactions, however, may be subject to attack under the Williams Act.

E. RULE 10b–5
Rule 10b–5 is a broad antifraud provision applicable to securities creating a federal cause of action.

1. History of Rule
Originally adopted for narrow purposes, rule 10b–5 grew without control until a series of narrowing Supreme Court decisions beginning in 1975.

2. Rule 10b–5 as Federal Law
The popularity of rule 10b–5 is in part a result of the preference of most plaintiffs for the federal forum if possible. Advantages are both procedural and substantive.

3. Limiting Principles on rule 10b–5
The post-1975 Supreme Court decisions require the plaintiff to establish "scienter." *Ernst & Ernst v. Hochfelder.* The plaintiff must himself be a purchaser or seller of securities. *Blue Chip Stamps v. Manor Drug Stores.* Rule 10b–5 only relates to deception not unfairness. *Santa Fe Industries v. Green.*

4. Rule 10b–5 as an Antifraud Provision
Virtually all cases involving fraud in the purchase or sale of securities may be brought under rule 10b–5. The test of fraud includes not only affirmative misrepresentations but also omissions of material facts. Rule 10b–5 covers closely held as well as publicly held corporations. In these cases there is no need to establish diversity of citizenship and the single

use of facilities of interstate commerce—e. g., the telephone, establishes federal jurisdiction.

5. Rule 10b–5 as a Prohibition Against Insider Trading

SEC v. Texas Gulf Sulphur establishes that rule 10b–5 is violated by a person who trades in publicly held securities on the basis of inside information. Suit may be brought by the SEC, possibly by the persons who bought from or sold to the insiders, and possibly by anyone who was buying or selling in the market at the same time as the insider.

Persons covered include not only officers, directors, or agents of the issuer, but their "tippees" as well. The person giving the tip may be liable for his tippees' profits. *Dirks v. SEC*, 463 U.S. 646, 103 S.Ct. 3255 (1983). In *Chiarella v. United States* the Supreme Court set aside a criminal conviction of a financial printer under rule 10b–5 holding that he had no duty to the public to stay out of the market. However, subsequent courts have accepted the suggestion that a violation of rule 10b–5 may be based on a breach of duty to a private employer. Following *Chiarella*, the SEC adopted rule 14e–3 which makes it unlawful for a person who wrongfully obtains inside information to use it in securities transactions.

6. Rule 10b–5 as a Protection Against Deception of the Corporation in Connection with the Acquisition or Disposition of Shares

Rule 10b–5 may be violated when a corporation is deceived in connection with the purchase or sale of shares since a corporation is a "person" within rule 10b–5.

7. Rule 10b–5 as a Regulator of Corporate Publicity

A corporation violates rule 10b–5 if it issues a false press release that affects public securities trading. Such an action must involve scienter under *Hochfelder*. Private shareholders who rely on an actionable press release may have a cause of action against the issuer. However, some cases have been reluctant to conclude that press releases issued by corporations have in fact been false or misleading or that a corporation had an affirmative duty to disclose a specific event.

Recent cases have adopted a "fraud on the market" theory that permits a person trading on false public information to recover without a showing of actual reliance on the false information.

F. SECTION 16(b) OF THE SECURITIES EXCHANGE ACT

Section 16(b) is designed to avoid in-and-out short term trading by specified classes of persons.

1.   **Scope of Section 16(b)**
      Section 16(b) applies only to officers, directors, or ten per cent
      shareholders of corporations registered under section 12 of the Securities
      Exchange Act.

      Section 16(b) only applies to purchases and sales, or sales and purchases
      within a six-month period and requires all profit from such transactions to
      be paid over to the corporation.

      Section 16(b) is broadly construed to effectuate its goal; transactions by
      covered persons must be disclosed publicly under section 16(a); and a
      champertous enforcement policy ensures that all section 16(b) violations
      will be vigorously prosecuted.

2.   **Application of Section 16(b) in Takeover Situations**
      The Supreme Court has held that a purchase by tender offer which
      causes the aggressor's ownership to exceed ten per cent of the target's
      shares is not a "section 16(b) purchase." *Foremost-McKesson Inc. v.
      Provident Securities Co.* Another Supreme Court case holds that a
      person holding more than ten per cent of the shares of a target may sell
      its shares in two transactions; if the first transaction reduces ownership
      below ten per cent the second transaction is not subject to section 16(b).

3.   **Section 16(b) and Trading Partnerships**
      Generally a partnership that has a partner who is a director of a covered
      corporation is not itself considered to be a director. An exception applies
      if the partnership has "deputized" the partner to serve on the board.

4.   **Section 16(b) and Trading in Different Classes of Securities**
      Generally, section 16(b) does not apply to a purchase of preferred and
      sale of common within six months. An exception applies if the two
      securities are trading as economic equivalents.

5.   **Section 16(b) in Perspective**
      Section 16(b) is erratic and catches innocent people. On the other hand, it
      has largely eliminated the evil of short term trading by corporate officers
      and directors against which it was primarily directed.

G. **SALE OF CONTROLLING SHARES**

1.   **Control Premiums**
      A person having voting control of a corporation may usually sell its
      shares at a premium representing the control element that accompanies
      these shares.

2.   **Tests for Sale of Control**
A controlling shareholder may have to account for a control premium in several situations:

a.   A controlling shareholder must make a reasonable investigation of the purchaser. If such an investigation would have revealed that the purchaser was likely to loot the corporation, the seller may be liable for losses suffered from such looting.

b.   If the court views the favorable sale opportunity as (1) a corporate opportunity belonging to all shareholders rather than to the majority shareholders, or (2) as a sale of a corporate office rather than a sale for the stock, a controlling shareholder may be compelled to share the control premium with minority shareholders. Some cases have imposed liability for the control premium on the basis of the unfairness of the transaction.

c.   Law review commentators have suggested that the best rule would be that all control premiums should be shared with all shareholders in every sale of control cases. Other commentators argue that transactions based on a control premium benefit all shareholders and that a rule requiring sharing would discourage many desirable transactions.

XVI.   INDEMNIFICATION AND LIABILITY INSURANCE

"Indemnification" permits the corporation to a limited extent to assume and pay the litigation expenses of corporate officers and directors. It may also permit the corporation to an even more limited extent to pay judgments, settlements and criminal fines.

Liability insurance for directors and officers ("D & O" insurance) provides traditional third party liability insurance against some of these items.

A.   INDEMNIFICATION AND PUBLIC POLICY

1.   **Policies Favoring Indemnification**
Given litigation costs today, indemnification may be essential if responsible persons are to be willing to serve as directors.

2.   **Policy Limitations on Indemnification**
A person absolved of charges of negligence or misconduct is entitled to indemnification. A person found guilty of willful misconduct is generally not eligible for indemnification of any kind. Between these two extremes lie the difficult cases.

B.   SCOPE OF INDEMNIFICATION UNDER MODERN STATE STATUTES
The Delaware statutes, the 1969 Model Act and the Revised Model Business Corporation Act form the basis for most modern indemnification statutes.

1.   **Indemnification when the Defendant Has Been Successful in the Proceeding**
Under modern statutes the defendant is entitled to indemnification as a matter of statutory right if he "is wholly successful on the merits *or otherwise*". As a result a director with a valid procedural defense is entitled to indemnification without regard to the merits. California omits the phrase "or otherwise."

2.   **Permissive Indemnification**
Under modern statutes, indemnification is permitted as a matter of discretion but not as a matter of right where the defendant acts in good faith and in the best interest of the corporation but is not completely successful in the litigation, for example, by entering into a settlement. Directors cannot compel corporations to grant indemnification for conduct falling within the category of permissive indemnification.

3.   **"Authorization" and "Determination" of Indemnification**
A "determination" relates to the eligibility of the officer or director for indemnification while an "authorization" is a corporate judgment that an appropriate use of corporate resources is to pay the director or officer the amount so "determined." Determinations of indemnification are to be made by directors who are not parties to the litigation, by the shareholders or by special legal counsel. Authorization may be made by the board of directors or by the shareholders.

4.   **Court-Approved Indemnification**
A person otherwise not eligible for indemnification may petition a court for a determination that he is "fairly and reasonably" entitled to indemnification of reasonable expenses. A corporation may avoid court-ordered indemnification by providing so in its articles of incorporation.

5.   **Advances for Expenses**
A corporation may advance expenses of a proceeding as they are incurred without waiting for a final determination of eligibility for indemnification if allowed by statute.

6.   **Indemnification of Officers, Employees and Agents**
Under the Revised Model Business Corporation Act, indemnification of an officer, agent or employee who is not a director is not subject to the limiting principles applicable to indemnification of directors. An officer (but not employees or agents) has the same right to mandatory indemnification as a director and may apply for court-ordered

indemnification. A director who is also an officer or employee is limited to the indemnification rights of a director.

7. Modification of Statutory Indemnification Policies
The Revised Model Business Corporation Act provides that a contractual or voluntary provision relating to indemnification is valid if consistent with the policies of the Act.

8. Indemnification of Witnesses
The Revised Model Business Corporation Act provides that the corporation has power to pay or reimburse the expenses of a director in a proceeding in which he is a witness but not a party.

9. Notification of Indemnification
The Revised Model Business Corporation Act requires the corporation to notify shareholders of all indemnifications or advances of expenses in connection with suits brought by or in the name of the corporation.

10. Indemnification in Federal Proceedings
The SEC believes that it is against public policy for a corporation to indemnify officers or directors against liabilities imposed by the Securities Act of 1933 except upon order of a court.

C. D & O LIABILITY INSURANCE

1. Insurable Risks
D & O policies only cover insurable risks, thereby eliminating wrongful misconduct and self-dealing transactions, among others, from coverage.

2. Policy Exclusions
D & O policies also contain significant exclusions so that the coverage does not include many potential risks.

3. Policy Coverage and Premiums
Policies are generally purchased to cover all officers and directors of the corporation. Premiums are usually shared, with the officers and directors paying a small percentage of the cost.

4. State Statutes
Many state statutes specifically empower corporations to purchase D & O insurance. In the absence of such a statute, a power to acquire such insurance is likely to be implied.

XVII. INSPECTION OF BOOKS AND RECORDS

A. INSPECTION BY DIRECTORS

As a manager of the corporation, a director has a broad though not completely limitless right of inspection.

B. INSPECTION BY SHAREHOLDERS

A shareholder has a more limited inspection right than a director because he does not have management responsibilities and has limited fiduciary duties.

1. Sources of the Shareholders' Right of Inspection

Shareholders' inspection rights may be found in (a) common law principles, (b) statute, (c) rights generally of litigants and (d) rights generally of members of the general public.

a. The common law right of inspection required judicial enforcement upon the showing of a proper purpose by the shareholder. Statutory rights of inspection also require a showing of "proper purpose" but many statutes provide that if the shareholder has owned shares for a specified period (usually six months) or of a specified percentage (usually five percent), the burden is on the corporation to show lack of a proper purpose. These statutes also often impose a statutory penalty on the corporation or its officers for not granting the statutory right of inspection without cause.

b. The Revised Model Business Corporation Act retains the "proper purpose" requirement but eliminates arbitrary time period or holding requirements. The shareholder must allege his purpose with particularity and only records relevant to that purpose need be produced. Enforcement is by summary judicial proceeding with the corporation being required to pay the shareholder's expenses if the refusal was without reasonable cause.

c. The statutory right of inspection provided by the Revised Model Business Corporation supplements the common law right of inspection. In many states the relationship between the statutory and common law rights of inspection is not clear.

2. Scope of Records Subject to Inspection

a. The Revised Model Business Corporation authorizes inspection of "accounting records" of the corporation, the record of shareholders, and minutes of meetings of shareholders and directors. The scope of the inspection right in other state statutes depends on the precise statutory language, which varies widely from state to state.

b.   A corporation may not avoid the right of inspection by offering substitute documents or summaries.

3. Scope of Inspection Right
Most statutes recognize the shareholder may be assisted by his accountant and attorney when inspecting books and records. The Revised Model Business Corporation Act also authorizes machine copies to be made at the shareholder's expense; most state statutes are silent on this matter though courts often authorize such copies where reasonable.

4. Restrictive Orders
Courts may condition or limit the right of inspection in any reasonable way, e.g. by prohibiting the shareholder from giving the information to a competitor.

5. What is a "Proper Purpose"?
A "proper purpose" is one that is reasonably related to the shareholder's interest in the corporation. There has been extensive litigation over what a "proper purpose" is.

6. Inspection Rights of a Beneficial Owner
Nonrecord owners usually have many if not all the inspection rights of a record owner.

C. MANDATORY RECORD KEEPING REQUIREMENTS

1. Record of Shareholders
Statutes usually require a list of persons eligible to vote to be available at a shareholders meeting. The Revised Model Business Corporation Act and many statutes also require that this list be available for a limited period before a meeting.

The list of shareholders (not the voting list prepared for meetings) is the most common object of a demand for inspection. Such a list is usually essential before a proxy fight or takeover attempt can be launched.

2. Mandatory and Discretionary Records
Some state statutes and the Revised Model Business Corporation Act require corporations to keep minutes of meetings and records of actions taken by directors and shareholders. Many statutes recognize that corporations may keep discretionary records of various types.

3. Mandatory Disclosure to Shareholders
Some states require mandatory disclosure to shareholders through annual reports or otherwise. The Revised Model Business Corporation Act

requires every corporation to furnish annual financial statements to shareholders. Many states have no such requirement.

4. Other Mandatory Disclosure Requirements
The Revised Model Business Corporation Act requires disclosure to shareholders of transactions involving issuance of shares for promissory notes or promises of future services as well as indemnification of directors in connection with suits brought by or in the name of the corporation.

XVIII. SHAREHOLDER LITIGATION

"Shareholder litigation" refers to litigation brought by a shareholder in connection with his capacity or role as shareholder.

A. "DIRECT," "DERIVATIVE," AND "CLASS" LITIGATION

1. "Direct" Defined
A direct suit involves the enforcement by a shareholder of a claim based on injury done to him directly as an owner of shares.

2. "Derivative" Defined
A derivative suit is a suit by a shareholder to remedy a wrong to the corporation as such, rather than to the shareholder individually.

3. Relationship with "Class Suits"
Most class suits are direct suits where the number of plaintiffs forming the class is large.

4. Practical Application of Distinctions
Different procedural and substantive rules are applicable to these types of suits. However, the line between them is sometimes hazy and artful pleading may sometimes permit a complaint to be framed either as direct or derivative.

B. DERIVATIVE SUITS IN FEDERAL COURTS

1. Classification of Parties for Diversity Purposes
The corporation is usually aligned as a defendant for diversity purposes.

2. Pendent Jurisdiction
In the absence of diversity, suit may often be brought under federal law and state claims may be attached under the concept of pendent jurisdiction.

C.   PREREQUISITES FOR MAINTAINING DERIVATIVE SUITS

1.   Demand on the Corporation and the Directors
Both the Revised Model Business Corporation Act and the Federal Rules of Civil Procedure require that the plaintiff allege either that he made a demand on the directors for redress or that such a demand would have been fruitless.

2.   Demand on Shareholders
The Federal Rules of Civil Procedure also require an allegation that a demand was made on shareholders or that such a demand was unreasonable. A number of states impose a similar requirement. Taken literally, a demand on shareholders would require an expensive proxy solicitation. The Revised Model Business Corporation Act does not require a demand on shareholders.

3.   Contemporary Ownership
The Federal Rules require that the plaintiff show that he was a shareholder when the cause of action arose or that he later obtained his shares by operation of law. Most states impose a similar requirement.

An equitable principle may prevent persons who acquired most of the shares by purchase from bringing a derivative suit based on pre-purchase claims.

4.   Security for Expenses
Statutes in many states require plaintiffs to post security for the defendants' expenses and allow defendants to be reimbursed for their expenses out of this security if the court finds suit was brought without just cause. These statutes are designed to discourage derivative suits brought solely for their settlement values.

Many statutes impose this requirement only on plaintiffs with small holdings. The Revised Model Business Corporation Act does not contain a security-for-expenses statute on the ground that the requirement unreasonably discriminates against small shareholders. Other statutes have been revised to give the court discretion to impose the security requirement only when the litigation appears frivolous or baseless.

5.   Verification
Both the Revised Model Business Corporation Act and the Federal Rules of Civil Procedure require that shareholders suits be "verified." This is designed to assure good faith litigation but does not require the plaintiff to know the details of his or her claim.

D. DEFENSES IN DERIVATIVE SUITS

1. Failure to Meet Unique Procedural Requirements

A plaintiff who fails to meet the security-for-expenses or similar procedural requirements will have his suit dismissed. Such a dismissal is without prejudice to a later refiling by the same or a different plaintiff.

2. Substantive Defenses

Defenses available to third party defendants may result in a dismissal with prejudice. Such defenses usually may not be raised by the corporation.

3. Plaintiff Disqualification

A third class of defense relates to the specific plaintiff. A disqualification of the plaintiff normally prevents him from thereafter serving as a plaintiff but does not bar subsequent refiling of the suit by another plaintiff.

E. MISCELLANEOUS PROCEDURAL PROBLEMS

1. Necessary Party

The corporation is a necessary party to any derivative litigation.

2. Combination of Claims

A plaintiff normally may not combine direct and derivative claims in the same suit; personal counterclaims usually may not be filed against a derivative plaintiff.

3. Multiple Suits

Multiple derivative suits may be brought by different plaintiffs arising out of a single transaction. Courts have broad discretion to determine which one will proceed and which one will be stayed. Intervention may be permitted.

4. The Role of Counsel

The interests of the corporation and the other defendants are different and normally separate counsel are required. Other problems involve the scope of the attorney-client privilege and the possible role of the plaintiff's counsel with the corporation.

5. Jury Trials

While derivative suits are equitable in nature, a right to a jury trial may exist for issues that are legal in nature.

6. **Merger of Corporate Defendant**
   The merger of a corporate defendant may require that the new or surviving corporation be added to the litigation. In the case of a cash-out merger in which the plaintiff receives cash for his or her shares, the plaintiff may no longer maintain the suit since he or she is no longer a shareholder.

7. **Collateral Estoppel**
   Principles of collateral estoppel may prevent defendants in a derivative suit from relitigating issues previously resolved against them in an enforcement proceeding.

F. SETTLEMENT OF A DERIVATIVE SUIT
Historically, secret settlements have been a serious problem in derivative litigation.

1. **Judicial Approval**
   Most states now require judicial approval of a proposed settlement in an effort to resolve the problem of secret settlements.

2. **Discretionary Review of Proposed Settlements**
   Courts attempt to ascertain that proposed settlements are reasonable, fair, and adequate to the corporation and the shareholders.

3. **Notice and Hearing on Settlement**
   Shareholders are entitled to notice and hearing on proposed settlements.

4. **Derivative Pursuit of Secret Settlement**
   A secret settlement may be itself made the subject of a derivative suit.

5. **Settlement of Underlying Claim**
   A corporation may itself settle a claim that is in litigation without court approval and that settlement also may be made the basis of a later derivative suit.

G. RECOVERY IN DERIVATIVE SUITS
Generally, recovery goes to the corporation not the plaintiff shareholder.

1. **Justification of Rule**
   The general rule protects all interests in the corporation, including creditors.

2. **Exception Where Wrongdoers are Major Shareholders**
   Some courts have allowed innocent shareholders to recover directly on the theory that wrongdoers should not be permitted to control the use of the proceeds. These cases are the minority view.

    3.   Other Relief
    In appropriate cases, plaintiffs may obtain injunctive or other relief.

H.   RES JUDICATA

    1.   Final Judgment on the Merits
    A final judgment on the merits binds not only the plaintiffs but also all other shareholders.

    2.   Settlements
    Court approved settlements are normally binding on all shareholders.

    3.   Dismissal of Suit
    A dismissal may or may not have res judicata effect depending on the grounds of the dismissal.

I.   PLAINTIFF'S EXPENSES

    1.   Creation of a Fund
    A successful plaintiff is entitled to have his or her expenses, including attorneys' fees, repaid out of any fund created by the successful suit.

    2.   Non-Fund Cases
    Attorneys' fees for successful plaintiffs may also be paid if the suit is of substantial benefit to the corporation even if no fund is created.

    3.   Amount of Plaintiff/Attorneys' Fees
    A variety of factors are taken into account in establishing the amount of the fee to be awarded the attorney for the successful plaintiff.

XIX. ORGANIC CHANGES

Organic changes include a variety of basic changes in the structure of the corporation. Such changes require approval of the shareholders. Traditionally, approval by two-thirds of all shares, voting and nonvoting alike, was required but the Revised Model Business Corporation Act and the statutes of many states now only require approval by a majority of all outstanding voting shares, whether or not present at the meeting.

A.   AMENDMENT OF ARTICLES
    Under modern statutes there are no "vested rights" in certain provisions of articles of incorporation. Any provision may be amended by the statutory procedure.

1.   **Mandatory Requirements**
An amendment may only include provisions that permissibly may be included in original articles of incorporation. Amendments that make changes in issued securities must also be accompanied by a description of how the changes are to be effectuated. Under the Revised Model Business Corporation Act, the implementing provisions may appear in the articles of amendment.

2.   **Procedural Requirements**
Generally, an amendment need be approved only by the required majority or greater percentage of shareholders set forth in the statute. Under the Revised Model Business Corporation Act, a majority of the votes present at a meeting at which a quorum is present is sufficient to approve an amendment unless the amendment creates dissenter's rights with respect to a class in which case the amendment must be approved by a majority of all of the shares of that class. Such a class is entitled to vote as a separate voting group on the amendment. A nonvoting class of shares may be entitled to vote as a class on a change burdensome to it. Dissenting shareholders may also have a right of dissent and appraisal on amendments that affect a class in specified ways, for certain types of amendments.

3.   **Remnants of the Vested Rights Theory**
Some states impose legal or equitable restrictions on amendments to articles of incorporation that are burdensome to a specific class of shares.

B.   **STATUTORY MERGERS AND CONSOLIDATIONS**
Statutes authorize certain transactions which combine two or more corporations.

1.   **Definitions**
A "merger" is a combination of two corporations in which one disappears and another survives. A "consolidation" involves the combination of two corporations into a new corporation. The Revised Model Business Corporation Act does not include the concept of a "consolidation."

These combinations are usually called "statutory mergers" or "Class A reorganizations."

2.   **Procedures**
A merger must be approved by the board of directors and recommended to the shareholders for approval. The traditional percentage was two-thirds of all outstanding shares but the Revised Model Business Corporation Act and many state statutes require a majority of the voting shares to approve the transaction.

Shareholders that have a right to vote have the right of dissent and appraisal if the plan of merger contains a provision that would create a right of dissent and appraisal if it were contained in an amendment to the articles of incorporation.

3. Triangular Mergers, Cash Mergers and Short Form Mergers

A triangular merger involves the merger of a corporation into a subsidiary of the acquiring corporation; the shareholders of the disappearing corporation receive shares of the acquiring corporation, not shares of its subsidiary.

A cash merger is a merger in which some minority shareholders are required to accept cash or property rather than shares in the continuing enterprise.

A short form merger is a merger between a parent corporation and its subsidiary which usually must be 90 per cent or 95 per cent owned to qualify under the short form merger section of the statute. The parent corporation must be the surviving corporation.

Delaware law imposes an "entire fairness" and "full disclosure" test to such transactions.

These types of mergers are permitted by the statutes of many but not all states.

4. Reverse Triangular Mergers and Share Exchanges

In instances where the continued existence of the acquired corporation is important, the process of a "reverse triangular merger" may be used. Such process involves the formation of a new subsidiary of the acquiring company, followed by a merger of that subsidiary into the corporation to be acquired. Securities of the parent are exchanged for securities of the corporation to be acquired. Ultimately the acquired corporation becomes a wholly owned subsidiary of the acquiring corporation.

C. SALES OF SUBSTANTIALLY ALL ASSETS

A sale of substantially all the assets of the corporation is usually treated as an organic or fundamental change in the corporation.

1. Sales in Ordinary Course of Business

A sale in the ordinary course of business usually does not require shareholder approval. The Revised Model Business Corporation Act also provides that a transaction in which assets are distributed to a wholly owned subsidiary does not require shareholder approval.

2. Right of Dissent and Appraisal
The right of dissent and appraisal usually exist in connection with a sale not in the ordinary course of business.

D. NONSTATUTORY AMALGAMATIONS

1. Types of Transactions
A stock-acquisition or asset-acquisition transaction may have the same economic effect as a statutory merger.

A stock-acquisition transaction is often called a "Class B reorganization;" an asset-acquisition transaction is often called a "Class C reorganization."

2. Selection of Form of Transaction
The selection of the form of the transaction may have substantive legal, economic, and tax consequences. Persons in control of a corporation may negotiate for the form which is most beneficial to them.

A few courts have held that a transaction which has the same economic effect as a statutory merger must be treated as if it were such a merger. This is the de facto merger doctrine.

E. RECAPITALIZATIONS
A recapitalization is a restructuring of the capital structure of the corporation, typically an elimination of large arrearages on cumulative preferred shares.

1. Economics of Transaction
A recapitalization may be beneficial to all interests in a corporation, even those who are asked to give up some rights.

2. Form of Transactions
A recapitalization typically takes the form of an articles amendment or a merger into a wholly owned subsidiary.

3. Validity of Transactions
While arguments based on "vested rights" are not likely to succeed, recapitalizations may be subject to attack on grounds of "fraud" or "manifest unfairness."

F. "GOING PRIVATE"
"Going private" refers to the once popular transaction involving the elimination of public shareholders to avoid reporting and other legal requirements.

1. **Economics of Transaction**

   A corporation may go public when market conditions are favorable for a high price. Years later, the going private transaction occurs when the market is depressed.

2. **Form of Transaction**

   A going private transaction usually takes the form of a cash merger with the public shareholders being compelled to accept cash. It may also take the form of a reverse stock split with fractional interests being compelled to accept cash. The split is set at a level at which all public interests become fractional interests.

3. **Regulation of Going Private Transactions**

   The state law applicable to cash mergers is applicable to going private transactions. In addition, the SEC has adopted disclosure regulations relating to going private transactions.

G. LEVERAGED BUYOUTS

A leveraged buyout (LBO) is a transaction by which an outside entity, not itself a publicly held corporation, acquires all the outstanding shares of a publicly held corporation. After the LBO is completed, the corporation is no longer publicly owned. Often the management is interested in the acquiring entity. Advantages of an LBO include cost savings of compliance with the securities acts and tax savings arising from the transaction.

H. RIGHTS OF DISSENT AND APPRAISAL

1. **Scope of Right**

   Shareholders have the statutory right to dissent and to obtain the appraised value of their shares through a judicial proceeding in connection with specific transactions described in the statute. Several state statutes provide that the statutory dissent and appraisal procedure is the exclusive remedy for dissenting shareholders. The Revised Model Business Corporation Act provides the remedy is exclusive "unless the action is unlawful or fraudulent" with respect to the shareholders.

2. **Procedure for Appraisal**

   Precise statutory procedures are usually established; these procedures must be strictly complied with if the appraisal right is to be obtained. The price is set by judicial proceeding if a negotiated price cannot be established. The Revised Model Business Corporation Act provides that payment of the undisputed portion of the value of the shares must be made promptly after the transaction. Most states provide for payment only at the termination of the judicial proceeding.

3. Evaluation of Appraisal Remedy

Appraisal is often not a preferred remedy from the standpoint of minority shareholders because it requires expensive and time consuming litigation and because the corporation with its extensive assets is an active participant seeking to establish the lowest possible valuation.

I. VOLUNTARY DISSOLUTION

1. Dissolution Before Commencement of Business

A simplified process of dissolution before commencement of business is usually available.

2. Dissolution by Consent of Shareholders

Dissolution by unanimous consent of shareholders is permitted in many states. Such consent can only be obtained as a practical matter in closely held corporations. The Revised Model Business Corporation Act does not contain a special provision to this effect; though shareholders may act by unanimous consent, action by directors is also required.

3. Regular Dissolution

Dissolution requires adoption of a resolution to dissolve by directors, followed by approval by the specified percentage of shareholders.

4. Notice of Intent to Dissolve

Some state statutes require a corporation planning to dissolve to file a preliminary notice of intent to dissolve. Many state statutes dispense with this requirement.

5. Dissolution Procedure

Notice must be given to creditors. Final dissolution is permitted only after all debts and taxes have been paid, and all statutory requirements complied with.

6. Equitable Limitations on Dissolution

The power to dissolve a corporation voluntarily may sometimes be abused. Some courts have imposed equitable limitations on the otherwise unlimited power to dissolve upon compliance with the mandated statutory procedures.

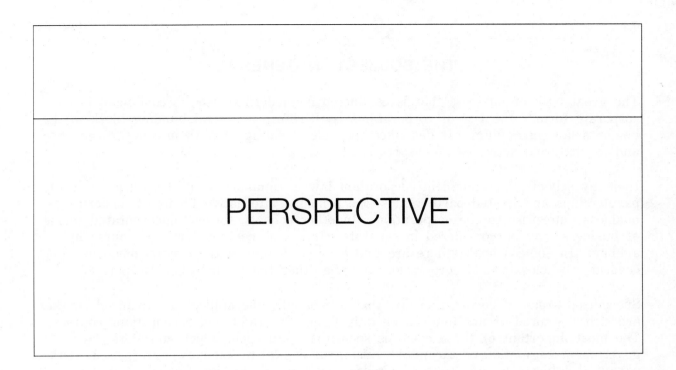

PERSPECTIVE

Analysis

The Subject in General
Relationship With Agency
Relationship With Federal Income Taxation
How to Prepare for and Do Well on Corporation Examinations

THE SUBJECT IN GENERAL

The great bulk of business that is conducted in modern society is conducted in corporate form. The law of corporations is therefore a central building block in the business law curriculum. It describes the rules relating to both internal governance and the external activities of corporations.

In many schools, the course in corporation law is combined in part with a study of partnerships and limited partnerships, the principal alternative forms of modern business enterprise to the corporation. In other schools, these unincorporated forms of business may be considered in separate courses or combined with a course in agency. In some schools, there are two courses dealing with corporations, one covering the closely held corporation and the other the publicly held corporation.

Specialized areas of corporation law that are usually the subject of advanced courses are either ignored or are touched on only lightly in traditional corporations courses. The most important of these areas is securities regulation, which considers government regulation of the public raising of capital by business enterprises. Other advanced subjects include corporate reorganization, corporation finance, and the taxation of business enterprises.

This outline discusses corporations, both closely held and publicly held. It does not cover partnerships or limited partnerships, or the specialized advanced subjects described in the previous paragraph, though it does discuss some of the topics covered in these advanced courses.

RELATIONSHIP WITH AGENCY

Many problems discussed in the corporations course involve agency principles. Corporation teachers generally assume that students have received a grounding in fundamental agency concepts either in the first year of law school or in separate agency/partnership courses, or in both. Some casebooks contain brief discussions of agency concepts for the benefit of students who feel their grounding in this important area is weak. In general, for the purposes of the corporations course, it is more important that the student understand the fundamental principles of the law of agency, such as the difference between actual and apparent authority, than the technical rules about subjects such as when actual authority is revoked.

RELATIONSHIP WITH FEDERAL INCOME TAXATION

The relationship between the courses in corporations and federal income taxation is somewhat like the relationship between the chicken and the egg. Many areas discussed in the law of corporations are shaped to some degree by federal tax concepts; on the other hand, many issues discussed in tax courses presuppose a working knowledge of corporate concepts. While there is no rigid rule about which course should be taken first, or whether it is desirable to take the two courses simultaneously, it is customary for most students in most schools to take corporations without previously having had a course in federal income taxation. As a result, many individual corporation teachers do not emphasize tax concepts (depending to some extent on the casebook that is chosen); even where tax-related concepts are discussed, they can almost always be understood without a broader knowledge of federal income taxation generally. On the other hand, a basic working knowledge of corporations is usually assumed without discussion in federal income taxation courses.

HOW TO PREPARE FOR AND DO WELL ON CORPORATION EXAMINATIONS

The law of corporations is derived partially from state and federal statutory provisions and partly from common law sources. Some teachers use the corporations course as largely an exercise in statutory construction and analysis of the law of a particular state, while others emphasize the broader common law or general issues. In either event, some attention is normally paid to federal law dealing with corporate issues as well as state law. In preparing for an examination a student must recognize the emphasis the instructor has placed on these areas and concentrate his time accordingly. Further, account must be taken of the nature of the examination itself: a short answer or multiple choice examination in a course that has heavily emphasized the statutes and case law of a particular state, should be prepared for quite differently from an essay examination in a course that concentrated on general or federal legal principles without considering as a unit the law of any particular state.

The practice questions included in this outline are designed to give students experience with both short answer and essay questions, though it must be recognized that questions based on state statutory provisions can only be answered correctly by reference to the rules in the specific state in question.

When answering essay questions, a student in corporation law should follow basically the same method of analysis of the question that is applicable to every law school essay exam. However, in considering his response, the student must take into account the possibility that the question raises issues of statutory construction or application of federal law as well as traditional common law principles. A student virtually guarantees himself or herself a low grade if he or she answers a question that revolves around the construction of a specific statutory provision on the basis of general equitable principles. The same unfortunate result follows if a student applies principles of federal law to a situation in which no federal jurisdiction exists. The following suggestions may help to avoid these common errors in examination analysis:

1)   The first step in any examination is to read the question very carefully and identify the issues and questions raised. While this may seem self-evident, probably more poor answers are the result of inadequate analysis of the question than any other single cause. It may be helpful to ask yourself: Why is the instructor asking me about this factual situation? What areas of the course are involved in this situation?

2)   The second step is to isolate the legal principles that are applicable to the issues and questions raised. In corporations, the legal principles may be found (a) in a corporation statute or code (either that of a specific state, of Delaware, or possibly, the Revised Model Business Corporation Act); (b) in the general case law dealing with corporations that form the bulk of the cases in each of the casebooks; or (c) in the federal law arising under either the Federal Securities Act of 1933 or the Securities Exchange Act of 1934, or conceivably under the Federal Securities Code that has not yet been enacted. It is possible that a single question may have one or more facets arising under different sources.

3)   Having isolated the issues and the sources of legal principles, organize your answer and respond to the issues raised in the same manner as in any other examination. Conclusions should be supported by reasons; if you have rejected an argument that appears to be plausible, it is desirable to refer to both the argument and the reason for its rejection; make sure that your answer responds to all the issues raised by the question, and so forth.

4)   Be careful about "just throwing things in" because you know about them. A canned essay on an irrelevant topic almost certainly will not help you, and may well detract from the overall evaluation of your answer. Also, some exam questions in corporations (and in other subjects as well) may be designed to test whether you know that some principle is *not* applicable; for this reason you should concentrate on why the principle is not applicable, not on what would happen if the inapplicable principle were applicable.

I

CORPORATION LAW
IN GENERAL

Analysis

A. "Corporation" Defined
B. Constitutional Incidents of the Corporate "Personality"
C. Sources of Law
D. Functional Classification of Corporations

A. "CORPORATION" DEFINED

A corporation is a type of legal institution or concept that defines relationships among people. It is "more nearly a method than a thing." *Farmers' Loan & Trust Co. v. Pierson*, 222 N.Y.S. 532, 543 (Sup.Ct. 1927). Several different theories have been proposed to describe these relationships; each is to some degree a correct picture of what a corporation is.

1.   ENTITY THEORY
A corporation can be most readily envisioned as an artificial, fictitious entity created for the purpose of conducting a business. The basic elements of this artificial entity are the following:

   a.   The corporation has the power to conduct its business entirely in its own name, including entering into contracts, buying or selling land, bringing suits or being sued, filing tax returns, paying taxes, and the like.

   b.   The artificial entity is formed by a grant of authority by a government agency, in most states, the secretary of state. A document, usually entitled "articles of incorporation," must be filed, a filing fee paid, and other formal steps taken to form the entity.

   c.   The artificial entity must be generally recognized as such by the creating state, the Federal Government, and private citizens who deal with the corporation.

   d.   The artificial entity in a fundamental sense is a fiction. In the bright eye of reality, real people conduct a business, whether or not it is in corporate form, and real people enjoy the profit or suffer the loss from the business. In some limited situations courts may refuse to follow the artificial entity analysis to its logical conclusions, if it leads to fraudulent or significantly unfair consequences, frustration of clearly defined statutory policies, or other undesirable results. *Farmers' Loan & Trust Co. v. Pierson*, 222 N.Y.S. 532 (Sup.Ct. 1927). These situations are discussed in somewhat greater detail below under the doctrine "piercing the corporate veil." (See part IV.A).

2.   CONCESSION THEORY
A second theory of corporateness is that a corporation is a "grant" or "concession" from the state. Cf. *Association for the Preservation of Freedom of Choice, Inc. v. Shapiro*, 174 N.E.2d 487 (N.Y. 1961). This theory is based on the role of the state in the formation of a corporation described above.

   a.   This theory was more popular at an earlier time when the grant of corporate charters was ringed with restrictions or limitations.

b.   This theory is sometimes referred to today in the debate over "social responsibility" of corporations. The argument is that because a corporation is a grant or concession, it may be qualified by the state as it sees fit; the state may therefore validly impose restrictions on corporate behavior and withdraw the corporate privilege completely if the restrictions are not complied with.

3.   CONTRACT THEORY

A third theory of corporateness is that the charter of a corporation represents a contract (a) between the state and the corporation, or (b) between the corporation and its shareholders, or (c) among the shareholders themselves. The implications of this theory are as follows:

a.   The argument that a corporate charter represents a contract between the state and the corporation has less appeal today than in an earlier day. It was relied upon by the United States Supreme Court in *Dartmouth College v. Woodward,* 17 U.S. (4 Wheat) 518 (1819) to prevent the state of New Hampshire from enacting a statute amending the charter of the College. However, the case is primarily of historical interest today because, following a suggestion in the opinion in that case, all modern state statutes specifically reserve the power to subject outstanding charters to subsequent statutory amendments.

b.   The argument that a corporate charter represents a contract between the shareholders or between the corporation and the shareholders is likely to surface in the current context in disputes between different classes of shareholders, or in disputes in which one class of shareholders claims that the class is being discriminated against in some way. Rights of senior classes of securities (e. g., preferred shares) are defined and limited by the basic corporate documents; the provisions in these documents relating to the rights of the senior securities are often described as the "contract" between the senior securities holders and the common shareholders.

> *Example:*   Articles of incorporation provide that preferred shares are "entitled to receive, when and as declared by the board of directors, dividends equal to but not exceeding two dollars per share per year before any dividend is declared or paid on common shares." The corporation has an exceptional year and the directors are considering paying dividends in excess of $20.00 per share. The preferred shares are nevertheless only entitled to receive two dollars per share; if the directors attempt to declare a discretionary dividend of, say, ten dollars per share on the preferred, that is a "breach of the common shareholders' contract" which entitles them to enjoin any dividend on the preferred in excess of two dollars per share.

4.   NEXUS OF CONTRACTUAL RELATIONSHIPS

The economist has evolved his or her own theory of corporateness that permits analysis of the corporation as an economic phenomenon. This theory rejects the notion that the shareholders are the ultimate owners of the enterprise but treats them, along with bondholders and other creditors, as providers of capital in anticipation of receiving a desired return. The "nexus of contractual relationships" includes all arrangements by which capital, labor, material, and managerial services are obtained by the corporation.

It should be noted that under this theory shareholders and creditors explicitly share the risk that total revenues will be less than total costs during an accounting period.

B.   CONSTITUTIONAL INCIDENTS OF THE CORPORATE "PERSONALITY"

A corporation is entitled to some but not all of the constitutional protections available to individual persons. The process of deciding which constitutional protections are available to corporations and which are not is a matter of constitutional construction.

1.   PRIVILEGES AND IMMUNITIES

A corporation is not a citizen of a state or of the United States for purposes of the privileges and immunities clause. *Paul v. Virginia*, 75 U.S. (8 Wall.) 168 (1868). Therefore states may validly impose restrictions on a foreign corporation's activities within the state, *Eli Lilly & Co. v. Sav-On-Drugs, Inc.*, 366 U.S. 276, 81 S.Ct. 1316 (1961), though such restrictions may relate only to *intrastate* activities and may not burden interstate commerce. *Allenberg Cotton Co., Inc. v. Pittman*, 419 U.S. 20, 95 S.Ct. 260 (1974).

2.   FREE SPEECH

A corporation has rights of free speech which may not be restricted as such by state statute. *Pacific Gas & Elec. v. P.U.C. of California*, ___ U.S. ___, 106 S.Ct. 903 (1986); *First Nat'l Bank of Boston v. Bellotti*, 435 U.S. 765, 98 S.Ct. 1407 (1978); *Consolidated Edison Co. v. Public Service Commission*, 447 U.S. 530, 100 S.Ct. 2326 (1980).

3.   SELF INCRIMINATION

A corporation does not have a privilege against self incrimination. *Wilde v. Brewer*, 329 F.2d 924 (9th Cir. 1964).

4.   DUE PROCESS AND EQUAL PROTECTION

A corporation is protected against deprivations of property without due process of law, *Oklahoma Press Pub. Co. v. Walling*, 327 U.S. 186, 66 S.Ct. 494 (1946), and is entitled to the constitutional right of equal protection of the law,

Munn v. Illinois, 94 U.S. (4 Otto) 113 (1877); *Wheeling Steel Corp. v. Glander*, 337 U.S. 562, 69 S.Ct. 1291 (1949).

C. SOURCES OF LAW

The law of corporations is derived from several sources.

1. STATE INCORPORATION STATUTES

Every state has a general incorporation statute which describes the incorporation process, defines generally the rights, powers and roles of shareholders, directors, and officers within the corporation, and provides rules about fundamental corporate changes. While these statutes vary from state to state, there has been a substantial trend toward modernization and liberalization in all states with the result that variations from state to state are declining in importance. Two sources of statutes have been particularly influential:

a. The Model Business Corporation Act prepared and maintained by the committee on corporate laws of the section on corporation, banking and business law of the American Bar Association; and

b. The Delaware General Corporation Law. Several important commercial states, including New York and California, have retained their own statutes; because of the commercial importance of these states, these statutes have also been influential.

2. STATE COMMON LAW PRINCIPLES

Because of the importance of statutory provisions in the law of corporations, the common law inheritance of rules and principles is now less important than in some other subjects. Many judicial decisions are interstitial in nature, either supplying supplementary principles when the statutes are silent or construing statutory provisions. Such decisions of course are authoritative. Nevertheless, in some areas broad common law principles are still generally applied on the theory that they define basic rights and duties within a corporation and were not affected by statutory enactments.

3. FEDERAL STATUTES

The Securities Exchange Act of 1934 and the Securities Act of 1933 are the major federal statutes applicable to broad categories of corporations. Under these statutes, the Securities and Exchange Commission (SEC) has broad rulemaking power which it has not hestitated to exercise. A significant portion of the law applicable to publicly held corporations is federal in origin, based on these statutes, and rules promulgated thereunder.

4.   FEDERAL COMMON LAW
Prior to 1970 several federal cases and law review commentaries suggested
that a "federal law of corporations" was developing under these federal
securities acts.   However, with a series of restrictive decisions by the United
States Supreme Court beginning in about 1975, it now is clear that a general
federal jurisprudence of corporations has not been created, and federal law
applied to corporations must be grounded in the securities acts and regulations.
The principal cases involved in the growth and decline of federal corporation
law are set forth in XV, infra.

D.   FUNCTIONAL CLASSIFICATION OF CORPORATIONS

The basic distinction underlying much of the law of corporations is between the
closely held corporation (or "close corporation") and the *publicly held corporation*
(or "public corporation").   While the same statutes are often applicable to both
classes of corporations, the problems and concerns are usually quite different and in
most courses are discussed separately.

1.   DEFINITION OF A CLOSELY HELD CORPORATION
A closely held corporation is a corporation with most of the following
attributes:

    a.   It has a few shareholders, all or most of whom are usually active in the
management of the business;

    b.   There is no public market for its shares;

    c.   Its shares are subject to one or more restrictions on transfer; and

    d.   It has never registered a public distribution of shares under the federal
or state securities acts.

2.   DEFINITION OF A PUBLICLY HELD CORPORATION
A publicly held corporation is a corporation with most of the following
attributes:

    a.   Some of its shares are held by members of the general public and the
overall number of shareholders is usually large;

    b.   There is a public market for its shares which may be on a securities
exchange or among brokers "over the counter;"

    c.   The corporation is subject to reporting and disclosure requirements under
the securities acts;

    d.   It has made a distribution of shares to members of the general public.

3. **THEORETICAL SIGNIFICANCE OF THE DISTINCTION BETWEEN CLOSELY HELD AND PUBLICLY HELD CORPORATIONS**

While many publicly held corporations are relatively large in terms of assets and many closely held corporations are relatively small in terms of assets, the importance of the distinction is not the size of assets as much as the number of shareholders and the marketability of their shares.

a.   The presence or absence of a public market for the corporation's shares is the most important difference between the two types of corporations.

1)   A shareholder in a publicly held corporation who is dissatisfied with management may sell his shares on the public market; a shareholder in a closely held corporation may have no place to sell his shares except to other shareholders in a face-to-face transaction in which the other shareholders may be willing to buy only at relatively low prices.

2)   In the publicly held corporation, the value of shares may be more readily estimated because the public market for shares provides a benchmark as to what numerous buyers and sellers believe the shares to be worth; in contrast, in the closely held corporation, there may be no external way to estimate the value of corporate shares.

3)   Because of the nonexistence of a market for shares in the closely held corporation, a minority shareholder may be "locked in" to an unsalable asset and be subject to "freeze out" or "squeeze out" tactics; these concepts have only limited application to publicly held corporations.

b.   A second major difference is that in a closely held corporation, most of the shareholders are likely to be employed by or earn their livelihood through the corporation's business while in a publicly held corporation, most of the shareholders are not connected with management and have only a limited say in the policies adopted by the corporation. As a result, "ownership" and "control" are likely to be widely separated in a publicly held corporation but closely interconnected in a closely held corporation.

c.   A third difference is that the presence of public shareholders unconnected with the business of a publicly held corporation is thought to present a strong case for governmental regulation of internal aspects of a public corporation's affairs, while in a closely held corporation, there is usually thought to be only a relatively weak (or nonexistent) case for governmental regulation of the internal affairs of the corporation.

Caveat: Corporations form a continuum rather than a polar concentration. At the margin there may be uncertainty whether a specific corporation has more of the attributes of a publicly held or a closely held corporation. The issue that must be resolved with respect to such an "in between" corporation may dictate its classification as closely held or publicly held in the specific case, though in some instances a comparison with both publicly and closely held corporations may be helpful. Numerically, the "in between corporation" is quite common, much more numerous than the publicly held corporation.

Example: *Y* Corporation is owned by six persons, three of whom participate full-time in the management of the business. Shares were originally sold to four persons; when one withdrew, he sold his shares to three other investors. Thereafter share transfer restrictions on the shares were imposed by unanimous agreement. The corporation is a closely held corporation.

Example: *AB* Corporation was wholly owned by two brothers in 1969, when they decided to "go public" by selling ten per cent of the outstanding shares through a registered public offering. At the present time, *A* and *B* own 87 per cent of the stock; the balance of the shares are owned by members of the general public. *A* and *B* continue to operate the business, electing themselves as directors. One brokerage firm "makes a market" in *AB* Corporation stock by quoting bid and asked prices for shares from time to time. Sales, however, are infrequent. *AB* Corporation is a publicly held corporation; if the number of shareholders is over 500 and corporate assets exceed three million dollars, it has additional registration obligations under the Securities Exchange Act of 1934.

Example: *X* Corporation was originally formed and wholly owned by two brothers who died in 1936 and 1938. They left the bulk of their shares to their fourteen children, though one brother made several gifts of shares to trusted employees. Of the fourteen children and employees owning shares, several have died leaving shares to children, nephews, nieces, spouses, etc. By 1980, there are a total of 123 shareholders and no shareholder owns more than 20 per cent of the outstanding shares. There has never been a public offering of the shares and there is no trading in *X* Corporation shares, though a few isolated sales have occurred from time to time. Despite the large number of shareholders, *X* Corporation has more of the characteristics of a closely held corporation than a publicly held corporation, though it is not clearly one nor the other. If the number of shareholders grows to over 500 when it has over three million dollars of assets, it too, like *AB* Corporation, will be obligated to register under the Securities Exchange Act of 1934. Of course, as the number of shareholders increases, the probability that a public market in the corporation's shares will also develop increases.

Caveat: The economist views the market for many publicly held shares to be "efficient" and to reflect the best estimates of value of the shares at any point in time. Considerable empirical evidence supporting this view exists for the broadest securities markets, including the New York Stock Exchange. The market for many publicly held securities, however, is much thinner and there is little empirical evidence as to the nature of these markets. Like the distinction between publicly held and closely held corporations, the "efficiency" of markets may be a matter of degree, and one should not assume that merely because a corporation is classified as "publicly held" an efficient and broad market necessarily exists for its shares.

REVIEW QUESTIONS

I–1. Corporate problems are easy. One simply should visualize the corporation as a separate person and answer the question.

True _____   False _____

I–2. Corporate problems are easy. One should simply view the corporation as a contract among the various participants.

True _____   False _____

I–3. If one person owns all of the stock of a corporation he is that corporation, and all the fictions in this world cannot dispute that fact.

This comment is largely true _____   largely false _____

I–4. The state grants the corporation its charter and may impose any restrictions it wishes. A corporation therefore does not have any constitutional rights.

True _____   False _____

I–5.   The rights of a preferred shareholder are set forth in articles of incorporation and common shareholders may limit the rights of the preferred shareholders to what is set forth in the articles.

True ——————————   False ——————————

I–6.   The state grants the corporation its charter and its law therefore controls all aspects of the corporation's conduct.

True ——————————   False ——————————

I–7.   How does a closely held corporation differ from a publicly held corporation?

II

FORMATION OF CORPORATIONS

Analysis

A. SELECTION OF STATE OF INCORPORATION

The first question that must be resolved in forming a corporation is what state should be the state of incorporation.

1. **LOCAL OR CLOSELY HELD BUSINESSES**
    For local or closely held businesses, the choice of the state of incorporation usually comes down to the state in which business is principally conducted or a state with a "liberal" statute, such as Delaware.

    a. The costs of incorporating in Delaware and qualifying to transact business as a foreign corporation in the local state are almost always higher than local incorporation.

    b. With the "modernization" of state statutes and the elimination of onerous requirements, the disadvantages of local incorporation have tended to diminish or disappear.

    c. Incorporation in Delaware may create later problems, for example, the corporation or its directors may be subject to suit in Delaware even though no business is conducted there and none of the directors are present in Delaware.

2. **INTERSTATE OR NATIONAL BUSINESS**
    For interstate or national businesses, incorporation in any one of several states is usually feasible, since in any event the corporation must qualify to transact business as a foreign corporation in the other states in which it does business. Most large publicly held corporations are interstate or national in character and may incorporate in any one of the 50 states. Many such businesses incorporate in a "liberal" jurisdiction, usually Delaware, for the following reasons:

    a. A "liberal" statute is by definition a statute designed to simplify the problems faced by management in conducting business under that statute;

    b. There are a large number of judicial decisions in Delaware construing the statute so that uncertainties are minimized;

    c. There is a sophisticated judiciary and bar in Delaware familiar with corporation problems and corporation laws; and

    d. There is a "climate" favorable to corporations and business in Delaware that may be reflected in prompt amendments to the statute if unsuspected problems arise.

Caveat: Are the Delaware statute and the Delaware judiciary more management-oriented and permissive than the statutes and judiciaries of other states? It is tempting to conclude that they must be because of the number of large public corporations that have elected to incorporate in Delaware. Some respected commentators have made such accusations, but there also have been staunch defenders of the Delaware law and judiciary. It is difficult to find any hard empirical evidence to establish such charges. Indeed, empirical studies show that shares of corporations reincorporating in Delaware do not decline in value as a result of the reincorporation. Certainly some recent Delaware court opinions stress protection of minority shareholders and hold management responsible for abuses of their position. Further, a comparison of the Delaware statute with the Revised Model Act or the corporation statutes of several other leading states do not reveal any consistent promanagement bias in the Delaware statute. It may be that the popularity of Delaware today is based in part on tradition and in part on the relatively high degree of certainty and specificity that marks the Delaware corporation law.

Caveat: California is usually viewed as a "strict" state. The California statute contains a number of "pro-shareholder" provisions that do not appear in the statutes of most states. California also has adopted a provision by which it seeks to impose certain of these pro-shareholder provisions on foreign corporations that have substantial contacts with California. New York also has a somewhat similar, but considerably narrower, provision.

B. VARIATIONS IN STATUTORY REQUIREMENTS AND NOMENCLATURE

1. STATUTORY REQUIREMENTS

It is obviously essential to comply with the specific statutory requirements of the state chosen for the state of incorporation.

a. While numerous variations exist from state to state, there is a surprising degree of uniformity and consistency in most modern statutes. Virtually all onerous substantive requirements have been eliminated in most states.

b. Procedural variations in the incorporation process may still exist in some states. While most states simply require a filing with a state official and nothing more, some states, such as Delaware, also require a local filing in the county in which the registered office is located. Other states, such as Arizona, also require a public advertisement in a newspaper of general circulation of the fact of incorporation. Some states also continue to require the filing of additional documents to establish compliance with various statutory requirements.

c. Variations may also exist with respect to filing fees, franchise taxes, stock issuance or transfer taxes, and similar items.

2. NOMENCLATURE

The Revised Model Business Corporation Act (1984) nomenclature is followed in most states. In this nomenclature, the document filed with the secretary of state is called "articles of incorporation." Under earlier versions of the Model Act (and the statutes of a number of states), the secretary of state issued a document called a "certificate of incorporation" when he or she accepted the articles for filing. In the Revised Model Act (and the statutes of an increasing number of states), the paper work is simplified by requiring the Secretary of State simply to issue a fee receipt as indicating acceptance of the filing.

In some states the document filed with the secretary of state is called a "certificate of incorporation" or "charter"; in some states, the document issued by the secretary of state may be called a "charter."

C. DOCUMENTS FILED IN THE OFFICE OF THE SECRETARY OF STATE

The basic filing requirement is that articles of incorporation which conform to statutory requirements must be filed accompanied by the appropriate filing fee.

1. PROCEDURE UNDER OLDER STATUTES

Under most older state statutes, duplicate originals or an original and a copy of the articles of incorporation, must be filed with the secretary of state.

a. "Duplicate originals" means that both copies must be manually executed with original notarial seals and the like. As a practical matter, the document is prepared and copies made before it is executed; the original and one copy are then executed and filed. An "original and a copy" means that the original is fully executed and then copied by xerography or similar means so that signatures and seals are reproduced but not original.

b. If the articles conform to the statute, the office of the secretary of state attaches the certificate of incorporation to the copy or duplicate original and returns them to the incorporators or their representative.

c. A receipt for the filing fee also usually accompanies the certificate.

2. PROCEDURE UNDER NEWER STATUTES
To reduce the problems of handling many pieces of paper, some states authorize the filing of only a single original executed copy of the articles; the incorporators receive only a receipt for the filing fee as the sole evidence of incorporation. Such receipt is the equivalent of a certificate of incorporation. Of course, a certified copy of the original articles on file with the secretary of state often may be obtained for a nominal fee.

3. PROCEDURE UNDER THE REVISED MODEL BUSINESS CORPORATION ACT
RMBCA §§ 1.20 and 1.25 standardize and simplify the filing requirements and filing procedures for most documents. Requirements that documents be verified or acknowledged are eliminated; the executing officer must simply designate the capacity in which he signs. One exact or conformed copy of the executed document must be filed with the document; the secretary of state attaches the fee receipt (or acknowledgement of receipt if there is no fee) to the copy and returns it to the filing party. The purpose of this procedure is to provide, for the benefit of the corporation, a copy of the filed document which shows on its face that it is an exact copy.

The Act seeks to limit the discretion of the secretary of state in reviewing documents submitted for filing. This officer's duty is described as "ministerial" and he or she is directed to file documents even though they contain material not referred to in the Act [RMBCA § 1.25(d)]. RMBCA § 1.21 prohibits the secretary of state from prescribing mandatory forms (with a couple of minor exceptions). RMBCA § 1.30 grants this officer power "reasonably necessary to perform the duties required of him by this Act," but the Official Comment adds that this provision "is not intended to give him general authority to establish public policy." These restrictions on the authority of the secretary of state are narrower than the authority enjoyed by that officer in most states.

D. INCORPORATORS

Articles of incorporation are executed by one or more persons called "incorporators." Historically, three incorporators who were natural persons were required and many states imposed special residency or other requirements for incorporators. The signatures of incorporators usually had to be verified or under oath.

1. MODERN RELAXATION OF REQUIREMENTS
Since the role of incorporators is a formal one without significant responsibilities, duties, or liabilities, virtually all states have simplified the requirements.

a.   Only a single incorporator is required, who may be an individual or corporation, or in many states, a trust, estate or partnership.   There are usually no age or residency requirements.

b.   Requirements of oaths, verifications and seals have been eliminated in some states by statute or judicial decision.   See e. g., *People v. Ford*, 128 N.E. 479 (Ill. 1920).

c.   Incorporators execute the articles of incorporation and receive back the certificate of incorporation.   In most states, they serve no other function.

d.   In some states the incorporators meet to complete the formation of the corporation.   In jurisdictions that follow earlier versions of the Model Act, the incorporators do not meet and formation of the corporation is completed by initial directors named in the articles of incorporation. RMBCA § 2.02(b)(1) and 2.05(a) give each corporation the option of having the formation completed by the incorporators or by initial directors named in the articles of incorporation.   The Official Comment to RMBCA § 2.05 states that "it is expected that initial directors will be named [in the articles of incorporation] only if they will be the permanent board of directors and there is no objection to the disclosure of their identity in the articles of incorporation."

2.   DUMMY INCORPORATORS

Since incorporators have no substantive responsibilities in most states, the practice is widespread of using "dummy" incorporators.   These may be a secretary or employee of the law firm creating the corporation or any other person unconnected with the future business who is willing to allow his name to be used as an incorporator.

E.   CONTENT OF THE ARTICLES OF INCORPORATION

1.   MANDATORY REQUIREMENTS

a.   Older state statutes generally require the following *minimum* information to appear in every articles of incorporation:

1)   The name of the corporation;

2)   Its duration, which may be perpetual;

3)   Its purpose or purposes which may be, or include the conduct of any lawful business;

4)   The securities it is authorized to issue;

5)   The name of its registered agent and the address of its registered office;

6)   The names and addresses of its initial board of directors (in states where the initial board completes the formation of the corporation);

7)   The name and address of the incorporator or incorporators.

b.   Experience has shown that virtually all corporations elect the duration to be "perpetual" and their purposes to be "the conduct of any lawful business." As a result, the RMBCA omits these two provisions, instead providing that every corporation has perpetual duration unless a shorter period is chosen (RMBCA § 3.02) and a purpose of engaging in "any lawful business" unless a more limited purpose is set forth in the articles of incorporation [RMBCA § 3.01(a)].

2.   DISCRETIONARY PROVISIONS

In addition to the required minimum provisions, state statutes usually provide that certain additional provisions may be included in the articles of incorporation at the election of the corporation.

a.   State statutes often provide that specified rules of fundamental corporate governance are applicable unless the corporation elects to eliminate or modify them by specific provision in the articles of incorporation.

   Example: In many states each shareholder has preemptive rights (see part V, F) and a right to vote cumulatively (see part VII, C) unless such rights are specifically limited or excluded by provisions in the articles of incorporation. Most publicly held corporations eliminate both preemptive rights and cumulative voting on the theory that they greatly complicate the raising of capital and voting for directors and are of little direct benefit in most publicly held corporations.

   Example: A publicly held corporation desires that a quorum of shareholders should consist of holders of one third or more of the shares rather than a majority. The statutes of many states require all provisions reducing the quorum requirement applicable to shareholders to appear in the articles of incorporation.

b.   State statutes authorize additional discretionary provisions to be placed either in the articles or the bylaws. A careful attorney may prefer that an essential governance provision appear in the articles of incorporation where it is a matter of public record and more difficult to amend.

Example: A corporation proposes that the board of directors may act only by unanimous vote. Even though such a clause is effective if placed in either the bylaws or the articles under the state statute in question, an attorney may recommend that it be included in the articles because it is unusual and has the potential of creating a deadlock.

c. State statutes generally authorize corporations to include any provisions they desire relating to corporate powers. Though it is unnecessary (and, indeed, undesirable) to refer to powers specifically and unambiguously granted to corporations by statute, references to specific powers may be helpful where the state statute is silent or unclear on whether corporations generally possess the specific power.

Example: Old case law in State X makes it clear that corporations generally do not have power to act as general partners in general or limited partnerships. The present state incorporation statute contains an oblique reference to "investing in partnerships" but does not specifically authorize a corporation to act as a general partner. A careful attorney recommends that a specific grant of power that the corporation may act as a general partner in a general or limited partnership be routinely included in the articles of incorporation of every corporation she forms. Such a clause effectively broadens the power of the corporation, reduces the likelihood that later transactions may be questioned, and possibly avoids future litigation.

d. Special clauses relating to the purposes of a corporation are sometimes included in articles of incorporation in states where the statute, like RMBCA § 3.01, automatically grants every corporation the power to engage in any lawful business. A recitation of the purpose of a corporation may be required by a regulatory statute or agency if the corporation is to engage in a specific business. Some persons prefer that articles of incorporation provide somewhat more information about the objects of the corporation than the bare minimum required by modern statutes. Also, the creators of the corporation may desire to narrow the broad purposes authorized by the statute as part of a desired control arrangement. See part H below.

Example: Professional corporation statutes usually require that a corporation specify in its articles of incorporation which profession it proposes to engage in and permits the corporation to engage only in that one profession.

F. THE CORPORATE NAME

Under most state statutes, a corporate name must usually (i) contain a reference to the corporate nature of the entity (using the words "corporation," "incorporated," "inc." or similar word), (ii) not be the same as or deceptively similar to a name already in use or reserved for use, and (iii) not imply that a corporation is engaged in a business in which corporations may not lawfully engage. The RMBCA substitutes the test of "distinguishable upon the records of the Secretary of State" for the "same or deceptively similar" test (see 1. below). Secretaries of state usually maintain lists of names that are reserved or currently in use (and hence unavailable) and also may have internal rules about name availability. As a result, it is usually desirable to check whether a specific name is available with the secretary of state before it is used.

Example: Articles of incorporation are filed under the corporate name "Chicago Allied Steel Company." The name is rejected because an existing corporation is using the name "Allied Steel Company" and the internal rules of the secretary of state's office require that geographical names be ignored in determining whether names are identical. (Whether or not the secretary of state is right is usually irrelevant in such situations; it is so much easier to choose another name that is acceptable to the secretary of state than to litigate over name availability that even the most arbitrary rules are unlikely to be tested.)

1. NAME UNIQUENESS
The requirement that each corporation have a unique name is primarily to avoid confusion in such matters as sending tax notices and naming defendants in law suits.

    a. In many states, the name requirements are partially designed to prevent unfair competition. These statutes prohibit the use of names that are the "same or deceptively similar;" some states distinguish further between names that are the "same" or "deceptively similar," or merely "similar." The "same" or "deceptively similar" names may not be used under any circumstances while a "similar" name may be used if the proposed corporation obtains a letter of consent from the other corporation. The latter requirement seems clearly based on unfair competition considerations. The following examples are drawn from regulations adopted in a state that follows this pattern:

        Example: "Sampson Inc.," "Sampson Company," "Sampson Corporation" and "The Sampson Company" are all "the same."

        Example: "Van Lines of North America, Inc." and "North American Van Lines, Inc." are "deceptively similar."

Example: "Chicago Service and Supply, Inc." is similar to "Chicago Service Co." and would need a letter of consent.

Example: "E. G. Williams Electric Company" is not the same, deceptively similar, or similar to "Williams Electric Company" and no letter of consent is required.

Caveat: These examples are drawn from the principles applied by the secretary of state of one state. Not all state agencies might agree with these conclusions.

b.   RMBCA § 4.01 and the statutes of a few states, including Delaware, have changed the "same or deceptively similar" to "distinguishable upon the records" of the secretary of state. The RMBCA adopted this standard on the theory that the secretary of state "does not generally police the unfair competitive use of names and indeed, usually has no resources to do so." Confusion "in the absolute or linguistic sense" is the test for name availability under this simpler standard.

Example: "ABC Co.," "ABC Inc.," "AbC Co." and "Abc Inc." would probably not be viewed as distinguishable upon the records of the secretary of state under this standard.

Example: "Transamerica Airlines, Inc." is distinguishable upon the records of the secretary of state from "Transamerica, Inc." and "Trans International Airlines, Inc." Trans-Americas Airlines, Inc. v. Kenton, 491 A.2d 1139 (Del.1985).

2. RESERVATION OF NAME

Persons planning to form a corporation may "reserve" an available name for a limited period of time (usually 120 days) for a small fee. The reservation of a name permits the preparation of corporate documents, ordering of stationery, etc., with assurance that the proposed name will be available if the articles are filed within the period the name is reserved. Reservations of name may not be renewable in some states.

3. REGISTRATION OF NAME

A foreign corporation not transacting business in a state may register its name with the secretary of state to assure that no local business will obtain the right to use its name. Registration of a name thus protects the foreign corporation's good will reflected in its name and its option to later expand its operations into the state and use its current name. In most states, registration is on an annual basis and may be renewed indefinitely. Some states, however, do not authorize the registration of names of foreign corporations.

4. USE OF ASSUMED NAME BY FOREIGN CORPORATION

A foreign corporation that has not previously registered its name may discover that its own name is not available when it seeks to qualify to transact business in a new state. In this situation, the statutes of many states require the foreign corporation to qualify to transact business under an assumed name in the new state and file an assumed name certificate with the secretary of state.

Caveat: Business corporation acts generally do not require a corporation to conduct business in its corporate name. A corporation therefore has the same right as an individual to conduct business under an assumed name so long as the use of the name is not fraudulent and does not constitute unfair competition with some other person already using the same or a similar name. Many states have assumed name statutes that require individuals or corporations using assumed names to file an assumed name certificate with the county clerk or some other state or local official. A corporation that elects to transact business under a name other than its corporate name usually must comply with such a statute in the same way as an individual. However, a corporation that uses its own name is usually not considered to be using an assumed name and therefore is not subject to the filing requirement of such statutes. Assumed name statutes vary widely from state to state, and many states do not have statutes relating to this practice.

G. PERIOD OF DURATION

Modern statutes authorize the corporation to have "perpetual" existence, and while it is possible to specify a shorter period of existence, it is almost never desirable to do so. A period of existence less than perpetual creates the risk that the corporate existence may expire without renewal with uncertain rights and liabilities of participants thereafter. The RMBCA provides that every corporation has a perpetual duration unless a shorter period is specified in the articles of incorporation.

H. PURPOSES

Many modern statutes authorize very general purposes clauses, e. g., "the purpose of the corporation is to engage in any lawful business or businesses" without further specification. The use of such clauses, however, is a recent phenomenon. The RMBCA and the statutes of several states go further and provide that every corporation automatically has an "any lawful business" clause unless a narrower clause is specified in the articles of incorporation.

1.   **HISTORY OF PURPOSES CLAUSES**
The nature of purposes clauses has evolved over a long period of time, reflecting varying attitudes of mistrust toward the corporation. They were formerly of much greater importance than they are today.

a.   In the earliest period, all corporations were formed by special legislative enactment. In effect each purposes clause was separately developed in the legislative process.

b.   In the nineteenth and early twentieth centuries corporations could be formed under the early general incorporation statutes only for a limited and specific purpose, e. g., "to conduct a mill for the grinding of wheat, corn, and other grain." Corporations were usually limited to a single specific purpose, though ancillary powers might be implied from such a purposes clause.

   Example: A railroad corporation was authorized "to purchase, hold, and use . . . real estate and other property as may be necessary for the construction and maintenance of its road and canal and the stations and other accommodations necessary to accomplish the objects of its incorporation . . ." The U.S. Supreme Court held that a lease of a seaside hotel by the corporation was not ultra vires. *Jacksonville M., P. Ry. & Nav. Co. v. Hooper,* 160 U.S. 514, 16 S.Ct. 379 (1896).

c.   A major advance occurred when state statutes were modernized to permit corporations to include a number of specific purposes clauses. Since the number of such clauses was unlimited, many corporations adopted the practice of including tens or even hundreds of specific purposes clauses routinely in every articles of incorporation. This practice quickly eliminated any significance the purposes clauses might have.

d.   Many early statutes restricted the power of corporations to amend articles of incorporation to broaden purposes clauses. These restrictions were gradually eliminated as the practice of using multiple purposes clauses grew.

e.   A general purposes clause of the type described above is a logical simplification of the practice of using multiple purposes clauses. However, as a result, in the modern practice there is little or no reason to have a purposes clause at all, and doctrines based on the premise that purposes clauses are limiting in nature, such as ultra vires or implied powers, have little modern relevance.

2.   **LIMITED PURPOSES CLAUSE AS A PLANNING DEVICE**
A limited purposes clause may be used today despite broader statutory authorization as a planning device or to limit corporate activities as a

protection for investors. A corporation that pursues a business that exceeds such a limited purposes clause is acting ultra vires. (See part II, M below.)

Example: The statute of State *X* provides that every corporation has the power to engage in any lawful business unless a narrower purpose is specified in the articles of incorporation. *A* is an investor in a new corporation which is to be operated by *B* and *C* who are each making much smaller investments. *A* wants to ensure that the corporation will only engage in the retail drug business. He insists that a clause restricting the purposes of the corporation be included in the articles of incorporation. The clause is valid within a limited extent and *A* may be able to enjoin *B* and *C* from engaging in a broader business if the rights of third persons have not intervened.

Caveat: Because of modern rules relating to ultra vires (see part II, M), it is doubtful that the narrow purposes clause requested by *A* will effectively limit the activities of the corporation. *A* should seek to establish more effective voting or control devices if he wishes to assure himself that his capital will be invested only in the retail drug business.

I. SECURITIES

The securities a corporation is authorized to issue must be described in the articles of incorporation. See part V.

J. INITIAL CAPITALIZATION

Some states require that a corporation have a minimum amount of capitalization before it may commence business. One thousand dollars is the most common amount, but some states have selected other amounts. Most states, however, have eliminated all minimum capitalization requirements.

1.   CURRENT TREND
The modern trend is clearly in the direction of eliminating such requirements. The theory behind this trend is that minimum capitalization requirements are arbitrary and do not provide any meaningful protection to creditors.

2.   FAILURE TO MEET MINIMUM CAPITAL REQUIREMENTS
In states that retain minimum capitalization requirements, directors are usually made personally liable, if business is commenced without the required minimum capital.

a.   In most states this liability is limited to the difference between minimum required capitalization and the amount of capital actually contributed.

> *Example:* In such a state, with a minimum $1,000 capital requirement, a corporation commences business with $700 in capital. The directors are usually liable for $300; this liability disappears if the corporation thereafter obtains additional capital of $300 or more.

b.   A few state statutes have been construed to impose unlimited liability on directors for all debts incurred before the minimum capitalization was paid in.

> *Example:* In such a state, with a minimum $1,000 capital requirement, a corporation commences business with capital of $700. In the course of its business, the corporation incurs liability of $10,000. The directors are liable for $10,000 and this liability is not eliminated if thereafter capital contributions of $300 or more are received. E. g., *Sulphur Export Corp. v. Caribbean Clipper Lines, Inc.*, 277 F.Supp. 632 (E.D.La. 1968). *Tri-State Developers, Inc. v. Moore*, 343 S.W.2d 812 (Ky. 1961).

K.   REGISTERED OFFICE AND REGISTERED AGENT

The registered office and registered agent at that office must be specified in the articles. They serve the purposes of providing a location where the corporation may be found (for service of process, tax notices, and the like) and a person on whom process may be served. State statutes require filings with the Secretary of State to reflect changes in the registered office or registered agent, or both.

L.   CORPORATE POWERS

Every state statute lists general powers that every corporation possesses. It is unnecessary and undesirable to list some or all of these powers in the articles of incorporation. RMBCA § 3.02 provides that every corporation "has the same powers as an individual to do all things necessary or convenient to carry out its business and affairs, including without limitation" a traditional list of powers. This broadening language was drawn from the statutes of California and a few other states.

1.   GENERAL POWERS

The general powers possessed by corporations under most modern statutes include:

    a.   To sue and be sued;

    b.   To have a corporate seal;

    c.   To purchase, receive, lend, sell, invest, convey and mortgage personal and real property;

    d.   To make contracts, borrow and lend money, and guarantee the indebtedness of third persons;

    e.   To conduct its business within or without the state;

    f.   To elect or appoint officers or agents, define their duties, fix their compensation, and provide pension, profit sharing, and stock option plans;

    g.   To make charitable, scientific or education contributions or donations for the public welfare;

    h.   To be a partner or manager of a partnership or other venture;

    i.   To make and alter bylaws for the administration and regulation of its internal affairs.

2. ACTS IN EXCESS OF POWERS

If a corporation does an act which it does not have power to do, it is usually considered to be acting ultra vires. See part M below.

3. PARTIAL ENUMERATION OF POWERS

The danger of a partial enumeration of statutory powers in an articles of incorporation is the danger that a negative inference will be drawn that the inclusion of some enumerated powers implies the exclusion of unenumerated ones.

M. ULTRA VIRES

The dictionary definition of "ultra vires" is beyond the scope of the powers of a corporation. It is used to describe acts that exceed either the stated purposes or the powers of the corporation.

Example: A corporation is formed for the purpose of "selling or lending all kinds of railway plant, carrying on the business of mechanical engineers, etc." The corporation contracts to build a railroad in a foreign country. In a famous decision the English courts held the contract to be ultra vires. *Ashbury Railway Carriage & Iron Co. v. Riche*, 7 L.R.–E. & I. App. 653 (1875).

1. THE COMMON LAW ULTRA VIRES DOCTRINE

The early common law view was that an ultra vires transaction was void since the corporation simply lacked the power to enter into the transaction. Such a doctrine, however, led to potentially undesirable results and was gradually modified:

a. A transaction that was purely executory might be enjoined if it was ultra vires with respect to either party.

b. If the transaction was wholly executed by both parties, the transaction cannot be attacked on the ground of ultra vires. *Herbert v. Sullivan*, 123 F.2d 477 (1st Cir. 1941).

c. If the transaction was partially executed, ultra vires may be raised, but doctrines of estoppel, unjust enrichment, or pure fairness might mitigate the strict common law view. *Goodman v. Ladd Estate Co.*, 427 P.2d 102 (Or.1967).

d. Ultra vires transactions might be ratified by all the shareholders. See *Lurie v. Arizona Fertilizer & Chem. Co.*, 421 P.2d 330 (Ariz. 1966) [corporation entering partnership].

e. Generally, the defense of ultra vires is not available to a corporation in a suit based on tort or in a prosecution for criminal conduct. Such liability, of course, is based on agency principles of respondeat superior.

f. Directors and officers causing the corporation to enter into ultra vires transactions are not automatically liable for losses suffered thereby, though the fact that the conduct was ultra vires might cause courts to be more willing to "pierce the corporate veil" or otherwise impose personal liability on the directors and officers. See *Lurie v. Arizona Fertilizer & Chem. Co.*, 421 P.2d 330 (Ariz. 1966).

g. The attorney general of the state may attack corporations engaging in ultra vires transactions by injunction, quo warranto, or suits to dissolve the corporation. As a practical matter, such suits by the state are extremely rare.

2. CURRENT TRENDS

Three factors have greatly reduced the importance of the ultra vires doctrine:

a. The use of multiple purposes clauses, and more recently, the use of general purposes clauses;

b. The broadening of the general powers that every corporation possesses by statute;

c.   The power of a corporation to amend its articles of incorporation in order to broaden its purposes to accommodate desirable transactions; and

d.   The ultra vires statutes described below.

3.   STATUTORY TREATMENT OF THE ULTRA VIRES DOCTRINE

Modern statutes sharply limit the ultra vires principle. A typical statute states that "no act of a corporation and no conveyance or transfer of real or personal property to or by a corporation shall be invalid by reason of the fact that a corporation was without capacity or power to do such act or to make or receive such conveyance or transfer" with three exceptions:

a.   In a suit by a shareholder against the corporation to enjoin an ultra vires act, if all affected parties are present in the litigation and the court finds that it is equitable to enjoin the ultra vires act;

b.   In a proceeding by the corporation against incumbent or former officers or directors of the corporation; and

c.   In a proceeding by the state attorney general to dissolve the corporation or enjoin the ultra vires act.

> *Example:*   A corporation formed for the purpose of dealing in pleasure boats and motors signs a lease to rent a motion picture theatre for a long period. The landlord regrets entering the lease and seeks to cancel it on the ground it is ultra vires from the standpoint of the tenant. The landlord loses under the above statute whether or not the tenant has amended its articles to broaden its purpose. *711 Kings Highway Corp. v. F. I. M.'s Marine Repair Serv., Inc.*, 273 N.Y.S.2d 299 (Sup.Ct. 1966).

> *Example:*   A corporation is sued on a guarantee of indebtedness which is ultra vires under the law of the state in question. The corporation may not defend on the ground that the guarantee is ultra vires under the statute. However, a shareholder may intervene and raise the ultra vires issue, though the court has discretion whether or not to enforce the ultra vires contract on the ground of equity or fairness. The plaintiff may also seek to avoid the claim of the intervening shareholder on the ground that he is not in fact acting independently of the corporation. *Inter-Continental Corp. v. Moody*, 411 S.W.2d 578 (Tex.Civ.App. 1966).

4.   MODERN AREAS OF ULTRA VIRES CONCERN

Ultra vires issues may continue to arise in some states on the question whether or not the corporation has power to enter into the following acts:

a. Making charitable or political contributions;

b. Granting employee fringe benefits;

c. Entering into partnerships;

d. Acquiring shares of other corporations;

e. Guaranteeing indebtedness of others; and

f. Making loans to officers or directors.

Caveat: Even when not expressly referred to, a court may conclude that a corporation implicitly has power to engage in the foregoing acts. E.g. *Union Pac. Railroad Co. v. Trustees, Inc.*, 329 P.2d 398 (Utah 1958) (charitable contribution).

Caveat: Even where state statutes grant the power to enter into such transactions in broad terms, courts may impose a limitation of reasonableness based on public policy or common sense.

Example: A state statute authorizes a corporation to "make donations for the public welfare or for charitable, scientific or educational purposes." A closely held corporation with income in excess of $19,000,000 per year proposes to make a gift of over $500,000 to a charitable corporation controlled by the majority shareholder. The gift is valid; even though the statute should be construed to permit only "reasonable" charitable gifts, the proposed contribution is reasonable under the circumstances. *Theodora Holding Corp. v. Henderson*, 257 A.2d 398 (Del.Ch. 1969). In concluding that a $500,000 gift was reasonable, some reliance was placed on the federal income tax law that permits the deduction of up to ten percent of taxable income as charitable donations in any year.

Example: After the death of two corporate officers, the board of directors of the corporation voted to pay certain bonuses to their widows. The Court held that such payments were ultra vires since they were not charitable and, under the circumstances, not supported by consideration or justifiable as a species of executive compensation. *Adams v. Smith*, 153 So.2d 221 (Ala. 1963). Some courts disagree, *Chambers v. Beaver Advance Corp.*, 140 A.2d 808 (Pa. 1958), and in any event a program by which stipends are paid to widows or widowers of employees generally can readily be justified as a species of employment compensation.

Example: X, an 80 per cent shareholder, causes the corporation to place a second mortgage on its property to secure a loan made to another corporation that is wholly owned by X. Such a mortgage is gratuitous and ultra vires, and may be set aside at the suit of the 20 per cent shareholder. *Real Estate Capital Corp. v. Thunder Corp.*, 287 N.E.2d 838 (Ohio Com.Pleas 1972). It was unclear whether the holder of the mortgage had reason to know that the mortgage was gratuitous; such a transaction might also constitute a breach of fiduciary duty by X.

Example: In order to secure passage of legislation, a corporation agreed to make certain payments to local taxing authorities in lieu of taxes; as a result of that agreement, the local taxing authorities withdrew their opposition to the legislation. The lower court held such payments not to be ultra vires; they were donations to local taxing authorities though not contributions and not lobbying expenditures; *Kelly v. Bell*, 254 A.2d 62 (Del.Ch. 1969). The Supreme Court affirmed, commenting that personal liability should not be imposed on the directors for such questionable payments since they exercised business judgment in agreeing to make them.

N. COMPLETION OF THE FORMATION OF THE CORPORATION

The filing of articles of incorporation is only the first step in forming a corporation.

1. ADDITIONAL STEPS
Lawyers generally are expected to take the following additional steps to complete the formation of the corporation:

a. Prepare bylaws;

b. Prepare minutes of the various organizational meetings, including waivers of notices or consents to action without formal meetings;

c. Open a bank account;

d. Obtain a minute book and seal;

e. Obtain share certificates and make sure they are properly prepared and issued;

f. Prepare shareholders' agreement, if any;

g. Obtain necessary tax identification numbers and comply with other state and federal legal requirements;

h. Generally oversee the preparation and execution of the various forms, certificates and other documents.

2. **CONSEQUENCES OF FAILURE TO COMPLETE FORMATION**

The consequences of a partial formation of a corporation usually arise in the context of a suit against the officers, directors, or shareholders to hold them liable for an obligation incurred in the name of the corporation. A number of cases hold that no such personal liability is created so long as articles of incorporation were filed. E. g., *Moe v. Harris*, 172 N.W. 494 (Minn. 1919). If personal liability is imposed after the filing of articles of incorporation, the result is likely to be analyzed as a case involving:

a. Promoters' liability;

b. Piercing the corporate veil; or

c. The failure to comply with a mandatory condition subsequent.

The last alternative is becoming less common with the simplification of incorporation statutes.

REVIEW QUESTIONS

II–1. Delaware is the best state in which to incorporate.

True _____   False _____

II–2. Incorporation is an expensive process not suitable for small businesses.

True _____   False _____

II–3. When forming a corporation, it makes no difference who you use as incorporators.

True _____   False _____

II–4. Articles of incorporation may contain only the information specified in the statute.

True _____   False _____

II–5.   Why would provisions relating to internal governance ever be included in articles of incorporation rather than in the bylaws?

II–6.   A corporation must do business under its official name and may not use a fictitious name.

True _____   False _____

II–7.   What is the difference between a reserved and a registered name?

II–8.   When should a period of duration less than perpetual be elected?

II–9.   Corporations must specify the purposes for which they are formed and limit their activities to those purposes.

True _____   False _____

II–10.   Corporations should always use the broadest possible purposes clause permitted by the state statute.

True _____   False _____

II–11.   Why does a corporation need a registered agent and registered office?

II–12.   Should corporate powers ever be listed in articles of incorporation?

II–13.   What does ultra vires mean?

II–14.   Why do modern statutes restrict or eliminate the doctrine of ultra vires?

II–15.   What factors have led to the decline of ultra vires?

II–16.   What steps are required to complete the formation of a corporation after articles of incorporation have been filed?

II–17.   What is the consequence of filing articles of incorporation and commencing business without completing the organization of the corporation?

II–18.   Two lawyers, one practicing real property and estates law and the other specializing in the trial of negligence cases, share an office. Each pays half the rent, the salaries of the employees, the cost of office equipment, supplies, utilities, and the upkeep of the library. They each have their own clients and receive their respective fees. Would they enjoy any advantages, including minimizing their taxes and maximizing their tax benefits, by incorporating? To what extent would they have to change their manner of operations? [This question and answer is drawn from Ballantine, Problems in Law 230 (5th Ed. 1975).]

III

PREINCORPORATION TRANSACTIONS

Analysis

A. Promoters
B. Promoter's Contracts
C. Promoter's Fiduciary Duties
D. Agreements to Form Corporations
E. Preincorporation Subscriptions

A. PROMOTERS

"Promoters" are persons who assist in putting together a new business. The term is not one of opprobium; rather, promoters are often shrewd, visionary individuals who serve important social and economic functions.

1.   BASIC FUNCTIONS OF PROMOTERS
    In promoting a new venture, promoters:

    a.   Arrange for the necessary business assets and personnel so that the new business may function effectively. This may include obtaining or renting a plant, assembling work and sales forces, finding sources of raw materials and supplies, finding retail outlets, making long term commitments of various types, and so forth.

    b.   Obtain the necessary capital to finance the venture. The sources of capital include (i) equity capital contributed by investors, (ii) loans from third parties, either secured or unsecured, and (iii) loans from the investors supplying the equity capital.

    c.   Complete the formation of the corporation.

2.   LOCATION OF DISCUSSION OF PROMOTERS IN THIS OUTLINE
    Part B of this section of the outline deals exclusively with problems of contracts entered into by promoters in connection with function (1)(a) above. Problems of capital raising (function (1)(b) above) are discussed in part IV. Promoters' fiduciary duties relating both to promoters contracts and the raising of capital are discussed in part C of this section of the outline.

B.   PROMOTER'S CONTRACTS

Promoters may enter into contracts on behalf of the venture being promoted either before or after articles of incorporation have been filed. Most problems are created by preincorporation contracts since under modern statutes the corporate existence begins when articles of incorporation are accepted for filing, and contracts entered into by the promoter after that date will normally bind only the corporation. The legal consequences of preincorporation contracts entered into by promoters vary, depending in part on the form of the contract itself.

1.   CONTRACTS ENTERED IN THE NAME OF A CORPORATION "TO BE FORMED"
    In contracts of this type, the promoter enters into a preincorporation contract which on its face shows that the corporation has not yet been formed. A typical form of execution of a contract of this type is in the name of "ABC Corporation, a corporation to be formed."

a. Such a contract can be analyzed in several different ways, depending on the facts and the context, which have widely different legal consequences.

    1) The most common analysis is that the promoter is personally liable on the contract and he is not relieved of liability if the corporation is formed and adopts the contract. Assuming that the corporation is formed and adopts the contract both the promoter and the corporation are thereafter severally liable on the contract. Presumably the promoter may look to the newly formed corporation for indemnification if the contract benefits the corporation but the promoter is held personally liable.

    2) A second possible analysis is that the promoter is personally liable on the contract, but is thereafter relieved of liability if the corporation is later formed and adopts the contract. This is an example of a "novation."

    3) A third possible analysis is that the promoter is not personally liable on the contract. While the corporation may become liable if it is later formed and adopts the contract, no one is liable under this analysis until that event occurs. Legally, under this analysis the third party has made only an offer to the corporation which may be revoked by the third party (unless it is supported by consideration or is otherwise made irrevocable by law).

    4) A final possible analysis is that the promoter is not personally liable on the contract but has agreed to use his best efforts to cause the corporation to be formed and to adopt the contract. The promoter's "best efforts" promise may be consideration for the third party's promise under the contract. This differs from (3) in that both parties have incurred liability: the promoter may be liable on his or her promise if no steps are taken to form the corporation though not liable on the contract itself.

b. The test of which of these four alternatives is the appropriate one in a specific case depends on the "intention" of the parties; where the intention is not clearly expressed considerable uncertainty as to legal analysis may exist. However, most cases find the promoter personally liable on one theory or another. The issue of novation (alternative (2)) is considered further later in this part of the outline.

    Example: O'Rorke enters into a contract to build a bridge for "D. J. Geary for a bridge company to be organized and incorporated." O'Rorke was to commence work within 10 days and payments were to be made to him periodically after work was commenced. Geary is personally liable on the obligation: the court relied in part on the fact that payments were required to be made (presumably by Geary personally) before the bridge company was formed. *O'Rorke v. Geary*, 56 A. 541 (Pa. 1903). Accord: *Stanley J. How & Associates, Inc. v. Boss*, 222 F.Supp. 936 (S.D.Iowa 1963).

Example: Quaker Hill, Inc. sells nursery stock to a corporation to be formed by Parr and Presba. At the urging of Quaker Hill's representative, the contract is entered into in the name of "Mountain View Nurseries, Inc. by Parr, President" even though Quaker Hill's representative knew no corporation had been formed. Quaker Hill cannot hold Parr and Presba personally liable because Quaker Hill, by its conduct, clearly indicated it intended to look for payment only to the newly formed corporation. *Quaker Hill, Inc. v. Parr*, 364 P.2d 1056 (Colo. 1961). Since Parr and Presba are not personally liable and no corporation was formed, no bilateral contract exists, and Quaker Hill could have revoked its offer to ship the nursery stock at any time before the corporation's acceptance. Accord: *Sherwood & Roberts-Oregon, Inc. v. Alexander*, 525 P.2d 135 (Or. 1974); *Stewart Realty Co. v. Keller*, 193 N.E.2d 179 (Ohio App. 1962).

2.   CONTRACTS ENTERED INTO IN THE CORPORATE NAME

These cases differ from the preceding cases in that the contract is entered into in the corporate name and one or both parties erroneously believe the corporation has been formed. The factual patterns under this heading may vary because the contract may be entered into at various times during the incorporation process. For example, the contract may be entered into when no steps toward incorporation have been taken, or after articles have been filed but before the certificate of incorporation is executed. Under earlier statutes, essentially the same problem also arose if the contract was entered into after the certificate of incorporation was issued but before other mandatory steps for incorporation were completed.

a.   The common law developed concepts of corporations *de facto* and corporations *de jure*. In a suit brought by a private plaintiff against a promoter, the conclusion that either a *de facto* or a *de jure* corporation existed absolved the promoter of liability. However, the state could attack the existence of a corporation *de facto* while a *de jure* corporation was valid for all purposes.

    1)   A corporation *de jure* had sufficiently complied with the incorporation requirements so that a corporation was legally in existence for all purposes. A *de jure* corporation involved compliance with all *mandatory* statutory requirements; failure to

comply with less important requirements (called *directory* requirements) did not affect the *de jure* status of a corporation. The distinction between mandatory and directory requirements is obviously a matter of degree; *People v. Ford*, 128 N.E. 479 (Ill. 1920) holds over the dissent of one Justice that the statutory requirement of a seal is a directory requirement; however, in evaluating this case it should be noted that the contrary conclusion would have called into question the validity of over 4,300 corporations.

> *Example:*   Articles of incorporation fail to comply with the statutory requirement that addresses be stated in that two addresses of directors or incorporators are incorrect.   All other statutory requirements are complied with.   The corporation is a *de jure* corporation.

> *Example:*   Under the state statute, articles of incorporation must be filed with the secretary of state and recorded with the county recorder of the county in which the registered office is located.   The statute does not set forth the consequences of failure to file locally.   A corporation files articles with the secretary of state but fails to file locally.   Such a corporation is probably not a *de jure* corporation but may be a *de facto* corporation (defined below).

2)   A corporation *de facto* is a corporation that is partially but defectively or incompletely formed; it is sufficiently formed, however, to be immune from attack by everyone but the state. Since virtually all litigation in this area involves private plaintiffs rather than the state, a holding that a corporation is *de facto* is "virtually as good" as a holding that it is *de jure*.

(i)   The traditional test of *de facto* existence is threefold:

(A)   There is a valid statute under which the corporation might incorporate;

(B)   There has been a "good faith" or "colorable" attempt to comply with the statute; and

(C)   There has been actual use of the corporate privilege.

> *Example:*   A corporation files articles of incorporation with the secretary of state but does not file the articles locally as required by statute.   In

most states the corporation is considered a *de facto* corporation.

Example: A corporation prepares articles of incorporation but because of a clerical mistake by the attorney no filing is ever made with the secretary of state. The corporation is not a *de facto* corporation. *Conway v. Samet,* 300 N.Y.S.2d 243 (Sup.Ct. 1969).

Caveat: The *de facto* doctrine in practice tends to be result-oriented rather than objective.

Example: In a tort case, a defect in formation might be deemed sufficient to prevent the formation of a *de facto* corporation; in a contract case where the third person clearly relied only on the credit of the "corporation," a court might hold on essentially the same facts that a *de facto* corporation existed.

Caveat: State statutes often provide for the legal consequences of a failure to comply with some statutory requirement; such statutes should provide a substitute for the *de facto* doctrine.

Example: A corporation commences business with less than $1000 in capital, the minimum requirement in the state statute. However, the statute also provides that directors who permit the corporation to commence business with less than the minimum capital are jointly and severally liable for the difference. The statutory liability should be deemed exclusive. In a suit to impose personal liability on shareholders (other than the directors liable under the statute) an argument that the failure to provide the minimum capital prevents the creation of a *de facto* corporation should be rejected and the statutory liability should be exclusive.

Example: The foregoing transaction occurs in a state that does not expressly limit the liability of the directors to the unpaid portion of the minimum capital. The directors and officers are personally liable for all debts or liabilities incurred before the minimum capital is paid in. *Sulphur Export Corp. v. Caribbean Clipper Lines, Inc.*, 277 F.Supp. 632 (E.D.La. 1968).

(ii)   Modern statutes often substitute a more objective test for the common law *de facto/de jure* distinction. All modern statutes have a provision that states in substance "the corporate existence shall begin upon the issuance of the certificate of incorporation." Several state statutes also provide in substance that persons who act as a corporation without authority to do so should be liable as partners. The apparent objectivity of these statutes, however, is as illusory as the objectivity of the *de facto* doctrine itself.

(A)   Some courts have read these statutes literally to provide that the issuance of the certificate of incorporation is the "bright line" that distinguishes the corporation from the "noncorporation." Under such reasoning, personal liability exists on all precertificate obligations, before the secretary of state acts on the articles of incorporation.

Example: A person mails articles of incorporation to the secretary of state and the following day executes a note in the corporate name on behalf of the corporation. A day after the note is executed, the secretary of state receives the articles of incorporation, reviews them, rejects them, and returns them for correction. Corrections are made and the articles later accepted and the certificate of incorporation issued. In many states the person signing the note is personally liable, though he may be able to avoid liability on the theory of a "corporation by estoppel" described below. *Robertson v. Levy*, 197 A.2d 443 (D.C.App. 1964).

Example: Articles of incorporation are filed and accepted, and a certificate of incorporation issued. However, no further steps are taken to complete the formation of the corporation. No meetings are held, no shares are issued, and so forth. A note is executed in the corporate name. In many states the person signing the note is not automatically personally liable since the certificate of incorporation conclusively establishes the existence of the corporation. An argument to hold such a person liable may be based on the concept of "piercing the corporate veil." (See part IV)

Caveat: Some secretaries of state have adopted the practice of backdating certificates of incorporation or fee receipts to the date the articles are filed, in effect ignoring processing time. This practice, which is not uniform, may eliminate some time-of-issuance questions.

Example: The articles of incorporation are filed on May 1, and the corporation executes the promissory note in question on May 3. On May 4, the secretary of state issues the certificate of incorporation but follows the standard practice in his office of dating it May 1, the date of filing. It is probable that the corporate existence would be considered to have begun on May 1 so that the promissory note is solely a corporate obligation.

Example: The articles of incorporation are filed on May 1, but are returned to the incorporators because of the absence of a notarial certificate. The certificate is added, and the same articles are refiled on May 3. Some secretaries of state will issue the certificate of incorporation dated back to May 1. However, if the articles are reexecuted on May 3 so that the notarial certificate bears that date, it is unlikely that any secretary of state would date the certificate earlier than May 3.

(B) Some courts have distinguished between active participants in the "corporation" and passive investors; the latter are not personally liable on transactions entered into before the certificate of incorporation is issued. This view may be based on the statutory language in older versions of the Model Business Corporation Acts as referring only to persons "who assume to act" as being liable as partners. *Timberline*

Equipment Co., Inc. v. Davenport, 514 P.2d 1109 (Or. 1973).

(C)   Some statutes contain provisions making the issuance of the certificate of incorporation conclusive of the existence of the corporation but not referring to persons "who assume to act" as corporations.   In such states, an additional argument may be made that the common law concept of the *de facto* corporation may continue to exist because the statute does not purport to deal explicitly with precertificate obligations.

> *Example:*   In a state that does not follow the practice of backdating articles of incorporation, an incorporator prepares articles of incorporation on April 1 and mails them to the secretary of state.   Because of a delay in the mails the articles are not received until April 5, and a certificate of incorporation is issued on April 7, showing that date as the date of issuance. The corporation enters into a contract on April 4; even though the *de jure* existence of the corporation did not begin until April 7, a corporation *de facto* exists from and after April 1, and only the corporation is liable on the April 4 obligation.   *Cantor v. Sunshine Greenery, Inc.*, 398 A.2d 571 (N.J.Super.App.Div. 1979).

(D)   RMBCA § 2.04 provides that "all persons purporting to act as or on behalf of a corporation, knowing there was no incorporation under this Act," are jointly and severally liable for liabilities incurred.   This provision is consistent with the results reached in most of the above cases, and is analogous to a similar provision in the Uniform Limited Partnership Act and Revised Uniform Limited Partnership Act.

b.   Some cases have applied a concept of "corporation by estoppel" that appears to be potentially independent of modern statutes and the common law *de facto* corporation concept.

> *Example:*   *X* executes articles of incorporation and reasonably but erroneously believes that they have been filed as required by statute by his attorney.   *X* negotiates the purchase of typewriters in the corporate name and executes notes in the

corporate name to pay for them. The seller relies solely on the corporate credit. Some courts have held the seller "estopped" to deny the existence of the corporation under these circumstances. *Cranson v. IBM*, 200 A.2d 33 (Md. 1964). Other courts have held the "shareholder" personally liable but recognize that he or she may have a claim over against the attorney for malpractice. *Conway v. Samet*, 300 N.Y.S.2d 243 (Sup.Ct. 1969).

1) This is "reverse estoppel" since *X*, the person who made the representation, is being permitted to escape liability while the person who *relied* on the representation is being estopped from disputing the representation. In normal estoppel cases, only the person *making* a representation is estopped from later denying it.

2) If carried to its logical conclusion, the concept of "corporation by estoppel" would permit shareholders to obtain the benefits of limited liability simply by consistently representing the corporation's existence. Notions of public policy and the need to preserve the incorporation process therefore dictate that only persons who honestly but erroneously believe that articles have been filed should be able to take advantage of the corporation by estoppel concept. See RMBCA § 2.04 described in part a. above.

3) If the defendant seeks to avoid liability on the theory that the plaintiff is not a lawful corporate entity, the doctrine of corporation by estoppel is usually applied. *Timberline Equipment Co., Inc. v. Davenport*, 514 P.2d 1109 (Or. 1973).

c. This area of the law of corporations reflects the interplay of basically conflicting general principles. In such situations, unpredictability of result and irreconcilable precedents often result, and this area is no exception.

1) The statutes and common sense say—"no certificate of incorporation, no corporation." Under this approach there should be unlimited personal liability for all obligations entered into in the corporate name before the corporation was formed.

2) Where third persons deal on a corporate basis with an apparent corporation, they receive a "windfall" if they may subsequently hold other persons liable. The failure to form the corporation usually is discovered long after the transaction in question was entered into, when the third person learns after litigation has commenced through discovery that the corporation was not fully formed when the transaction was entered into. Some courts have accepted the "windfall" argument and refuse to impose personal liability even in

circumstances where no steps toward incorporation have been taken. E. g., *Frontier Refining Co. v. Kunkel's Inc.*, 407 P.2d 880 (Wyo. 1965).

3.   LIABILITY OF CORPORATION ON PROMOTER'S CONTRACTS

The corporation is not automatically liable on promoters' contracts made for its benefit before it came into existence. Rather, a newly formed corporation may accept or reject all preincorporation contracts.

a.   Technically, an acceptance of a preincorporation contract by a corporation is an "adoption" not a "ratification." Ratification assumes that the principal was in existence when the agent entered into the unauthorized contract, when a principal "ratifies" such a contract the principal is deemed bound on the contract from the time it was entered into. Since the corporation was not in existence when the contract was entered into, ratification cannot be the proper technical term. Some courts, however, loosely use the word "ratification" to describe the corporate adoption of a preincorporation contract.

b.   This rule allows subsequent investors in some cases to review promoters' contracts and reject those that seem improvident. However, the rule is uneven since the time for adoption may occur before the outside investors appear or while the promoter is the dominant force in the newly formed corporation.

c.   Adoption may be express or implied and presupposes knowledge of the terms of the contract. However, a recovery in quasi contract will normally be available where benefits are accepted even if the contract is not adopted.

> ***Example:***   A one-year employment contract involving a salary of $500 per month is negotiated by a promoter. With knowledge of the terms, the directors of the newly formed corporation accept the benefits of the employment contract for four months. Whether or not the contract was formally adopted by the board of directors, the corporation has adopted the contract, is bound by it, and may enforce it. This is implied adoption. *McArthur v. Times Printing Co.*, 51 N.W. 216 (Minn. 1892). Accord: *Kridelbaugh v. Aldrehn Theatres Co.*, 191 N.W. 803 (Iowa 1923).

> ***Example:***   In the foregoing illustration, the promoter also secretly promises the employee a year-end bonus of $1,000. The directors of the corporation are unaware of this promise and the circumstances are not such as to give reason to believe that additional compensation was promised. The corporation

has not adopted the contract and is not bound by the promise to pay the bonus since adoption requires knowledge of the terms of the contract; however, the employee will have a quasi-contractual claim for the fair market value of his services, which may or may not be greater than $500 per month.

d. Where the contract relates to services leading to the formation of the corporation (e. g., the lawyer's fee for forming the corporation), mere existence of the corporation does not constitute "adoption" of the contract. The lawyer may recover in quasi contract for the reasonable value of his services.

4. RELATIONSHIP BETWEEN PROMOTER'S LIABILITY AND CORPORATE ADOPTION

Generally, corporate adoption of a contract will release the promoter from further liability only if the parties agree that a novation will occur.

Example: The promoter executes a contract with a third party which contains the following clause: "It is understood by the parties hereto that it is the intention of the Purchaser to incorporate. If such incorporation is completed by closing, all agreements, covenants, and warranties contained herein shall be construed to have been made between Seller and the resultant corporation and all documents shall reflect same."

This clause does not expressly release the promoters from liability upon the adoption of the contract by the corporation and some courts hold that the promoter remains liable as a co-obligor with the corporation. *RKO-Stanley Warner Theatres, Inc. v. Graziano*, 355 A.2d 830 (Pa. 1976). Other courts might construe the last quoted sentence as an indication that the third person intended to look solely to the corporation after its formation and might therefore infer that a novation was intended.

Example: In the foregoing example the corporation is formed but does not adopt the contract. The corporation is not bound despite the language of the agreement and it is probable that the promoter remains personally liable on the theory that the third person intended someone always to be liable.

a. Williston's position is that a novation is almost always contemplated on the theory that the third person usually intends to look solely to the corporation after it is formed.

b.   This "complete novation" theory may lead to promoters deciding to form "shell corporations" solely to escape personal liability even after it is clear that the promotion will fail.

Caveat: Many cases have refused to follow Williston's suggestion and find novations only where there is some indication that a novation was actually intended.   See *Frazier v. Ash*, 234 F.2d 320 (5th Cir. 1956).

C.   PROMOTER'S FIDUCIARY DUTIES

Co-promoters of a venture owe fiduciary duties to each other as though they were partners to the corporation and to subsequent financial interests in the venture.

1.   THE CORPORATION AS THE BENEFICIARY
After the corporation is formed it may obtain from the promoter any benefits or rights the promoter obtained on its behalf.

Example: *A*, a co-promoter, secretly obtains land needed by the corporation and sells it to the corporation after it is formed at a profit.   The transaction constitutes a breach of fiduciary duty and the corporation may recover the secret profit.

2.   CO–PROMOTERS AS THE BENEFICIARY
Co-promoters are essentially partners in the promotion of the venture, and any benefits or rights one promoter obtained must be shared with the co-promoters.

Example: *A*, a co-promoter, secretly obtains land needed by the corporation, planning to convey it to the corporation.   However, the promotion fails, no corporation is ever formed, and *A* resells the land profitably.   His co-promoters may recover their share of the secret profit.

3.   SUBSEQUENT INVESTORS AS THE BENEFICIARY
The major issue relating to promoters' fiduciary duties is the extent to which *subsequent* shareholders or investors may be protected by such duties. According to the "Massachusetts Rule" the corporation may attack the earlier transaction if the subsequent sale to public investors was contemplated when the earlier transaction was entered into. *Old Dominion Copper Mining & Smelting Co. v. Bigelow*, 89 N.E. 193 (Mass. 1909).   According to the "Federal Rule" the corporation may not attack the earlier transaction since all the shareholders at the time consented to the transaction. *Old Dominion Copper Mining & Smelting Co. v. Lewisohn*, 210 U.S. 206, 28 S.Ct. 634 (1908).

Example: At a time when only *A* and *B* are shareholders of a corporation, *A* and *B* enter into a transaction with the corporation. Thereafter shares are sold to public investors who later learn of the earlier transaction between *A* and *B* and the corporation and object to it on the ground that the compensation to *A* and *B* is excessive. Under the Massachusetts Rule the corporation or the subsequent investors may successfully attack the earlier transaction if the subsequent sale to investors was contemplated; under the Federal Rule neither can successfully do so.

a. The two rules suggested were both established in two cases arising out of a single promotion in the early years of the twentieth century.

b. The "Massachusetts Rule" has been more popular than the "Federal Rule."

c. The real issue in this type of case is the lack of full disclosure about the promoters' transaction when the public investors decided to make their investments. If there is full disclosure presumably the public investors will reduce the price they are willing to pay for the shares to reflect the transaction in question.

d. Many cases of this nature have arisen in the modern era as "disclosure" or "securities fraud" cases rather than as "promoters fraud" cases. See the discussion in part XV below, particularly the discussion of rule 10b–5.

4. CREDITORS AS THE BENEFICIARY

Some cases apply fiduciary concepts to protect creditors against unfair or fraudulent transactions by promoters. *Frick v. Howard*, 126 N.W.2d 619 (Wis. 1964). Most such cases also may be analyzed as simple fraudulent conveyance cases.

D. AGREEMENTS TO FORM CORPORATIONS

A preincorporation agreement to create a corporation is enforceable in the same ways as any other contract. Many modern promotions are cast in the form of such a contract.

1. SURVIVABILITY OF AGREEMENT

The major issue relating to preincorporation contracts is which provisions survive the formation of the corporation. Since the articles of incorporation, bylaws, shareholder agreements, and minutes of meetings on their face appear to provide a complete set of rules of governance, the contract will normally not survive the formation of the corporation unless specific and precise provisions to that effect are included. Where such provisions are included, they may be enforced so long as they do not violate public policy.

E. PREINCORPORATION SUBSCRIPTIONS

A preincorporation subscription is a written promise by a person to purchase a specific number of shares of a corporation at a specific price after the corporation is formed. Such promises may be obtained by promoters as part of their capital-raising efforts.

1. Historically most capital for new ventures was raised through preincorporation subscriptions. Their public use was made impractical by the enactment of the securities acts which imposed registration requirements on both the subscription and the subsequent sale of shares. They still may be used in closely held corporations, though simple contractual agreements with the corporation are now more common.

2. Preincorporation subscriptions may be obtained independently of each other and some courts held that such subscriptions were not supported by consideration.

   a. In some instances subscriptions may be made in a form that permitted an argument that the promises were made in exchange for each other; in these instances courts often held that preincorporation subscriptions were contractual and therefore irrevocable.

   b. Modern statutes provide that preincorporation subscriptions are irrevocable for a stated period, often six months, without regard to whether they are supported by consideration. RMBCA § 6.20(a).

3. Modern statutes provide that payments on subscriptions that have been accepted by the corporation must be uniform.

4. Modern statutes permit a forfeiture of partial payments on subscriptions in the event later installments are not paid. Notice must be given before a subscription may be forfeited.

REVIEW QUESTIONS

III–1. A promoter and an incorporator perform the same functions.

True _____ False _____

III–2.   A promoter enters into a contract in the form "ABC Corporation, a corporation to be formed, By X." The promoter is not personally liable on that transaction.

            True _____   False _____   Uncertain _____

III–3.   A promoter who enters into a contract in the form described in question III–2, even if liable originally on the contract, will certainly be released from liability if the corporation is formed and takes over the contract.

            True _____   False _____   Uncertain _____

III–4.   How do cases involving corporations de facto and by estoppel differ from the promoters' cases?

III–5.   The Revised Model Business Corporation Act abolishes the concept of de facto corporation?

            True _____   False _____   Uncertain _____

III–6.   What is a corporation by estoppel and what is wrong with the concept?

III–7.   The corporation after it is formed automatically picks up all promoters' contracts.

            True _____   False _____

III–8.   A and B are promoters. B purchases an inventory of furniture for $60,000 which she represents to A cost $75,000. A agrees to the $75,000 figure. B has breached a duty to A.

            True _____   False _____   Uncertain _____

III–9.   A corporation after it is formed can sue promoters for unfair or fraudulent transactions.

            True _____   False _____   Uncertain _____

III–10.   Preincorporation subscriptions for shares are contracts.

            True _____   False _____

III–11. D entered into a contract with P for the building of a bridge across the Allegheny river. The contract recited that it was between "P and D for a bridge company to be incorporated." The bridge was built and *subsequently* the corporation was formed. P sues D personally to recover on the contract contending that D is personally liable inasmuch as the corporation was not in existence at the time the contract was entered into. D contends that in executing the contract he acted for a corporation to be formed and that the corporation and not D is liable on the contract. Is D personally liable to P?

III–12. A, a promoter of XYZ Publishing Co., engaged M to solicit advertisements for XYZ Publishing Co. prior to its incorporation. M's contract was for one year beginning October first. M started work October first. XYZ was incorporated on October 16. M worked six months and then was discharged by XYZ. XYZ never took formal action through its board of directors to adopt the contract with M but its shareholders, officers and directors knew of the contract and M was paid by the corporation until the time of his discharge. M sues XYZ for breach of contract. XYZ defends on the basis that it was not in existence at the time the contract was made and cannot be bound by acts of its promoters without adoption by the board of directors. Is XYZ liable on the contract?

IV

PIERCING THE CORPORATE VEIL

The phrase "piercing the corporate veil" is a metaphor to describe the cases in which a court refuses to recognize the separate existence of a corporation despite compliance with all the formalities for the creation of a *de jure* corporation. The phrase "piercing the corporate veil" is abbreviated to "PCV" in the balance of this part.

Analysis

A. Traditional Tests
B. Individual Shareholder Liability for Corporate Debts
C. Parent Corporation's Liability for Obligations of Subsidiary Corporation
D. Use of the Separate Corporate Existence to Defeat Public Policy
E. Piercing the Corporate Veil in Taxation Cases
F. Piercing the Corporate Veil in Bankruptcy

A.   TRADITIONAL TESTS

The traditional tests for PCV are to "prevent fraud" or to "achieve equity."   Many courts add the goals of "preventing oppression" or "avoiding illegality."   These tests are obviously result oriented and give little indication of the circumstances in which a court will refuse to recognize the separate existence of a corporation.   Other courts have applied a concept of "shareholder domination" or "alter ego" as the basis for PCV.   Since a majority or sole shareholder always "dominates" the corporation, and that corporation in a sense is always the "alter ego" of the majority or sole shareholder, these tests also do not provide a sound basis for application of the concept of PCV.

1.   ONE PERSON CORPORATIONS
One or two person corporations are treated no differently than other corporations in PCV cases.

2.   MOTIVE
Motive is unimportant in the sense that the separate corporate existence may be recognized even though the corporation was formed solely for the purpose of avoiding unlimited liability.

> *Example:*   *X* is the sole owner of a retail drug business which includes home deliveries.   *X* decides to incorporate solely because he fears potential liability for (1) accidents by his delivery trucks and (2) adverse drug reactions from the products he sells.   If the corporation is formed and operated consistently with the principles set forth below, its separate corporate existence should be recognized despite the liability-avoiding motive of the sole shareholder behind its formation.

3.   BROTHER–SISTER CORPORATIONS
PCV cases are not limited solely to the liability of individual shareholders for corporate obligations.   In appropriate cases, the separate existence of related corporations, i. e., corporations with common shareholders, may be ignored so that the two corporations are treated as a single entity.   This may occur even though the common shareholders are not found to be personally liable for corporate obligations under a PCV theory.

4.   INACTIVE SHAREHOLDERS
PCV is not an all-or-nothing principle.   In appropriate cases, active shareholders may be held liable for corporate debts on a PCV theory but inactive shareholders may be found not to be personally liable on such obligations.

5.   ESTOPPEL AGAINST SHAREHOLDERS
PCV is basically an equitable doctrine available to creditors of the corporation whose separate existence is being questioned.   It generally is not available to the corporation itself or its shareholders who now regret having formed the

corporation; it also may not be available to the bankruptcy trustee of the corporation whose separate existence is being questioned, though individual creditors may be able to assert a claim under the PCV doctrine. *Stodd v. Goldberger*, 141 Cal.Rptr. 67 (Cal.App. 1977).

B. INDIVIDUAL SHAREHOLDER LIABILITY FOR CORPORATE DEBTS

Many PCV cases involve attempts to hold shareholders who are individuals liable for corporate obligations. (The rules relating to *corporate* shareholders are somewhat different and are discussed in the following subsection.)

1.   CONSENSUAL TRANSACTIONS
   In cases involving *contract* claims the third person has usually dealt voluntarily with the corporation in some way. Hence, absent unusual circumstances he has "assumed the risk" that the corporation will be unable to meet its obligations and should not be able to PCV and hold the shareholders personally liable. Many but not all cases accept this approach.

> *Example:*   X creates a corporation of which he is sole shareholder with a capital of $1. Y sells $50,000 worth of goods to X's corporation on credit without making any credit check and without being misled in any way. Y may not recover from X on a PCV theory and is limited to his suit against X's corporation. See *Brunswick Corp. v. Waxman*, 599 F.2d 34 (2d Cir. 1979); Texas Industries, Inc. v. Dupuy & Dupuy Developers, Inc., 227 So.2d 265 (La.App. 1969).

   a.   "Unusual circumstances" in which shareholder liability for contract claims might be imposed include:

   1)   The shareholder conducts business in such a way as to cause confusion between individual and corporate finances. See *Zaist v. Olson*, 227 A.2d 552 (Conn. 1967).

   > *Example:*   For convenience, X pays all bills of his corporation by his personal checks and reimburses himself at the end of each week by a single corporate check. X is probably personally liable on corporate obligations to persons who are aware that bills in the past have been paid from X's personal funds.

   2)   The third party is in some way misled or tricked into dealing with the corporation.

Example: X negotiates a contract directly with Y, believing that he is dealing with Y on an individual basis. After the deal is concluded in principle, Y presents a contract in which his wholly owned corporation is the sole obligor on the contract. X does not notice this change. If the change is not conspicuous or X is misled in some way, X may hold Y personally on the contract. However, if the change is conspicuous and there is no deception, it is likely that X must look solely to the corporation on the theory that a person who signs a contract without reading it is bound by the contents.

3)   The corporation is operated in an unusual way so that:

(i)   It can never make a profit;

(ii) All available money is siphoned off to the shareholder without regard to the needs of the corporation; or

(iii) It is operated so that it is always insolvent. *Iron City Sand & Gravel Div. v. West Fork Towing Corp.*, 298 F.Supp. 1091 (N.D.W.Va. 1969); *DeWitt Truck Brokers, Inc. v. W. Ray Flemming Fruit Co.*, 540 F.2d 681 (4th Cir. 1976).

It is probable that many such transactions can be attacked on the theory that they constitute fraudulent conveyances or frauds on creditors independently of the PCV doctrine.

Example: A corporation is formed by a group of persons to build houses to be sold to the shareholders. The corporation prices each home at less than cost so that the corporation must ultimately fail. Creditors who are unaware of the pricing practice probably can hold the shareholders individually liable, *Yacker v. Weiner*, 263 A.2d 188 (N.J.Super. Ch.Div. 1970), though there is some case law to the contrary, *Bartle v. Home Owners Cooperative, Inc.*, 127 N.E.2d 832 (N.Y. 1955).

Example: X forms two corporations, one to manufacture a product and the other to sell it. The price at which the manufacturing corporation sells the products to the selling corporation determines in which corporation the profits will accumulate. X conducts the business so that liabilities end up in the manufacturing corporation and assets in the selling corporation. If the distinction between the two corporations is not sharply maintained and creditors believe they are dealing with a single enterprise, both corporations may be jointly liable for all corporate obligations.

4) The capitalization of the corporation is in some way misrepresented. Of course, an affirmative misrepresentation by the shareholder of the capitalization of his corporation might constitute actionable fraud independent of the PCV doctrine.

> *Example:* A creditor considering an extension of credit to *AB* Corporation requests financial information. A two-week old balance sheet is supplied showing substantial liquid assets and relatively few current liabilities; this balance sheet is accurate as of the time it was prepared, but in the intervening two weeks the shareholders have caused the corporation to make a substantial distribution of liquid assets to themselves as dividends. It is likely that the shareholders would be held personally responsible to the creditor; the theory may be PCV, fraudulent misrepresentation, or a fraud on creditors.

5) The shareholder promises unconditionally to be personally responsible for the corporate obligations under circumstances where it is inequitable to permit the shareholder to rely on the statute of frauds.

> *Example:* A supplier to the corporation refuses to make further shipments unless paid for in cash on delivery. The shareholder promises to pay for the goods personally if the corporation does not, as an inducement to encourage the supplier to ship the goods immediately. The supplier ships the goods in reliance on the shareholder's promise. In most jurisdictions, the supplier may enforce the shareholder's promise even though not in writing. This may be based on a PCV analysis, on the "main object" exception to the statute of frauds, on a reliance exception to the statute of frauds, or conceivably on other theories as well. *DeWitt Truck Brokers, Inc. v. W. Ray Flemming Fruit Co.*, 540 F.2d 681 (4th Cir. 1976).

b. Inadequate or nominal capitalization should normally not be a factor in contract cases. Indeed, the formation of a nominally capitalized corporation may be an integral part of a carefully devised plan by the parties to allocate the risk of loss; courts should normally not change such allocation of risks in the absence of fraud or other abuse of the contract process.

> ***Example:*** A agrees to supply widgets to *B* at a specified price for resale. The understanding is that *A* will be paid only out of the proceeds of the resale of the widgets and *B* will not be personally responsible for any deficit or for any unsold widgets. To effectuate this understanding, *B* forms a wholly owned corporation with a capital of one dollar and all sales of widgets are made to or by the corporation. Sales are unprofitable and some widgets are unsalable. *B* is not liable on a PCV or any other theory; the application of any such theory would change the allocation of loss agreed to by the parties in an arms-length negotiation.

2. NONCONSENSUAL TRANSACTIONS

In cases involving nonconsensual transactions (usually torts) there is usually no element of voluntary dealing. As a result, one cannot usually argue that the third person "assumed the risk" by dealing with a nominally capitalized corporation.

a. To recognize the separate corporate existence of a nominally capitalized (and therefore judgment proof) corporation engaged in a hazardous activity may shift the risk of loss or injury to some random member of the general public who happens to be injured by the activity.

b. The individual tortfeasor is personally liable whether or not he was acting as an agent of the corporation. If he was acting as an agent, the corporation is also liable for the tort under the theory of respondeat superior. If the tortfeasor is also a corporate shareholder, officer or agent, he is liable because he is a tortfeasor and it is unnecessary to argue PCV. However, usually the tortfeasor is judgment proof, the corporation is also unable to satisfy the claim, and attempts are made to hold the shareholders personally liable on a PCV theory.

c. Lack of adequate capitalization is usually considered a major factor in PCV in tort cases. If the capital was originally reasonably adequate in light of the probable risks, a PCV argument is likely to be rejected even if unavoidable business reverses have reduced the amount of capital so that the tort creditor cannot be fully compensated. A PCV argument is likely to be accepted where the original capital is nominal or small in light of contemplated business risks.

d. Generally, many courts are more willing to accept PCV arguments in tort cases than they are in contract cases. Most litigated cases, however, involve only the sufficiency of a complaint to withstand a motion to dismiss rather than review of a judgment on the merits.

Example: A corporation is formed to operate a taxicab in New York City with the minimum capitalization and minimum insurance required by law. The cab seriously injures a pedestrian. While the case law is split, some authority would apply a PCV analysis to hold the controlling shareholder automatically liable. Others would require a showing that the policy of the corporation was to distribute all assets to the shareholder as promptly as possible so as to maintain minimum capitalization and insurance. Others require some kind of showing that the shareholder was himself involved in the corporate business. *Walkovsky v. Carlton*, 223 N.E.2d 6 (N.Y. 1966). Most cases finding liability involve some aggravating circumstances of the latter types.

Example: A corporation is formed to lease and operate a swimming pool. The corporation is formed but no capital is paid in by the shareholders. A child is drowned at the pool due to the negligence of an employee. An attorney who was an officer and may have been an investor was involved in the operation of the corporation and was held personally liable for the damages. *Minton v. Cavaney*, 364 P.2d 473 (Cal. 1961). Again, aggravating circumstances may be involved such as the failure to complete the formation of the corporation, to provide any capital at all, or to follow corporate formalities in connection with the corporate business.

e. A PCV argument is likely to be adopted where the corporation is formed specifically to engage in ultrahazardous activities which cause injury to person or property.

Example: A corporation is formed to do blasting pursuant to a contract. As a result of the blasting operations damage occurs to adjoining property. The shareholders are indirectly involved in decisions as to the conduct of the business: the corporation was nominally capitalized with the bulk of the assets loaned to the corporation by the shareholders. The shareholders are personally liable for the damages caused by the blasting operations.

3. FAILURE TO FOLLOW CORPORATE FORMALITIES

In PCV cases, a factor that is often significant if not decisive is the failure to follow corporate formalities.

a.   A PCV argument is much more likely to be accepted if the plaintiff can show:

1)   Failure to complete the formation of the corporation;

2)   Failure to contribute capital or to issue shares;

3)   Failure to hold elections, meetings and to follow the other trappings of corporate formality;

4)   Shareholders making business decisions much as though they were partners; and

5)   Mixing of personal and corporate activities, such as informal loans, use of corporate funds for personal loans, or vice versa.

See generally: *Zaist v. Olson*, 227 A.2d 552 (Conn. 1967). Not all cases, however, impose liability merely because of some informality and intermixing of personal and corporate assets. *Zubik v. Zubik*, 384 F.2d 267 (3d Cir. 1967).

b.   While such activities may lead to confusion or deception in some cases, liability is not dependent on a showing that third persons were misled or confused. The most likely justification for the principle is to provide a sanction to assure that corporate formalities are followed.

Example: Articles of incorporation are filed but no further steps are taken to complete the corporation. The corporation commences business. The active shareholders are likely to be held personally liable for corporate debts.

Example: The corporation is properly formed in the sense that articles of incorporation are filed, bylaws adopted, shares issued, and minutes of the organizational meetings are prepared. However, thereafter no shareholders' or directors' meetings are held. All decisions are made in the corporate name by the shareholders after talking among themselves. Even though no third party is harmed by such informal conduct or informal decision-making, active shareholders are likely to be held personally liable for corporate debts.

4.   ARTIFICIAL DIVISION OF A SINGLE BUSINESS ENTITY

In all PCV cases, an important factor is whether a single business is artificially divided into several different corporations to reduce exposure of assets to liabilities. Professor Berle referred to this phenomenon as the theory of "enterprise entity."

a.   The normal response to an artificial division of a single business entity is to hold the entire entity responsible for the debts of the business rather than to hold the shareholders personally liable for such debts.

> *Example:*   *X*, the owner of a fleet of taxicabs in New York City, forms a separate corporation for each taxicab, a separate corporation for the garage that services the cabs, and a separate corporation for the paging service that takes telephone calls and relays them to individual cabs.   Except for the separate incorporations, the business is operated as a single unit but the shareholder uniformly conducts business in the name of one or more of the corporations.   Each corporation is liable for the debts of each other corporation. *Mangan v. Terminal Trans. System, Inc.*, 284 N.Y.S. 183 (S.Ct. 1935), aff'd per curiam, 286 N.Y.S. 666 (1936).   Whether or not *X* is personally liable depends on the nature of the claim asserted, the adequacy of the capitalization of the individual corporations, and other factors.

b.   Two or more corporations owned by a single shareholder or owned approximately proportionally by several shareholders are often referred to as "brother-sister corporations."   Such corporations may also be analyzed as a type of "parent-subsidiary" relationship discussed below.

C. PARENT CORPORATION'S LIABILITY FOR OBLIGATIONS OF SUBSIDIARY CORPORATION

Courts are more likely to PCV when the shareholder is itself a corporation than when the shareholder is an individual.

1. CONFUSION OF AFFAIRS

Parent liability for the subsidiary's debts usually arises from a failure to maintain a clear separation between parent and subsidiary affairs.   Conduct that may lead to parental liability includes:

a.   Referring to the subsidiary as a "department" or "division" of the parent;

b.   Mixing business affairs, such as using parental stationery to respond to inquiries addressed to the subsidiary;

c.   Having common officers who do not clearly delineate the capacity in which they are acting, i. e., a failure to identify "which hat he (or she) is wearing;"

d.   Mixing assets, such as having the subsidiary sign a pledge of assets to secure parental indebtedness, transferring funds informally from one entity to the other without the formalities normally involved in a loan, or having a common bank account. *Bernardin, Inc., v. Midland Oil Corp.*, 520 F.2d 771 (7th Cir. 1975).

2.   PERMISSIBLE ACTIVITIES

If practices similar to those described in paragraph 1. are avoided, a PCV argument should be rejected even though:

a.   One corporation owns all the shares of the corporation;

b.   The corporations have common officers or directors; and

c.   The corporations file a consolidated tax return or report their earnings to their shareholders on a consolidated basis. *Berger v. Columbia Broadcasting System, Inc.*, 453 F.2d 991 (5th Cir. 1972).

3.   FRAUD OR INJUSTICE

Some cases have concluded that in a contract case a parent is liable for its subsidiary's liabilities only upon a showing of "fraud or injustice." *Edwards Co., Inc. v. Monogram Industries, Inc.*, 730 F.2d 977 (5th Cir. 1984), rev'g 713 F.2d 139 (5th Cir. 1983).

4.   CONCLUSION

The willingness to PCV in the parent-subsidiary relationship appears to be based on the view that it is less serious to hold an additional corporate entity liable than it is to hold an individual shareholder liable.

D.   USE OF THE SEPARATE CORPORATE EXISTENCE TO DEFEAT PUBLIC POLICY

The flexibility of the corporate fiction often permits it to be used in a way that arguably tends to defeat or undercut statutory policies.

Example: A statute prohibits bank directors from borrowing from their bank. A corporation that is wholly owned by a bank director seeks to obtain a loan from the bank. The argument that the corporate borrower has a separate identity from the shareholder and that therefore the loan may be validly made would defeat a clearly defined public policy expressed in the statute; the loan should therefore be held to violate the statute. This result might be rationalized on the ground that the corporation is the "alter ego" of its shareholder and that a loan to the "corporation" is therefore a loan to the "shareholder."

1. **GENERAL PRINCIPLE**

   The issue in such cases revolves around the strength and purpose of the state public policy rather than the degree or extent of formation or method of operation of the corporation.

   Example: A statute prohibits branch banking, i. e., a bank is prohibited from conducting business at more than one location. A bank buys all the capital stock of another bank and plans to continue the banking business at both the parent and subsidiary bank locations. Whether this violates the anti-branch banking statute depends on an evaluation of the policies underlying that statute, not on an examination of the way in which the parent and subsidiary banks conduct business. If the policy underlying the statute is not a strong one, the parent-subsidiary bank relationship should not be viewed as a violation of the statute.

2. **QUALIFICATION OF SHAREHOLDER FOR EMPLOYEE BENEFITS**

   A corporation may also be used to qualify a person for public benefits available to employees which he would not be entitled to if he conducted business in his own name. The validity of this practice also depends on an evaluation of the policies underlying the grant of benefits.

   Example: X, a 63-year old farmer learns that his social security benefits may be increased if he establishes a favorable employment record during the last two years before his retirement. Accordingly, he incorporates his farm, becoming the sole shareholder and hires himself as an employee of the corporation to improve his earnings record. The establishment of the corporation to improve a person's social security entitlement is not of itself an improper use of a corporation in light of the purpose of the social security system to assure persons an adequate retirement income. *Stark v. Flemming,* 283 F.2d 410 (9th Cir. 1960). However, a court may revise the "salary" downward to a reasonable amount to prevent an artificially high entitlement.

   Example: In the foregoing situation, the farmer incorporates in order to obtain unemployment benefits during the winter months when little farm work is done. He "lays himself off" during these slow periods, and files for unemployment compensation. This claim should be rejected since the unemployment benefit system was basically not intended to cover employers or owners of a business. *Roccograndi v. Unemployment Compensation Board of Review,* 178 A.2d 786 (Pa.Super. 1962).

3. OTHER POLICY ISSUES

A PCV analysis may also be used to determine whether a parent corporation is bound by a subsidiary's union contract. *United Paperworkers Int'l Union v. Penntech Papers, Inc.*, 439 F.Supp. 610 (D.Me. 1977) *aff'd* 583 F.2d 33 (1st Cir. 1978).

E. PIERCING THE CORPORATE VEIL IN TAXATION CASES

Under the Internal Revenue Code the government has broad power to ignore or restructure fictional transactions which have as their sole purpose the avoidance or minimization of taxes.

1. RECOGNITION OF CORPORATION IN GENERAL

Generally, the separate corporate existence of a corporation will be recognized for tax purposes if it is carrying on a bona fide business and is not merely a device to avoid taxes.

2. ESTOPPEL AGAINST TAXPAYER

The taxpayer, if he or she selects the corporate form of business, is generally bound by that selection and cannot argue that the separate existence of the corporation should be ignored.

F. PIERCING THE CORPORATE VEIL IN BANKRUPTCY

Under the Federal Bankruptcy Act, courts have considerable flexibility in dealing with corporations and shareholders for the purpose of preserving the rights of creditors.

1. PIERCING THE CORPORATE VEIL

The court may ignore the separate corporate existence and hold the shareholders liable for all corporate obligations.

2. RECLASSIFICATION OF TRANSACTION

The court may refuse to recognize, may reclassify, or change the form of a transaction between shareholder and corporation where it is equitable or reasonable to do so.

Example: A loan by a shareholder to his corporation which is essentially part of the initial capital needed by the corporation to conduct business may be treated as a contribution of equity capital and subordinated. *Costello v. Fazio*, 256 F.2d 903 (9th Cir. 1958). On the other hand, where the initial capital is more than nominal and the corporation was organized apparently in good faith, subsequent loans to cover losses should not be subordinated. *In re Mader's Store for Men, Inc.*, 254 N.W.2d 171 (Wis. 1977).

> *Example:* In the previous example, essentially the same result may be reached by rejecting the shareholder's claim in its entirety.

3. SUBORDINATION

The court may subordinate claims of shareholders to claims of other creditors where the claim of the shareholder is in some sense inequitable. This power was viewed by the Supreme Court as inherent in the bankruptcy jurisdiction of federal courts. *Pepper v. Litton*, 308 U.S. 295, 60 S.Ct. 238 (1939). It is now codified in section 510(c)(1) of the Bankruptcy Act of 1978.

a. The power to subordinate inequitable claims (e.g., for excessive salaries) is known as the "Deep Rock" doctrine from the name of the subsidiary in the leading case applying the doctrine. *Taylor v. Standard Gas & Electric Co.*, 306 U.S. 307 (1939).

> *Example:* A sole shareholder transfers funds to his corporation in the form of loans and backdated deeds of trusts, at a time when the corporation was insolvent. The original capital was about $5,000 while the "loans" aggregated $77,500. The "loans" are in fact capital contributions, the deeds of trust are frauds on creditors, and the shareholder's claims should be subordinated to all other creditors. *In re Fett Roofing & Sheet Metal Co., Inc.*, 438 F.Supp. 726 (E.D.Va. 1977), aff'd without opinion 605 F.2d 1201 (4th Cir. 1979).

b. Subordination theoretically simply changes the "order of payment" so that the shareholder's claim may be paid after other creditors are satisfied in full; as a practical matter, however, the claims of other creditors will usually exhaust the estate so that if a claim is subordinated under the "Deep Rock" doctrine, it will not be satisfied in whole or in part.

c. Where both the parent and subsidiary are bankrupt, proceedings may be consolidated and priorities between the parent's and subsidiary's creditors determined on an equitable basis. *Stone v. Eacho*, 127 F.2d 284 (4th Cir. 1942).

REVIEW QUESTIONS

IV–1. How does the piercing the corporate veil concept differ from promoters' transactions, corporations de facto, and similar concepts?

IV–2.   X forms a corporation for a risky business solely because of fear of unlimited liability. The corporate veil of X's corporation may be pierced for this reason.

True _____   False _____

IV–3.   X forms a corporation with one dollar of capital as permitted by the statutes of his state. The corporation enters into a lease but defaults after six months because of business losses. X is personally liable on the lease.

True _____   False _____

IV–4.   In the same situation as question IV–3, the corporation is found liable for a tort committed by an employee in which X did not participate. The corporate form protects X against this liability.

True _____   False _____

IV–5   In the same situation as question IV–3, X commingles business and personal finances and does not keep separate corporate records. X is liable for both liabilities described in questions IV–3 and IV–4.

True _____   False _____

IV–6.   X Corporation creates a subsidiary, Y Corporation, with the same officers and directors. Because of this confusion of personnel, X Corporation is liable for Y Corporation's debts.

True _____   False _____

IV–7.   In question IV–5, X Corporation often refers to Y Corporation as a "division" and transfers money to assist Y Corporation simply by check. X Corporation is liable for Y Corporation's debts.

True _____   False _____

IV–8.   X, an individual aged 60, decides to incorporate her own business and employ herself to establish the necessary earnings record for social security purposes. This is a fraud on the Federal Government and X is ineligible.

True _____   False _____

IV–9.   P sued A Corporation for damages on the ground that P had been fraudulently induced to enter into a training course contract. P served

A Corporation under a state long-arm statute allowing service on "any person who transacts any business" in the state. A Corporation is incorporated in another state and directly transacted no business in the state. However, P contended that A Corporation was doing business because it was a holding company for S which was doing business in the state. The trial court found that A Corporation owned 100% of the stock of S but allowed S's management autonomy as to achievement of goals set in conjunction with A's management; A Corporation provided S with a general financial, legal, tax and administrative services, and acted as its banker but S kept separate books and records, S and A had separate auditors, officers and office staffs. Should the court hold that A was transacting business in the state?

IV–10.   D purchased Blackacre for the purpose of mining coal. He formed "A Corporation" and posted on Blackacre a sign, "A Corporation Mines." There was issued to D all of the shares of the corporation except one share which was issued to D's wife. Neither D nor his wife paid any money for these shares. There was no meeting of shareholders, no directors were elected, no corporate control was exercised and no corporate books were kept. The mine was operated as though it were the private business of D: the expenses of the mine were paid by D from his private bank account and the income was deposited in D's private account. One of the employees in the mine is killed as a result of negligence in the mining operations. His executor sues D. Is D liable?

V

FINANCING THE CORPORATION

Analysis

141

A. IN GENERAL

The following are the likely sources of capital for a corporation:

1. **EQUITY CAPITAL**
   Capital contributed by shareholders in exchange for shares of stock is usually referred to as "equity capital" or "equity financing."

2. **LOANS FROM SHAREHOLDERS**
   Capital loaned by the shareholders to the corporation may be substituted for equity capital in whole or in part. Such loans therefore have many of the characteristics of equity capital and may be treated as equity capital for some purposes.

3. **LOANS FROM THIRD PERSONS**
   The raising of capital through loans from third persons is usually referred to as "debt financing." Capital loaned by third persons to the corporation should be distinguished from loans by shareholders because of the significantly different economic and legal consequences of such loans. For example, there is little likelihood that bona fide loans from third parties will be treated as equity capital; there is a real possibility that shareholder loans will be so treated.

4. **INTERNALLY GENERATED FUNDS**
   Capital internally generated from the corporation's business through the retention of earnings, creation of reserves, sales of appreciated assets and the like is a final source of funds needed by a corporation.

B. THE ISSUANCE OF "COMMON SHARES"; AN INTRODUCTION TO "PAR VALUE"

RMBCA § 2.02(a)(2) provides that the articles of incorporation must set forth "the number of shares the corporation is authorized to issue." RMBCA § 6.01(a) provides that the articles of incorporation must prescribe "the classes of shares and the number of shares of each class" that the corporation is authorized to issue; in addition, if more than one class of shares is authorized, the articles of incorporation "must prescribe a distinguishing designation for each class, and, prior to the issuance of shares of a class, the preferences, limitations, and relative rights of that class must be described" in the articles of incorporation.

1. **THE TREND TOWARD THE ELIMINATION OF MANDATORY PAR VALUE**
   In more than 40 states, the articles of incorporation must also state the par value of the shares of each class (or state that the shares are issued "with no par value" or "without par value"). The remaining states, like the Revised Model Business Corporation Act (1984), have eliminated the concept of par

value, and the current trend is toward the elimination of this concept as an historical anomaly.

(a)   "Par value" is an artificial value set forth in the articles of incorporation and appearing on the face of certificates for shares. The complex operation of this concept is described in parts 4, 5, and 6 below.

(b)   RMBCA § 2.02(b)(2)(iv) permits the use of par value as a discretionary matter. The Official Comment explains that such provisions may be of use "to corporations which are to be qualified in foreign jurisdictions if franchise or other taxes are computed upon the basis of par value."

(c)   Optional par value may also be given effect or meaning "essentially as a matter of contract" between the parties. In other words, the par value rules described below may be elected by the parties if they so desire by creating a par value for shares.

2.   THE CONCEPT OF "COMMON SHARES"

When a corporation issues only one class of shares, the shares need no formal designation but are usually described as "capital shares," "common shares," "capital stock" or "common stock." The rights of those shares need not be described in the articles of incorporation since they have the two basic rights of common shares:

(a)   They are entitled to vote for the election of directors and on other matters coming before the shareholders; and

(b)   They are entitled to the net assets of the corporation (after making allowance for debts), when distributions are made in the form of dividends or liquidating distributions.

RMBCA § 6.01(b) permits these essential attributes of common shares to be placed in different classes of shares but requires that classes with these attributes must always be authorized. RMBCA § 6.03(b) also requires that at least one share of each class with each of these basic attributes must be outstanding.

3.   AUTHORIZED AND ISSUED SHARES

It is customary in modern corporate practice to authorize additional shares over what is planned to be issued at the outset in the event additional capital is needed at a later date. Shares authorized but not issued may be issued at a later date by the board of directors without approval of the shareholders or amendment to the articles of incorporation.

Caveat: Where par value shares are involved, the capital accounts created therefrom (described below) are based on *issued* shares, not *authorized* shares. State statutes, on the other hand, may compute taxes either on the basis of authorized shares or on the basis of issued shares.

Example: A and B plan to contribute $10,000 each for fifty per cent of the stock of a new corporation. The attorney forming the corporation recommends that 500 shares of common stock be authorized with a par value of $1, and that 100 shares be issued each to A and B for $100 per share. Three hundred shares have the status of "authorized but unissued shares."

Example: In the previous example essentially the same economic result may be achieved by issuing 10 shares each for $1000 each. There are two differences: (1) the number of authorized but unissued shares of the corporation will be 480 instead of 300; and (2) as described below, if the shares are issued under a par value statute, the transaction will be reflected differently in the capital accounts of the corporation.

Example: The authorized but unissued shares in the two previous examples may be later issued by the board of directors at any price then decided upon by the board of directors, though if the shares have a par value, they should not be issued for less than par value (see below). If conditions warrant, the authorized shares may be issued at more (or less) than the original issue price.

4. PAR VALUE AS THE PRICING FLOOR

Where par value shares are involved, the one basic rule is that such shares should never be issued for less than par value. (The consequence of issuing par value shares for less than par is the creation of "watered shares" and a resulting liability on the part of the recipient to pay to the corporation the difference between par value and what the shareholder actually paid.) It is customary in modern practice to use "low par" or "nominal par" value shares rather than "high par" value shares.

Example: In the previous examples, the attorney may set the par value of $1 per share but issue the shares at $100 per share. He might set the par value at any amount up to $100 per share (in the first example) or $1000 per share (in the second example). However, the par value is set in the articles of incorporation, and once set, cannot be changed except by formal amendment to the articles of incorporation.

Example: In the previous example, if the attorney set the par value at the issue price of $100 per share, several undesirable consequences would follow: (i) no shares of the corporation could be thereafter issued by the corporation at less than $100 per share without creating a watered stock liability, (ii) for many years the federal documentary stamp tax was computed on the basis of par value so that in the past this alternative increased federal stamp taxes with no offsetting benefits (some state taxes may still be computed on the same basis); and (iii) as described below, the transaction will be reflected in the capital accounts of the corporation in a way that is less advantageous to the corporation than if nominal par shares were used.

5. PAR VALUE AND THE CAPITAL ACCOUNTS

Most corporation statutes provide that the aggregate of the par values of issued shares constitutes the "stated capital" of the corporation and any excess received for the issuance of shares over stated capital is "capital surplus."

Example: When 100 shares of $1 par value shares are issued each to *A* and *B* for $100 per share (or an aggregate of $10,000 each), the balance sheet of the corporation immediately after its formation will be as follows:

Assets		Liabilities	–0–
Cash	20,000		
		Equity Capital	
		Stated Capital	200
		Capital Surplus	19,800
	20,000		20,000

Example: If in this corporation a par value of $100 per share had been assigned, the balance sheet would be as follows:

Assets		Liabilities	–0–
Cash	20,000		
		Capital	
		Stated Capital	20,000
		Capital Surplus	–0–
	20,000		20,000

a. A major advantage of reflecting the bulk of the capital contributions as capital surplus is that under most state statutes stated capital is "locked in" the corporation for the benefit of creditors while capital surplus may be distributed to the shareholders or used to reacquire outstanding shares merely with the approval of shareholders.

Example: In the preceding example, *B* suffers business and gambling reverses and would like to withdraw half of his $10,000 contribution. *A* agrees to this so long as *B*'s shares are reduced correspondingly. Under most state statutes, capital surplus may be used to reacquire outstanding shares but stated capital may not. As a result, a corporation formed under "low par" principles could reacquire one half of *B*'s shares at cost, but a corporation formed under "high par" principles could not. The balance sheet of the "low par" corporation might look like this after reacquiring fifty of *B*'s shares for $5,000:

Assets		Liabilities	–0–
Cash	15,000		
		Equity	
		Stated Capital (150 shares outstanding, 50 treasury shares)	200
		Capital Surplus (5,000 restricted to reflect treasury shares)	14,800
	15,000		15,000

6. NO PAR VALUE SHARES

In most states that have mandatory par value statutes "no par" shares are permitted. However, in these states, these shares are generally tied into "par value" concepts though they may provide some protection against watered stock liability. No par shares may be issued for any amount of consideration specified by the directors; there is no floor below which the price may not be set.

Example: *A* and *B* decide to issue 100 no par shares out of a total authorization of 500 shares. (i) The directors may set, without limitation, the price at which no par shares are issued, and may set, e. g., $.01, $1.00 or $100 per share. (ii) The entire consideration is initially allocated to "stated capital" but in most states the directors may allocate a specified fraction (e. g., one-third) or all the consideration to "capital surplus." If no part is allocated to "capital surplus" the no par alternative is treated for accounting purposes like the high par alternative. If all or nearly all of the consideration is allocated to "capital surplus," the no par alternative is treated for accounting purposes like the low par alternative.

a. Where property (other than cash) is received in some states the directors must still specify in dollars the consideration to be received for no par shares. In other states, the directors may simply specify the property to be received without setting a dollar value.

b.   "No par" shares have no other significant advantage over "low par" shares in most states and the choice between them is more a matter of custom with the particular attorney than questions of practical or economic significance.

c.   Under the since-repealed federal documentary stamp tax no par shares were valued at the price at which the shares were actually issued while par value shares were valued at par value, no matter what price the shares were actually issued. To the extent state taxes reflect this treatment today, there is a continuing tax inducement to issue low par rather than no par shares.

> *Caveat:*   It is important to distinguish conceptually between "no par shares" in states that retain the par value structure, and shares issued in states that, like the RMBCA, have eliminated par value. The issuance of "no par shares" in par value states affect the stated capital and capital surplus account, may create a watered stock liability in certain circumstances, and may affect the distributions a corporation may lawfully make. States that have eliminated the par value structure have also generally eliminated the mandatory capital accounts and have established rules relating to when distributions may be made that are independent of any allocation of the consideration received when the shares are issued. See part G. below.

7.   WATERED STOCK

"Watered stock" is a generic term used to describe the issuance of shares below par value. Depending on the language of the state statute, watered stock may also arise if low par value or no par value shares are issued for a price below the price set by the directors for the issuance of such shares, even if the price at which the shares are actually issued is above the par value of the low par value shares.

a.   There are three subtypes of watered stock:

1)   "Bonus" shares are shares issued for no consideration usually in connection with the valid issuance of senior securities and as an inducement to invest in the senior securities;

2)   "Discount" shares are shares issued for a consideration less than the legally established price, either the par value or the price set by the directors; and

3)   "Watered" shares are technically shares issued for property the value of which has been artificially inflated. Historically, many fraudulent transactions took the form of shares issued for overvalued property. The phrase "watered stock" has gradually come to refer to bonus or discount stock as well.

b.   The par value of issued shares was early viewed as a public representation that at least that amount of equity capital had been received by the corporation. This concept gave rise to the idea that shareholders who knowingly received watered shares were involved in a potential misrepresentation to creditors and might be liable to them for any short-fall between the par value and the amount actually paid for shares. This is the classic "watered stock liability."

1)   This liability has sometimes been rationalized on the theory that the capital of a corporation is a "trust fund" for creditors. Under this theory any creditor might bring suit against the recipient of watered shares for failing to make the required payment to this "trust fund." This theory is largely a fiction because:

(i)   The capital of a corporation is not a "trust fund" in any more meaningful way than the assets of an individual may be considered a "trust fund" for his or her creditors; and

(ii)   The corporate creditors are no more the "beneficiary" of such a trust than are creditors of an individual debtor.

2)   In an early case, the theory of this liability was refined to a "holding out" theory. *Hospes v. Northwestern Mfg. & Car Co.*, 50 N.W. 1117 (Minn. 1892). The practical differences between the "holding out" and the "trust fund" theories are that under a "holding out" theory:

(i)   Only creditors who extended credit subsequent to the issuance of the watered shares might enforce the liability; and

(ii)   Creditors who knew that the shares were watered when they extended credit could not recover at all.

3)   The holding out theory is also fictional in the sense that reliance on the capital of the corporation by a creditor is presumed; indeed, the defendants can avoid liability only by an affirmative showing that the plaintiffs knew that the stock was watered or that they did not rely on the capital of the corporation when they extended credit.

4) Many modern par value statutes substitute a statutory liability for the above theories. Under these statutes, every shareholder is obligated to pay at least the price set as required by law for shares, and if a shareholder fails to do so, the corporation or any creditor may enforce the liability. The "price set as required by law" of course means a price at least equal to the par value of shares.

Example: A corporation issues 1,000,000 shares of $10 par value for an aggregate consideration of $5,000,000 in cash. Since the capital accounts automatically reflect a stated capital equal to the number of shares issued (1,000,000) times the par value ($10.00 per share), the asset accounts must be "watered" in some way if the balance sheet is to balance:

Cash	5,000,000	Liabilities	–0–
"Water"	5,000,000	Equity Capital	
		Stated Capital	10,000,000
	$10,000,000		$10,000,000

A person who extends credit to the corporation after the watered stock is issued without knowledge that the stock was watered may sue each recipient of the shares for $5.00 per share under all three theories. If he or she became a creditor before the shares were issued or knew that they were watered when extending credit, he or she cannot recover under the "holding out" theory but might recover under the other theories.

Example: In the foregoing example, under modern statutes the corporation itself might recover $5.00 per share from each recipient as the basic statutory liability a shareholder owes to his corporation for issuance of shares. This liability might be enforced by the corporation, a creditor, a bankruptcy trustee, or similar representative of the corporation, apparently without limitation. *Bing Crosby Minute Maid Corp. v. Eaton,* 297 P.2d 5 (Cal. 1956); *Frink v. Carman Distributing Co.,* 48 P.2d 805 (Colo. 1935).

c. Watered stock may give rise to unexpected and crushing liabilities and may make high par value shares unmarketable.

Example: A corporation originally issues shares with a par value of $100 per share at a sales price of $100. The corporation suffers financial reverses so that its outstanding shares are now worth less than $100 per share. The corporation decides to issue additional authorized shares to raise much needed capital; these shares can only be sold at the current market price of $60 per share. Since they are $100 par value shares, any person who purchases the new shares at $60 per share may also incur a potential watered stock liability of $40 per share. Sophisticated investors will naturally refuse to purchase shares under such circumstances and the shares are unmarketable.

Example: In the foregoing situation, the corporation may amend its articles of incorporation to reduce the par value of the authorized shares or may create a new class of low par value common shares.

d.   Watered stock liability may also arise if the directors set a specified dollar price for low par or no par shares and shares are issued at a lower price. *Milberg v. Baum*, 25 N.Y.S.2d 451 (App. Term 1941) (low par shares); *G. Loewus & Co. v. Highland Queen Packing Co.*, 6 A.2d 545 (N.J.Ch. 1939) (no par shares).

Example: The directors set a price of $10 per share for an issue of no par shares. For some reason one shareholder is permitted to buy shares for $8.00. That shareholder has a liability to the corporation for the additional $2.00 despite his contract with the corporation to pay only $8.00.

Example: No par shares may have an advantage where property of highly uncertain value is being contributed because the directors may be able to specify the property that is to be received for the no par shares without setting a dollar value on it. However, even where a dollar value must be set, the directors' valuation is likely to be accepted under the statutory provisions that make the determination of the directors as to value conclusive in the absence of fraud. *Johnson v. Louisville Trust Co.*, 293 F. 857 (6th Cir. 1923).

e.   Shares issued for no consideration, whether par or no par, may in some cases be cancelled at the suit of other shareholders and votes cast by such shares may be invalidated. *Triplex Shoe Co. v. Rice & Hutchins, Inc.*, 152 A. 342 (Del. 1930).

8. CONSIDERATION FOR SHARES

When shares are issued for property or services rather than cash, further problems arise.

a. Under most state statutes, only certain types of property qualify as valid consideration for shares. A typical statute provides that consideration may consist only of "cash, tangible or intangible property actually received or services actually performed." Many statutes add that promissory notes do not constitute eligible consideration. Several of these statutory provisions are grounded on state constitutional prohibitions against the watering of stock. If ineligible property or services are received for shares, the shares so issued are watered shares.

Example: *A* and *B* agree to form a corporation each to have one half of the stock. *A* is to contribute $10,000 in cash and *B* is to work full time for the corporation for one year. The consideration for the shares is recited to be $10,000 each, *A* to pay cash and "*B* to perform services of the value of $10,000 over the next year." If *B*'s shares are issued immediately, a watered stock liability of $10,000 on the part of *B* has been created despite the agreement by *A* and *B* that *B* is to contribute only services, since a promise of future services is not valid consideration for shares.

Example: In the above situation, *B*'s shares are to be issued only after *B* has performed services for one year. Since the services have been "actually performed" no watered stock liability has been created. *Eastern Oklahoma Television Co. v. Ameco, Inc.*, 437 F.2d 138 (10th Cir. 1971). However, *B* does not have the rights of a shareholder during the period he or she is rendering services, though *B* may have contract rights against *A*.

Example: In the above situation, *B*'s shares are to be issued immediately for a promissory note which is to be repaid by the performance of services over the year. Under most statutes, a watered stock liability has been created since promissory notes do not constitute permissible consideration. *Cahall v. Lofland*, 114 A. 224 (Del.Ch. 1921).

Example: In the above situation, *B*'s shares are to be issued immediately, not for services but for "six store fixtures having the value of $10,000." In fact the store fixtures are valueless. Most state statutes provide in effect that "in the absence of fraud the values established by the board are conclusive." Hence, if this transaction is not fraudulent, the values established for the store fixtures must be accepted. If the directors know the valuation is not an honest one, watered stock liability would arise. *See v. Heppenheimer*, 61 A. 843 (N.J.Ch. 1905); *Pipelife Corp. v. Bedford*, 145 A.2d 206 (Del.Ch. 1958).

Example: In the above situation, *B*'s shares are to be issued, not for services but for "secret contract rights." Most state statutes refer to "intangible" property as qualifying for the issuance of shares. Hence, it is likely that for reasons described in the previous examples, such a transaction does not give rise to watered stock liability unless the value placed on the contract rights is fraudulent. There is, however, some risk that a court may accept the argument that "secret contract rights" are so ephemeral that they do not qualify as "intangible" property and that therefore the shares are issued without consideration and are watered.

Example: *B*'s shares are to be issued for a promissory note secured by a lien on valuable real estate. While in many states a promissory note is not proper consideration for the issuance of shares, some courts have held that a secured promissory note may qualify as consideration for shares. In any event, the note itself is not void and may be sued upon by the corporation.

b.   If shares are issued for services already performed, the fair value of the shares so received is subject to income tax as ordinary income. This tax bill may create practical problems since the shareholder normally wishes to retain all his shares and must find the cash to pay the tax from other sources.

c.   The contribution of property to a corporation in exchange for its shares is not a taxable disposition of the property contributed if immediately after the exchange the persons contributing the property own at least 80 per cent of the voting and nonvoting shares of the corporation. This nonrecognition of gain is limited to transactions in which no property other than shares is received by the contributor and the liabilities assumed by the corporation to which the property is subject do not exceed the basis of the property in the hands of the contributor. I.R.C. § 351. No gain or loss is recognized by the corporation in connection with the raising of capital by the issuance of shares. I.R.C. § 1032.

d. RMBCA § 6.21(b) of the Revised Model Business Corporation Act (1984) authorizes shares to be issued for consideration consisting of "any tangible or intangible property or benefit to the corporation, including cash, promissory notes, services performed, contracts for services to be performed, or other securities of the corporation."

  1) The corporation may escrow shares issued for future services or benefits or a promissory note until the consideration is received. RMBCA § 6.21(e).

  2) The Official Comment states that "in the realities of commercial life, there is sometimes a need for the issuance of shares for contract rights or such intangible property or benefits."

  3) The traditional rules create anomalous results.

    Example: Jane Fonda agrees to make a film in exchange for a twenty-five per cent interest in the film. Under traditional rules she could not be issued shares upon the execution of her contract; on the other hand, a bank might lend the new corporation $10,000,000 solely on the basis of Jane Fonda's contract.

    Example: John D. Rockefeller could not give his promissory note for shares even though his note is "as good as gold." On the other hand, someone else, owning John D.'s promissory note, could acquire shares for John D.'s note.

  4) The issue of the types of consideration permitted for shares is independent of the issue whether to eliminate par value. States may follow the RMBCA in eliminating par value concepts and retain restrictions on the types of consideration permitted for shares.

C. ISSUANCE OF MORE THAN A SINGLE CLASS OF SHARES

Common shares are the residual ownership interests in the corporation. Corporations may also issue other classes of shares. The traditional classification of shares is between common and preferred shares. The RMBCA does not use the terms "common shares" and "preferred shares" since it is possible to create classes of shares that have some characteristics of both types of shares. These terms, however, are generally used in corporate practice.

1.   PREFERRED SHARES

"Preferred" shares may have preference either as to dividends or on liquidation or both. A "preference" simply means that the preferred shares are entitled to a payment of a specified amount before the common shares are entitled to anything. Most preferred shares have both dividend and liquidation preferences; such preference rights are defined in the articles of incorporation and are usually limited to a right to a specified amount and no more.

Example: A "$3.50 preferred" means that the preferred share is entitled to a dividend preference of $3.50 per share before any dividend may be paid on the common shares. Such a share is not entitled to, and will never receive more than, $3.50 per share no matter how much is available for distribution. The $3.50 payment is a dividend, however, and is discretionary with the board of directors. Unlike interest, it is not a debt owed by the corporation.

Example: The above preferred share may also be entitled to a preferential liquidating payment of $75.00. On liquidation, $75.00 must be first set aside for each such share and nothing may be paid on the common until the $75.00 is paid to the preferred. On the other hand, once the preferred receives $75.00 it will receive nothing more no matter how much is available. The question whether unpaid preferential dividends must also be satisfied in liquidation depends on the language of the articles of incorporation. *Matter of Chandler & Co.*, 230 N.Y.S.2d 1012 (Sup.Ct. 1962).

a.   A dividend preference may be noncumulative, cumulative, or cumulative-to-the-extent-earned.

1)   A cumulative dividend that is not paid in one year carries over to the next and must be satisfied in addition to the current year's preferred dividend before any dividend can be paid on the common stock in the second year.

Example: A preferred carries a $5 cumulative dividend. Because of shortage of working capital, the directors do not declare (in technical terms, they "omit") the dividend for three years. In the fourth year a dividend is declared: however, $20 in dividends must be paid to the holders of the preferred before any common dividend may be paid.

2) A noncumulative dividend treats each year as a unit; a noncumulative dividend not paid in any year is gone. In New Jersey, equitable principles have been held to limit the power of the corporation to refuse the payment of noncumulative dividends despite sufficient earnings. This New Jersey "dividend credit" rule has not been adopted elsewhere. See *Sanders v. Cuba R.R. Co.,* 120 A.2d 849 (N.J. 1956); *Lich v. United States Rubber Co.,* 39 F.Supp. 675 (D.N.J. 1941); compare *Guttmann v. Illinois Central R. Co.,* 189 F.2d 927 (2nd Cir. 1951).

Example: If the foregoing preferred were noncumulative, the directors could pay a dividend on the common the fourth year after paying only the $5.00 current dividend on the preferred. Indeed, an attempt to pay past noncumulative dividends could probably be enjoined by the common shareholders as a violation of their rights.

3) A cumulative-to-the-extent earned dividend is cumulative only to the extent earnings exist; in any year if earnings fail to "cover" the preferred dividend, the portion of the dividend that is not covered does not cumulate and is gone.

b. Preferred shares may be made *redeemable* by the corporation at a price set forth in the articles of incorporation. When shares are redeemed they are reacquired by the corporation and either disappear or become treasury shares, i. e., shares held in the "treasury" of the corporation. The holder of redeemable shares is entitled only to the "redemption price" set in the articles.

Example: Preferred shares sold for $50.00 per share may be made redeemable at $60.00 plus unpaid cumulative dividends. The corporation may at any time thereafter at its option elect to redeem those shares at the specified price.

Example: Under most state statutes, it is permissible to make shares redeemable at the option of the holder. Such shares have many characteristics of a demand promissory note. Such shares may be used (instead of a debt instrument) for financing when the lender is a corporation and desires to take advantage of the credit for intercorporate dividends under the Federal income tax law. The S.E.C. requires preferred shares redeemable at the option of the holder to be shown on balance sheets as a separate category under neither the "debt" nor "equity" accounts.

c.   Preferred shares may be made *convertible* into common or other shares at a ratio set forth in the articles of incorporation. Such ratios are usually adjusted to take account of share splits, share dividends, and recapitalizations—usually referred to as protection against "dilution."

> *Example:*   A preferred share may be made convertible into two shares of common; in technical terms the "conversion ratio is 2 for 1." Any shareholder may deliver one share of the preferred to the corporation and receive two shares of common; upon the conversion, the share of preferred disappears. If a "stock split" occurs in the interim by which one share of common has become, say, three shares of common, the antidilution provision would normally adjust the conversion ratio to 6 for 1. See *Merritt-Chapman & Scott Corp. v. New York Trust Co.*, 184 F.2d 954 (2d Cir. 1950).

> *Example:*   Most state statutes prohibit "upstream conversions," that is the right of common to convert to preferred, or either common or preferred to convert to debt. The RMBCA permits the creation of such shares on the theory that upstream conversions are potentially less damaging to creditors and other senior security holders than the redemption of shares for cash.

d.   Preferred shares, particularly in corporations whose common shares are publicly traded, are usually *cumulative* and *redeemable*, and also may be made *convertible*. Corporations often call the preferred for redemption at a time when the market price for the common into which the share may be converted is greater than the redemption value. The conversion right typically exists for a limited period after the call for redemption is announced; since it is obviously to the financial advantage of each shareholder to convert his shares before they are redeemed, one would normally expect all the preferred shareholders to convert their shares. Such a conversion is described as "forced." In practice, some shares are usually not converted because of inadvertence, the shares have been lost, etc.

> *Example:*   A preferred share is redeemable at $70 per share and convertible on a two for one basis. When the price of the common exceeds $35 per share, the shares should be converted promptly if they are called for redemption.

> *Example:*   In *Zahn v. Transamerica Corp.*, 162 F.2d 36 (3d Cir. 1947), convertible shares were called without disclosing that it would be advantageous for shareholders to elect to convert shares. In a second case, *Van Gemert v. Boeing Co.*, 520 F.2d 1373 (2d Cir. 1975), *cert. denied*, 423 U.S. 947, 96 S.Ct. 364, shares

were called without giving adequate notice so that shareholders could elect the conversion right. Liability exists in such cases for breach of a duty to adequately advise shareholders of their rights. See *Speed v. Transamerica Corp.*, 235 F.2d 369 (3d Cir. 1956); Broad v. Rockwell International Corp., 642 F.2d 929 (5th Cir. 1981).

e. Preferred shares are infrequently made participating. Participating shares differ from traditional preferred shares in that they are entitled to share in excess declarations of dividends along with common shares. Because they are "open-ended" participating preferred shares have some characteristics of a class of common shares.

> *Example:* In *Zahn v. Transamerica Corp.*, 162 F.2d 36 (3d Cir. 1947), a corporation created a class of preferred stock called "Class A stock." Class A stock was entitled to a dividend of $3.20 per year plus the right to share equally with the common stock in all declarations of dividends in excess of $4.80 per share. In effect, $3.20 was first paid to the Class A stock, then $1.60 to the common, and excess distributions were shared equally on a share-for-share basis. The Class A stock was a participating preferred. In the absence of specific provision, it is unlikely that a dividend-participation right of this nature would be construed to include an implied liquidation-participation right on the same terms. *Squires v. Balbach Co.*, 129 N.W.2d 462 (Neb. 1964).

f. Preferred shares have a par value (or are issued "without par value") in the same way as common shares and are subject to the same rules as common shares in this regard.

g. A single corporation may issue several classes of preferred shares, each having varying dividend and other rights specified in the articles of incorporation. While a class of preferred may be junior to other classes of preferred, it is nevertheless a preferred stock since it is preferred in comparison to the common stock.

2. CLASSIFIED COMMON STOCK

Common stock may also be issued in classes. Under the RMBCA and most state statutes there are virtually no restrictions or limitations on the rights of common shares that may be varied from class to class. Because of this flexibility, classes of common shares are often used as planning devices in closely held corporations.

> *Example:* A class of nonvoting common shares may be created under the statutes of most states. In many (but fewer) states, classes may be

created with the same financial rights but with multiple or fractional votes per share. Limited case law also permits the creation of a class of shares with voting power but with little or no financial interest in the corporation. *Stroh v. Blackhawk Holding Corp.*, 272 N.E.2d 1 (Ill. 1971); *Lehrman v. Cohen*, 222 A.2d 800 (Del. 1966).

Example: Two classes of shares may be created, one with twice the dividend right per share of the other class. Such classes are often uniquely designated, e. g., as "Class A stock" and "Class B stock."

Example: A class of shares may be created with one tenth of the liquidation right per share of the other class.

Example: Classes of shares may be created each with the right to elect a specified number of directors.

Caveat: A class of shares with preferential rights may be called "Class A common" or be given some other designation that does not use the word "preferred" and does not indicate that it has preferential rights. Similarly, a class of shares with only nominal or unimportant preferential rights may be given a designation such as "Senior preferred shares" which may give the impression that its preferential rights are greater than they actually are.

3.   PREFERRED ISSUED IN SERIES

Many state statutes authorize the creation of "series" of preferred shares the financial terms of which may vary from series to series. The board of directors is usually vested with authority to set the terms of each series from time to time by resolution in order to allow corporations to tailor the terms of each series to the market conditions existing at the time without formally amending the articles of incorporation.

a.   Such preferred shares are usually called "blank shares" since the board may "fill in" the terms.

b.   A formal certificate describing the terms of the series must be filed with the Secretary of State after the series has been established.

c.   Today, the difference between "classes" and "series" is usually one of nomenclature without substantive difference. In most states the board of directors may fix all terms of a series so that two "series" within a single "class" may have no terms in common.

d.   Historically, rights of "classes" are fixed in the articles of incorporation while rights of "series" may be fixed either in the articles or by the directors. However, the RMBCA, and several state statutes, permit the board of directors to fix the terms of "classes" as well as "series" if that power is given the board by the articles of incorporation. This is primarily a matter of nomenclature without substantive significance.

4. EQUIVALENCE OF SHARES WITHIN A CLASS OR SERIES

All shares of a class or series must have identical preferences, limitations, and relative rights with those of other shares of the same series or class (except to the extent shares of a class may be divided into series).

Caveat: It is unclear in many states whether classes or series of shares that have rights that vary with outside events may be created. These classes or series are often used as defensive tactics against takeovers and are usually called "poison pills." See part XIII, C, 3, infra.

D. THE USE OF DEBT IN THE INITIAL CAPITALIZATION OF THE CORPORATION

Debt securities are bonds, debentures, and notes. All such securities are often subsumed under the generic terms "bonds" or "debt securities."

1. BONDS AND DEBENTURES DESCRIBED

Bonds and debentures are usually long-term debt instruments while notes are usually (but not always) short-term instruments.

a. Bonds and debentures are usually unconditional written obligations to pay a specific amount at a future date. Bonds and debentures are usually negotiable instruments payable to bearer; interest obligations are usually represented by coupons which are themselves negotiable bearer instruments. Bonds or debentures may be registered in the name of the owner; such instruments are negotiable by endorsement rather than by mere delivery.

b. A bond is a secured debt while a debenture is unsecured. Bonds may be secured by liens on all or specific parts of the property of the issuer; the rights of the bondholders to foreclose are typically vested in a trustee pursuant to a written instrument known as an indenture. The rights and duties of the trustee are defined in the indenture. *United States Trust Co. v. First Nat'l City Bank*, 394 N.Y.S.2d 653 (App.Div. 1977).

c. A note is a negotiable instrument representing an unconditional promise to pay that may be secured or unsecured. It differs from a bond or debenture in that:

1)   It is usually payable to the order of the creditor; and

2)   The obligation to pay interest is not represented by coupons.

    d.   Bonds or debentures are usually issued in units of $1,000 or larger round numbers. They are often publicly traded.

2. DEBT INSTRUMENTS COMPARED WITH PREFERRED STOCK

Bonds or debentures differ from preferred stock (which is an equity security) from a legal standpoint in several basic respects:

    a.   Interest on bonds or debentures is an unconditional obligation of the corporation while dividends on preferred stock are discretionary with the board of directors.

    b.   A bond or debenture has a maturity date at which time the principal becomes due while preferred stock never becomes due. A debenture without a maturity date (called a "consol") is not unknown but is extremely rare in the United States.

    c.   A bond or debenture may have legal rights of foreclosure on default of payments while a preferred stock does not.

    d.   Despite these legal differences the economic differences between these two types of securities may be slight, depending on the specific terms of the two instruments being compared.

    e.   "Hybrid" securities are securities that have some of the attributes of debt and some of the attributes of preferred stock. The major problem with such securities is often uncertainty as to whether the instrument will be treated as equity or debt for tax purposes. *John Kelley Co. v. C.I.R.*, 326 U.S. 521, 66 S.Ct. 299 (1946). Marketability of hybrid securities may also be complicated by uncertainty as to the "true" nature of the instrument.

3. ADVANTAGES OF PROVIDING A PORTION OF THE INITIAL CAPITAL IN THE FORM OF DEBT

Persons who contribute the initial capital of the corporation often desire to lend a portion of that capital to the corporation. There are both tax and non-tax advantages in doing this.

    a.   The tax advantages generally arise only where subchapter S is not elected.

        1)   Interest on debt is deductible by the corporation while dividends on common or preferred shares are not. Thus the use of debt may

allow the shareholders some return from the corporation without incurring the double taxation on dividends that is a feature of the current federal income tax.

2) Also, a repayment of debt may be a tax-free return of capital rather than a taxable dividend. The use of debt may therefore permit the tax-free return of a portion of a shareholder's investment. A partial redemption of a taxpayer's shares often is treated as a dividend for tax purposes.

3) Generally, the existence of shareholder debt in the capital structure reduces taxes. Hence, the shareholder usually desires the greatest amount of debt possible in the structure.

4) The Internal Revenue Service has general power to reclassify excessive debt as equity contributions for tax purposes. Generally, if the debt is excessive, it is reclassified as equity in its entirety. Hence, there can readily be "too much of a good thing" in the wholesale creation of debt. See *Taft v. C.I.R.*, 314 F.2d 620 (9th Cir. 1963).

b. A second advantage of debt financing is that it simplifies non-tax planning where some investors are contributing more capital than others.

Example: *A* proposes to contribute $10,000 in cash; *B* proposes to contribute $6,000 in property of various types. Both plan to contribute services so as to roughly equalize aggregate contributions. *A* and *B* desire each to own 50 per cent of the shares. In order to equalize contributions, the attorney suggests that common shares be issued to reflect the $6,000 contribution by *A* and *B*, and that *A* separately lend the corporation $4,000. The terms of repayment of this loan, the interest rate, and the rate of compensation for services are matters for negotiation.

c. A final advantage of debt financing is that the shareholders may seek parity with general trade creditors if the business fails. See the "Deep Rock" doctrine discussed earlier; *Costello v. Fazio*, 256 F.2d 903 (9th Cir. 1958).

4. THIRD PARTY DEBT

Loans from third persons to the corporation do not provide the tax or planning benefits of loans from the original investors. The advantage of third party loans as a capital raising device from the standpoint of the shareholders principally revolves around the principle of leverage. Leverage arises when the venture can earn more on each borrowed dollar than the interest cost of borrowing that dollar.

Example: A corporation is capitalized with $50,000 of long-term bonds carrying an interest cost of 10% per year and 1,000 shares of common stock issued for $10 each, or an aggregate capital of $10,000. The $5,000 interest cost of the bonds must of course be paid each year whether or not there are earnings. The effect of leverage is shown by comparing the rate of return on total dollars invested with the rate of return on the common shares at various levels of hypothetical income (before making allowance for the interest charge).

(1) Income (before interest expense)	(2) Total Dollars Invested	(3) Earnings Per Total Dollar Invested	(4) Interest Cost	(5) Earnings Per Share (after interest expense)
2,000	60,000	0.03	5,000	−.03
5,000	60,000	0.08	5,000	0
20,000	60,000	0.33	5,000	1.50
50,000	60,000	0.83	5,000	5.00

The effect of leverage is shown by the much more rapid increase of earnings per share than earnings per total dollar invested. The explanation is simply that at higher levels of earnings, each borrowed dollar is earning more than its cost and the entire excess is allocable to the common shares.

5.   DEBT/EQUITY RATIO

a.   The ratio between a corporation's equity capital and its long term debt is often called the corporation's debt/equity ratio.

Example: The debt/equity ratio of the corporation in the previous example is 5:1 [$50,000 of debt to $10,000 of equity].

b.   The Miller-Modigliani theorem states (with certain simplifying assumptions) that the aggregate value of a corporation's securities [the market value of its equity securities plus the market value of its debt securities] is independent of the corporation's debt/equity ratio.

Example: In the previous illustration under ideal market conditions, any enhanced value of the common stock because of the advantages of leverage would be precisely matched by a decline in value of the bonds.

c.   A debt/equity ratio of greater than 4:1 between shareholder debt and equity is often viewed as creating the likelihood that the Internal Revenue Service will insist that the debt be viewed as equity capital.

d.   A corporation with a high debt/equity ratio is often called a "thin corporation."

E.   APPLICATION OF THE FEDERAL AND STATE SECURITIES ACTS

When raising capital, the possible impact of the federal Securities Act of 1933, 15 U.S.C.A. § 77a, the Securities & Exchange Act of 1934, 15 U.S.C. § 78a, and the state securities acts (colloquially called "blue sky laws") must always be considered.

1.   GENERAL DESCRIPTION OF PURPOSE

These statutes are designed to protect the public investor from fraudulent or misrepresented promotions or sales of securities. These statutes often require a registration of a securities issue before it may be publicly sold. The goal is usually full disclosure of all relevant facts about the securities being sold. A failure to register securities when required to do so gives rise to substantial civil liabilities to purchasers of the securities and may give rise to criminal liability as well. The leading cases relating to the obligations of persons preparing and signing registration statements are *Escott v. Barchris Constr. Corp.*, 283 F.Supp. 643 (S.D.N.Y. 1968), and *SEC v. National Student Marketing Corp.*, 457 F.Supp. 682 (D.D.C. 1978). The role of lawyers in the disclosure process is discussed in *Escott* and in *In the Matter of Carter & Johnson*, SEC Rel. 17597 (1981).

2.   COST OF REGISTRATION

The registration process, particularly at the federal level, is so expensive as to be impractical for most small and medium-sized (e. g., up to say, $500,000) public offerings. The current minimum cost of a full scale registration by a corporation that has never previously registered an issue exceeds $100,000.

3.   EXEMPTIONS FROM REGISTRATION

As a result attention must be focused on the availability of exemptions for a particular offer. At the federal level, the principal exemptions under the Securities Act of 1933 are the following:

a.   Regulation D is the SEC's principal "small offering" exemption. It contains three exemptions, together with accompanying definitions, terms, and conditions.

1)   Rule 504 exempts offers by corporations of up to $500,000 in any one year. The offers may not be made by general solicitation or

general advertising except in states where the offer is registered under state law and that law requires delivery of a disclosure document.

2) Rule 505 exempts offers by corporations of up to $5,000,000 in any one year if the number of unaccredited investors is less than 35 and no general solicitation or general advertising is used. Under rule 505, there is no limit on the number of accredited investors.

3) Rule 506 permits offers in unlimited amounts if the issuer reasonably believes that every unaccredited investor "has such knowledge and experience in financial and business matters, that he is capable of evaluating the merits and risks of the prospective investment," and no general solicitation or general advertising is used. Under rule 506 there is a limit of 35 on the number of sophisticated unaccredited investors but no limit on the number of accredited investors.

4) Rule 501(a) lists eight categories of "accredited investors:" institutional investors; private business development companies; tax exempt organizations, directors and officers of the issuer; purchasers of more than $150,000 of the securities; investors with a net worth of $1,000,000 or with an income in excess of $200,000 per year, on an entity made up of certain accredited investors.

b. Section 4(2), 15 U.S.C.A. § 77d exempts "transactions by an issuer not involving any public offering." Offerings not complying with Regulation D may nevertheless be exempt under section 4(2) if they meet the tests established by the case law for the availability of the exemption. The test is not dependent on the mathematical number of offerees; the basic requirement is that all offerees must have sufficient access and sophistication so that they do not need the protection of the act. *SEC v. Ralston Purina Co.*, 346 U.S. 119, 73 S.Ct. 981 (1953).

1) It should be noted that Regulation D relates to investors or *purchasers* of securities, the general section 4(2) exemption requires each *offeree* to meet the requirements of access and sophistication.

2) Large private offerings of securities to sophisticated institutional investors are known as private placements; in the aggregate private placements involve billions of dollars each year. Such placements will normally be exempt under rule 506 as well as under section 4(2).

c. Regulation A, adopted by the SEC under section 3(b) of the Securities Act, 15 U.S.C.A. § 77c (which authorizes the SEC to exempt issues of less than $5,000,000 where the SEC determines that registration "is not necessary in the public interest and for the protection of investors"), exempts offerings of up to $1,500,000 upon following a simplified registration process, including filing with a regional office of the SEC rather than in Washington. This simplified registration process is colloquially known as "Reg A;" its use has declined since the adoption of Regulation D.

d. Section 4(6), 15 U.S.C.A. § 77d, added in 1980, exempts offerings or sales solely to one or more accredited investors if the aggregate amount does not exceed $5,000,000 and there is no advertising or public solicitation. Most offerings exempt under this section will also be exempt under Regulation D.

e. Section 3(a)(11), 15 U.S.C.A. § 77c, exempts securities which are part of an issue offered and sold only to persons resident within a single state where the issuer is incorporated and doing business in that state. This so-called "intrastate exemption" is very narrowly and restrictively construed: a single offer of a security to a nonresident totally destroys the availability of the exemption. Section 3(a)(11) should be read in conjunction with Rule 146 that describes the SEC's position with respect to that exemption.

4. RESTRICTIONS ON TRANSFER OF UNREGISTERED SECURITIES

The availability of several exemptions is dependent on the ultimate investors having certain knowledge or sophistication, or being residents of specific states. In order to ensure that persons acquiring securities are the ultimate investors and do not buy them with a view toward further distribution to persons who might destroy the availability of the exemption, SEC regulations and accepted corporate practice require restrictions to be imposed on resale of securities sold pursuant to an exemption.

a. The restrictions will be noted on certificates issued pursuant to the exemption and "stop transfer" orders will be issued to the transfer agent, the person handling transfers of the corporation's securities. Under these certificate notations and "stop transfer" orders, the shareholder may be required to establish that the proposed transfer is consistent with the original exemption.

b. A person who buys shares with a view toward further distribution is called an "underwriter." An underwriter may be either a large commercial organization in the securities business or equally an individual planning to resell securities he originally acquired.

c. Securities originally sold pursuant to the private offering exemptions (§ 4(2) or Regulation D) may be resold pursuant to rule 144; this rule basically requires a two-year holding period. Sales during this period may be consistent with the original exemption (though not protected by rule 144) if there is a bona fide change in circumstances justifying the decision to sell the securities.

5. CONTROL PERSONS AND SECONDARY DISTRIBUTIONS
A secondary distribution is a public distribution of unregistered shares by a person other than the issuer.

    a.   Secondary distributions arise in two basic contexts:

        1)   Under the Federal Securities Act, a person who is in control of a registrant (usually referred to as a "control person") is subject to registration requirements upon the sale of his shares that are substantially the same as those applicable to the registrant itself; and

        2)   A person holding unregistered shares obtained from the issuer in a transaction that is exempt from registration may seek to resell them publicly; such sales are also a kind of secondary distribution that may require registration.

    b.   Secondary distributions must be registered unless an exemption is available. They are often registered in conjunction with or as part of a registration of an issue by the issuer itself.

6. WHAT IS A SECURITY?
The securities acts are used to police a variety of marginal investment schemes which may not involve "securities" in the traditional sense.

    a.   Securities acts define "security" broadly, usually referring to "investment contracts" and "other instruments" that evidence an investment. These phrases have been judicially defined to include within the scope of "security" any contract, transaction or scheme whereby a person invests money *in a common enterprise* and *is led to expect profits solely from the efforts of others*.

        1)   "Solely" has not been construed literally; a scheme may involve a security even if the investor is required to put forward a small amount of individual effort.

        2)   Golf club memberships, condominiums, scotch whiskey in warehouses, chain letter or pyramid schemes, fractional royalty interests, earthworm farms, commodity options, and other schemes have all been held to constitute "securities" in some circumstances.

> ***Example:*** An owner of a citrus grove sells land in "units"
> consisting of a row of trees per "unit." The original
> owner usually enters into a contract with the investor
> purchasing the unit by which he agrees to provide
> services such as cultivation, pruning, insect control, and
> protection from freezing. The owner also usually
> harvests and markets the crop, dividing the proceeds with
> the investors purchasing the units. The units constitute
> "securities" even though an investor theoretically might
> cultivate and harvest his own row of trees on his own
> and use or sell the crop as he sees fit. *S. E. C. v. W.
> J. Howey Co.*, 328 U.S. 293, 66 S.Ct. 1100 (1946).

b.   Since such investment schemes are almost never registered under the
securities acts, these cases make unlawful the public sale of most such
schemes.

c.   In *Landreth Timber Co. v. Landreth*, ___ U.S. ___, 105 S.Ct. 2297 (1985),
the Supreme Court rejected the so-called "sale of business doctrine" and
held that the sale of all or a majority of the shares of a closely held
corporation constituted the sale of a "security" subject to the federal
securities acts. This holding is of importance primarily because it makes
available the protections of federal antifraud provisions to all sales of
closely held shares (assuming that the facilities of interstate commerce are
used) even where the purchaser is intent on acquiring control of the
business rather than making a passive investment.

7.   STATE BLUE SKY LAWS

The provisions of state "blue sky" statutes often parallel the federal securities
acts but many do not.

a.   Some state statutes do not adopt the "full disclosure" philosophy of the
Securities Act of 1933 but permit distributions to be registered and sold
in the state only if their terms are "fair, just, and equitable."

b.   The private offering and other exemptions in state statutes are often
more numerical and objective than the corresponding exemptions in the
Federal Act.

c.   Generally, the registration requirements of the state statutes are in
addition to the requirements of the Securities Act of 1933. Thus, a
national distribution of new securities may require registration in fifty
states as well as with the SEC. The state registration process, known as
"blue skying an issue" is greatly simplified by reason of the fact that
most states have integrated or coordinated their registration process with
the federal process. This is known as "registration by coordination."

Other types of registration at the state level are "registration by notification" for issuers that regularly raise capital publicly and "registration by qualification." The latter is imposed on public distributions that are exempt from federal registration, e. g., under the intrastate exemption or Regulation D.

F. ISSUANCE OF SHARES BY A GOING CONCERN

Shares issued by a going concern create unique problems because the new shares will have an effect on outstanding shareholders. The issuance of shares at bargain prices or otherwise than in proportion to prior holdings may "dilute" the financial or voting powers of existing shareholders, or both.

1. PREEMPTIVE RIGHTS

The classic common law protection for existing shareholders is the doctrine of "preemptive rights," which gives outstanding shareholders the right to subscribe and pay for their proportionate part of any new issue of securities by the corporation at the price established by the board of directors. *Stokes v. Continental Trust Co.*, 78 N.E. 1090 (N.Y. 1906). If all shareholders exercise their preemptive rights no dilution occurs and the additional capital needed by the corporation is entirely raised from its present shareholders.

Example: A corporation is formed with an authorized capital of 200 shares with a par value of one dollar each. Shares were issued for a consideration of $10 each as follows: A—100 shares, B—50 shares, and C—50 shares. After several years of successful operation, A and B decide to amend the articles to increase the number of shares to 400 shares, and sell to themselves 100 shares each at $50 per share. C has a preemptive right to acquire 50 of the new shares at the same price as the shares being acquired by A and B—$50 per share.

a. There are, however, substantial limitations on modern preemptive rights:

1) Preemptive rights are discretionary. In many states, a corporation has preemptive rights unless a specific provision excluding them appears in the articles of incorporation (an "opt out" clause). RMBCA § 6.30, and the statutes of several states provide for an "opt in" provision: corporations have preemptive rights only, and to the extent, they specifically so designate.

As an aid to draftsmen, RMBCA § 6.30 contains a model provision relating to preemptive rights that may be elected by a simple clause, e.g. "This corporation elects to have preemptive rights." This model provision may be modified as appropriate. It deals with the scope of preemptive rights and other issues, such as waiver and resale of securities offered preemptively but not purchased.

2) Preemptive rights do not apply to treasury shares (i.e., shares that were once issued but have been reacquired by the corporation). The theory is that the dilution represented by treasury shares has already occurred and existing shareholders should have no complaint if a prior dilution is restored. Some modern statutes specifically extend preemptive rights to treasury shares. RMBCA does not contain an exemption for previously issued shares.

3) Preemptive rights do not extend to shares issued for property, including shares of other corporations. RMBCA § 6.30(b)(3)(iv). This exemption is based on considerations of practicability or necessity. Some courts have construed this exemption narrowly since in many instances the corporation could sell shares for cash, recognizing the preemptive right, and use the cash to acquire the property. *Dunlay v. Avenue M Garage & Repair Co.*, 170 N.E. 917 (N.Y. 1930).

4) Preemptive rights extend not to authorized but unissued shares to the extent they represent part of the contemplated initial capitalization of the corporation. RMBCA § 6.30(b)(3)(iii) [six months after incorporation]. This exemption is based on the assumption that preemptive rights extend only to new issues of shares after the corporation has raised its initial capital. It is inconsistent in principle with the modern practice of authorizing more shares than it is presently contemplated to issue. Some cases and state statutes refuse to recognize this exemption as being inconsistent with modern practice. *Fuller v. Krogh*, 113 N.W.2d 25 (Wis. 1962).

5) Preemptive rights do not extend to shares of different classes unless the other class is convertible into the class held by the shareholder. RMBCA §§ 6.30(b)(5), (b)(6), (c).

Example: Common shareholders do not have a preemptive right to acquire shares of preferred stock unless the preferred is convertible into common.

Example: Preferred shareholders may have a preemptive right to acquire new preferred shares of the same class. They do not, however, have preemptive rights to acquire common shares. Some early case law to the contrary, e. g., *Thomas Branch & Co. v. Riverside & Dan River Cotton Mills, Inc.*, 123 S.E. 542 (Va. 1924), has been overruled by statutory provisions defining the preemptive right.

    b.   Preemptive rights serve little purpose in publicly held corporations since they complicate the raising of capital. Also, the availability of a public market for shares renders the preemptive right less important since any shareholder may add to his or her shareholdings simply by purchasing shares in the open market.

2.   FIDUCIARY RESTRICTIONS ON THE OPPRESSIVE ISSUANCE OF SHARES

Where preemptive rights are inapplicable or have been eliminated, the power of controlling shareholders to issue new shares may be limited by the fiduciary duties they owe to minority shareholders. *Schwartz v. Marien*, 335 N.E.2d 334 (N.Y. 1975); *Ross Transport, Inc. v. Crothers*, 45 A.2d 267 (Md. 1946).

    a.   These fiduciary duties may also extend to bad faith issuances of shares where preemptive rights exist but circumstances are such that it is unreasonable to expect the minority shareholder to exercise his preemptive right.

    Example: A 20 per cent shareholder is totally excluded from management. With the specific intent of reducing her interest in the corporation, the majority shareholder proposes to issue new shares which will require the 20 per cent shareholder to invest $100,000 in new capital to exercise her preemptive right and retain her current percentage interest. The management-connected shareholders plan to pay for their portion of the new issue by cancelling loans they have previously made to the corporation. As a result of the new issue, the 20 per cent shareholder's proportional interest in the corporation is reduced to less than one per cent. Courts in some states have enjoined transactions of this type on the theory that they are oppressive and serve no business purpose. *Katzowitz v. Sidler*, 249 N.E.2d 359 (N.Y. 1969). Not all courts have agreed, however, though factual differences may partially explain the result. *Hyman v. Velsicol Corp.*, 97 N.E.2d 122 (Ill.App. 1951).

    b.   Issuance of shares at favorable prices to controlling shareholders may be set aside even though the transaction has a valid business purpose. *Adelman v. Conotti Corp.*, 213 S.E.2d 774 (Va. 1975); *Bennett v. Breuil Petroleum Corp.*, 99 A.2d 236 (Del.Ch. 1953). Equally suspect are transactions that affect the balance of power within a corporation without apparent business purpose. *Schwartz v. Marien*, 335 N.E.2d 334 (N.Y. 1975). However, where there is a good faith business purpose and no personal benefit, issuance of shares may benefit one class at the expense of another. *Bodell v. General Gas & Electric Corp.*, 140 A. 264 (Del.Ch. 1927).

c. Bad faith transactions which greatly reduce the proportional interest of minority shareholders are often called "squeeze outs" or "freeze outs."

G. DIVIDENDS AND DISTRIBUTIONS

A "dividend" is a payment out of current or past earnings; other distributions, to the extent permitted, may be called "capital distributions," "distributions in partial liquidation" or by other names that indicate that they are distributions of capital, not distributions of earnings. Terminology, however, is not precise, a liquidating distribution is often referred to as a "liquidating dividend" even though the payment constitutes a return of capital.

1. DIVIDEND POLICIES IN PUBLICLY HELD CORPORATIONS
Publicly held corporations generally adopt stable dividend policies that permit regular periodic distributions even though corporate income fluctuates.
Changes in dividend rates by publicly held corporations are generally publicly announced, not made lightly, and tend to reflect only important or apparently permanent changes in earnings experience.

Example: A publicly held corporation establishes and publicly announces a "regular" dividend of $0.25 per quarter. This rate will be retained despite fluctuations in earnings; if excess cash accumulates the corporation may declare a "special" or "extra" dividend that carries with it no promise that anything more than the regular dividend will be paid in the future. In the event of a temporary decline in earnings, the "regular" dividend may be "omitted" for one or two quarters and then resumed consistent with the general philosophy of preserving a stable dividend policy.

Example: In the prior situation, the corporation suffers a loss in one year but continues to pay the regular dividend of $0.25 per quarter. If the corporation has accumulated undistributed earnings from earlier years, the payment is a dividend out of those earlier years' accumulated earnings for tax and accounting purposes.

Example: A corporation announces that it has ceased paying dividends and probably will not resume dividends for at least five years in order to accumulate funds for expansion and modernization. Shareholders have no basis for objecting to such a policy even if the corporation had a policy of paying dividends in the past. *Berwald v. Mission Development Co.*, 185 A.2d 480 (Del. 1962).

2. DIVIDEND POLICIES IN A CLOSELY HELD CORPORATION
In a closely held corporation, the dividend policy generally adopted is "no dividends." The payment of dividends is likely to carry a higher tax cost than

the payment of the same amount in the form of salaries, rents or other payments that are deductible by the corporation. This policy may give rise to internal dispute and dissatisfaction since some shareholders may receive larger payments than others. In particular, if some shareholders are excluded from management they may receive nothing with respect to their shares while shareholders connected with management may benefit from substantially the entire corporate income.

a. The tactic of "softening up" minority shareholders by not paying dividends is often referred to as a "freeze out." The goal of such tactic is to compel the shareholder to sell his or her shares at a low price either to the corporation or to other shareholders.

b. Suits to compel the payment of a dividend have been successful only rarely since the payment of dividends is generally a matter of business policy for the directors to establish and is generally not subject to review by courts. *Sinclair Oil Corp. v. Levien*, 280 A.2d 717 (Del. 1971). Where such suits have been successful the plaintiff has been able to show (1) the availability of surplus cash not needed in the corporate business and (2) affirmative indications of bad faith on the part of management. *Keough v. St. Paul Milk Co.*, 285 N.W. 809 (Minn. 1939); *Dodge v. Ford Motor Co.*, 170 N.W. 668 (Mich. 1919); *Miller v. Magline, Inc.*, 256 N.W.2d 761 (Mich.App. 1977). Excessive compensation to insiders is an indication of bad faith.

> ***Example:*** A corporation pays "bonuses" to four of its employees who constitute the original incorporators but not to one person who later became an employee and a shareholder. The "bonuses" are computed on the basis of the excess earnings of the corporation and without a review of the employment performance of any of the employees. The "bonuses" are disguised dividends and are not pro rata; as a result the shareholder who did not receive a dividend may recover his pro rata share. *Murphy v. Country House, Inc.*, 349 N.W.2d 289 (Minn.App. 1984).

c. Some corporate charters have been construed as requiring the mandatory payment of dividends, particularly on preferred stock, *Crocker v. Waltham Watch Co.*, 53 N.E.2d 230 (Mass. 1944); *New England Trust Co. v. Penobscot Chemical Fibre Co.*, 50 A.2d 188 (Me. 1946); *Arizona Western Insurance Co. v. L. L. Constantin Co.*, 247 F.2d 388 (3d Cir. 1957); the desirability of such a construction is questionable, and some courts have refused to treat apparently mandatory language as creating an unqualified right to a dividend. *L. L. Constantin & Co. v. R. P. Holding Corp.*, 153 A.2d 378 (N.J.Super.Ch.Div. 1959).

d. The Internal Revenue Code contains a penalty tax applicable to corporations that unreasonably accumulate surplus. Section 531 imposes the penalty tax on accumulations that exceed the "reasonable needs of the business" but a minimum accumulation of $250,000 is permitted in any case. This penalty tax may often be avoided by the corporation agreeing to pay a dividend.

3. LEGAL REQUIREMENTS FOR DIVIDENDS AND DISTRIBUTIONS

State statutes impose widely varying tests for the legality of dividends and distributions.

a. The tests may differ depending on whether the state retains par value concepts, or whether, like the RMBCA, it has eliminated par value and the related concepts of "stated capital" and "capital surplus."

b. RMBCA § 6.40 imposes two tests to determine whether a distribution may be lawfully made:

1) An "equity insolvency" test that requires the corporation to be "able to pay its debts as they become due in the ordinary course of business" after giving effect to the distribution (RMBCA § 6.40(c) (1)); and

2) A "balance sheet" test that prohibits a distribution if, after giving it effect, "the corporation's total assets would be less than the sum of its total liabilities plus * * * the amount that would be needed" to satisfy preferential liquidation rights of other classes of shares (RMBCA § 6.40(c)(2)).

c. All states apply some form of equity insolvency test for distributions. In Massachusetts, that is the sole test. In most other states that test is combined with some form of balance sheet test as described below.

d. Most state statutes permit dividends to be paid only out of "earned surplus," a term that is defined as the sum of net accumulations of income from all earlier periods reduced by dividends paid in earlier years and similar items.

e. States with an "earned surplus" test for dividends, also usually permit non-dividend distributions out of capital surplus or other surplus accounts. In effect, the capital accounts created from the par value concept control the scope of distributions in these states.

f. Some states permit dividends or distributions that do not "impair capital" or use a similar phrasing that is broader than "earned surplus." However, statutes that permit dividends only out of "earned surplus" but then broadly permit distributions of capital or other surplus come out at about the same place as statutes that broadly permit all dividends or distributions that do not "impair capital."

Caveat: Paragraphs d. and e. describe the 1969 Model Act restrictions on dividends or distributions. Some states still have statutes still based on the 1950 Model Act that refer to distributions of capital or other surplus as "partial liquidations."

Caveat: State statutes, particularly from non-Model Act states may not fit neatly into the above categories. Determining the precise restrictions applicable on distributions in non-Model Act states may not always be easy since the language often does not address many issues. Some states, furthermore, have unique provisions. California, for example, requires capital to be preserved equal to five-fourths of the corporation's liabilities.

g. The validity of certain kinds of transactions that affect the dividend-paying or distribution-making capacity of a corporation depends on the language of the specific statute:

1) "Quasi reorganizations" are bookkeeping entries by which deficits of earned surplus are eliminated by the transfer of capital or other surplus to earned surplus; future earnings are thereafter available for the immediate payment of dividends.

2) "Nimble dividends" are dividends paid out of current earnings even though a deficit in earned surplus may exist from prior years. *United States v. Riely*, 169 F.2d 542 (4th Cir. 1948). Current earnings may also be used to pay dividends even though a capital deficit exists because of the issuance of watered stock. *Goodnow v. American Writing Paper Co.*, 69 A. 1014 (N.J. 1908). See also: *Morris v. Standard Gas & Electric Co.*, 63 A.2d 577 (Del.Ch. 1949) applying the Delaware statute which prohibits a nimble dividend if the value of corporate capital is less than the capital represented by the capital stock.

3) "Reevaluation surplus" is surplus created by the directors' decision to "write up" the value of appreciated assets; distributions of "reevaluation surplus" are permitted in some states. *Randall v. Bailey*, 23 N.Y.S.2d 173 (Sup.Ct. 1940); *Dominguez Land Corp. v. Daugherty*, 238 P. 697 (Cal. 1925).

4) Surplus may also be created by recognizing and placing a value on goodwill or other intangible assets not previously shown in the corporation's books; the use of such surplus for distributions has

been permitted in some cases. *Randall v. Bailey*, 23 N.Y.S.2d 173 (Sup.Ct. 1940).

5) "Reduction surplus" is surplus created by the reduction of stated capital by amendments to the articles of incorporation or the retirement of shares; the use of such surplus for distributions is permitted by some state statutes with the consent of the shareholders.

4. CONTRACTUAL RESTRICTIONS ON DIVIDENDS AND DISTRIBUTIONS
Because state statutes provide few restrictions on distributions and therefore little or no protection for creditors, the practice has developed of creditors imposing contractual restrictions on dividends and distributions in loan agreements.   Such agreements often provide more meaningful restrictions than state statutes.

Example: *ABC* Company plans to borrow $15,000,000 from *X* Life Insurance Company.   The loan is in the form of a sale of bonds in a private placement.   *X* Life Insurance Company declines to make the loan unless *ABC* Corporation agrees to the following limitations on dividends and distributions:

(a) *ABC* Corporation may pay a dividend of up to $0.25 per share per quarter so long as its annual income in the preceding year was $5,000,000 or more.

(b) *ABC* Corporation may pay an extra or special dividend not to exceed $1.00 per share if its net earnings exceed $25,000,000 and not to exceed $2.00 per share if its earnings exceed $50,000,000 in the preceding year.

(c) No other dividend or distribution or redemption or reacquisition of shares by *ABC* Corporation may be made without the prior written approval of *X* Life Insurance Company.

H. REDEMPTIONS AND REPURCHASES OF OUTSTANDING SHARES

A redemption or repurchase by a corporation of some of its outstanding shares has the same economic effect as a dividend or distribution to the shareholders whose shares are redeemed or purchased.   The assets of the corporation are reduced by the purchase price of the shares while the shares of itself owned by the corporation cannot be considered to be assets.   (This can be appreciated by comparing the status of repurchased shares with the status of authorized but unissued shares.)   As a result, the legal restrictions applicable to dividends are also generally applicable to share repurchases or redemptions. RMBCA §§ 6.40, 1.40(6).

1.   REASONS FOR REDEMPTIONS IN PUBLICLY HELD CORPORATIONS

Share redemptions or repurchases may occur in publicly held corporations for several reasons: e. g., to provide shares for employee share purchase plans, for the acquisition of other businesses, or to eliminate the interest of major shareholders without affecting the market for the shares. Such repurchases are often made in the public market at current market prices and create relatively few problems, unless they occur in the context of a struggle for control, e. g., *Cheff v. Mathes*, 199 A.2d 548 (Del. 1964); *Unocal Corp. v. Mesa Petroleum Co.*, 493 A.2d 946 (Del. 1985); or as part of a plan to force out all public shareholders (a "going private" transaction). *Kaufmann v. Lawrence*, 386 F.Supp. 12 (S.D.N.Y. 1974).

2.   REASONS FOR REDEMPTIONS IN CLOSELY HELD CORPORATIONS

Share redemptions or repurchases raise quite different problems in closely held corporations. Since there is no public market for shares in closely held corporations, a shareholder who wishes to sell his shares has only limited purchasers: either other shareholders or the corporation itself. Also there is no public market price by which the fairness or reasonableness of the repurchase price can be judged. Redemptions in such situations are usually designed to permit a shareholder to withdraw from the corporation and liquidate his or her investment.

   a.   When the other shareholders are willing to acquire the interest of the shareholder who wishes to sell, repurchases by the corporation are often simpler and more convenient than pro rata purchases by the other shareholders. The corporation may acquire life insurance policies on the lives of its shareholders to have funds available to acquire their shares on their death.

   b.   Repurchases by the corporation often are made on the installment basis over a period of years with the shareholder accepting promissory notes of the corporation for the bulk of the purchase price.

      1)   The payment of the purchase price over time may allow the corporation to pay for the shares out of expected future earnings.

      2)   The tests for the validity of a share purchase or redemption—usually that the corporation have available earned surplus from which the purchase may be made and the corporation not be rendered insolvent by the transaction—may be applied in either two ways:

(i) Only at the time of the original sale at which the promissory notes are issued; or

(ii) Sequentially to each payment on the notes.

3) The early case law generally tested the validity of each payment separately; *Matter of Trimble Co.*, 339 F.2d 838 (3d Cir. 1964); *Robinson v. Wangemann*, 75 F.2d 756 (5th Cir. 1935); *Mountain State Steel Foundries, Inc. v. C. I. R.*, 284 F.2d 737 (4th Cir. 1960) (holding that a promissory note covered by earned surplus when it came due was enforceable even if not covered by such surplus when it was issued). RMBCA § 6.40(e) and some cases take the first position and apply the tests only to the original purchase. *Williams v. Nevelow*, 513 S.W.2d 535 (Tex. 1974). Under this approach promissory notes representing the purchase price of shares, if covered by earned surplus when they are issued, are considered to be no different from any other ordinary corporate obligation, and are enforceable on a parity with other creditors even if there is no earned surplus to cover the note at the time of payment. California apparently takes an intermediate position and invalidates the note if there is not available earned surplus at the time of payment but allows a lien securing the note to be enforced. *In re National Tile & Terrazzo Co., Inc.*, 537 F.2d 329 (9th Cir. 1976).

c. One court has enforced a contractual obligation on the part of the corporation to repurchase shares at cost when they were originally sold pursuant to a contract that contained such a promise by the corporation, despite the potential unfairness to other shareholders. *Grace Securities Corp. v. Roberts*, 164 S.E. 700 (Va. 1932).

d. Redemptions by a corporation are usually more favorable from a tax standpoint than direct purchases by the other shareholders.

3. STATUS OF REACQUIRED SHARES

a. Reacquired shares under most early statutes were classed as "treasury shares." Such shares had an intermediate status, i.e. they were not viewed as "issued" for purposes of dividends, quorum and voting purposes, but they were also not viewed as "unissued shares" for purposes of restrictions imposed by par value statutes and restrictions on the types of consideration that may be paid for authorized but unissued shares.

b. In par value states, stated capital was not reduced by the par value of treasury shares; such shares were reflected on the financial statements by a special entry showing that they were held as treasury shares and restrictions were placed on the earned surplus and/or capital surplus accounts to reflect that the purchase price for the treasury shares had been charged to those accounts. Accounting for treasury shares was complicated; it was based on the assumption that those shares were not permanently retired but would be reissued at a later date.

c. Many corporations acquired treasury shares so as to avoid the statutory restrictions on the issuance of authorized shares.

Example: Corporation A, a publicly held corporation, wishes to contribute 10 shares as a door prize for a benefit for an employee who had been seriously injured in an automobile accident. It may not use authorized but unissued shares for this purpose under the state statute that permits shares to be issued only for "money or property actually received or services actually performed." Corporation A may lawfully contribute 10 treasury shares for this purpose.

Caveat: One court has applied the limitations on the issuance of authorized shares to the reissuance of treasury shares. *Public Inv. Ltd. v. Bandeirante Corp.*, 740 F.2d 1222 (D.C.Cir. 1984). This result reached by the court is reasonable on the facts of that case, but it is not consistent with generally understood principles relating to treasury shares.

d. RMBCA § 6.31 eliminates the concept of treasury shares. Reacquired shares under this Act have the status of authorized but unissued shares. This change was made in recognition of the fact that with the elimination of restrictions on the issuance of shares, there is no reason to retain the concept of treasury shares.

4. REDEMPTIONS AT OPTION OF CORPORATION

Corporations may issue preferred shares that are redeemable at the option of the corporation. In many states common shares may not be made redeemable at all or may be made redeemable only if there exists another class of common shares that is not redeemable. See *Lewis v. H. P. Hood & Sons, Inc.*, 121 N.E.2d 850 (Mass. 1954). RMBCA permit redeemable common shares without limitation or restriction.

a. If the redeemable shares have voting power, the redemption may affect control of the corporation. Such redemptions, however, have been permitted if made in good faith. *Hendricks v. Mill Engineering & Supply Co., Inc.*, 413 P.2d 811 (Wash. 1966). Some commentators have argued that redeemable voting shares should be prohibited as a matter of public policy because of the coercive threat the power of redemption may create.

b.   The corporation may purchase redeemable shares from individual shareholders at a negotiated price without necessarily triggering the redemption obligation. *Snyder v. Memco Engineering & Mfg. Co., Inc.,* 257 N.Y.S.2d 213 (App.Div. 1965).

5.   REDEMPTIONS AT OPTION OF SHAREHOLDER

Many states permit shares to be made redeemable at the option of the shareholder. Such shares have some of the characteristics of a demand promissory note. Such shares are a financing device that is more attractive than debt where the supplier of capital is a corporation so that a dividend is entitled to the dividend received credit under the federal income tax law.

I. ILLEGAL DIVIDENDS OR REDEMPTIONS

Generally, assenting directors are liable for an illegal dividend or redemption; shareholders who receive such a dividend are generally liable to repay it only if they knew it was unlawful when they received it. *Reilly v. Segert*, 201 N.E.2d 444 (Ill. 1964). Directors, however, may generally rely on the records of the corporation and the opinion of the corporation's accountant in good faith without incurring liability for an illegal dividend. See RMBCA § 8.33. Liability for illegal dividends or distributions generally run to the corporation rather than to individual creditors. *Schaefer v. DeChant*, 464 N.E.2d 583 (Ohio Ct.App. 1983).

J. SHARE DIVIDENDS AND SHARE SPLITS

Unlike cash or property dividends, a share dividend or share split does not dissipate corporate assets. In effect, the total number of shares having claims to the pool of assets are increased but the pool of assets is neither increased nor decreased. (In contrast, when shares are repurchased or redeemed, the size of the pool of assets is reduced by the purchase price for the shares and the number of shares having claim to the remaining assets are reduced by the number of redeemed shares.)

1.   DEFINITIONS

A share dividend differs from a share split principally in accounting treatment. In a share split, the par value of each old share is divided among the new shares while in a share dividend the par value of each share is unchanged and the stated capital of the corporation is increased by the number of shares issued as a dividend. RMBCA § 6.23 refers only to "share dividends".

a.   A share dividend is usually described as a percentage increase while a share split is described in the form of a "new-for-old" ratio.

Example: A corporation declares a 6% stock dividend. Each shareholder's holdings are increased by one share for every 16⅔ shares held;

fractional shares may be paid in cash or in the form of scrip which may be sold for cash. Funds will be transferred from earned surplus (or some other account) to stated capital to reflect the increase in the number of outstanding shares.

Example: A corporation declares a 2-for-1 stock split. Each shareholder is issued one new share for each share held; as a result, each shareholder has two shares where before he or she had one. The par value of or capital represented by each share is cut in half and as a result, the aggregate capital is not increased by the stock split.

b.   In a stock split, the regular dividend rate is adjusted, though often the combined rate on the new shares is greater than the rate on the old shares. No change in dividend rate is normally made as a result of a share dividend.

Example: In a 2-for-1 split, the corporation announces the regular dividend rate of 0.50 per quarter year rate on the old shares will be replaced by a 0.30 per quarter year rate on the new. The new rate is the equivalent of 0.60 rate on the old shares.

Example: The corporation declares a 6 percent share dividend. The old dividend rate of 0.50 per quarter year is retained on a per share basis; total quarterly dividends will therefore increase with the additional number of shares.

2.   EFFECT ON MARKET PRICES

The market price of new shares after a stock split is often somewhat greater than the price of the old shares. This may partially be explained by the dividend increase though partially it may be a psychological reaction by the market. A share dividend rarely has a noticeable effect on market prices. Many shareholders may sell shares received as a dividend or in a split without realizing that they are reducing slightly their proportional interest in the corporation.

Example: In the preceding example, the shares before the split sold for $20 per share. The new shares sell for about $13.00 per share. Only part of this increase can be explained by the dividend increase.

Caveat: Miller and Modigliani have established that (with certain simplifying assumptions) the value of a corporation's common shares is independent of the dividend policy adopted by the corporation. Under these assumptions, the retention of corporate earnings increases the market value of the corporation's common shares by precisely the amount the payment of a dividend would have reduced that value.

3. **TREATMENT OF SHARE DIVIDENDS AND SPLITS**

Since share dividends or splits have some characteristics of income and some of principal, it is not surprising that litigation has arisen over the proper classification of such distributions in various contexts. In most of these situations, the intention of the creator of the interest, if clearly expressed, will control; litigation arises because no intention is expressed or the expression is ambiguous.

    a. A recurring question that arises in trusts or testamentary bequests is whether a share dividend should be awarded to the life tenant or to the remainderman.

        1) One view is that share dividends should be classified as income and not principal if earnings are capitalized to reflect the dividend. *Matter of Fosdick*, 152 N.E.2d 228 (N.Y. 1958).

        2) A second view is that share dividends should be classified as income to the extent they are paid out of income that accrued subsequent to the creation of the life interest. This is often referred to as the Pennsylvania rule.

        3) A third view is that share dividends should be treated as income up to an amount equal to six per cent of the principal each year.

        4) A fourth view is that all share dividends should be treated as principal. This is often referred to as the Massachusetts rule.

    b. A similar issue is whether a testamentary gift of a specified number of shares should be deemed to carry with it shares later received in a share split. Again, the intent of the testator ultimately controls: did he or she intend to give a specified number of shares or a specified interest in the corporation? Where intent is ambiguous or uncertain, diversity of views may prevail. *Compare In re Estate of Marks*, 255 A.2d 512 (Pa. 1969) with *In re Howe's Will*, 224 N.Y.S.2d 992 (App.Div. 1962).

REVIEW QUESTIONS

V–1. How does a corporation obtain its capital?

V–2. What function does par value serve today?

V–3.   Why doesn't the use of no par shares solve problems of corporate capitalization?

V–4.   Watered stock is a historical concept that has no practical importance today.

True _____   False _____

V–5.   What does the Revised Model Business Corporation Act do about par value?

V–6.   In what sense is preferred stock preferred?

V–7.   What is the difference between a bond and debenture?

V–8.   In these days of inflation, Ben Franklin's old statement that "the best corporation is a debt-free corporation" is more true than ever.

True _____   False _____

V–9.   So long as one offers shares to fewer than 35 persons, there can be no problem under the federal or state securities acts.

True _____   False _____

V–10.   What are preemptive rights?

V–11.   A corporation that eliminates preemptive rights may issue shares at any time in the future at any price the directors decide appropriate.

True _____   False _____

V–12.   Why is a repurchase of outstanding shares by a corporation similar to a dividend?

V–13.   Creditors should always impose restrictions on dividends by contract. The protection given creditors by the legal restrictions on the distribution of dividends by state corporation statutes are almost totally illusory.

True ＿＿＿＿＿＿   False ＿＿＿＿＿＿

V–14.   A publicly held corporation decides to issue a dividend in the form of shares of stock rather than in the form of money. As a matter of economics, there is no significant difference in these two types of distributions.

True ＿＿＿＿＿＿   False ＿＿＿＿＿＿

V–15.   Commerce, Inc. is incorporated in a state with a par value statute; it has a single class of shares listed on the New York Stock Exchange. It has recently engaged in an extensive mail-order sales campaign in order to stimulate its sagging economic fortunes. Commerce, Inc., although it had a large accumulated deficit in earned surplus from losses from prior years, declared and paid a dividend out of its net profits for last year. Commerce, Inc. was not insolvent at the time of the declaration or payment of the dividend.

Commerce, Inc. now finds itself in deep financial trouble. Plagued by creditors and unable to meet presently due liabilities, it files a petition in bankruptcy. Its trustee-in-bankruptcy sues both the directors and the shareholders of Commerce, Inc. who received the dividend. What are the potential liabilities of the directors who authorized the dividends and the shareholders who received them? Would it make any difference if Commerce, Inc. were incorporated in a state that has enacted the Revised Model Business Corporation Act? [This question and answer is drawn in part from Ballantine, Problems in Law 241 (5th Ed. 1975).]

V–16.   B owned a mining claim worth $100,000. She formed X corporation in a state with a par value statute and transferred to X the mining claim for shares having a par value of $250,000. The corporation became insolvent and R was appointed its receiver. R sued B for $150,000. May R recover?

V–17.   P entered into an agreement with D Corporation whereby P agreed to sell to D 150 shares of D's stock for $40,000. D Corporation was to pay the purchase price in installments of $1,000 every 3 months. At the time of the purchase D Corporation has sufficient surplus to make the purchase without impairing capital. After the corporation had paid $13,000 on the purchase price it became insolvent. Is P entitled to file a claim for $27,000 as a creditor in a subsequent bankruptcy?

V–18.   X corporation has been in business for 10 years, has made substantial profits every year, and yet has never paid a dividend. In addition to its capital of $2,000,000 it has accumulated $8,000,000 surplus without clear plans to expand its business. Of its $10,000,000 in assets, $2,000,000 is cash. Z, a stockholder, sues to have the court order the board of directors of X to declare a dividend. Should the order issue?

VI

THE STATUTORY SCHEME OF MANAGEMENT AND CONTROL

Analysis

A. The Statutory Scheme in General
B. Attempts to Vary the Statutory Scheme
C. The Statutory Scheme as an Idealized Corporate Model

A. THE STATUTORY SCHEME IN GENERAL

State corporation statutes provide an idealized distribution of the power of management and control among the three tiers of a corporation—shareholders, directors and officers.

Caveat: This part outlines the broad principles of corporate management and control; later parts describe in detail the roles and functions of shareholders (part VII), directors (part VIII), and officers (part IX).

1. SHAREHOLDERS

The shareholders are viewed as the ultimate owners of the corporation. They have, however, only limited powers of management and control in the corporation, including:

a. The power to select directors.

b. The power to remove directors. At common law shareholders could remove directors only for cause; in many state statutes this power has been broadened to include removal with or without cause. *Scott County Tobacco Warehouses, Inc. v. Harris,* 201 S.E.2d 780 (Va. 1974). See RMBCA § 8.08; Del.Gen.Corp.Law § 141(k).

c. The power to make recommendations to the board of directors about business and personnel matters. *Auer v. Dressel,* 118 N.E.2d 590 (N.Y.1954). Shareholders, however, do not have direct power to implement these recommendations and some courts have refused to compel corporations to submit issues of this type to the shareholders. *Carter v. Portland General Electric Co.,* 362 P.2d 766 (Or. 1961).

   Caveat: Regulations adopted by the Securities and Exchange Commission require certain corporations to submit certain issues to shareholders. See part XII, below. The *Carter* case involved a corporation not subject to the SEC requirements.

d. The power to amend or repeal bylaws in many states. RMBCA § 10.20. But See *Somers v. AAA Temporary Services, Inc.,* 284 N.E.2d 462 (Ill.App. 1972) holding that if this power is delegated to directors, the shareholders may lose this power. Under the RMBCA, shareholders would not lose their power under the circumstances of this case.

e. In conjunction with the board of directors, the power to approve fundamental corporate changes:

   1) Amendments to articles of incorporation [RMBCA § 10.03];

2)   Mergers or consolidations with other corporations [RMBCA § 11.03];

3)   Sale of substantially all the assets of the corporation not in the ordinary course of business [RMBCA § 12.02]; and

4)   Dissolution [RMBCA § 14.02].

f.   The power to select the corporate auditor (in corporations subject to SEC regulation).

g.   Where an internal struggle for control exists, the power to definitively resolve which faction shall be entitled to manage the corporation, *Campbell v. Loew's Inc.*, 134 A.2d 852 (Del.Ch. 1957).

2.   DIRECTORS

The board of directors of a corporation is entrusted with the general power of management of the business and affairs of the corporation. All significant business decisions are generally entrusted to the directors, *Continental Securities Co. v. Belmont*, 99 N.E. 138 (N.Y. 1912), though they may delegate many decisions to corporate officers or agents.

a.   Many state business corporation acts state that powers of the corporation "shall be exercised by," and the business and affairs of a corporation "shall be managed" by, the board. In several states, this statutory language has been modified in recent years to *"exercised by or under authority of"* and *"managed by or under the direction of"* the board. See RMBCA § 8.01; Del.Gen.Corp.Law § 141(a).

1)   These latter descriptions more accurately reflect the role of the board of directors in large publicly held corporations where, perforce, most of the detailed control over and management of huge aggregations of assets must be performed by management.

2)   The earlier descriptions more accurately reflect the role of the board in smaller, closely held corporations where it is often feasible for boards to manage the business and affairs of the corporation.

b.   The board of directors selects the corporate officers and has the power to remove them. The board also may employ employees or agents, or create new officers and employ persons to fill them. It is customary for boards to delegate the power of employing lower level employees and agents to the corporate president or other officers.

c.   Certain corporate decisions are viewed as being peculiarly within the scope of discretion of directors. These functions, such as determining the amount that should be distributed as dividends to the shareholders, are often specifically assigned to the board's discretion by statute.

d.   In the statutory scheme directors are not viewed as agents or representatives of shareholders but as persons with independent authority, independent fiduciary duties, and some tenure to office. The independent office and role of directors are created by statute, not by decision of the shareholders.

3.   OFFICERS
The officers of the corporation in the statutory scheme generally have the limited role of carrying out the policies and decisions of the board rather than the broader role of creating policy. While officers have limited authority to bind the corporation by their actions within the scope of their responsibilities, this power is not broadly construed. In other words, the essence of the statutory scheme is that discretionary power within the corporation is in the board of directors not the officers or shareholders.

B.   ATTEMPTS TO VARY THE STATUTORY SCHEME

Attempts to reallocate the corporate powers in a way different from the statutory scheme historically have been viewed with suspicion and many have been held to be against public policy and unenforceable.

1.   COMMON LAW APPROACH
The strict common law view was that agreements between shareholders that attempted to resolve questions vested in the board of directors were unenforceable and may be ignored by the other parties to the agreement. *McQuade v. Stoneham*, 189 N.E. 234 (N.Y. 1934).

Example: Two shareholders, *A* and *B* with a combined majority of the voting shares, enter into an agreement that provides: (a) They will vote for themselves as directors; (b) They will establish *A* as president and *B* as vice president; (c) The salary of the president will be $50,000 per year and the salary of the vice president will be $40,000 per year.

The agreements referred to in (b) and (c) invade the discretionary power of the directors and are unenforceable. The agreement (a), however, does not interfere with the discretion of directors (since the selection of directors is purely a function of the shareholders) and is therefore not subject to attack on the same ground. Its enforceability depends on whether it is severable from the unenforceable portions.

Example: C agrees to invest in a corporation only if the other two shareholders, A and B, agree that the corporation will not borrow in excess of $10,000 without the prior consent of C. A and B agree in writing to this proposal and C purchases shares. Since borrowing money is within the discretionary power of the directors to manage the business, the agreement is against public policy and unenforceable. The board of directors may ignore the agreement and borrow money in excess of $10,000 without obtaining the prior consent of C.

2. RELAXATION OF STRICT COMMON LAW RULE

As illustrated by the foregoing examples, the strict common law rule sometimes led to significant injustice because apparently reasonable and sensible contracts were invalidated. As a result, the same court that decided *McQuade* shortly thereafter modified the strict common law rule by holding that contracts which involved only slight impingements on the statutory scheme and hurt no one should not be invalidated under this general principle. *Clark v. Dodge*, 199 N.E. 641 (N.Y. 1936). It is likely that some courts might consider the veto in the second example above as a "slight impingement." The modern trend is to relax even further the test for invalidating such agreements. *Galler v. Galler*, 203 N.E.2d 577 (Ill. 1964).

Example: Two shareholders agree that the corporation should pay dividends of $50,000 per year if there are funds available after the board of directors has set aside whatever funds it believes necessary for future contingencies and growth. In most states such an agreement today would be deemed a "slight impingement" and the agreement would be held valid.

a. Courts have also stated that the rule about interfering with the board's discretion was designed to protect minority shareholders (or, at least, shareholders who are not parties to the contract); therefore, if all the shareholders entered into the agreement, somewhat broader impingements on the discretion of the directors may be permitted. However, major impingements that radically change the locus of power or scheme of corporate governance would not be permitted even if all the shareholders agreed.

   Example: All the shareholders agree that all internal decisions within the corporation shall be made as though the shareholders were partners and that the corporation shall not have a board of directors. Absent specific statutory authorization, such an agreement is not enforceable.

   Example: All the shareholders agree that directors must always approve and agree to all transactions that a majority of the shareholders approve. Such an agreement is not binding on the directors.

Example: A shareholder's agreement providing for an option to purchase shares also contains provisions relating to the naming of officers and the fixing of their compensation. These provisions were in fact never implemented. The court may ignore the provisions dealing with the officers (which violate the statutory scheme) and enforce the balance. *Triggs v. Triggs,* 385 N.E.2d 1254 (N.Y. 1978).

3. SPECIAL STATUTORY RULES FOR CLOSE CORPORATIONS

A number of states have adopted statutes that modify the common law rules set forth in paragraphs 1 and 2. Many of these statutes permit a close corporation to dispense with the board of directors entirely and have the business and affairs managed directly by the shareholders. Others expressly permit restrictions on the discretion of directors to be included in articles of incorporation; these provisions may be applicable to all corporations.

a.   RMBCA § 8.01(c) allows corporations with less than 50 shareholders to dispense with the board of directors entirely. RMBCA § 8.01(b) allows restrictions on the power of the board of directors to be placed in the articles of incorporation without regard to the number of shareholders.

b.   Where the board of directors has been eliminated, the shareholders are often referred to as "managing shareholders" and have the rights and duties of directors. *Graczykowski v. Ramppen,* 477 N.Y.S.2d 454 (App.Div. 1984).

c.   In *Zion v. Kurtz,* 405 N.E.2d 681 (N.Y. 1982), the court upheld an agreement between two shareholders that the corporation would not enter into transactions or new business without the consent of both shareholders despite the fact that no reference to the agreement appeared in the articles of incorporation and the corporation had not elected close corporation status. The court viewed these omissions as technical and subject to the power of the court to order the articles of incorporation reformed. The vote was 4–3; the dissenters argued that public notice of agreements restricting the power of directors was essential for their validity under these statutes.

4. ORDERS AND DIRECTIONS OF MAJORITY SHAREHOLDERS

The directors are not agents of the shareholders and may not be compelled to approve transactions merely because a majority or even all the shareholders approve them. *Continental Securities Co. v. Belmont,* 99 N.E. 138 (N.Y. 1912). The sole remedy of the majority shareholders in this situation is to elect different directors.

> *Example:* *A*, owner of a majority of the shares of a corporation, wishes for the corporation to buy a piece of land. The directors decline. *A* cannot compel the directors to do so but may, of course, elect more compliant directors at the next election of directors. *Automatic Self-Cleansing Filter Syndicate Co., Ltd. v. Cuninghame*, 2 Ch. 34 (Ct.App. Eng. 1906).

a. Even though the shareholders may not order the directors to approve a transaction, they may recommend a transaction and urge its approval by the board.

> *Example:* *A*, in the above example, may properly bring before a shareholder's meeting a resolution urging the directors to approve the land purchase. *Auer v. Dressel*, 118 N.E.2d 590 (N.Y. 1954).

b. As indicated above, at common law directors could be removed only for "cause," a term that implies dishonesty, misconduct, or incompetence. Hence, at common law the selection of more compliant directors would have to await the next annual meeting. *Auer v. Dressel*, 118 N.E.2d 590 (N.Y. 1954), *Campbell v. Loew's, Inc.*, 134 A.2d 852 (Del.Ch. 1957). However, in most states today, shareholders may remove directors without cause; in such states, the majority shareholders may immediately remove the present board and elect different directors willing to enter into the transaction. *Scott County Tobacco Warehouses, Inc. v. Harris*, 201 S.E.2d 780 (Va. 1974). See RMBCA § 8.08; Del.Gen.Corp.Law, § 141(k).

> *Example:* *A*, in the above example, in most states may call a special shareholder's meeting, remove the recalcitrant directors, and elect himself and friends to the board; the land purchase may then be approved.

c. The principal justification for requiring removal of the old board and election of a new is that directors have fiduciary duties to the corporation, creditors and shareholders. A director should not be compelled to follow the wishes of a majority shareholder if he believes the transaction breaches a fiduciary duty. The election of successor directors imposes fiduciary duties on them and they must decide whether the desired transaction is consistent with their duties.

5. DELEGATION OF DUTIES

The directors may not delegate their entire duties of management to third persons and agreements entered into by the corporation which purport to do so may be unenforceable as against public policy.

Example: A corporation enters into a management contract with a third person which vests "sole and exclusive power to manage all affairs of the corporation" in that third person for a period of 25 years. Such an agreement has been held to be against public policy and unenforceable. *Sherman & Ellis, Inc. v. Indiana Mutual Cas. Co.,* 41 F.2d 588 (7th Cir. 1930); *Kennerson v. Burbank Amusement Co.,* 260 P.2d 823 (Cal.App. 1953). It is unlikely that a power to fire the third person for "cause" would save such an agreement from invalidity.

Example: A corporation enters into a management contract of the general type described in the previous example but the agreement reserves to the board the power to review the performance of the manager annually and to replace him if the board considers it appropriate. This qualification probably makes the agreement valid since the delegation of authority is no longer total.

6. DIRECTORS' VOTING AGREEMENTS

The directors may not enter into agreements among themselves relating to how they will vote.

Example: A and B are directors. They agree that B will support proposals presented by A and that A will support proposals presented by B. Such an agreement is against public policy and unenforceable, though, of course, A and B may vote together on a voluntary basis.

7. TESTAMENTARY DIRECTIONS

Majority shareholders may seek to guide the fortunes of their corporation after their death by testamentary directions to their trustees. Such directions may be held to be unenforceable on the ground they restrict the discretion of directors, though the inflexibility of testamentary directions may indicate a broader basis for their invalidity.

Example: A 68 per cent shareholder leaves his shares in trust and directs his trustees (i) to elect themselves as directors, (ii) to name his widow as chairman of the board at a salary of $1,000 per month, and (iii) to elect X as president, also at a specified salary. Instructions (ii) and (iii) violate public policy and are unenforceable. *In re Estate of Hirshon,* 233 N.Y.S.2d 1018 (App.Div. 1962), *modified* 192 N.E.2d 174 (N.Y. 1963).

Caveat: If trustees name themselves as directors, testamentary instructions may create unavoidable conflicts between the duty of the trustee to follow the directions of the testator and the duty of a director to make decisions based on the best interests of the corporation. Testamentary trustees/directors faced with such a conflict may petition a court for instructions, but this itself may be a cumbersome drawn-out process, particularly if there is an appeal.

C. THE STATUTORY SCHEME AS AN IDEALIZED CORPORATE MODEL

The statutory scheme is an idealized corporate model of corporate governance that, in some respects, does not accurately reflect the structure of power in either the very large, publicly held corporation, where shares may be owned by thousands or millions of shareholders, or in the very small corporation, with very few shareholders.

1. THE PUBLICLY HELD CORPORATION

In the publicly held corporation, the power of management is in fact vested not in the board of directors but in the full time, professional corporate officers and employees. This group is usually referred to as "management."

a.   Management has the detailed knowledge about business affairs necessary to make business decisions. The board of directors usually contains several outsiders, who have only limited knowledge of business affairs, and several members of management. These persons are usually referred to as "outside directors" or "independent directors".

b.   The board of directors meets only periodically while management is a full time professional staff.

c.   The board of directors does not have its own staff or independent sources of information but is dependent on management to decide which issues should be brought to the board and what information should be given to the board.

   Example: When Penn Central went into bankruptcy the board of directors had not been advised of the steadily deteriorating financial position of the railroad or of the plans of the management to file for receivership. As a result, the board was as shocked and surprised as the ordinary man-in-the-street.

d.   While the board theoretically selects the chief executive officer (CEO) and other top management, in practice, usually the current CEO names his successor and the board in effect ratifies that selection.

e.   New members of the board of directors are usually selected by the management or by the present board. As a practical matter, the shareholders have an opportunity only to vote for or against the persons so designated, thereby in effect ratifying the choices previously made.

f.   Most shareholders vote by proxy in publicly held corporations based on information provided by the corporation. The number of shareholders who attend shareholders' meetings in person are usually an infinitesimal proportion of all the shareholders. Most shareholders routinely vote in favor of management's recommendations.

2.   THE CLOSELY HELD CORPORATION

The statutory scheme also does not accurately reflect the manner of operation of corporations owned by a very small number of shareholders.

a.   Such corporations are usually called "close corporations" or "closely held corporations".

b.   The shareholders in close corporations are usually simultaneously officers and directors. Business decisions may be made by consensus and without regard to whether the person is acting as officer, director, or shareholder.

c.   Requirements of meetings, appointments, elections, and so forth are all likely to be considered meaningless formalities. Indeed, many such corporations go for years without ever having a formal shareholders' or directors' meeting.

d.   A number of states have adopted statutes relaxing the statutory requirements applicable to closely held corporations. See part X, G.

3.   INTERMEDIATE CORPORATIONS

There are many corporations that do not have the characteristics of the publicly held corporation or of the closely held corporation. These "in between" corporations may have some characteristics of either type of corporation, and in many such corporations, the idealized statutory scheme may be a reasonable description of the allocation of power and control within the corporation.

REVIEW QUESTIONS

VI–1.   What is the "statutory scheme" or "statutory norm" in the law of corporations?

VI–2.   In a corporation with two shareholders, it is silly to talk about the statutory scheme. The shareholders should simply run the corporation in the same way that they run a partnership.

   True _____   False _____

VI–3.   X corporation has a provision in its articles of incorporation that states, "no act of the board of directors of this corporation concerning the management of its business affairs shall be of any effect unless consented to or ratified by a unanimous vote of all its shareholders." A, B and C were the sole shareholders and the sole directors of X corporation. They had earlier elected A president, B vice president and C secretary-treasurer of the corporation. They now meet as a board of directors and vote to relieve C of his duties as secretary-treasurer and make B secretary-treasurer in addition to his being vice president. C votes against his removal as secretary-treasurer and contends that he cannot be removed under the above charter provision without unanimous vote of the shareholders, and he being one, does not consent to his own removal. C brings suit against A and B to compel them to admit him to the office of secretary-treasurer and to compel them to deliver to him the books of such office. What result?

VII

SHAREHOLDERS' MEETINGS, VOTING, AND CONTROL ARRANGEMENTS

Analysis

A. SHAREHOLDERS' MEETINGS

The rules with respect to shareholders' meetings are rather straight-forward. There is a considerable degree of uniformity from state to state in these statutory requirements.

1. **ANNUAL MEETINGS**
    Annual meetings are required to be held for the purpose of electing directors and conducting other business. The time and place of the annual meeting may be specified in or fixed in accordance with the bylaws. The failure to hold an annual meeting does not affect the validity or continued existence of the corporation. The failure to hold an annual meeting also does not affect the incumbency of sitting directors. See part VIII, E; RMBCA § 7.01.

2. **SPECIAL MEETINGS**
    All meetings other than the annual meeting are called special meetings. Such meetings may be called by the board of directors, and under many state statutes by the President, the holders of a specified number of shares (often 10 per cent), and other persons named in the bylaws. RMBCA § 7.02.

3. **NOTICE**
    Shareholders must be given written notice of annual or special meetings as provided in the statute or in the bylaws. Many statutes require at least ten but not more than fifty days' notice. RMBCA § 7.05 requires 10 to 60 days notice.

    a. The purposes of a special meeting must be stated in the notice and the business to be conducted at that meeting is limited to that specified in the notice. RMBCA § 7.02(d). No purposes of an annual meeting need be stated and any relevant business may be conducted at such a meeting.

    b. Notice may be waived by a written document executed before, at, or after the meeting in question. RMBCA § 7.06.

    c. In the absence of statute, there is no common law requirement that shareholders be permitted to vote on matters not required to be considered by shareholders. *Carter v. Portland General Electric Co.*, 362 P.2d 766 (Or. 1961).

4. **QUORUM REQUIREMENTS**
    A quorum at a meeting is typically a majority of the voting shares though some statutes allow the quorum to be reduced either without limitation or to a specified fraction (e.g. one third). Earlier versions of the Model Act allowed the quorum to be reduced to one third; RMBCA § 7.25(a) permits the quorum requirement to be reduced without limitation.

> *Example:* A quorum by statute consists of a majority of the voting shares. A corporation has 100 shares outstanding and 52 shares are represented at the meeting. A quorum is present and therefore a majority of those present—27 shares—may validly approve actions unless a greater percentage is required by the statute or bylaws.

a.   Shares represented by proxy are deemed present for purposes of a quorum. *Duffy v. Loft Inc.*, 151 A. 223 (Del. Ch. 1930).

b.   Non-voting shares, treasury shares (i. e., shares once outstanding but reacquired by the corporation) and shares owned by a majority-owned subsidiary of the corporation are not counted toward a quorum under most state statutes.

c.   Most courts hold that if a quorum is once present, the meeting may continue even though a faction removes itself from the meeting in an effort to break the quorum. *Levisa Oil Corp. v. Quigley*, 234 S.E.2d 257 (Va. 1977) (minority view). RMBCA § 7.25(b) codifies the majority view.

5.   VOTING

The general rule is that a majority of votes at a meeting at which a quorum is present is necessary to adopt a measure. Earlier versions of the Model Business Corporation Act so provided but RMBCA § 7.25(c) changes the approval requirement to "the votes cast * * * favoring the action exceed the votes cast opposing the action." This change was designed to eliminate the negative way the traditional rule treated abstentions.

a.   An abstention may be reflected by casting of a blank ballot, or by casting a ballot marked "abstention" or by casting no ballot at all.

> *Example:* Assume a corporation has 100 shares of a single class outstanding, all entitled to cast one vote each. A quorum consists of 51 shares. If 60 shares are represented and the vote on a proposed action is 28 in favor, 23 opposed and 9 abstaining, the action is not adopted under the traditional language of most statutes since the affirmative vote by 28 shares is not a majority of the shares present. On the other hand, if the 9 abstaining shares were not present at all, the action would have been approved since 51 shares were present and 28 voted in favor of the proposal.

b.   RMBCA § 7.28 also establishes a plurality vote requirement for the election of directors in order to take into account the possibility of three or more factions competing for directorships. Earlier versions of the

Model Act and the statutes of most states do not contain a special rule for elections of directors.

Caveat: The RMBCA phrases quorum and voting requirement in terms of "voting groups" in order to apply these requirements separately in class voting situations, where different classes of shares are entitled to vote separately on an issue. See RMBCA § 1.40(26). In most situations, there will be only one voting group, the group consisting of all shares entitled by the articles of incorporation to vote on the matter, acting on a matter.

6. SUPERMAJORITY QUORUM AND VOTING REQUIREMENTS

Statutes generally allow the quorum and vote requirements to adopt a measure to be increased up to and including unanimity. See RMBCA § 7.27. A case finding such an increase in voting or quorum requirements to be against public policy, *Benintendi v. Kenton Hotel*, 60 N.E.2d 829 (N.Y. 1945), was promptly rejected by legislative enactment.

a. Supermajority requirements are often imposed in closely held corporations to ensure that a minority shareholder has a veto power over matters coming before the shareholders.

Example: An owner of 20 per cent of the outstanding shares may obtain a veto power by insisting that no action may be taken by the shareholders unless a quorum consists of 90 per cent of the outstanding shares and that actions to be approved must be voted upon affirmatively by all the shareholders present at a meeting at which a quorum is present.

b. Supermajority requirements are also used as defensive weapons to protect publicly held corporations against unwanted takeover attempts.

Example: A publicly held corporation amends its articles of incorporation to provide that if any person obtains a majority of the outstanding shares of a corporation without the approval of the board of directors, the voting requirement for all actions by the shareholders will be increased to seventy per cent. This provision deters takeovers because an outsider will not have voting control of the corporation unless he either obtains approval of the board or purchases over seventy per cent of the outstanding shares of the corporation.

7. ACTION WITHOUT A MEETING

Under most state statutes, a written consent signed by all the shareholders is as valid as an action taken at a meeting. RMBCA § 7.04. In some states, a consent signed by the percentage of shares needed to approve a transaction is also effective. This majority-consent procedure may be used in publicly-held as well as closely-held corporations. A majority consent provision permits a purchaser of a majority of the shares of a publicly held corporation immediately to replace the board of directors and take control of the corporation.

Example: A corporation with 120,000 shares outstanding receives a consent signed by holders of 61,000 shares in a state with a majority-consent procedure. The action is validly taken. No account is taken of the quorum requirement in this computation.

8. MULTIPLE OR FRACTIONAL VOTES

Under older statutes the rule is one vote per share (except possibly for nonvoting shares). A number of state statutes now permit multiple or fractional votes per share. In these states all computations must be based on an aggregate-votes rather than aggregate-voting shares basis. RMBCA §§ 6.01, 7.21.

Example: Articles of incorporation provide that for purposes of determining a quorum, a shareholder has one vote for each share owned up to fifty shares and one vote for each twenty shares owned in excess of fifty shares, but no shareholder may cast more than one fourth of all the votes at a meeting (except as proxy for other shareholders). The provision, which prevents a single shareholder from constituting a quorum no matter what his holdings, is valid under the Delaware statute. *Providence & Worcester Co. v. Baker,* 378 A.2d 121 (Del. 1977).

9. MANIPULATION OF MEETING DATES FOR ULTERIOR PURPOSES

Cases are divided on whether a court should intervene if the persons in control of a corporation manipulate the meeting date in order to avoid a proxy fight or in order to make a successful proxy fight more difficult. *Schnell v. Chris-Craft Industries, Inc.,* 285 A.2d 437 (Del. 1971) holds that such manipulation may constitute a breach of fiduciary duty by the persons in control of the corporation; *In re Unexcelled, Inc.,* 281 N.Y.S.2d 173 (App.Div. 1967) permits such manipulation based on a literal reading of the applicable business corporation act.

B. ELIGIBILITY TO VOTE

Eligibility to vote shares at a shareholders' meeting is determined by "record ownership" on a specified date, called the "record date."

1. THE CONCEPT OF RECORD OWNERSHIP

Corporations issue shares in the name of designated persons and the names and addresses of those persons are recorded in the records of the corporation. That person is called the "record owner."

a.   A person who buys shares from a current shareholder may present the old shares to the corporation (along with an executed power of attorney from the old owner) and have new certificates issued in his name, thereby becoming the new record owner.

b.   A person may acquire shares without going through the mechanics of becoming the record owner. Such a person is called the "beneficial owner"; the record owner has mere naked title and may be compelled to transfer that title to the beneficial owner by executing the necessary power of attorney to enable the beneficial owner to become the record owner.

2. RECORD DATE

Persons entitled to vote at a meeting are the record owners on a specific date called the "record date." The record date may be established by the board of directors; if it does not do so the record date is the date of the notice of the meeting. RMBCA § 7.07.

a.   Shares may be transferred on the books of the corporation after the record date, but such subsequent record owners do not thereby obtain the power to vote.

b.   A record date may also be set by "closing the transfer books" on a specific date, thereby refusing to recognize subsequent transfers of securities and in effect freezing the transfer books until after the meeting. This is practically never used today in modern corporations and was eliminated as an option in the RMBCA.

c.   Even though the record owner on the record date is entitled to vote at the meeting, the beneficial owner on the date of the meeting may compel him to vote as the beneficial owner directs. This is usually done by requiring the beneficial owner to execute a blank proxy in favor of the beneficial owner. A court may compel the record owner to execute such a proxy.

d.   These rules are designed to simplify the meeting for the corporation which deals exclusively with the record owners and does not concern itself with the identity of the beneficial owner. *Salgo v. Matthews*, 497 S.W.2d 620 (Tex.Civ.App. 1973).

e. RMBCA § 7.23 authorizes corporations to establish procedures to recognize beneficial owners as owners of shares.

3. VOTING LIST

Corporations must prepare an accurate voting list of the record owners entitled to vote at a meeting. This list must be available for inspection at the meeting, and under most statutes must also be available for inspection for a period of time before the meeting. RMBCA § 7.20. The failure to prepare this list does not affect the validity of any action taken at a meeting. Some state statutes impose a penalty on the corporate officer who is obligated to prepare a voting list but fails to do so.

4. MISCELLANEOUS VOTING RULES

Statutes of many states set forth rules as to who may vote shares in certain circumstances. RMBCA § 7.24 contains more elaborate rules than most statutes. Older statutes provide:

a. Shares owned by a trustee may be voted by the trustee only if the shares are transferred to his or her name.

b. Shares held by an administrator, executor, guardian or conservator may be voted directly by him or her without transfer of the shares to his or her name. (Unlike a trustee, such fiduciaries will have official evidences of their appointment.)

c. Shares held by a receiver may be voted directly by the receiver without transfer of the shares to his or her name if the order of appointment specifically authorizes the receiver to vote shares.

d. A shareholder who pledges shares may vote them until the shares are transferred to the name of the pledgee, who thereafter may vote the shares.

5. INSPECTORS OF ELECTION

Disputes as to entitlement to vote are usually resolved by inspectors of election who may be granted discretionary authority to resolve disputes on the basis of the statutory voting rules and the records of the corporation. *Salgo v. Matthews*, 497 S.W.2d 620 (Tex.Civ.App. 1973).

C. CUMULATIVE VOTING

Elections of directors may involve cumulative or straight voting. In some states constitutional or statutory provisions require cumulative voting; in most states, however, each corporation may elect by appropriate provisions in its articles of incorporation whether or not to have cumulative voting.   RMBCA § 7.28.

1.   STRAIGHT VOTING

In straight voting each shareholder may cast the number of votes equal to the number of shares he or she holds for candidates for each position to be filled on the board of directors.

> *Example:*   A shareholder with 30 voting shares in an election to fill three directorships may cast up to 30 votes for each of three candidates.

   a.   Under straight voting, shareholders holding a majority of the voting shares will elect the entire board of directors.

   b.   Straight voting is simple and easy to understand.   As a result, it is widely used in publicly held corporations.

2.   MECHANICS OF CUMULATIVE VOTING

In cumulative voting each shareholder determines the aggregate number of votes he or she may cast in an election by multiplying the number of shares he or she holds by the number of positions to be filled.   Each shareholder may cast that number of votes for one or more candidates.

> *Example:*   In the foregoing example, the shareholder with 30 shares may cast an aggregate of 90 votes since there are three positions to be filled. Under cumulative voting she may cast all 90 votes for a single candidate or divide them between two or more candidates as she sees fit.

   a.   In directoral elections, all candidates run at large and not for or by places, e. g., in an election to fill three vacancies, the top three vote getters are elected by plurality vote.   RMBCA § 7.28(a).

> *Example:*   In the foregoing example, if the shareholder with 30 shares votes all 90 votes for herself, she will be elected to the board unless three other candidates receive 91 or more votes each.

   b.   The effect of cumulative voting is to give minority shareholders the possibility of representation on the board of directors.

> *Example:*   In the foregoing example, the shareholder with 30 shares may elect a director even though the other shareholders have 85 shares.   The other shareholders may cast 255 votes (3 × 85) but that is not enough to give each of three candidates 91 votes each.   They may give candidate X_1 and X_2 91 votes each, but they then have only 73 remaining votes to give to X_3, and

hence cannot prevent the election of the minority shareholder as the third director.

c. The basic formula for determining whether a single block of shares may elect a director under cumulative voting is

$$\frac{S}{D+1} + 1$$

where S equals the total number of shares voting and D equals the number of directors to be elected. The analogous formula to elect N directors is

$$\frac{nS}{D+1} + 1.$$

3. ADVANTAGES AND DISADVANTAGES OF CUMULATIVE VOTING
The claimed advantages of cumulative voting are that it is more democratic, that it permits minority representation, and that it permits the election of a "watchdog director" to oversee the majority's management of the corporation. The claimed disadvantages are that it increases partisanship and divisiveness on the board, and that it is complex and confusing to shareholders.

4. MINIMIZATION OF THE EFFECT OF CUMULATIVE VOTING
Several devices minimize the impact of cumulative voting:

a. In states where cumulative voting is not required, a majority or other specified percentage of the shareholders may amend the articles of incorporation to eliminate cumulative voting entirely. *Maddock v. Vorclone Corp.*, 147 A. 255 (Del.Ch. 1929).

b. The majority shareholders may be able to remove without cause the director or directors elected by the minority. RMBCA § 8.08(a). However, the statutes of a number of states avoid circularity by limiting the power to remove a director elected by cumulative voting to situations where the vote to retain the director is insufficient to have elected him if the vote were cast in an election for directors in which cumulative voting was permitted. RMBCA § 8.08(c).

Example: In the foregoing example the shareholder with 30 shares has elected one director; the shareholders with 85 shares have elected two directors. The shareholders with 85 shares call a special meeting of shareholders to remove the minority director without cause, as shareholders may do under the state statute in question. On the removal motion, the minority shareholder casts her 30 shares against the removal. Since that vote would have been enough to elect one director at an election of directors, the removal motion fails even though 85 shares were voted in favor of it and on other issues a simple majority of the shareholders may resolve all questions.

c. Under many state statutes, if the board of directors consists of nine or more members, the board may be "classified" or "staggered" so that members are elected for two or three year terms with one half or one third being elected each year. RMBCA § 8.06. While the formal justification for classification is to ensure continuity of service on the board, *Bohannan v. Corporation Comm'n*, 313 P.2d 379 (Ariz. 1957), the traditional practical justification is usually more closely related to its impact on cumulative voting. *Stockholders Committee v. Erie Technological Products, Inc.*, 248 F.Supp. 380 (W.D.Pa. 1965). In the 1980s staggering the board of directors and preventing removal of directors without cause have become favored defenses against unwanted takeover attempts in publicly held corporations, since these provisions prevent the purchasers of a majority of the shares from immediately replacing a majority of the board of directors.

Example: A publicly held corporation incorporated in a state in which cumulative voting is mandatory has 10,000,000 voting shares outstanding and a board of directors consisting of 17 members. If all members of the board are elected each year, a bloc of 555,555 shares is sufficient to elect one director. If the board is "classified" or "staggered" so that six members are elected in each of two years and five are elected in the third year, it will take a bloc of 1,428,572 shares to elect a single director. A "public interest" organization might seek to find one half million sympathetic votes but one and one half million may be beyond its vote generating capacity.

Example: In the foregoing illustration, if directors cannot be removed without cause, an outside aggressor who purchases more than 5,000,000 voting shares could not elect a majority of the entire board until at least two annual elections of directors have been held.

Caveat: A single case, *Wolfson v. Avery*, 126 N.E.2d 701 (Ill. 1955) has invalidated a staggering system on the ground that it violates the right of cumulative voting granted by the state constitution.

Caveat: A single case, *Humphrys v. Winous Co.*, 133 N.E.2d 780 (Ohio 1956) upheld a staggering system that placed only a single director in each class. Such a plan destroys cumulative voting in that corporation and is prohibited under the statutes of all states, the Ohio statute having been amended to reverse this decision.

Caveat: Some state statutes provide that a board of three or more members may be classified if cumulative voting is not permitted; if cumulative voting is permitted, the board may be classified only if it consists of nine or more.

d. The board might be permanently reduced in size to reduce the impact of cumulative voting in much the same way as "staggering" the board does.

Example: In the mathematical formula relating to cumulative voting set forth earlier, reduction of the number of directorships to be filled reduces the size of the denominator of the fraction and therefore increases the value of that fraction.

e. Work of the board may be delegated to committees and the minority-elected director may not be named to committees.

f. The board may be "stage managed" so that all important decisions are made beforehand through informal discussions that do not include the minority-elected director. The meeting thereafter is entirely pro forma, without discussion, and conducted with a "quick gavel."

D. PROXY VOTING

A proxy is the grant of authority by a shareholder to someone else to vote his shares. The relationship is one of principal and agent. Depending on the context, the term "proxy" may refer to the piece of paper granting the authority, to the grant of authority itself, or to the person holding the authority. The RMBCA uses the term "proxy" in the last sense; it uses the phrase "proxy appointment" in the first sense and "appointment form" in the second sense. See RMBCA § 7.22.

1. PREVALENCE

Voting by proxy is the norm in publicly held corporations where the large number of shareholders would often make personal voting completely impractical. The use of proxies in such corporations is regulated by the Securities and Exchange Commission; such regulation is described below in part XII. Voting by proxy is less universal but still widely used in closely held corporations when a shareholder will not be personally present at a meeting.

2.   FORMAL REQUIREMENTS

A proxy appointment must be in writing. Under many statutes a proxy appointment is valid for eleven months only, thus necessitating a new solicitation for every annual meeting. Under RMBCA § 7.22(c) a proxy appointment is valid for a longer period if specified in the appointment form (but such an appointment would normally be revocable).

3.   REVOCABILITY

Most proxy appointments are revocable. Where revocable, the act of revocation may consist of any action inconsistent with the continued existence of the grant of authority.

Example: A shareholder executes a proxy appointment form solicited by management on April 1. Four days later he executes a competing appointment form on behalf of an insurgent group. The later appointment revokes the earlier one and the shares may be voted by the proxy named by the insurgent faction.

Example: A shareholder executes an appointment form but later decides to attend the meeting in person. If she attempts to vote in person, her act constitutes a revocation of the earlier proxy appointment.

a.   A proxy appointment is revocable even if it is stated to be irrevocable or a consideration for the appointment is stated. *Stein v. Capital Outdoor Advertising, Inc.,* 159 S.E.2d 351 (N.C. 1968).

   Example: A shareholder executes an appointment form that states it is irrevocable for five years. The appointment is valid for five years under the RMBCA if it is not revoked, which it may be at any time.

   Caveat: A purchased vote is generally thought to be against public policy and unenforceable. Case law involving a purchased vote has invalidated the proxy appointment but the cases are not numerous. In *Schreiber v. Carney,* 447 A.2d 17 (Del.Ch. 1982), the court refused to invalidate an arrangement in which a major shareholder contracted, for a consideration, to vote its shares in the same manner as a majority of the independent shareholders. There was full disclosure of the arrangement to the independent shareholders.

b.   To be irrevocable a proxy appointment must (i) state that it is irrevocable; and (ii) be "coupled with an interest." Examples of appointments that are "coupled with an interest" include:

1)   A proxy who is a pledgee under a valid pledge of the shares;

2) A proxy who is a person who has agreed to purchase the shares under an executory contract of sale;

3) A proxy who is a person who has lent money or contributed valuable property to the corporation;

4) A proxy who is a person who has contracted to perform services for the corporation as an officer; and

5) A proxy appointment given in order to effectuate the provisions of a valid pooling agreement (described in the following part).

c. Some courts have upheld irrevocable proxy appointments that do not squarely fall within any of the above categories or meet the above requirements. Some statutes define the five situations described above as the only ones in which an irrevocable proxy appointment may be recognized.

E. SHAREHOLDER VOTING AGREEMENTS

Agreements between shareholders that they will vote their shares cooperatively or as a unit are generally enforceable. RMBCA § 7.31.

1. SCOPE OF VALID SHAREHOLDERS AGREEMENTS

Shareholder voting agreements, often called "pooling agreements," are valid so long as they relate to issues, such as the election of directors, on which shareholders may vote. *E. K. Buck Retail Stores v. Harkert*, 62 N.W.2d 288 (Neb. 1954); *Weil v. Beresth*, 220 A.2d 456 (Conn. 1966); *Ringling Bros.-Barnum & Bailey Combined Shows, Inc. v. Ringling*, 53 A.2d 441 (Del. 1947). If the agreement deals with issues that are within the discretion of directors, the agreement may be invalid on the basis of principles discussed earlier (see: part VI).

Example: Two shareholders agree that they will vote for each other as directors, that they will use their best efforts to elect one as president and the other as secretary, and that each will be paid a salary of $1,000 per month. The first agreement is a valid pooling agreement; the other two are invalid unless enforceable under close corporation statutes. The distinction is that valid shareholder agreements may relate only to matters that are within the province of shareholders under the statutory scheme. Whether or not such an agreement is severable depends on the language of the agreement and the extent to which the valid portions standing alone are sufficient to effectuate the underlying purpose of the agreement.

2. FORMAL REQUIREMENTS

A few states have adopted statutes regulating pooling agreements, often limiting the period during which a pooling agreement may continue (e. g., to ten years), requiring that copies of the pooling agreement be deposited at the principal office of the corporation, and so forth. However, in most states, the pooling agreement is a contractual voting device that may continue indefinitely.

3. DETERMINATION OF HOW POOLED SHARES SHOULD BE VOTED

Pooling agreements may provide directly for the manner in which shares are to be voted, that is, for or against a specified proposal or motion. Or such matters may be the subject of subsequent negotiation and decision of the shareholders with some method of determining how the shares are to be voted in the event of a failure to agree. Resolution of disagreements is usually by arbitration, an arbiter, or by a decision of some person mutually trusted by all the participants.

4. ENFORCEMENT OF POOLING AGREEMENTS

Enforcement of a pooling agreement creates special problems since the shares are registered in the names of the individual shareholders on the books of the corporation.

a. Many courts will enforce a pooling agreement by decreeing specific performance. However, in one leading case the Delaware Supreme Court enforced a pooling agreement by disqualifying the shares sought to be voted in violation of the agreement. *Ringling Bros.-Barnum & Bailey Combined Shows, Inc. v. Ringling*, 53 A.2d 441 (Del. 1947). The effect of this was to utterly defeat the purpose of the agreement since the disqualified votes were essential for control of the corporation.

b. Some state statutes specifically address the enforcement issue by authorizing specific performance of pooling agreeements. See RMBCA § 7.31(b).

c. New York makes irrevocable a proxy granted in connection with a pooling agreement. To take advantage of this enforcement device, the agreement probably should contain specific reference to the irrevocable nature of the proxy appointment, and should designate who may exercise the irrevocable proxy and under what circumstances.

F. VOTING TRUSTS

Voting trusts are formal arrangements by which shares are registered in the name of one or more voting trustees on the books of the corporation. Voting trust agreements usually provide that all dividends or other corporate distributions pass through to the beneficial owners of the shares so that all attributes of ownership other than the power to vote remain in the beneficial owners. Voting trusts are thus a device by which the power to vote may be temporarily but irrevocably severed from the beneficial title to shares. Trustees may issue voting trust certificates to represent the beneficial interests; these certificates may be traded much as shares of stock are traded.

1.   COMMON LAW ATTITUDE

At common law there was great suspicion of voting trusts. While this attitude has been partially reversed by state statutes specifically recognizing and validating such trusts, some of the rules discussed below can be traced to early judicial hostility to the voting trust device. See generally *Tankersley v. Albright*, 514 F.2d 956 (7th Cir. 1975), refusing to grant summary judgment on the validity of a common law voting trust.

On the other hand there has been some recognition that a voting trust should be viewed as simply another control mechanism that may in certain situations be the subject of abuse but generally is not more subject to criticism than other control devices. This perspective is most clearly set forth in *Oceanic Exploration Co. v. Grynberg*, 428 A.2d 1 (Del. 1981).

2.   STATUTORY REQUIREMENTS

State statutes uniformly recognize the validity of voting trusts that meet statutory requirements. See RMBCA § 7.30. The most common such requirements are the following:

a.   The agreement may not extend beyond ten years.

b.   The agreement must be in writing.

c.   A counterpart of the agreement must be deposited with the corporation at its registered office, to be subject to the same right of inspection by (i) shareholders or (ii) holders of a beneficial interest in the trust, that is provided a shareholder to inspect books and records of the corporation.

d.   Some states have imposed the further requirement that the essential purpose of the trust must be a proper one. Such a requirement probably serves little substantive purpose since carefully prepared testimony may validate a trust otherwise vulnerable while an unusually forthright or honest witness may inadvertently give testimony that may lead to invalidation of the entire trust.

> ***Example:***   The purpose of securing control of, or lucrative employment with, the corporation is not a proper purpose, and a trust formed for this purpose is invalid in some states.

> ***Example:*** The purpose of assuring the continued benefit of skilled and experienced management to the corporation is a proper purpose and a trust created for this purpose would probably be valid in the same state.

e. Because of the common law attitude toward voting trusts, discussed above, a voting trust agreement that fails to comply with all statutory requirements is considered invalid in its entirety in most states. Further, an arrangement that has most of the characteristics of a voting trust must fully meet these requirements if it is to be upheld, even though it is formally a voting agreement or proxy arrangement rather than a trust. *Abercrombie v. Davies*, 130 A.2d 338 (Del. 1957). Even though these requirements are basically simple ones that may be easily complied with, a number of cases have arisen in which these requirements have been ignored.

f. A voting trust may be set aside if later events cause its essential purpose to fail. *Selig v. Wexler*, 247 N.E.2d 567 (Mass. 1969).

3. USES OF VOTING TRUSTS

Voting trusts may be used for a wide variety of purposes, including:

a. The preservation, retention or securing of control in a closely held corporation.

b. Assurance of temporary stability in control of a corporation coming out of bankruptcy or receivership or being divested from another corporation pursuant to the anti-trust laws. *Brown v. McLanahan*, 148 F.2d 703 (4th Cir. 1945).

c. Elimination of a troublesome shareholder from control of a corporation; sometimes imposed by creditors as a condition of securing needed financing for the corporation.

4. VOTING TRUSTS IN PUBLICLY HELD CORPORATIONS

Voting trusts are generally considered to be inconsistent with basic concepts of corporate democracy in corporations with publicly traded securities. The New York Stock Exchange, for example, will usually refuse to list for trading a security that is partially held in a voting trust.

5. POWERS OF TRUSTEES OF VOTING TRUSTS

The power of trustees to vote on fundamental corporate changes has given rise to some litigation. The issue may depend on the specific language of the voting trust, *Clarke Memorial College v. Monaghan Land Co.*, 257 A.2d 234 (Del.Ch. 1969), though some decisions have found equitable limitations on the ·

power of trustees to approve damaging fundamental changes despite clear and broad language. *Brown v. McLanahan*, 148 F.2d 703 (4th Cir. 1945).

G. CLASSES OF SHARES AS A VOTING DEVICE

A device that permits the effective divorce of voting power from the ownership of a significant financial interest in the corporation without restriction or limitation is the creation of classes of shares with disproportionate voting and financial rights. In most states, no limitation is placed on the creation of classes of shares without voting rights, with fractional or multiple votes per share, with power to select one or more directors, and with limited financial interests in the corporation. RMBCA § 6.01. As a result classes of shares offer the maximum degree of flexibility and adaptability.

Example: Two shareholders each own 50 per cent of the stock of a corporation. After a series of fights or disagreements, they agree to restructure the corporation so that each shareholder will hold all the shares of one class of shares with the power to elect two directors. In addition a third class of shares, consisting of one share, with the power to elect one director, is issued to the corporation's attorney. The third class has a par value of $10 per share, is not entitled to receive dividends, and may receive only its par value of ten dollars upon dissolution of the corporation. A leading case has held that a class with such limited financial rights is nevertheless a valid class of shares. *Lehrman v. Cohen*, 222 A.2d 800 (Del. 1966).

Example: A corporation is to have two shareholders, one putting in $100,000, the other $50,000. They desire to share equally in control but in the ratio of their contributions (2:1) for financial purposes. The attorney suggests that an equal number of shares of two classes of common stock, Class A common and Class B common, be authorized. Each class is entitled to elect two directors, but the dividend and liquidation rights of the Class A are twice those of Class B. The corporation then issues all the Class A common to one shareholder for 100,000 dollars and all the Class B common to the other shareholder for 50,000 dollars. If shares with multiple votes per share are authorized in the particular state, the shares may be identical in all financial respects, with the class received by the smaller contributor having two votes per share.

Example: A minority shareholder wishes to be assured of being treasurer of the corporation and to have a veto over all amendments to the articles of incorporation. The attorney suggests that a special class of common shares be issued to the minority shareholder, and the articles of incorporation provide that (1) the treasurer must be a holder of that class of shares, and (2) the articles may be amended only by an affirmative vote of two-thirds of each class of shares, voting by classes. In other respects the classes have equal rights.

Example: There are three shareholders, each contributing the same amount of capital, but *C* is also contributing the basic idea and wants the same voting power as *A* and *B* combined. To effectuate this structure, voting and non-voting common shares (with equal dividend and liquidation rights) are issued in the following amounts:

	Voting	Non-Voting
A	50	50
B	50	50
C	100	–0–

Somewhat the same result can be obtained by the use of non-voting preferred shares or indebtedness rather than non-voting common shares.

Example: *A, B,* and *C* are each contributing the same amount of capital, but *A* wants to be sure that *B* and *C* will not combine to oust him and cut off his income. The attorney suggests that *A* execute a five-year employment contract with the corporation guaranteeing him the specified income, renewable for a second five years at the option of *A*. To assure that *A* will be assured of a right to participate in the board deliberations, the attorney suggests that three classes of stock be created, each with the power to elect one director.

H. SHARE TRANSFER RESTRICTIONS

Share transfer restrictions are contractual restrictions on the free transferability of shares. They are increasingly the subject of statutory recognition. See RMBCA § 6.27. They serve important functions in modern corporate practice.

1. USE IN CLOSELY HELD CORPORATIONS

In the closely held corporation share transfer restrictions typically constitute contractual obligations to offer shares either to the corporation or to other shareholders, or to both successively, on the death of the shareholder or before his selling or disposing of the shares to outsiders.

a.   The restriction may take the form of—

1)   An option in the corporation or shareholders to purchase at a designated or computable price. *Allen v. Biltmore Tissue Corp.,* 141 N.E.2d 812 (N.Y. 1957) (purchase option at original purchase price enforceable).

2)   A mandatory buy-sell agreement obligating the corporation or shareholders to purchase the shares at a designated or computable price.

3)   A right of first refusal, giving the corporation or the shareholders an opportunity to meet the best price the shareholder has been able to obtain from outsiders.

b.   The choice between these three forms of share transfer restrictions depends on the business needs of the shareholders.

Example: An option or a right of first refusal does not guarantee the shareholder a specified price, whereas a buy-sell agreement does.

Example: Because of the limited marketability of small blocs of minority shares in a closely held corporation, a right of first refusal is not likely to be meaningful since no outsider is likely to offer to purchase such a bloc.

c.   Share transfer restrictions enable participants in the venture to decide who shall participate in the venture. In effect they achieve the corporate equivalent of the partnership notion of *delectus personae*.

d.   Share transfer restrictions ensure a stable management and protect against an unexpected change in the respective proportionate interests of the shareholders which might occur if one shareholder is able to quietly purchase shares of other shareholders.

e.   Share transfer restrictions may materially simplify the estate tax problems of a deceased shareholder.

1)   If the corporation or other shareholders are obligated to purchase the shares owned by the deceased shareholder (a buy-sell agreement) the estate is assured that a large, illiquid asset will be reduced to cash.

2)   Either an option or a buy-sell agreement, if established in good faith, will be accepted by the Internal Revenue Service as establishing the value of the shares for Federal estate tax purposes, thereby avoiding a probable dispute with the tax authorities since closely held shares have no market on which value can be based and the Internal Revenue Service is apt to take an optimistic attitude as to the value of such shares in the absence of an agreement establishing the value.

> ***Example:*** *A* and *B* are brothers without families of their own. They enter a contract by which each agrees that the corporation will buy the shares of a deceased shareholder at a price of $50 per share. *A* dies at a time when it is clear that the shares are worth much more than $50.00. The agreement is not binding on the Internal Revenue Service since the contract indirectly benefits the natural object of the decedent's bounty and appears to be a device to minimize estate taxes.

> ***Example:*** *A* and *B* are unrelated individuals each with families that include small children. They enter into the same agreement. If the agreement is binding on the shareholder's estate (as it normally would be) it is also binding on the Internal Revenue Service.

f. Share transfer restrictions may be imposed to ensure the continued availability of the subchapter S election, e. g., to ensure that the thirty-five shareholder maximum is not exceeded and that shares are not transferred to an ineligible shareholder which would cause the loss of the subchapter S election.

g. Share transfer restrictions in the form of buy-sell agreements may be used as a device to resolve deadlocks arising from equal voting power being held by two persons or factions.

2. USE IN PUBLICLY HELD CORPORATIONS

In a publicly held corporation, share transfer restrictions are used to prevent violations of the Federal Securities Act where the corporation has issued unregistered shares pursuant to an exemption which would be lost if the shares are transferred to ineligible persons.

a. Share transfer restrictions are imposed on the unregistered shares, warning that transfers are prohibited, and instructions are placed with the transfer agent to refuse to accept unregistered shares for transfer, unless the transferee can establish that the transfer will not cause loss of the exemption.

b. Share transfer restrictions in publicly held corporations thus usually take the form of flat prohibitions on transfer unless the transferor can establish that the transfer is consistent with retention of the exemption. Typically, this requires an opinion of counsel, affidavits by the purchaser or transferee, and possibly the acceptance of further restrictions on transfer by the purchaser or transferee.

c. Shares subject to restrictions on transfer are called "restricted securities." A corporation may at the same time have securities that are publicly traded and otherwise indistinguishable from restricted securities. Rule 144 under the Securities Act of 1933 is the principal rule establishing when restricted securities may be sold on the public market; it basically establishes a two-year holding period requirement.

3. OTHER USES

Share transfer restrictions may be imposed where there are substantive limitations on who may be a shareholder or where governmental authorities wish to review, and possibly limit, who is participating in the ownership of a business.

Example: It may be unethical for persons who are not attorneys to share in the profits of a law practice. A professional corporation that is engaged in the practice of law may therefore impose share transfer restrictions prohibiting the conveyance or transfer of shares to a person who is not an enrolled attorney.

Example: The New York Stock Exchange for many years reserved the right to determine who may participate in the ownership of brokerage firms. This restriction was usually imposed by a share transfer restriction that prohibited transfers of shares of brokerage firms to persons without the prior consent of the Exchange. *Ling and Co. v. Trinity Sav. and Loan Ass'n,* 482 S.W.2d 841 (Tex. 1972).

4. LEGAL REQUIREMENTS WITH RESPECT TO SHARE TRANSFER RESTRICTIONS

Share transfer restrictions are restraints on alienation and many courts have stated that they therefore should be strictly construed, though a trend toward a more liberal approach appears to be developing.

Example: An option or buy/sell agreement that applies to sales or donations of shares to third persons will usually not be violated by a transfer or gift to children or grandchildren.

Example: A restriction against sales "to the public" may not prohibit a sale to another shareholder.

Example: A prohibition against sale to an "officer-stockholder" may not prohibit a sale to a corporation owned by an officer-stockholder.

Example: A restriction without specific language of survivability may expire on the death of a shareholder. *Vogel v. Melish,* 196 N.E.2d 402 (Ill.App. 1964).

a.   At common law, the validity of a share transfer restraint depends on whether it "unreasonably restrains or prohibits transferability." An "unreasonable" restraint may be apparent on the face of the restraint or it may be found in the circumstances in which the restraint is applied.

Example: An outright prohibition on transfers of shares is invalid.

Example: A restriction imposed by bylaw or charter amendment cannot apply to previously outstanding shares unless the particular shareholder assents to the restriction. *B & H Warehouse, Inc. v. Atlas Van Lines Inc.*, 490 F.2d 818 (5th Cir. 1974). [There is some contrary authority]. RMBCA § 6.27(a), second sentence, codifies the result reached in *B & H Warehouse.*

Example: Restrictions which prohibit transfers unless consent of the directors or other shareholders is first obtained are of doubtful validity since consent may be arbitrarily withheld. *Rafe v. Hindin*, 288 N.Y.S.2d 662 (App.Div. 1968) (consent arrangement invalid).

b.   The narrow common law view about the enforceability of share transfer restrictions has caused several states to adopt legislation broadening the types of restrictions that may be enforced.

1)   Delaware, for example, provides that a restriction may validly require the prior consent by the corporation or the holders of a class of securities to any proposed transfer, the approval of the proposed transferee by the corporation, or the prohibition of a transfer to designated persons or classes of persons, if such designation "is not manifestly unreasonable." Del.Gen.Corp.Law § 202.

2)   RMBCA § 6.27 follows the broad outline of the Delaware statute. RMBCA § 6.27(c) authorizes share transfer restrictions to maintain the legal status of the corporation (e.g. under subchapter S or the integrated close corporation statutes), to preserve exemptions under securities laws, or "for any other reasonable purpose." Share transfer restrictions in the form of buy/sell or option agreements are expressly authorized without limitation [RMBCA §§ 6.27(d)(1), (d)(2)] while consent restrictions [RMBCA § 6.27(d)(3)] and prohibitory restrictions [RMBCA § 6.27(d)(4)] are permitted so long as they are not "manifestly unreasonable."

c.   There is no outer limitation on the duration of share transfer restrictions. If the restriction is a traditional option or buy-and-sell agreement, it is probable that the restriction remains enforceable without regard to the rule against perpetuities or similar notions of "reasonableness."

1)   Valid restraints normally continue so long as the need or justification for them exists.

2)   Share transfer restrictions may terminate by:

(A)   Express agreement of the shareholders involved.

Example: All shareholders decide to sell their shares to an outside purchaser despite a restriction against such sales. The restriction is abandoned by agreement.

(B)   Abandonment or disuse.

Example: Shares are sold or transferred by two or three shareholders in isolated transactions without compliance with the restrictions and without objection by the various parties. The restrictions probably have been abandoned and later sales or transfers may be made free of the restrictions.

d.   Proper formalities must be followed when creating valid share transfer restrictions if they are to be binding on persons who may be unaware of them.

1)   Most restrictions appear in the articles of incorporation or bylaws of the corporation, though they may also be imposed by contract between the corporation and shareholders, or among the shareholders themselves. RMBCA § 6.27(a), first sentence.

2)   Statutes often require that a reference to a restriction appearing in articles or bylaws be placed or "noted" on the face or back of share certificates subject to the restriction. RMBCA § 6.27(b).

(A)   Article Eight of the Uniform Commercial Code adds that the reference or notation on the shares must be "conspicuous" if the restriction is to be enforceable against a person without actual knowledge of the restriction. RMBCA §§ 6.27(b), 1.40(3) contain the same requirement.

Example: A printed heading in capitals or larger of other contrasting type or color is "conspicuous" under the UCC and RMBCA.

(B) A person who knows of the valid restriction before he buys the shares is bound by the restriction, whether or not the above procedural requirements have been followed. RMBCA § 6.27(b), last sentence.

3) Copies of restrictions appearing in contracts may have to be filed with the corporation and be available for inspection under the statutes of some states.

5. TO WHOM OPTION OR BUY–SELL RESTRICTIONS SHOULD RUN

Share transfer restrictions that constitute option or buy/sell agreements to purchase the shares will usually run either to the corporation or to some or all of the shareholders. RMBCA §§ 6.27(d)(1), (d)(2), however, allows them to run to "the corporation or other persons (separately, consecutively, or simultaneously)". The choice is a matter of convenience.

a. The advantages of restrictions running to the corporation are:

1) The corporation may be able to raise the necessary cash more easily than the shareholders individually.

2) The proportionate interests of the remaining shareholders are necessarily unaffected by a corporate acquisition of shares.

3) If life insurance is to be used to provide funds to purchase shares on the death of a shareholder, it is usually simplest to have the corporation pay the premium and own the policies on the lives of each shareholder rather than having each shareholder attempt to insure the life of every other shareholder.

b. If the restriction runs to the corporation but the corporation lacks the necessary capital to lawfully repurchase the shares at the time the repurchase is to be made, the restriction may be unenforceable. In this situation, the agreement may require the shareholders or some of them to agree to buy the shares if the corporation is not legally permitted to do so.

c. In an option arrangement running to the corporation, the corporation may decline to purchase, and anticipated control arrangements may be adversely affected. Interested shareholders may generally participate in the decision whether or not the corporation should purchase and may vote their own self-interest. *Boss v. Boss*, 200 A.2d 231 (R.I. 1964).

d. A disadvantage of having share transfer restrictions run to other shareholders is that one or more of the shareholders may be unable or unwilling to purchase their allotment of shares.

1)   In this situation, the proportionate interests of the remaining shareholders will be affected if some purchase and some do not.

    (A)   The agreement may provide that shares not purchased should be reoffered proportionately to the remaining shareholders, even though the proportionate interests of the shareholders are changed thereby.

    (B)   In the absence of such a reoffer requirement it is likely that all unpurchased shares would be considered free of all repurchase obligations.

2)   An offer made simultaneously to all the shareholders may be withdrawn if some decline to accept. *Helmly v. Schultz*, 131 S.E.2d 924 (Ga. 1963).

3)   If the number of shareholders is large the mechanics of having restrictions run to shareholders become complicated, and it usually is preferable for the restrictions to run to the corporation.

e.   A shareholder may not always desire that his shares be offered proportionately to the other shareholders.

Example: A controlling shareholder with a son and daughter who are minority shareholders may wish to provide that all shares be first offered to his son and then to his daughter (or vice versa) rather than be offered proportionately. In this situation, the share transfer restriction is part of the shareholder's testamentary plan of disposition of his property.

6.   ESTABLISHMENT OF PRICE IN OPTION OR BUY–SELL ARRANGEMENTS

The price provisions of shareholder option or buy-sell agreements often raise the most difficult and important problems in drafting such agreements.

a.   Closely held shares by definition have no market or quoted price, and one simply cannot refer to a "fair," "reasonable," or "market" price.

b.   Since it usually is impossible to know whose shares will be first offered for sale under such an agreement, the basic goal in establishing such a mechanism is to be as fair as possible.

c.   The following methods are often used to establish a purchase price:

1)   A stated price. *Allen v. Biltmore Tissue Corp.*, 141 N.E.2d 812 (N.Y. 1957).

2)   Book value.

3)   Capitalization of earnings.

4)   Best offer by an outsider.

5)   Appraisal or arbitration, either by trained, impartial appraisers or arbitrators, or by directors or other shareholders.

6)   A percentage of net profits to be paid for a specified number of years following the event which triggers the sale. Some of these methods are discussed briefly below.

d.   Any price fixed in the agreement or by periodic negotiation is enforceable in the absence of fraud, overreaching, or breach of fiduciary duty. *Yeng Sue Chow v. Levi Strauss & Co.*, 122 Cal.Rptr. 816 (App. 1975); *In re Mather's Estate*, 189 A.2d 586 (Pa. 1963).

> *Example:*   Two shareholders agree that the shares of the one who dies first shall be bought by the other at $1.00 per share. A court has enforced such an agreement even though at the time of death the shares were worth over $1000 per share.

> *Example:*   In the foregoing example a court may deem the grossly inadequate price to necessitate a careful examination of the circumstances surrounding the execution of the agreement. Indications of overreaching or reliance by one shareholder on the other may constitute grounds for setting the argument aside for "unconscionability" or "fraud."

> *Example:*   A contract provides for the periodic adjustment of a fixed purchase price. A willful refusal by a younger shareholder to renegotiate the price under such an agreement might be considered fraudulent. A convenient "forgetfulness" on the part of such a shareholder might also be grounds for setting aside the obsolete price. See *Collins v. Universal Parts Co.*, 260 So.2d 702 (La.App. 1972).

e.   "Book value" is by far the most popular method of valuation. This value may be computed by a simple division of a balance sheet figure by the number of outstanding shares and tends to increase as the profitability of the business increases. However, courts may order adjustments in this value to reflect reality and avoid a "blind adherence" to whatever figures are set forth in the books of the corporation. *Aron v. Gillman*, 128 N.E.2d 284 (N.Y. 1955); *Jones v. Harris*, 388 P.2d 539 (Wash. 1964).

1) Book value is based on the application of certain accounting conventions to corporate transactions and as a result book value may not be a realistic estimate of value.

Example: One accounting convention requires assets to be valued at historical cost rather than current market value. A corporation which owns real estate acquired decades earlier at a low price may have a book value that considerably understates the true liquidating value of the assets.

Example: Investments in readily marketable securities may be shown on the books at cost even though current market values may be obtained from the financial tables of any newspaper.

Example: Accounting conventions allow corporations to include certain things as assets which may never be realized on liquidation; for example costs of initial formation or of "good will" acquired in connection with the purchase of another business. It may be appropriate to eliminate such "assets" from the balance sheet before computing book value.

Example: If a corporation utilizes accelerated depreciation schedules for tax purposes, it may be desirable to specify that straight line depreciation should be used to compute book value for valuation purposes.

Example: If inventory is valued on a LIFO ["last-in first-out"] basis for tax purposes, it may be desirable to require the inventory to be valued at a more realistic figure before computing book value.

f. Appraisal of the value of closely held stock usually involves in part a capitalization of earnings.

Example: If a corporation has average earnings of $50,000 a year over the last three years, and it is reasonable to capitalize those earnings at ten per cent, the capitalized value of the corporation is $500,000 $\left(\frac{\$50,000}{0.10} = \$500,000 \right)$.

Example: If the reasonable capitalization ratio were eight per cent, the business would be valued at $625,000 (625,000 × .08 = 50,000); if it were fifteen per cent, it would be valued at $333,333 (333,333 × .15 = 50,000).

1) The most appropriate capitalization ratio may be justified by the appraiser on the basis of earnings ratios of comparable publicly held businesses, the appraiser's general experience with valuing businesses in the particular industry, or simply the appraiser's intuitive "feel" as to how risky a specific business is.

2) Valuation based on capitalization of earnings may also be affected by different assumptions about the level of average earnings in the future, and whether different assets should be capitalized at different rates.

g. An appraiser or arbitrator will usually take into account all the various possible methods of valuation. He may consider, for example, (i) book value, (ii) capitalized value, (iii) estimated liquidation value if the assets were sold and (iv) sales prices of shares in isolated transactions in the past. He may take an average of these values, or if three closely agree, may base his valuation on only those three.

h. After the value of the overall business is obtained, the per share value is usually obtained by a simple division by the number of outstanding shares. However, complications may arise if senior securities must be valued and whether a further discount from the per share value should be taken if the shares are an isolated minority bloc with no chance of sharing in control.

REVIEW QUESTIONS

VII–1. If a corporation does not impose larger quorum and voting requirements than specified in the statute, what is the minimum number of shares necessary to enact an ordinary resolution at a shareholders meeting?

VII–2. May a corporation create shares with more or less than one vote per share?

VII–3. What is the difference between record ownership and beneficial ownership?

VII–4.   Why does a corporation need to set a record date for voting at a meeting or for payment of dividend?

VII–5.   Cumulative voting permits minority representation on the board.

True _____   False _____

VII–6.   The opposite of cumulative voting is noncumulative voting.

True _____   False _____

VII–7.   In a struggle for control, shareholder A gives a proxy appointment to the management faction. A week later A receives a solicitation from the insurgent faction and also signs their proxy appointment form. Which appointment form will control?

VII–8.   A proxy appointment may be made irrevocable if it is supported by consideration and is stated to be irrevocable.

True _____   False _____

VII–9.   What is the difference between a pooling agreement and a voting trust?

VII–10.   Why are share transfer restrictions commonly used in closely held corporations?

VII–11.   Are share transfer restrictions ever used in publicly held corporations?

VII–12.   The president of Compliance Corp. called a special meeting of shareholders expressly for the purposes of considering a merger with Ready, Ltd., and such other matters as might come before the meeting. Notice to such effect was sent to all shareholders. At the meeting the holders of a majority of shares were present.

Two shareholder-directors, N. E. Gative and Ken Servative, voiced strong opposition to the merger. A shareholder then proposed that Gative and Servative be removed as directors without cause. This proposal was passed by a majority vote. L. I. Berl and Red Stamp were then elected as successor directors. The shareholders decided that the board should retain counsel and continue negotiation with Ready, Ltd., concerning the proposed merger. Several months later, the plan of merger was finalized, approved by the board of directors, and proposed to the shareholders of Compliance Corp. The plan received the necessary shareholder vote of both Ready, Ltd. and Compliance Corp.

Meanwhile, prior to the filing of the articles of merger, Gative and Servative commenced an action to enjoin the merger and for their reinstatement as directors. What result? [This question and answer is drawn from Ballantine, Problems in Law 236 (5th Ed. 1975).]

VII–13. The shareholders of D Corporation requested in writing that the president of the corporation call a meeting for the following purposes: (1) to vote upon a resolution endorsing the administration of the former president who had been removed by the directors and demanding that he be reinstated as president; and (2) to vote upon a proposal to hear charges against certain directors and vote upon their removal. The president refused to call the meeting on the ground that neither of the proposals was proper for a meeting of the shareholders. Will an order in the nature of mandamus lie to require the president to call the meeting?

VIII

DIRECTORS

Analysis

A. NUMBER AND QUALIFICATIONS OF DIRECTORS

In most states the board of directors may consist of one member or more. RMBCA § 8.03(a). While, historically, many states had residential or shareholding requirements for directors, these requirements have been largely eliminated. RMBCA § 8.02. The RMBCA states expressly that only individuals may serve as directors; in some European legal systems an entity may serve as a director but there appears to have been no recent attempt to broaden state statutes to permit this practice.

1. NUMBER

Historically, three directors were required and some states retain this requirement. Some states allow boards of one or two directors only where there are one or two shareholders.

   a. The number of directors is usually established in the bylaws; if the bylaws are silent the number is set as either the minimum permitted in the state or the number of initial directors set forth in the articles.

   b. The number of directors may be increased or decreased by express amendments to the bylaws, but a decrease does not have the effect of eliminating or shortening the term of any sitting director.

   Caveat: Since the directors have power to amend bylaws under the statutes of most states, the board in effect has power to determine its own size under the foregoing principles. RMBCA § 8.03(b) of the RMBCA and the statutes of a few states, however, impose outside limits on the extent to which a board of directors may utilize its power to amend bylaws to dramatically increase or decrease its own size without shareholder approval.

   c. Many publicly held corporations have created a variable-sized board of directors: the shareholders or the bylaws establish a maximum and minimum size and authorize the board of directors to determine the actual size within those limits from time to time. This practice gives the board of directors needed flexibility in deciding to add one or more specific individuals to the board when necessary or not to fill vacancies as they occur yet minimizes the possible manipulation of the size of the board to serve narrower purposes and preserves the ultimate power of the shareholders over the size of the board. RMBCA § 8.03(c) expressly recognizes this practice.

   d. Some cases have recognized that bylaws setting the number of directors may be amended informally.

> *Example:* The shareholders elect four directors when the bylaws specify that the board shall consist of only three directors. In some states, this constitutes an implied amendment of the bylaws. However, this is not a desirable practice since it injects future uncertainty as to the number of directors to be elected and reduces the value of the written bylaws.

B. MEETINGS, QUORUM, NOTICE AND RELATED MATTERS

Regular meetings of the board occur at the times specified in the bylaws. Special meetings may be called by the persons specified in the bylaws.

1. NOTICE

No notice of regular meetings is required. RMBCA § 8.22(a). Special meetings may be called upon two days notice unless a longer or shorter notice is required or permitted by the bylaws. RMBCA § 8.22(b).

2. QUORUM

A quorum of directors consists of a majority of the directors except that a greater number may be specified by the bylaws. RMBCA § 8.24(b) and the statutes of a few states permit the bylaws to reduce a quorum to one-third of the board of directors. A majority vote of those present at a meeting where a quorum is present is binding action. RMBCA § 8.24(c). Generally, only lawfully elected directors may be counted toward quorum or voting requirements. *Dillon v. Scotten, Dillon Co.*, 335 F.Supp. 566 (D.Del. 1971). Directors personally interested in the transaction may not be counted towards these requirements unless the articles specifically so provide. *Sterling v. Mayflower Hotel Corp.*, 93 A.2d 107 (Del. 1952).

a. RMBCA § 8.24(c) makes it clear that a board may act on a matter only if a quorum is present when the action is taken. Most state statutes are silent on this matter.

> *Caveat:* The rule for shareholders is that once a quorum is present the meeting may proceed to its conclusion and the withdrawal of one or more shareholders does not destroy the quorum. RMBCA § 7.25(b). This is the opposite to the rule established for directors in RMBCA § 8.24(c).

b. A quorum is unnecessary only where vacancies exist and the action to be taken is the filling of such vacancies. Depending on the language of the specific statute, this power may exist:

1) Only when the number of directors *in office* is less than a quorum; or

    2)   When the number of directors *acting* is less than a quorum even though the number *in office* is greater than a quorum. *Jacobson v. Moskowitz*, 261 N.E.2d 613 (N.Y. 1970).

> ***Example:*** A board consists of eleven members. A quorum is six. Because of deaths and resignations the number in office is five. Under both constructions, the five remaining directors may meet and fill the seven vacancies.

> ***Example:*** In the same board, the number in office is eight. However, the remaining directors are bitterly divided on a five-three basis and the three minority directors refuse to attend meetings. Under some statutes the five directors may fill the vacancies even though the three director-minority refuses to attend the meeting. It will be noted that in this example, the number of directors in office is more than a quorum. Under some statutes the power to fill vacancies in this situation could not be exercised at a meeting attended only by five members.

    3)   RMBCA § 8.10(a)(3) adopts position 1) above.

c.   Some courts have treated a willful refusal to attend a meeting as a breach of fiduciary duty. *Gearing v. Kelly*, 182 N.E.2d 391 (N.Y. 1962). However, other courts have recognized this tactic as part of a struggle for control and have held that it should not be treated as improper.

C. COMPENSATION

Directors traditionally serve without compensation, it being assumed that their financial interest in the corporation or feelings of prestige will encourage them to serve on a gratuitous basis. Increasingly, in publicly held corporations, directors are receiving significant and substantial compensation as inducements to serve and to devote substantial attention to corporate affairs. See RMBCA § 8.11.

D. REMOVAL AND RESIGNATION OF DIRECTORS

1. REMOVAL OF DIRECTORS

Directors may be removed by shareholders, with or without cause, under the statutes of most states. RMBCA § 8.08. Articles of incorporation, however, may limit the power of removal to removal for cause. Under the statutes of some states, a court may also remove a director for cause specified in the statute, upon the petition of a specified percentage of the shareholders.

RMBCA § 8.09 permits court removal for "fraudulent or dishonest conduct, or gross abuse of authority or discretion.".

a.   The power to remove directors without cause tends to assure fealty by the board to the majority shareholder.

b.   Many publicly held corporations have eliminated the power of shareholders to remove directors for cause as a defensive measure against unwanted takeovers. This provision is usually coupled with the staggering of the election of directors.

c.   Removal for cause by court action may be less expensive than a shareholders' proceeding in a publicly held corporation. This procedure may also be adopted in a closely held corporation where the director charged with misconduct declines to resign and possesses the voting power as shareholder to prevent his removal.

2.   RESIGNATION OF DIRECTORS
The resignation of directors in most states is not expressly covered by statute. RMBCA § 8.07 permits resignation either immediately or at a future date; a resignation at a future date permits the departing director to participate in the selection of his or her successor.

E. FILLING OF VACANCIES

Vacancies created by resignation, death or removal of a director, may be filled either by the board of directors or the shareholders. RMBCA § 8.10(a). Under older statutes, vacancies created by increasing the size of the board could only be filled by the shareholders, but most modern state statutes permit all vacancies to be filled by the board of directors without regard to the way they were created. See also part VIII, B 2(a).

F. HOLDOVER DIRECTORS

Directors serve for their term and until their successors are elected and qualified. RMBCA § 8.05(e). Thus, if directors are not elected at an annual meeting for any reason, or the required annual meeting is not held, the directors then in office "hold over" until their successors are selected. This principle often applies (1) in closely held corporations where meetings are held erratically, if at all, and (2) in deadlock situations where the shareholders are evenly divided and unable to elect successors. *Gearing v. Kelly*, 182 N.E.2d 391 (N.Y. 1962).

Example: *A* and *B* are the sole shareholders in a corporation, each owning fifty per cent of the shares. There are four directors, elected by straight voting, two in effect having been named by *A* and two by *B*. One of *A*'s directors dies or unexpectedly resigns, and the vacancy is validly filled by *B*'s directors with a person acceptable to *B* but not to *A*. The person so elected will remain in office indefinitely since in the next election for directors the election will be deadlocked. [To appreciate this, set up a mock election in which *B* casts votes for three or four directors].

Example: In the foregoing example, directors are to be elected by cumulative voting. By casting all his votes for two candidates, *A* will be able to restore the prior two-two division of the board and the hold-over director provision will have no application.

G.   REQUIREMENT THAT DECISIONS BE MADE AT MEETINGS

The common law rule was that the power invested in directors to control and manage the affairs of a corporation was not "joint and several," but "joint only," and that directors could take action only "as a body at a properly constituted meeting."

1.   RATIONALE
The theory underlying this rather peculiar rule was that shareholders were entitled to a decision reached only after group discussion and deliberation. Views may be changed as a result of discussion, and the sharpening of minds as a result of joint deliberation improves the decisional process.

2.   IMPLICATIONS
This rule led to several subsidiary conclusions:

a.   The independent, seriatim approval of an act by each director individually, is not effective directoral action. *Baldwin v. Canfield*, 1 N.W. 261 (Minn. 1879), mod. 1 N.W. 276 (Minn.).

b.   Directors may not vote by proxy.

c.   Formalities as to notice, quorum, and similar matters must be fully adhered to.

3.   MODERN STATUS OF THE RULE
The rigid requirement that all directoral decisions must be made at a duly convened meeting makes very little sense today when applied to a close corporation where all the shareholders are active in the business. In that situation even the requirement of a formal meeting is likely to be considered a meaningless formality. The rule also had undesirable consequences which led to its gradual softening.

a.   Rigid application of the doctrine often permits a corporation to use its own internal procedural defects as a sword to undo undesired transactions. E. g., *Mosell Realty Corp. v. Schofield*, 33 S.E.2d 774 (Va. 1945). This basic injustice is heightened because a person dealing with a corporation usually has no way of verifying that formalities were in fact completely and fully followed.

b.   As a result, the broad principle has been riddled by judicially created exceptions. The most common exceptions are "estoppel," "ratification," and "acquiescence." E. g., *Meyers v. El Tejon Oil & Refining Co.*, 174 P.2d 1 (Cal. 1946).

> ***Example:*** Even though informal directoral action may be ineffective to formally authorize a transaction, it may be considered acquiescence in and ratification of the very same transaction, thereby binding the corporation. *Sherman v. Fitch*, 98 Mass. 59 (1867); *Phillips Petroleum Co. v. Rock Creek Mining Co.*, 449 F.2d 664 (9th Cir. 1971); *Mickshaw v. Coca Cola Bottling Co.*, 70 A.2d 467 (Pa.Super. 1950).

c.   It is dangerous to assume that the historical principle that directors may act only at meetings is totally obsolete. However, it is probable that one or more of the exceptions will be found applicable in specific situations where it seems equitable to hold the corporation liable. The original rule will likely be applied when it appears that no benefit was received from the transaction by the corporation. *Hurley v. Ornsteen*, 42 N.E.2d 273 (Mass. 1942); *Mosell Realty Corp. v. Schofield*, 33 S.E.2d 774 (Va. 1945).

d.   Most state statutes allow a board of directors or committee to participate in a meeting by means of a conference telephone or similar communications equipment by means of which all persons participating in the meeting can hear each other at the same time. See RMBCA § 8.20(b).

1)   Such participation constitutes presence in person at a meeting. This provision may be of considerable practical usefulness where directors are widely scattered, or where one or more of them are distant from the location where regular meetings are held.

2)   The fact that specific statutory authorization was felt to be necessary for a common sense idea such as telephonic meetings shows that the common law rule that directors can act only in meetings has some continued vitality.

e.   Most state statutes now also permit directors to act by unanimous written consent without a formal meeting. RMBCA § 8.21.

    1)   Under these statutes, a written consent has the same effect as a unanimous vote.

        Caveat: An informal action, not evidenced by a written consent, has been held to be invalid on the ground that the statute has "preempted the field." *Village of Brown Deer v. Milwaukee,* 114 N.W.2d 493 (Wis. 1962).

    2)   This modest and sensible provision solves most problems created by the common law rule requiring directors' meetings.

H. DIRECTORS' DISSENTS TO ACTIONS

Directors are sometimes faced with the issue of responding to a majority decision to authorize the corporation to enter into transactions which the director feels to be precipitate, risky, or outright illegal. In some circumstances the director may be held personally liable even though he or she objected to the transaction and voted against it.

1.   **AVOIDANCE OF LIABILITY BY FILING DISSENT**
To avoid liability a director must make sure that his or her dissent appears in the written minutes since otherwise the director is presumed to have assented to the action and may be liable therefor. RMBCA § 8.24(d).

    a.   If the dissent is not recorded in the minutes the director must file a written dissent to such action as required by the statute. A typical provision requires that the notice be sent to the secretary of the meeting or the secretary of the corporation by certified mail within a short period after the meeting.

    b.   Filing of a statutory written dissent not only eliminates liability, and obviates later questions of proof but also may have a psychological effect upon the other directors who realize that at least one director considers the conduct sufficiently questionable as to seek legal protection.

    c.   Filing of a written dissent may also afford notice to shareholders or others examining the records that at least one director questioned the propriety of a specific transaction.

2.   **AVOIDANCE OF LIABILITY BY RELIANCE ON OPINION OF OTHERS**
Depending on the language of the specific state statute, a director may be able to avoid liability in some situations by showing that he or she relied on the opinion of others in good faith. RMBCA § 8.30(b). Generally, this defense is not available to a director who has actual knowledge about, or expertise with

respect to, the issue in question.   RMBCA § 8.30(c).   Statutes permit reliance on one or more of the following:

a.   The written opinion of legal counsel for the corporation (though, as a practical matter, reliable and unqualified written opinions may be difficult to obtain on questionable transactions).

b.   Financial reports prepared by the corporation or by its auditors or accountants.

c.   Statements by officers or employees of the corporation with respect to matters within their authority.

d.   Reports by committees of the board other than committees on which the director serves.

3.   RESIGNATION
The director fearing liability may resign as director, though if the resignation occurs after the objectionable transaction is approved, liability may be avoided only if the director files the appropriate dissent.

4.   OBJECTION TO NOTICE
A director waives objection to the notice of a meeting by attending the meeting, unless he or she attends for the sole purpose of objecting to the transaction of any business and does not participate in the business undertaken at the meeting.   Even minimal participation is likely to be construed as a waiver.   RMBCA § 8.23(b).

I.   COMMITTEES OF THE BOARD OF DIRECTORS

Where a board of directors is large, it may be convenient to appoint one or more committees to perform the functions of the board of directors.   RMBCA § 8.25.   The committee may specialize on one area of concern to the board, e. g., a committee on executive compensation, or may function as a substitute for the full board between meetings of the full board, i. e., an executive committee.

1.   COMMITTEES UNDER THE RMBCA
RMBCA § 8.25 authorizes the creation of committees of the board of directors to exercise functions of the board of directors.   This section applies only to committees of the board exercising directoral functions; it does not cover advisory committees that may consist of board or non-board members.

a.   A board committee may be created by a majority of the directors in office (or the larger number required by a supermajority provision if one has been adopted).

b.   A committee must have two or more members.

c.   The creation of a committee and the delegation to it of authority does not alone constitute compliance with the directors' statutory duty of care.

d.   RMBCA § 8.25(e) lists eight nondelegable functions that must be exercised by the full board. This list is not based on the traditional ordinary/ extraordinary matters distinction but is designed to prevent delegation of matters that have immediate and irrevocable effect (such as the declaration of a dividend), matters that may well become irrevocable without swift action, and matters that will cause changes of position by others that cannot be rectified. All other matters are delegable to committees of the board.

> *Example:*   Nondelegable functions include authorization of dividends, approval or recommendation to shareholders of fundamental actions such as mergers, amendments to articles of incorporation, and the like, amendment of bylaws, approval of reacquisitions of shares or the sale of shares, and the creation of classes or series of shares out of blank shares.

2.   EXECUTIVE COMMITTEE
An executive committee generally provides oversight over general corporate matters during periods when the board of directors is not sitting.

a.   Executive committees often consist only of directors who are employees or executives of the corporation.

b.   An executive committee usually may be created only if specific provision therefor appears in the articles of incorporation or bylaws. Under the Revised Model Business Corporation Act § 8.25, any committee, including an executive committee, may be created by a corporation unless the articles of incorporation or bylaws provide otherwise.

c.   Many state statutes specifically authorize the creation of an executive committee and contain express provisions with respect to its compensation and duties. The Revised Model Business Corporation Act makes an executive committee subject to the same rules and restrictions as any other committee. See paragraph 1 above.

d.   In older statutes that specifically refer to executive committees limitations on powers of executive committees may be included to ensure that there is little possibility of a "run away" committee.

e. Delegation of authority to an executive committee generally does not relieve the board of directors, or any member, of any responsibility imposed upon it or them.

3. AUDIT COMMITTEE

Most publicly held corporations have audit committees; such committees are now required by the New York Stock Exchange as a condition for listing shares on that exchange. Audit committees usually perform functions such as the following:

a. Recommend the accounting firm to be employed by the corporation as its independent auditors.

b. Consult with the accounting firm so chosen to be the independent auditors with regard to the plan of audit.

c. Review, in consultation with the independent auditors, the report of audit and the accompanying management letter of response, if any.

d. Consult with the independent auditors (often out of the presence of management) with regard to the adequacy of the internal accounting controls and similar matters.

4. NOMINATING COMMITTEES

An increasing number of publicly held corporations have nominating committees. A 1982 survey showed that nearly 80 per cent of publicly held companies had such committees, a remarkable increase in a relatively few years. The role of the nominating committees often depends on the board and its relation to the Chief Executive Officer (CEO). Such committees often perform some or all of the following functions:

a. Establish qualifications for directors.

b. Establish procedures for identifying possible nominees who meet these criteria.

c. Review the performance of current directors and recommend, where appropriate, that sitting directors be removed or not reappointed.

d. Recommend the appropriate size and composition of the board.

5. COMPENSATION COMMITTEES

An increasing number of publicly held corporations also have compensation. Again, their role depends on the board and its relation to the CEO. Such committees often have the following functions:

a. Review and approve (or recommend to the full board) the annual salary, bonus and other benefits, direct and indirect, of the CEO, other management directors and other designated members of senior management.

b. Review and submit to the full board recommendations concerning new executive compensation or stock plans.

c. Establish, and periodically review, the corporation's policies in the area of so-called management prerequisites.

d. Review compensation policies relating to members of the board of directors.

> *Caveat:* The audit, nominating and compensation committees have particular importance in assessing the balance of power between management and the board of directors in the publicly held corporation. As described subsequently (see part IX), the CEO in the past has often dominated the board of directors; the extent to which the board of directors has been able to develop an independence from the CEO varies widely from corporation to corporation. As the independence of the board increases, the power and importance of these committees has also increased.

6.   PUBLIC POLICY COMMITTEES

An increasing number of publicly held corporations have created public policy committees to review such matters as the charitable activities of the corporation, the role of the corporation in community affairs, political activities by the corporation (to the extent permitted by public policy), equal opportunity policies established by the corporation, and non-financial policies such as worker safety, environmental impact, and product safety.

REVIEW QUESTIONS

VIII–1.   Directors who are unavoidably absent should vote by proxy.

True _____   False _____

VIII–2.   Directors may only act collegially in meetings.

True _____   False _____

IX

OFFICERS

Analysis

A. CORPORATE OFFICERS AND THE SOURCES OF THEIR AUTHORITY

State corporation statutes usually contain only skeletal provisions dealing with corporate officers. A typical statute merely states that there shall be a president, a treasurer, a secretary, and (usually) one or more vice-presidents, and that any person may fill two or more offices simultaneously except the offices of president and secretary. The statutes also usually grant unlimited authority to the board to create such additional offices as the board deems appropriate. The officers of a corporation, and the functions they are to perform, are usually defined in the bylaws and resolutions of the board.

RMBCA § 8.40(a) does not require any designated officers except an officer performing the functions usually performed by the secretary. See RMBCA §§ 8.40(c), 1.40(20). Little purpose is served by statutorily designated titles and problems of implied or apparent authority may be thereby created. RMBCA § 8.40(d) permits any individual to hold two or more offices at the same time without limitation or restriction.

1.   AUTHORITY OF OFFICERS IN GENERAL
Corporate officers, including the president, have relatively little inherent power by virtue of their offices. The principal repository of inherent power to conduct the business and affairs of the corporation is in the board of directors, not the officers.

    a.   Corporate officers may draw authority from the following sources:

        1)   The statutes (to a limited extent).

        2)   The articles of incorporation (though provisions dealing with officers in this document are uncommon).

        3)   The bylaws (which usually outline the functions of officers in some detail).

        4)   General resolutions of the board granting authority to officers.

        5)   Specific resolutions of the board authorizing the corporate officers to enter into specific transactions reviewed and approved by the board.

    b.   In addition, amorphous doctrines such as implied authority, ratification or estoppel, may provide *de facto* authority to officers to bind their corporations on the basis of informal conduct or acquiescence.

2.   INHERENT AUTHORITY OF CORPORATE OFFICERS

The bylaws of the corporation usually describe in general terms the roles of traditional corporate officers. The brief descriptions that follow are taken from typical bylaw provisions.

a.   The president is "the principal executive officer of the corporation," and, subject to the control of the board, "in general supervises and controls the business and affairs of the corporation." He or she is the proper officer to execute corporate contracts, certificates for securities, and other corporate instruments.

b.   The vice president performs the duties of the president in his absence or in the event of his death, inability or refusal to act. Vice presidents act in the order designated at the time of their election, or in the absence of designation, in the order of their election. Vice presidents may also execute share certificates or other corporate instruments.

c.   The secretary has several different "housekeeping" functions: he or she keeps the minutes of the proceedings of shareholders and the board of directors, sees that all notices are duly given as required by the bylaws, is custodian of the corporate records and of the corporate seal, sees that the seal of the corporation is properly affixed on authorized documents, keeps a register of the names and post office addresses of each shareholder (if there is no transfer agent), signs, along with the president or vice president, certificates for shares of the corporation, and has general charge of the stock transfer books of the corporation if there is no transfer agent.

d.   The treasurer has "charge and custody of and is responsible for" all funds and securities of the corporation, and receives, gives receipts for, and deposits, all moneys due and payable to the corporation. The treasurer may be required to give a bond to ensure the faithful performance of his duties.

B.   NON–STATUTORY OFFICERS

Boards of directors or bylaw provisions may create new or different offices. Many corporations have assistant secretaries or treasurers. In others, the "president" may be a senior officer but subordinate to other officers such as "Chairman of the Board of Directors" or "Chief Executive Officer". Other officers often created are "Chief Financial Officer" (CFO), "Chief Legal Officer" (CLO), and "Chief Operations Officer" (COO). These various offices are sometimes created by specific provisions in the bylaws; more commonly they are discretionary with the board of directors, being created or eliminated by simple resolution.

C. DETERMINATION OF OFFICERS' AUTHORITY

A person dealing with a corporate officer who purports to represent the corporation generally must satisfy himself or herself of the officer's authority.

1. **ORAL REPRESENTATIONS BY OFFICER**

   Reliance on the officer's oral representations is hazardous because usually an agent's representations about his or her own authority are not binding on the principal.

2. **RELIANCE ON OFFICER'S TITLE**

   Reliance on the office, e. g., dealing with the "President" of a corporation, is also hazardous because the common law view is that such offices carry with them only very limited authority to bind the corporation.

   Example: The president of an oil drilling corporation orders 45 miles of $4\frac{5}{8}''$ plastic pipe. Without more, it cannot be determined whether or not such a transaction was within his or her actual or apparent authority; litigation may be necessary to establish the liability of the corporation.

   Example: If in the preceding example the corporation received and used the pipe it would be liable to pay for it under principles of quasi contract or unjust enrichment.

3. **RELIANCE ON CERTIFIED RESOLUTION**

   The simple and foolproof way to ensure that the corporation is bound by a transaction is to require the person purporting to act for the corporation to deliver, prior to the closing of the transaction, a certified copy of a resolution of the board of directors authorizing the transaction in question. The certificate should be executed by the secretary or an assistant secretary of the corporation, the corporate seal should be affixed, and the certificate should recite the date of the meeting.

   a. There is no reason to go behind the certificate and attempt to ascertain whether or not the stated facts are true. The corporation is estopped to deny the truthfulness of facts stated in the secretary's certificate, since keeping and certifying corporate records is within the actual authority of the secretary. *In re Drive-In Development Corp.*, 371 F.2d 215 (7th Cir. 1966).

   b. Since the binding nature of the certificate rests on an estoppel, an inquiry into the circumstances behind the certificate may be counterproductive since it may develop information that may destroy the basis of estoppel. On the other hand, if one knows (or should know) that the representations are untrue, one cannot rely on estoppel.

c.   The small size of many transactions may make any formality, including a certified resolution, uneconomic.

D. INHERENT AUTHORITY OF THE PRESIDENT

Laymen often believe that the president of a corporation has wide discretion to enter into not only ordinary business transactions, but extraordinary transactions as well.

1.   TRADITIONAL VIEWS

Most courts have held that this view is erroneous. The present state of the law is that the president has only limited authority which may not extend beyond minor, ordinary, routine transactions. *Black v. Harrison Home Co.*, 99 P. 494 (Cal. 1909); *In re Westec Corp.*, 434 F.2d 195 (5th Cir. 1970). The locus of power to approve more significant transactions is in the board of directors, not the president. *Schwartz v. United Merchants & Manufacturers, Inc.*, 72 F.2d 256 (2d Cir. 1934).

a.   This narrow construction of the president's authority may lead to injustice since persons relying on appearances may discover that their reliance was ill-advised.

b.   Also, persons aware of the rule are forced to demand an exhibit of the president's authority before dealing with him.

2.   CURRENT TREND

There is a general trend to broaden the implied authority of the president (or chief executive officer). Some courts have concluded that a president presumptively has any powers which the board could give him. Others have given him authority to enter into transactions "arising in the usual and regular course of business," and have construed that phrase broadly. However, the scope of this broadening of authority is uncertain in application.

Example: The corporate president hires a salesman on a commission basis that is customary in the industry. Most courts today would hold the corporation bound on the theory that hiring agents and employees is within the regular course of business.

Example: The president of the corporation negotiates a settlement of a lawsuit in which the corporation is a defendant which involves the payment of a material amount. It is doubtful whether the president may bind the corporation to such a settlement, and the board of directors should approve it. A similar rule applies to the decision to file a lawsuit. *Covington Housing Development Corp. v. City of Covington*, 381 F.Supp. 427 (E.D.Ky. 1974), *aff'd* 513 F.2d 630 (6th Cir. 1975).

Example: The president promises a 30 year old person a pension of $1,500 per year commencing in thirty years if he will leave his present employment and become an employee of the corporation. Such a promise may be within the inherent authority of the president. *Lee v. Jenkins Bros.*, 268 F.2d 357 (2d Cir. 1959).

E.   APPARENT AND IMPLIED AUTHORITY OF OFFICERS

Where the authority of a person purporting to act for a corporation has not been specifically created by action of the board of directors, the following doctrines may be available to a third person seeking to hold the corporation on a transaction entered into by the person in the corporate name.

1.   RATIFICATION

The board of directors of a corporation may learn that an officer has entered into a transaction in the past without being specifically authorized to do so. If the board does not promptly attempt to rescind or revoke the action previously taken by the officer, it is probable that the corporation will be bound on the transaction on a theory of "ratification." *Scientific Holding Co., Ltd. v. Plessey Incorporated*, 510 F.2d 15 (2d Cir. 1974). Ratification may arise merely from knowledge of the transaction and failure to disaffirm or rescind it, it is particularly likely to arise where the corporation retains some benefit from the transaction.

2.   ESTOPPEL OR UNJUST ENRICHMENT

When elements of retention of benefits by the corporation and/or known reliance by the third party on the existence of the contract are added, "estoppel" or "unjust enrichment" might be applied. "Estoppel" differs from "ratification" mainly in that attention is placed on reliance by third persons, and the inequitableness of permitting the corporation to pull the rug out from under such persons.

Caveat: These doctrines are most commonly applied in situations involving silence and acquiescence; they may, however, be applicable to affirmative conduct as well.

Example: A corporation may expressly ratify a transaction, or a corporation may be estopped to deny that a transaction was authorized if it expressly creates the appearance of authority but withholds actual authority.

Example: One or more directors know that a third person is relying on the authority of the president in approving a questionable transaction. If the directors do not speak up until after it turns out that the result of the transaction is unfavorable to the corporation, the failure to speak up promptly may constitute ratification. *Yucca Mining & Petroleum Co. v. Howard C. Phillips Oil Co.*, 365 P.2d 925 (N.M. 1961).

Caveat: Courts are reluctant to find ratification of an unauthorized act by an officer where the act is fraudulent, unfair to minority shareholders, or against public policy.

3.   IMPLIED AUTHORITY

Implied authority usually arises when a third person seeks to hold the corporation on a current transaction by showing that the directors accepted or ratified prior similar transactions in the past. The acquiescence of the board of directors indicates that an actual grant of authority was informally made. *Hessler, Inc. v. Farrell*, 226 A.2d 708 (Del. 1967). The same facts which support a finding of ratification of transaction A_1 may be used to find implied authority for a later similar transaction, A_2.

4.   APPARENT AUTHORITY

Apparent authority theoretically involves conduct on the part of the principal that leads a reasonably prudent third person to suppose that the agent has the authority he purports to exercise. The classic example of apparent authority involves the third person who knows that an officer has exercised authority in the past with the consent of the board of directors and continues to rely on the appearance of authority.

a.   Apparent authority involves conduct on the part of the *principal* [that is, the corporation] which creates the appearance of authority; a mere representation by a corporate officer that he possesses the requisite authority is not sufficient. However, relevant corporate conduct may consist of silence, or of acquiescence in and ratification of acts performed in the past.

b.   Apparent authority differs from implied actual authority: for apparent authority, the third person must show that he was aware of the prior acts or holding out and that he relied on appearances, while implied actual authority may be found even in the absence of knowledge on the part of the third person. However, the same conduct may often tend to prove either implied actual authority or apparent authority.

Example: A corporate president has purchased pipe from a supplier four times in the past; each time the corporation has routinely paid for the pipe. The fifth time, involving a transaction of the same general order of magnitude, the corporation declines to accept the pipe. In a suit for damages, a court may rest a decision against the corporation on either apparent authority or implied actual authority and may rely on the prior transactions to justify either conclusion.

F. FIDUCIARY DUTIES OF OFFICERS

Corporate officers and agents owe a fiduciary duty to the corporation of honesty, good faith, and diligence. The scope of an officer's or agent's obligation to the corporation is determined in part by the nature of his employment with the corporation. The duty of subordinate officers or agents may be somewhat narrower than the analogous duty of a director. See part G below.

1.   GENERAL DUTIES OF ALL OFFICERS OR AGENTS

An officer or agent should act for the sole benefit of the corporation and give to it his or her best uncorrupt business judgment. Full disclosure of possibly conflicting transactions may be required, and the officer or agent may hold in trust for the corporation profits made personally in competition with, or at the expense of, the corporation.

2.   LIABILITY FOR EXCEEDING AUTHORITY

A corporate officer or agent may also be liable to the corporation if he or she exceeds his or her actual authority and binds the corporation in a transaction with a third person. Such a transaction, of course, must be within the officer's or agent's apparent authority if the corporation is to be bound.

3.   STATUTORY LIABILITY

RMBCA § 8.42 imposes a duty of care on officers analogous to the duty of care imposed on directors. Other duties of officers are generally not codified.

G. OFFICERS' LIABILITY ON CORPORATE OBLIGATIONS

A corporate officer or employee who acts within the scope of his or her authority as the corporation's representative in a consensual transaction is not personally liable on the transaction if he or she acted solely as an agent. However, personal liability may be imposed on an officer or employee in several circumstances.

1.   EXPRESS GUARANTY

The officer or employee may expressly guarantee the performance by the corporation, intending to be personally bound on the obligation. Such a guarantee may be written or oral, and may or may not be supported by consideration, depending on the sequence of events and what is requested.

a.   Of course, to be enforceable, a promise must be supported by consideration.

b. Whether or not it must also be in writing usually depends on the proper scope of the provision of the statute of frauds dealing with promises to answer for the indebtedness of another.

Example: The president of a corporation makes an oral promise to a supplier of merchandise that she will personally agree to pay for goods if they are delivered. Such a promise might be enforced despite the statute of frauds on the theory that the president was the primary obligor.

2. CONFUSION OF ROLES

The officer or employee may not intend to be personally bound, but may in fact become so by creating the impression that he or she is negotiating on an individual rather than corporate basis, or the agreement is executed in such a way as to indicate personal liability.

a. If a person negotiates a transaction without disclosing that he or she is acting on behalf of a corporation, there is personal liability to the third person on general agency principles relating to undisclosed principals.

b. If the existence of the corporation is disclosed, joint liability of the corporation and the officer may be created because of carelessness in the manner of execution.

Example: An officer executes a document in the name of, and on behalf of, a corporation as follows:

ABC Corporation

By _____
                     President

The officer is not personally liable on the obligation since the form of execution unambiguously indicates that only the corporation is liable.

Example: In the previous situation, the form of execution is as follows:

ABC Corporation

_____, President

This form of execution is ambiguous since the corporation and the president may be either joint obligors or the president may have intended to sign only in a representative capacity. *Harris v. Milam*, 389 P.2d 638 (Okl. 1964). The word "president" does not resolve the ambiguity since it may be an identification of the individual obligor or an indication that he or she signed only as a representative.

Caveat: In cases involving ambiguous forms of execution, courts appear to be more willing to allow corporate officers to testify about the "real intention of the parties" in executing general contracts than in executing promissory notes.

3. STATUTORY LIABILITY

Liability may arise because imposed by statute. Failure to pay franchise taxes or to publish a notice upon incorporation may, in some circumstances, lead to individual as well as corporate liability on corporate obligations.

Example: The Internal Revenue Code of 1954 provides for a personal penalty of one hundred per cent of the tax if a corporation fails to pay over income taxes withheld from employees. This penalty tax may be imposed on "any person required to collect, truthfully account for, and pay over" the tax. (I.R.C. § 6672.)

H. CORPORATE "NOTICE" OR "KNOWLEDGE"

A corporation can "know" or "have notice of" something only if one or more persons who represent the corporation know or have notice of the thing. The issue is the circumstances in which personal knowledge will be imputed to the corporate entity.

1. GENERAL RULE

Usually, knowledge acquired by a corporate officer or employee while acting in furtherance of the corporate business or in the course of employment is imputed to the corporation.

Example: If the president knows of a transaction, the corporation ratifies it if the corporation accepts the benefits of the transaction, even though one or more directors or other officers may not know all the details.

Example: Service of process on an authorized agent of the corporation supports a default judgment against the corporation even though the agent fails to forward the papers to the corporation's attorney.

2. AGENT ACTING ADVERSELY TO PRINCIPAL

Difficult problems arise when it is sought to impute knowledge of an agent to the corporation if the agent is acting adversely to the corporation. Generally, information or knowledge may be imputed from an agent who has ultimate responsibility for the transaction to his corporation even if the agent is acting adversely to and in fraud of the corporation.

Example: A corporate president learns that a low level employee is defrauding the corporation and "cuts himself in on the action" by demanding a percentage of the fraudulent gains. The president's knowledge is imputed to the corporation even though the president does not disclose his knowledge to the directors.

3.   CRIMINAL CORPORATE RESPONSIBILITY

An agent's wrongful intention may be imputed to a corporation so that a corporation may be subject to civil or criminal prosecution, including prosecution for traditional crimes such as murder or rape. Of course, for the corporation to be prosecuted such acts must be connected with, or be in furtherance of, the corporation's business.

I.   TENURE OF OFFICERS AND AGENTS

Corporate officers and agents generally serve at the will of the person or board having authority to elect or appoint the officers or agents. Corporate officers are elected by the board of directors, and corporation acts generally provide that they may be removed by the board of directors with or without cause. RMBCA § 8.43(b). So far as agents appointed by the president or general manager are concerned, the power to discharge is implicit in the power to employ.

1.   EMPLOYMENT CONTRACTS IN GENERAL

An officer or agent may be given an employment contract, and removal of such an officer or agent may give rise to a cause of action for breach of contract.

a.   The mere election or appointment of an officer or agent, even for a definite term, does not of itself give rise to a contract right. RMBCA § 8.44(a).

b.   Corporate bylaws usually provide that specified named officers, such as the president, vice president, secretary, and treasurer, are to be elected by the board of directors for a term of one year. The RMBCA uses the term "appoint" for officers rather than "elect." Generally, such provisions do not limit the power of a corporation to grant an officer an employment contract extending beyond the term of his office since, despite the contract, the officer or employee may be relieved of his or her duties at any time. But see the sharply divided opinions of the New York Court of Appeals in *Staklinski v. Pyramid Elec. Co.*, 160 N.E.2d 78 (N.Y. 1959). Of course, the corporation may be liable for breach of contract for the premature termination of the employment period if such an officer is not retained in office. RMBCA § 8.44(b).

c. Such long-term employment contracts may be upheld on a parity with other long-term contracts, e. g., leases which are valid if approved by the board despite the fact that they "bind" subsequent boards of directors. *Staklinski v. Pyramid Elec. Co.*, 160 N.E.2d 78 (N.Y. 1959); *In re Paramount Publix Corp.*, 90 F.2d 441 (2d Cir. 1937).

d. If the board has power to amend the bylaws, as most boards of directors do, an employment contract for more than one year may be deemed to be an implied amendment of the bylaws by the board. *Realty Acceptance Corp. v. Montgomery*, 51 F.2d 636 (3d Cir. 1930). The board may first amend the bylaws and then enter into a long-term employment contract.

> *Caveat:* Some courts have invalidated long-term employment contracts as being inconsistent with bylaw provisions that limit the terms of officers. Such cases have not always considered whether the directors have the power to amend bylaws. E.g., *Pioneer Specialties, Inc. v. Nelson*, 339 S.W.2d 199 (Tex. 1960).

2. LIFETIME EMPLOYMENT CONTRACTS

The claim that a person has been given a lifetime employment contract by a corporation has been treated with hostility by courts. Such contracts are usually oral and arise within the context of a family-run business.

a. While such a contract is not within the one year provision of the statute of frauds, courts often feel that the factual basis for such an open-ended commitment is inherently implausible.

b. Such contracts may subject a corporation to a substantial liability which may run for a long and indefinite period during which circumstances may substantially change.

c. Most cases which have refused to enforce such arrangements have done so on the ground the officer making the arrangement had neither actual nor apparent authority to enter into such an arrangement. See: *Lee v. Jenkins Bros.*, 268 F.2d 357 (2d Cir. 1959).

3. DISCHARGE FOR CAUSE

An officer or employee with an employment contract may always be discharged for cause.

a. "Cause" may consist of facts of dishonesty, negligence, refusal to obey reasonable orders, refusal to follow reasonable rules, or a variety of other acts such as engaging in an unprovoked fight.

b.   In effect, such conduct constitutes a breach of an implied (or express) covenant in the employment contract.

c.   Of course, if an officer does not have an employment contract, it is irrelevant as a legal matter whether or not "cause" for discharge exists.

4.   COMPENSATION PATTERNS

Employees sometimes request that they be compensated on a basis that reflects (a) corporate earnings or profits or (b) the market behavior of the corporation's shares rather than at a flat rate. No particular legal problem is raised by such contracts so long as the total amount of compensation is not so excessive as to constitute waste. See: part XIV, D., infra.

a.   The major question arising with respect to bonus arrangements based on corporate earnings and profits usually is one of computation. Profits may be computed in various ways, and often differences are material. The simple phrase "net profits," for example, is often ambiguous and its meaning may be elusive.

b.   Corporate officers and employees may also be paid in shares of stock. More commonly, compensation is in the form of options to purchase shares or plans by which employees may purchase shares at advantageous prices. Such arrangements, which are designed to give employees a long time investment interest in their employer, are more common in publicly held corporations (where a market for shares exists) than in closely held corporations.

c.   Employment contracts for highly paid personnel often provide for deferred compensation, fringe benefits, reimbursement of business expenses, and other tax-related benefits. Such benefits may also be provided to lower-paid employees on a more limited basis.

d.   In closely held corporations, an employment agreement may be an integral part of the basic understanding between shareholders.

1)   Terms relating to employment are often placed in shareholders' agreements so that they will be binding on all the other shareholders as well as the corporation.

2)   If there is disagreement between majority and minority shareholders, in the absence of an employment agreement the majority may exclude the minority totally from the corporation and its business.

REVIEW QUESTIONS

IX–1.   The reason that most persons believe that the president of a corporation has considerable authority is that the president is the most important person within the corporation and owns the most shares. Does this view accurately reflect the power of a president in a corporation?

IX–2.   An officer of a corporation cannot be given an employment contract for a period that exceeds the term for which the person was elected.

True _____   False _____

IX–3.   M is the president of P Corporation. P Corporation entered into a contract with D Corporation (which owned ½ the stock of P Corporation) to distribute D Corporation's products. D Corporation failed to deliver the product. M suggested to the board of directors of P Corporation that suit be instituted against D Corporation. A resolution to such effect was defeated by a majority of P Corporation's board of directors. M then instituted suit against D Corporation on behalf of P Corporation. Did M have power to institute the action in light of the decision by P Corporation's board of directors?

IX–4.   A, the president of D Corporation, without the consent of D Corporation's board of directors entered into a contract with P Corporation for the purchase of 45 miles of $6\frac{5}{8}''$ gas pipe. D Corporation refused to accept the pipe and P Corporation sued for breach of contract. At the trial the judge charged the jury that the corporation is bound by the act of the president in signing a contract. Is the jury charge correct?

X

MANAGEMENT OF THE CLOSELY HELD CORPORATION

Analysis

A. CHARACTERISTICS OF A CLOSELY HELD CORPORATION

A "close corporation" or "closely held corporation" is a corporation with a few shareholders. In such a corporation unique management problems arise because of the relationship that necessarily exists among shareholders.

1. LACK OF MARKET FOR MINORITY SHARES
Since a close corporation has only a relatively small number of shareholders, there is no public trading in, or public market for, its shares.

    a.   Potential purchasers of minority blocks of shares usually must be found among present shareholders, or rarely, among outsiders willing "to take a gamble." As a result, the market for minority blocks of closely held shares is at worst non-existent and at best a buyer's market; there are few alternative purchasers and therefore little or no incentive for buyers to offer reasonable prices for shares. Minority shares may have some value because they constitute a nuisance and may serve as the basis for litigation.

    b.   If the shares offered for sale constitute a controlling interest, they are often readily salable to outsiders interested in running the business in which the corporation is engaged.

    c.   Transferability of shares is usually restricted by contractual restrictions limiting free transferability. A shareholder desiring to sell his shares may have to comply with the restrictions before offering shares to outsiders.

2. SHAREHOLDER PARTICIPATION IN MANAGEMENT
The management of a close corporation is usually associated with the principal shareholders, or with all the shareholders. The majority shareholders may, of course, name the board of directors, and through them, the officers and employees. Usually they will name themselves to all important (and the highest salary-paying) positions.

3. DIVIDEND POLICY
The majority shareholders usually have little interest in paying dividends. Rather, to minimize income taxes, they usually prefer to distribute earnings in the form of salaries or other payments to the shareholders, or some of them, that are tax deductible by the corporation.

4. INFORMALITY OF MANAGEMENT
The management often operates the business in an informal manner, typically more as though it were a partnership rather than a corporation. Closely held corporations are therefore often called "incorporated partnerships."

5. NO COMPULSORY DISSOLUTION

Minority shareholders in a close corporation ordinarily have no power to force a dissolution of the corporation. Dissolution may occur voluntarily under state statutes only with the consent of a majority or greater fraction of the outstanding shares. In this respect a close corporation differs significantly from a partnership, in which each partner possesses a general power to dissolve the partnership.

6. FREEZEOUTS AND SQUEEZEOUTS

The foregoing factors, in combination, may readily result in a minority shareholder being "locked in" the corporation for a long period of time, being excluded from management by other shareholders, receiving little or no return on his or her investment, and being unable to dispose of it at a reasonable price. Indeed, over a period of time in which deaths, withdrawals, or fallings out are likely, the possibility that adverse and hostile interests will develop within a closely held corporation is fairly high.

7. FIDUCIARY DUTIES BETWEEN SHAREHOLDERS

The traditional view is that shareholders have no fiduciary duty as such to each other, and that transactions that constitute freezeouts or squeezeouts cannot generally be attacked as a breach of a duty of loyalty or good faith towards each other.

a. Massachusetts has developed a fiduciary duty theory in this context. In *Donahue v. Rodd Electrotype Co.*, 328 N.E.2d 505 (Mass. 1975) the court analogized the close corporation to a partnership and held that a "strict" fiduciary duty existed and that controlling shareholders owed a duty of the "utmost good faith and loyalty" to the minority. This case was followed by *Wilkes v. Springside Nursing Home, Inc.*, 353 N.E.2d 657 (Mass. 1976) in which the court ordered reinstatement of a minority shareholder to the corporate payroll after he had been fired in connection with an attempted freezeout. The *Wilkes* court recognized, however, that the controlling faction needed "some room to maneuver" and that the group's "selfish interest" should be balanced against its fiduciary duty. In *Hallahan v. Haltom Corp.*, 385 N.E.2d 1033 (Mass.App. 1979), the court ordered shares secretly acquired by an equal co-owner of shares in an effort to change the balance of power to be returned to the seller at cost.

b. For a recent development in the *Donahue* saga see *Leader v. Hycor, Inc.*, 479 N.E.2d 173 (Mass. 1985) where the court permitted a "reverse stock split" at the ratio of one new share for each 4,000 old shares, with fractional shares to be purchased for cash at a specified amount per share. See also *68th Street Apts., Inc. v. Lauricella*, 362 A.2d 78 (N.J.Super. 1976), *Knaebel v. Heiner*, 663 P.2d 551 (Alaska 1983), *Russell v. First York Savings Co.*, 352 N.W.2d 871 (Neb. 1984).

c.   Other cases recognizing a fiduciary duty (but not following the implications of *Donahue*) include *Zidell v. Zidell, Inc.*, 560 P.2d 1091 (Or. 1977), and *Masinter v. WEBCO Co.*, 262 S.E.2d 433 (W.Va. 1980).

B.   CONTROL DEVICES IN CLOSELY HELD CORPORATIONS

In the absence of special statutory treatment of closely held corporations, such corporations must establish control devices through the use of traditional and accepted shareholder control techniques.

1.   TRADITIONAL CONTROL TECHNIQUES
The following control techniques, all discussed earlier, may appropriately be used as control devices in close corporations.

a.   Shareholder pooling agreements (see part VII, E).

b.   Voting trusts (see part VII, F).

c.   Irrevocable proxies (see part VII, D, 3).

d.   Share transfer restrictions (see part VII, H).

e.   Multiple classes of shares (see part VII, G).

f.   Employment agreements between shareholders and the corporation (see part IX, I).

2.   HIGH QUORUM AND VOTING REQUIREMENTS
A useful device in effectuating shareholder control devices is increased voting requirements in order to give minority interests effectively a veto power. This veto power may be applicable at the shareholder level, at the board of directors level, or both.

a.   In most states, it is possible to increase the percentage needed to approve a measure to any desired number up to and including unanimity. Usually unanimity is imposed, but in some circumstances a lesser percentage may be sufficient to give the desired veto power.

b.   It is usually important to increase both the quorum requirement and the minimum vote requirement to make sure that it is impossible for the corporation to act without the assent of the minority shareholder.

c.   If the quorum requirement has not been increased, it is sometimes possible for the minority shareholder to prevent action by staying away from the meeting if that makes it impossible to obtain a quorum.

C. DISSENSION AND DEADLOCK WITHIN THE CLOSE CORPORATION

"Dissension" refers to internal squabbles, fights, or disagreements; "deadlock" to control arrangements that effectively prevent the corporation from acting. A deadlock may be the logical consequence of creating veto powers in minority shareholders. Many small corporations at one time or another in their history are wracked by dissension or deadlock; advance planning may help to reduce or eliminate such disagreeable incidents.

1. DISSENSION

Dissension without a deadlock may arise in a corporation in which one faction has effective working control. Typically, the minority faction is in a weak position, and attorneys may counsel such shareholders to adopt obstructionist tactics, including litigation, in an effort to improve their bargaining position. Of course, such tactics are likely to increase the enmity and friction within the corporation.

2. DEADLOCKS

If neither faction has effective working control, the corporation may become deadlocked.

a.   A corporation is potentially subject to deadlock if:

1)   Two factions own exactly fifty per cent of the outstanding shares;

2)   There are an even number of directors, and two factions each have the power to select the same number; or

3)   A minority shareholder has retained a veto power in one of the ways previously described.

b.   A deadlock may occur either at the shareholders' level or at the directors' level.

1)   If the shareholders are deadlocked, the corporation may continue to operate under the guidance of the board of directors in office when the deadlock arose. The general rule is that directors serve until their successors are qualified; if the deadlock prevents a subsequent election, those in office remain.

Example: Two shareholders each own 50 per cent of the outstanding shares. There are four directors, *A*, *Mrs. A*, *B*, and *Mrs. B*. *Mrs. B* resigns as a result of marital discord with *B*. Control of the corporation has been turned over permanently to *A* and *Mrs. A*. An attempt by *B* to elect two directors (and return to parity on the board) can itself be deadlocked by *A*.

> *Example:* In the foregoing example, *A* and *Mrs. A* fill the vacancy by electing their son, *XX*. *B* is now outvoted on the board, three to one. There may be no way for him to return to parity since *XX* remains in office until his successor is elected and all such elections are deadlocked. See *Gearing v. Kelly*, 182 N.E.2d 391 (N.Y. 1962).

2) A deadlock at the directoral level may prevent the corporation from functioning, though it is possible that the president or general manager may continue to operate the business, often to the complete exclusion of the other faction.

c. The most practical solution for the truly deadlocked corporation is usually for one faction to buy out the other since it is ordinarily preferable to preserve a going corporation rather than to dissolve it. The business assets of a corporation, including intangible good will, are ordinarily worth more as a unit than fragmented.

1) It sometimes may be possible for deadlocked parties to work out a sale after the deadlock has arisen.

2) The more logical solution, however, is to address the problem when the parties are in amity and to work out an agreement in advance by which one faction should buy out the other at a fair price in the event of a deadlock. Such an agreement is a form of buy-sell agreement. (See part VII, H). Such an arrangement must resolve several basic questions:

(A) Who is to buy out whom if both desire to continue the corporate business? Often the senior should buy out the junior, though if the age discrepancy is large, it may be more sensible to reverse the order and have the junior buy out the senior. An agreement may provide that one shareholder sets a price at which he is willing to buy out the other shareholder or to sell his own shares, and the other shareholder has the election to buy or sell.

(B) What events trigger the power to buy? Some kind of objective standard is usually desirable, such as the failure to agree on a slate of directors for some specified period.

(C)   Which pricing formulas should be used and which should be avoided?   The formula chosen should not rely on a cooperative effort to set the price.   Also, the formula should yield as "fair" a price as possible rather than one that arguably creates a bargain for one faction or the other.

(D)   May the person who is bought out form a competing business, and if so, where and on what terms?   A non-competition agreement is enforceable if it is reasonable under the circumstances.

(E)   In the event a buy-out has not been prepared in advance or cannot be worked out after the deadlock arises, the ultimate remedy for a deadlock is involuntary dissolution.   *In re Security Fin. Co.*, 317 P.2d 1 (Cal. 1957).

> *Caveat:*   The ultimate remedy of dissolution may very well benefit one faction of shareholders at the expense of another.   If a single shareholder's personal abilities largely explain the corporation's success, he or she may well desire liquidation.   By performing services on behalf of the corporation, the dominant shareholder is in effect sharing the fruits of his or her abilities with other shareholders.   If the corporation were dissolved, presumably the dominant shareholder could continue to operate the business without sharing the fruits with anyone.   However, if the dominant shareholder simply abandons the corporation and starts a new business in competition with the corporation, he or she may be subject to suit for unfair competition or usurpation of corporate opportunity.   Hence, he or she may desire dissolution.   This appears to have been the situation in *In re Radom & Neidorff, Inc.*, 119 N.E.2d 563 (N.Y. 1954).

D.   REMEDIES FOR DEADLOCKS

If a corporation is deadlocked and unable to break the deadlock, business corporation acts permit involuntary dissolution at the request of a shareholder.   Such dissolution, however, may be deemed discretionary with the court rather than automatic. *Wollman v. Littman*, 316 N.Y.S.2d 526 (App.Div. 1970); *In re Radom & Neidorff, Inc.*, 119 N.E.2d 563 (N.Y. 1954).   Further, other remedies short of involuntary dissolution may sometimes be available and some courts have declined to order dissolution until such other remedies have been tried. *Jackson v. Nicolai-Neppach Co.*, 348 P.2d 9 (Or. 1959); *Masinter v. WEBCO Co.*, 262 S.E.2d 433 (W.Va. 1980).

1. STATUTORY GROUNDS FOR INVOLUNTARY DISSOLUTION

Generally, dissolution may not be available to a shareholder unless he or she can establish that the situation comes within the precise language of the statute. There is no general common law right of dissolution and the statutes are often strictly construed. *Johnston v. Livingston Nursing Home, Inc.*, 211 So.2d 151 (Ala. 1968); *Kruger v. Gerth*, 210 N.E.2d 355 (N.Y. 1965); *Nelkin v. H. J. R. Realty Corp.*, 255 N.E.2d 713 (N.Y. 1969). Statutory grounds for involuntary dissolution vary from state to state.

Example: Wisconsin authorizes dissolution if the corporation is deadlocked so that "its business can no longer be conducted with advantage to its shareholders." Refusal to dissolve a deadlocked corporation that is unable to elect directors may itself be an abuse of discretion under this statute. *Strong v. Fromm Laboratories, Inc.*, 77 N.W.2d 389 (Wis. 1956).

Example: The California statute authorizes dissolution if "reasonably necessary for the protection of the rights or interests of any substantial number of the shareholders, or of the complaining shareholders." Dissolution may be ordered under this statute even in the absence of deadlock, mismanagement, or unfairness. *Stumpf v. C. E. Stumpf & Sons, Inc.*, 120 Cal.Rptr. 671 (Cal.App. 1975).

The following language (taken from § 14.30 of the Revised Model Business Corporation Act) is typical.

a. The directors must be deadlocked in the management of the corporate affairs, the shareholders are unable to break the deadlock and "irreparable injury to the corporation is threatened or being suffered, or the business and affairs of the corporation can no longer be conducted to the advantage of the shareholders generally, because of the deadlock." [RMBCA § 14.30(2)(i)]

b. The acts of the directors or those in control of the corporation are "illegal, oppressive, or fraudulent." [RMBCA § 14.30(2)(ii)] The word "oppressive" does not necessarily mean "imminent disaster;" it has been construed as involving lack of fair dealing or fair play, and in any event is a question for the trier of fact to resolve. *Mardikos v. Arger*, 457 N.Y.S.2d 371 (Sup.Ct. 1982); *White v. Perkins*, 189 S.E.2d 315 (Va. 1972); *Gidwitz v. Lanzit Corrugated Box Co.*, 170 N.E.2d 131 (Ill. 1960).

c. The shareholders are deadlocked in voting power, and have failed to elect successors to directors whose terms have expired during a period that includes at least two consecutive annual meeting dates. [RMBCA § 14.30(2)(iii)]

d.   The corporate assets are being "misapplied or wasted." [RMBCA
     § 14.30(2)(iv)]

2.   RECEIVERSHIPS

Some statutes contemplate the appointment of a receiver as an interim measure
before dissolution is decreed; courts in some states may appoint receivers for
deadlocked corporations within specific statutory authority. If a corporation is
placed in receivership, control passes from the hands of the deadlocked
shareholders to a court-appointed receiver; even if the business and assets are
preserved during the receivership, it is unlikely that the cause of deadlock will
be corrected and the business ever returned to its owners. In such situations,
dissolution is usually the ultimate solution. Receivership may encourage the
warring shareholders to reach an agreement by which one agrees to buy out
the other's interest; in such situations, the receivership should continue until
the sale is consummated. *Shaw v. Robison*, 537 P.2d 487 (Utah 1975).

3.   CUSTODIANS OR PROVISIONAL DIRECTORS

Some state statutes authorize courts to appoint custodians or provisional
directors where that appears to be an appropriate way to avoid a deadlock.
Many of these statutes are available only to a corporation that has elected
close corporation status. See Part G. below.

Example: Two shareholders each own 50% of the stock of a corporation. One
shareholder is in control of the board of directors and the deadlock
prevents the other shareholder from attaining parity. A custodian
may be appointed under Del.C. § 226(a)(1) despite the absence of
irreparable injury. *Giuricich v. Emtrol Corp.*, 449 A.2d 232 (Del.
1982).

4.   ARBITRATION

Mandatory arbitration is sometimes used as a device to avoid a deadlock short
of dissolution. In considering the desirability of arbitration, two questions
should be considered: first, what kinds of controversies is the arbitrator likely
to face, and second, what kinds of solutions will he or she be permitted to
adopt.

a.   Many disputes leading to deadlock in a closely held corporation involve
     personality conflicts or broad differences in policy. An arbitrator may
     have no criteria for resolving such disputes, and even if he or she does
     resolve a specific dispute, it is unlikely that he or she will have cured the
     basic disagreement which led to the original deadlock.

Example: A minority shareholder in a corporation deadlocked because of
an unanimity requirement seeks arbitration of a claim that the
majority shareholder should be removed as director. A decision
by the arbitrator to remove the majority shareholder would

turn control of the corporation over to the minority shareholder, and because there is an unanimity requirement for the election of directors, the turnover of control would be permanent, or until dissolution could be compelled pursuant to statute. Even if the majority shareholder has committed acts which might constitute cause for removal, it is doubtful whether an arbitrator should favor permanently one faction over another in a pure struggle for control. *Application of Burkin*, 136 N.E.2d 862 (N.Y. 1956). There are other remedies of the minority shareholder to correct the acts which constitute cause for removal—e. g., a derivative suit. Ultimately, if deep personal or policy conflicts continue, dissolution appears to be the only suitable remedy because arbitration cannot cure the root cause of the disagreement.

Caveat: Courts have often ordered arbitration in close corporation disputes when provided for by contract without consideration of the probable success of the arbitration. E. g., *Moskowitz v. Surrey Sleep Products, Inc.*, 292 N.Y.S.2d 748 (App.Div. 1968).

b. The advantages of arbitration are speed, cheapness, informality (as contrasted with a court proceeding), and the prospect of a decision by a person with knowledge and experience in business affairs. Where the reason for deadlock is a question not involving basic personal or policy matters, arbitration may satisfactorily resolve a dispute and permit the corporation to continue.

Example: The issue in disagreement is whether a corporation should exercise an option to purchase in a lease of real property. Such an issue is arbitrable. *Application of Vogel*, 268 N.Y.S.2d 237 (App.Div. 1966), *aff'd* 224 N.E.2d 738 (N.Y. 1967).

5. STATUTORY BUYOUT ARRANGEMENTS

Some statutes authorize a voluntary buyout of the shares of a shareholder who has filed a petition for involuntary dissolution or who has sought to have his or her shares acquired by the corporation or other shareholders. The price for a buyout is usually based on a judicial valuation of shares. The option to purchase is usually on the part of other shareholders and the failure to exercise the option may lead to a dissolution of the corporation. Some of these remedies are available only to a corporation that has elected close corporation status. See Part G. below.

Caveat: There has been little experience with these statutes, and it is not clear that they provide a significant benefit over a privately arranged transaction.

E. SPECIAL MANAGEMENT PROBLEMS IN THE CLOSE CORPORATION

The statutory norms embodied in most state statutes assume that corporations will be conducted with a degree of formality: shareholders will meet to elect directors who will in turn meet to elect or appoint officers and to direct the affairs of the corporation. These assumptions are obviously unjustified for most small closely held corporations. Corporate matters are likely to be resolved by unanimous consent with a minimum of formality and no regard for the statutory niceties.

1. CONSEQUENCES OF FAILING TO FOLLOW FORMALITIES
The failure to follow corporate formalities creates several possible legal issues:

a. Will the ignoring of corporate formalities result in the corporate veil being "pierced" and the participants being held personally liable on corporate obligations? (See part IV).

b. Will the participants' control arrangement be unenforceable because it violates the "statutory norms"? (See part VI).

c. Will decisions that are made informally and without following the statutory norms be binding on the corporation and third parties?

F. JUDICIAL RECOGNITION OF THE SPECIAL PROBLEMS OF THE CLOSE CORPORATION

The traditional view was that all corporations should be governed by essentially the same rules set forth in the corporation statutes, and that no special rules could or should be developed for the closely held corporation. *Kruger v. Gerth*, 210 N.E.2d 355 (N.Y. 1965).

1. DISSENTING VIEWS
Beginning in the 1960's this traditional view was challenged by several individual dissenting opinions urging a more relaxed and more realistic treatment of the closely held corporation. *Kruger v. Gerth*, 210 N.E.2d 355 (N.Y. 1965). These views usually urged:

a. Application of a greatly broadened fiduciary duty between shareholders in a closely held corporation;

b. Relaxation of the traditional statutory norms to permit more flexible control arrangements within the closely held corporation;

c.   Recognition that closely held corporations were "incorporated partnerships," and the selective application of partnership principles, including freedom to dissolve, to closely held corporations; and

d.   Enactment of special statutory provisions for the closely held corporation.

2.   ACCEPTANCE IN ILLINOIS AND MASSACHUSETTS

Strong and influential decisions favoring the special treatment of closely held corporations are *Galler v. Galler*, 203 N.E.2d 577 (Ill. 1964) and *Donahue v. Rodd Electrotype Co.*, 328 N.E.2d 505 (Mass. 1975).

a.   *Galler* applied a relaxed standard of statutory norms to uphold a reasonable control arrangement and strongly urged special statutory treatment for the closely held corporation.

b.   *Donahue* applied a broad fiduciary duty, not unlike that existing between partners in a general partnership, to shareholders in a closely held corporation.

c.   Decisions in a number of other states have accepted the general principles of these two leading cases.

3.   FIDUCIARY DUTIES OF SHAREHOLDERS

Based on language in *Donahue*, the Massachusetts court has broadly recognized that shareholders owe fiduciary duties to each other.

Example: A minority shareholder has a veto power over certain transactions because of a unanimity requirement. The shareholder exercises this power arbitrarily to prevent the payment of all dividends, thereby causing the corporation to incur a penalty tax for unreasonable accumulation of surplus. The minority shareholder has breached his duty to the other shareholders. *Smith v. Atlantic Properties, Inc.*, 422 N.E.2d 798 (Mass.App. 1981).

G.   SPECIAL CLOSE CORPORATION STATUTES

Special statutes relating to closely held corporations have been adopted in over a dozen states. These statutes are intended to permit such corporations to conduct their affairs with essentially the same freedom as if they were partnerships.

1.   STATUTORY PROVISIONS

While there is considerable variation in the state statutes relating to close corporations they generally provide the following:

a.   Agreements that restrict the discretion of directors are specifically
validated if they are set forth in the articles of incorporation.

   1)   The corporation may elect to dispense with the board of directors
entirely and have the business and affairs of the corporation
conducted by the shareholders as though they were partners.   If
this option is elected, the liabilities otherwise imposed on directors
are imposed on the shareholders as if they were directors.

   2)   In *Zion v. Kurtz,* 405 N.E.2d 681 (N.Y. 1980), the court upheld an
agreement between two shareholders that the corporation would not
enter into transactions or new business without the consent of both
shareholders despite the fact that no reference to the agreement
appeared in the articles of incorporation and the corporation had not
elected close corporation status.   The court viewed these omissions
as technical and subject to the power of the court to order the
articles of incorporation reformed.   The vote was 4–3, the dissenters
arguing that public notice of agreements restricting the power of
directors was essential for their validity under these statutes.

b.   The corporation may adopt special dissolution provisions that permit a
minority shareholder to compel the dissolution of the corporation.   This
provision, designed to eliminate the "locked in" feature of the close
corporation is the principal substantive provision of these statutes that
addresses the basic problem of the minority shareholder in a closely held
corporation.

c.   In the event of a deadlock at the directoral level, courts are empowered
to break the deadlock by the appointment of impartial custodians or
"provisional directors."

   (A)   This provision is designed to provide a simpler, more flexible
and less drastic solution to deadlocked corporations than either
the appointment of a receiver or dissolution.   *In re Jamison
Steel Corp.,* 322 P.2d 246 (Cal.App. 1958); *Giuricich v. Emtrol
Corp.,* 449 A.2d 232 (Del. 1982).

   (B)   It is likely that the mere threat of the appointment of a
custodian or one or more provisional directors will be a strong
stimulus to quarreling shareholders to make some kind of a
mutual accommodation.

   (C)   As is the case with arbitration, it is questionable whether the
appointment of a custodian or provisional director can cure a
deep-seated and fundamental difference of views between
equally divided shareholders.

    d.   In the event a petition for involuntary dissolution is filed, the corporation or the nonpetitioning shareholders may have the right to purchase the shares of the petitioning shareholder at a judicially determined fair valuation.

2.   CORPORATIONS ELIGIBLE FOR SPECIAL TREATMENT

The definition of an eligible corporation usually involves the following elements:

    a.   The number of shareholders may not exceed a specified number (ranging from as low as 10 in some states to 35 or more in others). The Model Close Corporation Supplement permits election by a corporation with up to 50 shareholders. See also RMBCA § 8.01.

    b.   The corporation never has made a registered public offering of shares.

    c.   Share transfer restrictions must be imposed on all outstanding shares limiting their free transferability.

    d.   Notations must be placed on all certificates describing which special provisions the corporation has elected to make applicable.

3.   ACTUAL USE OF CLOSE CORPORATION ELECTION

Even though a number of states have adopted close corporation statutes and this development has been widely praised, the actual experience in several states, including California, Delaware, Florida and Texas, indicates that this election has not been widely used.

    a.   It is probable that most attorneys are able to work out basic control relationships under the general corporation statutes and therefore do not feel it is necessary to use or experiment with these new and largely untried statutes.

    b.   The sheer complexity of some of these statutes may also have discouraged their widespread use. Some close corporation statutes are complex and prolix; much of the complicated language is addressed to problems related to eligibility, i. e., which corporations are eligible to take advantage of these special provisions and what happens when an electing corporation loses its eligibility.

    c.   Some lawyers may be concerned that the use of the close corporation election may have adverse tax consequences or may result in the possible loss of the shield of limited liability. The Model Close Corporation Supplement (MCCS § 25) and the statutes of some states expressly attempt to negate this result.

4. JUDICIAL RECEPTION OF CLOSE CORPORATION STATUTES

Despite the broad remedial purposes underlying modern close corporation statutes, some courts have given them narrow and literalistic readings not consistent with the underlying purposes. E. g., *Blount v. Taft*, 246 S.E.2d 763 (N.C. 1978). Other courts have been more generous. See e. g. *Zion v. Kurtz*, 405 N.E.2d 681 (N.Y. 1980).

REVIEW QUESTIONS

X–1. In a closely held corporation the shareholders today have essentially the same fiduciary duties to each other as partners in a partnership.

True _____   False _____

X–2. So long as an even division of shares between two shareholders is avoided, there is no possibility of a deadlock in a corporation.

True _____   False _____

X–3. What other solutions to the deadlock problem exist other than dissolution?

X–4. Every state should adopt a close corporation statute, since the experience in the states that have enacted them indicate that they are almost widely and universally used.

True _____   False _____

XI

MANAGEMENT IN THE PUBLICLY HELD CORPORATION

Analysis

A. Control of the Publicly Held Corporation
B. The Role of Shareholders in the Public Corporation

A. CONTROL OF THE PUBLICLY HELD CORPORATION

The theoretical structure of a corporation assumes that shareholders select directors who in turn select corporate officers to carry out their directives. In many ways the large public corporation bears little resemblance to this theoretical structure.

1.   LIMITED ROLE OF SMALL SHAREHOLDERS
The small shareholder is presented with a list of candidates for directors selected by the current managers of the corporation, and he may vote for or against them. However, the vote of any one shareholder is largely irrelevant, and since the overwhelming majority of the shareholders are going to vote in favor of the proposed directors, it really does not make very much difference whether or not he exercises his franchise. (See part B below.)

2.   WHO SELECTS THE DIRECTORS?
The real decision as to who will be directors is made not in the shareholder election process, but at some earlier point where an internal decision within the corporation is quietly made as to which candidates should be presented by management to the shareholders for approval. Shareholders basically ratify this selection by management.

3.   WHO RUNS THE BUSINESS?
In most publicly held corporations, the full time, professional management runs the business while directors serve a much more limited role.

    a.   The board of directors usually consists partly of management representatives ("inside directors") and partly of outsiders who are not officers or employees of the corporation and whose detailed knowledge of corporate affairs must of necessity be limited ("outside directors"). The modern trend is toward more outside directors but in many corporations management representatives continue to dominate the board. Some analysis divides outside directors into "affiliated" and "non-affiliated" outside directors. An "affiliated" outside director is one who has a substantial economic interest in the corporation, e. g. the corporation's outside counsel or a representative of its investment banker.

    b.   One important study revealed that the actual functions of boards of directors in publicly held corporations were as follows:

        1)   They provide advice and counsel.

        2)   They provide intellectual discipline for management (which must appear before the board and present views and defend recommendations).

3)   They act in crisis situations, such as where the CEO unexpectedly dies or is incapacitated, or where the affairs of the corporation are in such bad financial shape that a change of CEOs seems desirable.

c.   The same study concluded that by and large boards do *not* perform the following functions:

1)   They do not establish objectives, strategies and policies of the corporation.

2)   They do not ask discerning or "tough" questions at meetings of the board.

3)   They do not select the CEO though they may have a voice as a form of "corporate conscience".

4)   They do not decide what the corporation or the board of directors does.

d.   Outside directors also may provide assurance to shareholders that appropriate internal and external auditing and control devices within the corporation exist.

e.   During the 1970s and 1980s there was a trend toward increasing the number and influence of outside directors on boards of directors. A variety of factors have contributed toward this trend:

1)   Widespread disclosure of corporate misconduct during the 1970s;

2)   Pressure by the Securities and Exchange Commission and the national securities exchanges on corporations to "broaden" their boards;

3)   The Corporate Governance Project being conducted by the American Law Institute; and

4)   Holdings by courts that defensive tactics to avoid unwanted takeover attempts are more likely to be upheld as valid exercises of business judgment if they are approved by independent outside directors without large financial stakes in the outcome.

f.   Along with the trend toward more outside directors is heightened realization of the duties and responsibilities of directors.

g.   There is also wider use of committees of boards consisting primarily of outside directors. Audit committees are now widely used; many corporations have also formed nominating and compensation committees composed previously of outside directors in an effort to provide greater review of issues in these areas by the non-management members of the board. These committees are described in greater detail in part VIII, H, supra; they may gradually shift the locus of power in publicly held corporations away from management and toward the outside directors.

4. WHO SELECTS THE MANAGEMENT?

In publicly held corporations, the management tends to be a self-perpetuating body. Top management tends to rise gradually through the corporation until ultimately they are selected as top management by retiring top management. Such statements, however, are incomplete and often misleading.

a. If some blocks of shares approach working control, top management will usually be selected or approved by the persons in voting control of those blocks.

b. Personalities, loyalties, business relationships and the like may give considerable power to persons such as bankers, advisers, corporate counsel, and the like that is not dependent on the number of shares held or voted by them.

c. Where there is no single controlling block of shares, there always remains the possibility of management overthrow from internal or external mobilization of the disorganized body of shareholders. In the 1980s this phenomenon of purchase-type takeovers of large publicly-held corporations has become increasingly common.

d. Takeover or tender offer battles may determine corporate control through economic incentives to shareholders to sell their shares to aggressive outside interests.

B. THE ROLE OF SHAREHOLDERS IN THE PUBLIC CORPORATION

Shareholders, of course, have the ultimate power to determine who controls the business.

1. PRO–MANAGEMENT BIAS

On most matters shareholders vote in favor of management or as management recommends.

a. Management has control of the "proxy solicitation machinery" and views of management are routinely brought before the shareholders as the experienced voice of those actually managing the business. Persons seeking to challenge incumbent management must communicate with shareholders largely at their own expense. Hence, overthrow by way of a proxy fight is apt to be expensive and unlikely to be successful.

b. There is natural self-selection by shareholders. Most small shareholders consider their financial interest in their own investment as paramount, and if they are dissatisfied with the management of their corporation, they may sell their shares. Thus, shareholders unhappy with management tend to disappear by a process of self-elimination, and the remaining shareholders tend to be pro-management. This is often referred to as the "Wall Street Option".

c. The increased importance of institutional investors has also helped to solidify incumbent management. Institutional investors typically vote large numbers of shares and are natural supporters of management since they view themselves as investors, not controllers. On the other hand, these investors often hold the key to success of outside takeovers by purchase because of the size of the blocks of shares they hold.

2. LIMITATIONS ON MANAGEMENT CONTROL

Management control, however, is not limitless. There are several sources of external pressure which limit the power of management to do what it pleases.

a. A poor operating performance in terms of profits will result in depressed share prices and dissatisfied shareholders; these may lead indirectly to the ouster of management through a tender offer or similar maneuver.

b. Large shareholders or other members of the financial community— commercial bankers, investment bankers, or institutional investors—may have great power to limit the sources of the corporation's long and short term financing.

c. A "palace coup" may also be a possibility, particularly if there are large blocks of shares not participating in management.

d. The threat of filing of a shareholder's derivative suit may also have some effect.

e. The disclosure requirements of federal law create a gold fish bowl atmosphere which also exercises a cautionary effect on management.

Caveat: Economists argue that these limitations have substantial effect. They refer to a "market for control" that tends to ensure fidelity of management and to weed out less efficient managers.

3. THE ROLE OF INSTITUTIONAL INVESTORS
For many years the small shareholder was thought to epitomize the public shareholder. However, largely since World War II the institutional investor has grown tremendously in importance.

a. Institutional investors mainly collect and invest other people's money. They include:

   1)   Life insurance companies.

   2)   Pension funds.

   3)   Investment companies (the "mutual funds").

   4)   Bank trust departments, and similar organizations.

b. Assets of institutional investors have grown spectacularly, often by factors of 100 or more, in the last thirty years. In a sense, these institutional investors are the predominant owners of American industry today. Not only do they invest significant amounts of capital in a large variety of common shares traded on the major securities exchanges; their holdings in the aggregate are in excess of forty per cent of the outstanding shares of all listed publicly held corporations, and in specific corporations their percentage of ownership may exceed fifty per cent.

c. Since institutional investors handle funds that ultimately belong to members of the general public in the form of pensions, life insurance proceeds, savings, or financial investments, their growth in a sense has increased the broad base of ownership of the means of production in modern society. However in terms of the power to control, the growth of institutional investors represent a narrowing of the base, since relatively few persons now determine how large blocks of shares are voted.

d. Institutional investors often have the power, if they band together, to effectively control many large publicly held corporations.

   1)   Most institutional investors, however, act purely as investors and disavow any desire to control the business and affairs of corporations. In part as a result of this attitude, institutional investors also usually vote their shares in favor of management.

   2)   If they are dissatisfied with management, they prefer to sell their shares rather than engage in a struggle for control. In some instances, however, institutional investors may be compelled to take affirmative roles in management rather than acting as passive investors.

Example: In a struggle for control, the blocks controlled by institutional investors may be the critical swing blocks, and by deciding to sell or not to sell the investors effectively determine who will control the corporation.

Example: Institutional investors have sometimes opposed management proposals for "shark repellent" defensive amendments designed to make unwanted takeover attempts more difficult. This attitude reflects growing recognition that shark repellent amendments, by making takeovers more difficult, may entrench incumbent management and deprive shareholders of the opportunity to obtain premiums over market price for their shares in connection with takeover attempts.

e. Even though institutional investors act as passive investors, their sheer size often raises unique market problems.

    1) If an institutional investor decides to exercise its "market option" and sell its shares, the block may be so large that only other institutional investors have the capacity to absorb the shares.

    2) Large institutional holdings may increase the volatility of share prices since independent decisions by several large institutional investors to dispose of or increase their shares may markedly depress or inflate short-run prices.

4. NOMINEE REGISTRATION

Large institutional investors have developed the practice of holding securities in the names of *nominees*, usually a partnership of employees using names such as "Abel and Company."

a. This practice developed for innocuous reasons: to avoid onerous transfer requirements placed on corporations or fiduciaries selling shares.

b. A single institutional investor often uses several different nominees.

c. Central clearing corporations were created in the 1970s to facilitate trading in securities. Within a central clearing corporation many off-setting trades between brokers can be netted, thereby greatly simplifying the transfer of certificates and reducing paperwork. The major central clearing corporation now in operation is the Stock Clearing Corporation, a subsidiary of the New York Stock Exchange, whose nominee is Cede and Company.

5.   "STREET NAME" REGISTRATION

Millions of shares that are publicly traded are registered in "street names."
The "street" referred to is Wall Street, and the "names" referred to are the
names of well known brokerage companies with offices on Wall Street. Shares
registered in the name of such companies are endorsed in blank by the
registered owner and are transferred by delivery, often between brokerage
firms, to reflect transactions entered into over the New York or another stock
exchange.

a.   Where a speculator purchases shares with a view toward a prompt resale,
he will normally not want the shares registered in his own name. Indeed,
he probably will never take delivery of certificates but will let his broker
obtain certificates for the shares he buys and deliver certificates for the
shares he thereafter sells.

b.   Street name shares are bearer securities, but the problem of theft is not
a serious one since most transfers of street name securities are between
brokers.

c.   Where shares are registered in street name, the corporation does not
know who the beneficial owner is; indeed, it may not even know in which
brokerage firm the shares are currently held.

d.   A person who buys securities for investment may take delivery of
certificates registered in street name; more commonly, however, the
broker will arrange for new certificates to be issued in the name of the
investor.

e.   The number of shares in street name at any one time may be 20 or 30
per cent of the outstanding shares. These shares are often referred to as
the "float" or "floating supply." Shares borrowed to be sold short are
usually drawn from the float.

f.   RMBCA § 7.23 authorizes corporations to establish, on a voluntary basis,
procedures by which the corporation may recognize beneficial owners of
street name or nominee-owned shares, thereby avoiding the need to
communicate through different layers or tiers of record and non-beneficial
owners.

Caveat: This provision is experimental and there has been no experience
with how it might work in practice.

REVIEW QUESTIONS

XI–1.   What is the "Wall Street Option" in publicly held corporations?

XI–2.   In a publicly held corporation, who selects the directors?

XI–3.   The major role of directors in the publicly held corporation is to establish general business policies for the corporation.

True _____   False _____

XI–4.   A major function of directors is to decide who is to run the business, that is to select the chief executive officer.

True _____   False _____

XI–5.   What is "street name registration?"

XI–6.   What are institutional investors?

XI–7.   Do institutional investors usually support management or insurgents?

XII

PROXY REGULATION

Most modern law of proxy regulation is of federal rather than state origin and relates to the proxy solicitations of publicly held corporations. The basic provision of federal law is section 14(a) of the Securities Exchange Act of 1934, 15 U.S.C.A. § 78n, which makes it unlawful for any person to use the mails or any means or instrumentality of interstate commerce or the facilities of a national securities exchange to solicit proxies with respect to covered corporations "in contravention of such rules and regulations as the [Securities and Exchange] Commission may prescribe as necessary or appropriate in the public interest or for the protection of investors." Pursuant to this rather boundless grant of authority to regulate proxies, the SEC has issued the comprehensive and detailed regulations which are the subject of this chapter.

Analysis

A. CORPORATIONS SUBJECT TO FEDERAL PROXY REGULATION

The corporations subject to federal proxy regulation are those required to register under section 12 of the Securities Exchange Act, 15 U.S.C.A. § 78l, i. e., all corporations (1) having securities that are registered on a national securities exchange, or (2) having assets in excess of $3,000,000 and a class of equity securities held of record by 500 persons or more. The SEC increased the dollar minimum in 1982 by regulation from $1,000,000 to $3,000,000; in 1986 it has proposed a further increase to $5,000,000.

Example: A corporation has 400 shareholders of record holding common stock, and another 400 shareholders of record holding preferred stock, but no shares are registered on a national securities exchange. The corporation is not required to register under section 12 even though it has an aggregate of 800 shareholders since no class of shares is held by 500 persons.

Example: A corporation has 520 shareholders of record of common shares. The corporation is required to register under section 12 even though shares are not traded on an exchange.

B. TERMINATION OF REGISTRATION

Once a corporation is required to register under section 12, it remains subject to that section even though the number of shareholders drops below 500; registration under section 12 may be terminated only if the corporation has no class held of record by more than 300 persons. In 1982, the SEC added a new test for termination of registration: a corporation may also seek termination if its assets are valued at less than $3,000,000 and it has no class held of record by more than 500 persons. In 1986, the SEC proposed to make this provision applicable to corporations with assets valued at less than $5,000,000 and no class held of record by 500 or more shareholders.

C. CONSTITUTIONAL BASIS FOR FEDERAL REGULATION OF PROXIES

The constitutional basis for federal proxy regulation is the use of the mails or an instrumentality in interstate commerce. As a practical matter, it is probably impossible to solicit a large number of proxies in connection with a security registered under section 12 without some use of the mails or facilities of interstate commerce.

D. PROXY STATEMENTS AND ANNUAL REPORTS

The SEC proxy regulations (rule 14a–3) provide that with certain exceptions a solicitation of a proxy must be accompanied or preceded by the delivery of a proxy statement setting forth detailed information about the persons making the solicitation, about the background of all nominees, and in connection with solicitations by management, about remuneration and other transactions with management and with others, and about any matter on which the vote of shareholders is sought. These proxy statements are a major source of shareholder information about corporate affairs.

1. **ANNUAL REPORTS**

    The proxy regulations indirectly require the distribution of annual reports since rule 14a–3(b) provides that if a solicitation is made on behalf of management relating to an annual meeting of shareholders at which directors are to be elected, the proxy statement must be accompanied or preceded by an annual report of the corporation. This is the only basis in many states to require the distribution of annual information to shareholders.

2. **FORM OF PROXY DOCUMENTS**

    SEC regulations also prescribe the form of proxy document itself and prohibit certain devices such as undated or post-dated proxies or broad grants of discretionary power to proxy holders. Shareholders must be given the option to vote for or against candidates for directors, and proxy holders must actually vote the shares as shareholders direct for the election of directors and on other issues presented for decision to the shareholders.

3. **PRESOLICITATION REVIEW**

    The SEC conducts a presolicitation review process for proxy documents. Drafts of proxy statements and other soliciting materials (such as letters, press releases, and the like), must be filed with the SEC at least ten days prior to the date it is proposed to mail definitive copies to securities holders.

    a. Because the period for evaluation is short, as a practical matter the SEC review is based on an analysis of the filing and whatever else is in the Commission's files relating to the filing company.

    b. Most courts have recognized that this preliminary SEC review of proxy solicitation material should not be given great weight in subsequently evaluating the sufficiency of the disclosures.

    c. While the SEC does not pass upon the accuracy or adequacy of the disclosures, it does indicate that revisions should be made if it concludes that some materials are inaccurate.

4.   WHAT IS A SOLICITATION?

The SEC has consistently argued, and most courts have agreed, that the definitions of "solicitation" and "proxy" should be broadly construed to ensure the widest protection provided by the proxy regulations.

Example: An authorization to obtain a list of shareholders signed by 42 shareholders is a solicitation subject to the proxy regulations. *Studebaker Corp. v. Gittlin*, 360 F.2d 692 (2d Cir. 1966).

Example: Advertisements urging the approval or disapproval of certain transactions may constitute solicitations, though some courts have disagreed. E. g., *Brown v. Chicago R. I. & P. Ry.*, 328 F.2d 122 (7th Cir. 1964).

5.   EXEMPT PROXY SOLICITATIONS

The SEC proxy regulations exempt certain narrow classes of solicitations. The principal exceptions are:

a.   Solicitations to less than 10 persons;

b.   Solicitations by brokers to beneficial owners to obtain instructions on how to vote the shares;

c.   Solicitation by a beneficial owner to obtain a proxy from the record holder;

d.   Newspaper advertisements that describe only how holders may obtain copies of the proxy documents;

e.   Proxy advice furnished by a person who renders financial advice in the ordinary course of business and receives no special remuneration for the proxy advice.

6.   CORPORATIONS THAT NEED NOT SOLICIT PROXIES

Most corporate managements find it necessary to solicit proxies if there is to be a quorum at the meeting since most corporate managers own only a minute fraction of the outstanding shares. As a practical matter, the number of shares voted by shareholders who appear personally at a meeting is also usually numerically insignificant. In some corporations subject to registration under section 12, however, management may itself own or control enough shares to constitute a quorum without any solicitation of public shareholders. Section 14(f) of the Securities Exchange Act of 1934 requires such corporations to supply shareholders with information "substantially equivalent" to the information that would have been required if a proxy solicitation to its shareholders had been made.

7.   PROBLEMS CREATED BY STREET NAME AND NOMINEE HOLDINGS
The widespread practice of holding shares in street names or the names of nominees creates problems for the SEC proxy disclosure process since the beneficial owners of such shares are not the record owners and do not directly receive the required proxy statements or annual reports.

a.   SEC regulations require brokers and dealers to transmit proxy material to the beneficial owners of shares, and either:

1)   Execute proxy forms in blank (and deliver them to the beneficial owners so that the shares may be voted by them) or

2)   Solicit directions as to how to vote the shares and directly vote them as the beneficial owners direct.

Caveat: SEC regulations now require record holders to disclose names of beneficial owners (unless those owners object) so that direct communication can be established in the absence of objection by the beneficial owners.

b.   Stock exchange rules require brokers and dealers to transmit proxy information to beneficial owners if the solicitor of proxies reimburses the expenses of the broker or dealer. Regulations under the Securities Exchange Act also require issuers to provide registered owners who are nominees with sufficient copies of the proxy material so that a copy can be transmitted to each beneficial owner.

c.   Studies by the SEC reveal that these devices work reasonably efficiently and that there are not widespread abuses of the proxy solicitation process as a result of the nominee and street name registration practices.

d.   RMBCA § 7.23 proposes an alternative device that permits corporations to establish procedures to treat beneficial owners of shares as traditional record owners, thereby minimizing the routine transfer of voting-related documents by nominees and others. This section is experimental in nature.

E.   SHAREHOLDER PROPOSALS

Rule 14a–8 of the SEC regulations establishes an elaborate procedure by which a shareholder may submit one or more proposals for inclusion in the management's proxy solicitation material. If the proposal is an appropriate one for shareholder action, management may be required to include the proposal even if opposed to it. Management may explain the basis of its opposition; if management opposes a proposal the shareholder may include a further statement of not more than 200 words in support of the proposal.

1.   NUMBER OF PROPOSALS

A shareholder may submit a maximum of two proposals in any one proxy solicitation not exceeding an aggregate of 300 words. As described below, limitations are also imposed on repetitive proposals.

2.   PROPOSALS THAT MAY BE OMITTED

Because shareholders may seek action on proposals of dubious relevance or propriety, or simply for personal publicity, the SEC has imposed specific requirements and limitations on shareholders' proposals.

a.   Under present SEC regulations, a shareholder's proposal may be omitted if:

1) It is not a proper subject for action by security holders under the law of the issuer's domicile;

2) It would require the issuer to violate any state, federal or foreign law, if implemented;

3) It is contrary to any of the SEC's proxy regulations;

4) It relates to the enforcement of a personal claim or the redress of a personal grievance, against the issuer, its management, or any person;

5) It deals with a matter that is not significantly related to the issuer's business;

6) It deals with a matter that is beyond the issuer's power to effectuate;

7) It deals with a matter relating to the ordinary business operations of the issuer;

8) It relates to an election to office;

9) It relates to specific amounts of dividends;

10) It is moot in the sense that the issuer has substantially implemented the proposal;

11)   It is either counter to a proposal by management or substantially the same as a proposal by another shareholder which will be included in the proxy materials;

12)   It deals with substantially the same subject matter as a proposal that was previously submitted to the shareholders within the previous five years and failed to receive specified percentages of the vote, depending on the number of times it was submitted previously;

13)   The shareholder owns shares worth less than $1,000 or one percent of the outstanding shares, whichever is smaller; or

14)   The shareholder has another proposal that is being included in the proxy solicitation.

b.   The SEC has issued numerous rulings applying many of these exclusions; as a result, phrases such as "proper subject" or "ordinary business operations" have been given considerable practical content, and the tests are not as vague and open-ended as the language might indicate.   In *S.E.C. v. Transamerica Corp.*, 163 F.2d 511 (3d Cir. 1947) the court rejected an argument that a "proper subject" should be construed restrictively or legalistically.

Example: Important business-related proposals are "proper subjects" for shareholder action under state law if they are phrased as recommendations to the board of directors rather than specific directions to the corporation.

Example: A proposal to institute cumulative voting must be included in a proxy statement.

Example: A proposal that the corporation cease all dealings with the Union of South Africa until it changes its racial policies must be included in the proxy statement.

Example: A proposal that an electric utility not build a nuclear power plant may not be omitted on the ground that it involves only "ordinary business operations."

c.   The leading case is *Medical Committee for Human Rights v. S.E.C.*, 432 F.2d 659 (D.C.Cir. 1970), *vacated as moot* 404 U.S. 403, 92 S.Ct. 577 (1972).   The court held reviewable an SEC decision not requiring the inclusion of a shareholder's proposal relating to the manufacture of napalm and strongly intimated that proposals of this nature should be permitted to be considered by shareholders.

Rule 14a–8 has been controversial during the 1980s. In 1982, the SEC proposed three alternative approaches toward this rule: (1) to retain it in basically its present format with relatively minor changes designed to make it somewhat more difficult to obtain the inclusion of a proposal; (2) to permit corporations to establish their own rules with reference to shareholder proposals subject to certain regulatory minima; and (3) to retain the present rule but impose a numerical maximum on the number of proposals an issuer would be required to include in a proxy solicitation. In 1983, the SEC adopted the first alternative described above.

Some academic commentary during the 1980s has also been critical of the shareholder proposal rule.

F. FALSE AND MISLEADING STATEMENTS IN PROXY SOLICITATIONS

Rule 14a–9 makes it unlawful to solicit proxies by communications which contain "any statement which, at the time and in the light of the circumstances under which it is made, is false or misleading with respect to any material fact, or which omits to state any material fact necessary in order to make the statements therein not false or misleading."

1. PRIVATE CAUSE OF ACTION
For many years it was uncertain whether this broad prohibition created a private cause of action by shareholders or whether it was enforceable only by the Securities and Exchange Commission. This question was definitively answered in *J. I. Case Co. v. Borak*, 377 U.S. 426, 84 S.Ct. 1555 (1964). The Court held that rule 14a–9 created a private cause of action since, "private enforcement of the proxy rules provides a necessary supplement to Commission action. As in antitrust treble damage litigation, the possibility of civil damages or injunctive relief serves as a most effective weapon in the enforcement of the proxy requirements."

2. NATURE OF POST–BORAK LITIGATION
Since *Borak* there has been a substantial volume of private litigation under rule 14a–9. Such litigation is within the exclusive jurisdiction of the Federal courts and state "security for expenses" statutes are inapplicable. This litigation has been largely shaped by two other leading Supreme Court decisions:

a.   In *Mills v. Electric Auto-Lite Co.*, 396 U.S. 375, 90 S.Ct. 616 (1970), the Court held:

1)   It is not necessary to show that the omission of a material fact actually influenced votes; rather, it is enough to establish that the

vote itself was an essential step in the transaction being questioned, and

2)   If a material omission is established, the plaintiff's attorney is entitled to recover attorney's fees from the issuer even though no dollar recovery appears likely.

b.   In *TSC Industries, Inc. v. Northway, Inc.*, 426 U.S. 438, 96 S.Ct. 2126 (1976), an opinion widely read as narrowing the scope of the private cause of action under rule 14a–9, the Court:

1)   Defined a "material fact" as "an omitted fact if there is a substantial likelihood that a reasonable shareholder would consider it important in deciding how to vote;"

2)   Rejected the competing test that would have defined material facts to include all facts "which a reasonable shareholder *might* consider appropriate;" and

3)   Held that it was error to grant summary judgment on the issue that a misleading statement was "material" under the above tests. Thus, while the difference between the rejected and adopted tests may seem primarily semantic, the Court's distinction appears to constitute a warning to lower courts to limit rule 14a–9 to substantial misstatements; prior to this decision some courts had tended to find relatively minor misstatements or omissions to be "material" and therefore violations of rule 14a–9.

3.   REMEDIES IN RULE 14a–9 CASES
In an appropriate rule 14a–9 case, the court has several alternative remedies.

a.   A court may issue a temporary restraining order (TRO) to enjoin the distribution of proxy material, the voting of the proxies themselves, or the holding of the meeting.

1)   A TRO would normally terminate after all misstatements or deficiencies in the proxy solicitation material under rule 14a–9 have been corrected.

2)   In many cases the plaintiff does not seek a TRO because he or she is unable or unwilling to post the bond that may be required if the proxy solicitation involves approval of a merger or other large transaction.

b.   In the absence of a TRO, the meeting may be held, the proxies voted, and the transaction consummated before there is a judicial determination of whether or not the proxy solicitation material violates rule 14a–9. Thereafter, if a material omission in connection with a vote necessary to effectuate a transaction is established, the court may:

1) "Unwind" the merger;

2) Award money damages;

3) Do nothing.

c. Under *Mills,* attorney's fees might be awarded even if the transaction in question was not set aside or damages not awarded. The prospect of such an award probably led to vigorous prosecutions of violations of rule 14a–9 even if substantial relief seemed remote.

> *Caveat:* The narrowed definition of materiality in *TSC Industries,* however, has decreased the likelihood that attorney's fees will be awarded in close cases. Further, the refusal to grant summary judgment on the issue of liability in *TSC Industries* means that a decision on any such award of attorney's fees will probably be deferred until after the end of a long and expensive trial on the merits. Such a conclusion increases the necessary investment of time and resources before determination of fee eligibility from the standpoint of the attorney and may make vigorous prosecution of close cases less likely.

G. PROXY CONTESTS

SEC regulations with respect to proxy contests are described in the following chapter. See part XIII, B.

REVIEW QUESTIONS

XII–1. Since the solicitation of proxies is an internal function of corporate management, this subject is largely governed by state law.

True _____   False _____

XII–2. When is a corporation subject to federal proxy regulation?

XII–3. What is the constitutional basis for federal regulation of proxies?

XII–4. How does federal proxy regulation attempt to assure the transmission of complete and adequate information about corporate affairs to shareholders?

XII–5. If a corporation includes false or misleading statements in its proxy solicitation statement, may the individual shareholders object and bring suit if the statement is used to obtain shareholder approval of a transaction?

XII–6. In a suit by a shareholder, does the false or misleading statement have to be material and, if so, how is "materiality" defined?

XII–7. May a shareholder plaintiff obtain attorneys' fees in a suit described in question XII–6 if his suit is successful?

XII–8. A minority shareholder in a publicly held corporation subject to SEC regulation requests that the corporation include in its proxy statement a proposal that the corporation not develop nuclear energy facilities. May the corporation reject out of hand such a request?

XII–9. Even though a corporation is required to include a shareholder proposal in its proxy statement, history demonstrates that most such proposals are rejected by large pluralities. Why is any attention paid to such proposals?

XII–10. Expansion, Ltd. is a growing corporation that speculates in the recent boom in rural real estate. Its success has been erratic. The acquisition of Hideaway Ranch, Inc., a popular tourist resort, became its next objective. To this end, Expansion bought 39 percent of Hideaway's shares from a few large shareholders and then proposed a merger to the Hideaway management, which was inclined to support the merger, particularly because of Expansion's promise to retain them in managerial capacities in Expansion, the surviving corporation.

Hideaway solicited proxies for the proposed merger and received the necessary shareholder vote. However, the proxy material failed to disclose Expansion's erratic past or its speculative plans; nor did it mention the commitment made to Hideaway management. Under the merger Hideaway shareholders received two shares of Expansion for each of their Hideaway shares. No independent appraisal was made. An examination of Expansion's history reveals that its shares rarely reached a value as high as referred to in the prospectus. Expansion's securities are registered under the Federal Securities Exchange Act of 1934 but Hideaway's are not.

What rights and remedies might be available to Jack Case, a shareholder of Hideaway who dissented and is now seeking appraisal?

XIII

PROXY FIGHTS, TENDER OFFERS AND OTHER CONTESTS FOR CONTROL

Contests for control of publicly held corporations may take a variety of forms; in recent years new forms have evolved and it is likely that further developments will occur in the future.

Analysis

A. Principal Forms of Contests for Control
B. Proxy Contests
C. Tender Offers and Other Takeover Devices
D. Internal Struggles for Control

A. PRINCIPAL FORMS OF CONTESTS FOR CONTROL

Contests for control may take the following forms, among others:

1. PROXY FIGHT OR PROXY CONTEST

In a proxy fight a nonmanagement faction (the "insurgents") seek to obtain sufficient proxies from other shareholders to oust incumbent management. Management usually conducts a competing proxy solicitation. See part XIII, (B).

2. CASH TENDER OFFER

In a cash tender offer, the outside aggressor ("offeror") invites shareholders to tender their shares for purchase by the aggressor at a price specified by the aggressor. The price is set at a premium over current market price so as to attract tenders. Often the offeror seeks enough shares to ensure voting control; if more shares are tendered than called for, the offeror may take pro rata or may take all shares tendered. See part XIII, (C).

If a partial cash tender offer is successful, the offeror may announce that it will thereafter acquire the balance of the shares on terms less favorable than the original acquisition of the shares. This is usually called a "front end loaded transaction" or a "two tier" acquisition. The second transaction may be called a "mop up" transaction and may be set up so that shareholders are compelled to accept the proffered terms.

3. EXCHANGE OFFER

An exchange offer differs from a cash tender offer in that the aggressor offers a package of its own securities—often a combination of cash, debt, and equity securities—for the securities of the target corporation.

In a mop up transaction (see paragraph 2. above), securities rather than cash are traditionally offered.

4. "BEAR HUG" TRANSACTION

A "bear hug" is a forced embrace of the directors of a target corporation to persuade them to accept voluntarily a merger or other amalgamation which permits the take-over to proceed.

5. UNCONVENTIONAL TENDER OFFERS

Several cases have involved attempts to acquire a majority of the target's shares by unconventional means such as the private negotiated purchases of shares owned by institutional investors or substantial minority shareholders or by a campaign of open market purchases.

6.   "PALACE COUPS"
An overthrow from within the corporation occurs with some regularity; cases involving such struggles, however, are rare.

B.   PROXY CONTESTS

In a proxy contest, insurgents compete with management in an effort to obtain proxies. Usually the goal of insurgents is to elect a majority of the board of directors and thereby obtain control, but in some cases contests are waged solely to obtain representation on the board. While management has significant advantages in such a contest, insurgents are sometimes successful, thereby demonstrating that such advantages are not insurmountable.

1.   MANAGEMENT ADVANTAGES
Management's advantages in a proxy fight include:

a.   Insurgents may have to go to court to get the current list of shareholders;

b.   Within a broad range, management may finance its solicitation from the assets of the corporation, while the insurgents must finance their campaign from outside sources; and

c.   For the reasons discussed earlier (See part XI, A), shareholders tend to have a pro-management bias.

2.   INSURGENT TACTICS
An insurgent group, desiring to contest management control, usually first purchases a substantial block of shares in the open market before openly announcing its intentions. However, under the Williams Act (discussed below) it must make an SEC filing if it acquires over 5 per cent of the corporation's securities. Following this acquisition, it must conduct what is essentially a political campaign to persuade shareholders to cast proxies in their favor.

a.   A shareholders list is essential so that substantial shareholders may be contacted personally.

1)   A court proceeding may be necessary to obtain the list.

2)   In addition to seeking a list of shareholders by court proceeding under state law, an insurgent faction has limited rights under rule 14a–9, which requires management to provide minimal assistance to insurgent factions. Rule 14a–9 provides that:

(A) Each issuer must either mail to all shareholders the documents prepared by the insurgents at the insurgents' expense no later than the time management mails its proxy solicitation to shareholders, or

(B) The corporation may provide the shareholder with a reasonably current list of names and addresses by which the shareholder can substantially duplicate the mailing by management.

b. Specialized proxy contest firms are available to assist both management and insurgents in the campaign.

c. Large shareholders may be courted individually; with the modern growth of institutional investors, the support of this segment of the financial community may be essential if a proxy fight is to have a chance of succeeding.

d. Such a campaign may be expensive, running into the hundreds of thousands or millions of dollars.

3. CORPORATIONS SUBJECT TO PROXY CONTESTS

Proxy fights are not feasible in the very large corporation with hundreds of thousands or millions of shareholders, since the cost of solicitation is prohibitive. The most likely candidate for a proxy fight is a small or medium-sized publicly held company with a poor earnings record and, often, elderly management that has not paid attention to shareholders' relations.

In several recent takeover attempts against very large corporations, however, proxy fights have been threatened as part of the aggressor's strategy. Where an aggressor is contemplating the purchase of a multi-billion dollar company, often in large part for cash, the cost of solicitation of even millions of shareholders is likely to be viewed as a relatively small expenditure.

4. REGULATION OF PROXY CONTESTS

Proxy contests in corporations subject to section 12 of the Securities Exchange Act of 1934 are subject to regulation by the Securities and Exchange Commission under its proxy regulations. State law may also be applicable but there are few reported state cases dealing with proxy fights. See, however, *Salgo v. Matthews*, 497 S.W.2d 620 (Tex.Civ.App. 1973).

a. SEC regulations require all "participants" in a proxy contest (including nonmanagement groups) to file specified information with the SEC and the securities exchanges at least five days before a solicitation begins.

1) "Participant" is defined to include anyone who contributes more than $500 for the purpose of financing the contest.

2) Information that must be disclosed includes the identity and background of the participants, their interests in securities of the corporation, when they were acquired, financing arrangements, participation in other proxy contests, and understandings with respect to future employment with the corporation.

b. These regulations reject the view that such contests should be viewed as political contests with each side free to hurl charges with comparative unrestraint on the assumption that the opposing side may refute misleading charges. Rather, each participant's statements are subject to objective standards of accuracy and truthfulness. *SEC v. May*, 229 F.2d 123 (2d Cir. 1956).

5. WHO PAYS THE COST OF PROXY CONTESTS

a. There appears to be no doubt that the corporation should pay for the cost of printing and mailing the notice of meeting, the proxy statement required by federal law, and the proxies themselves. These are legitimate corporate expenses because without the solicitation of proxies it is likely that no quorum of shareholders could be obtained.

b. Most courts have allowed management also to charge to the corporation the reasonable expenses of educating shareholders if the controversy involves a "policy" question rather than a mere "personal" struggle for control. *Rosenfeld v. Fairchild Engine and Airplane Corp.*, 128 N.E.2d 291 (N.Y. 1955); *Levin v. Metro-Goldwyn-Mayer, Inc.*, 264 F.Supp. 797 (S.D.N.Y. 1967).

1) Virtually every issue may be dressed up as a "policy" rather than "personal" issue.

2) "Education" usually favors the management's side of the controversy.

c. The effect of a. and b. is probably to permit the deduction of all reasonable management expenses. Some judges have unsuccessfully suggested that a narrower test should be applicable to the reimbursement of management expenses.

d. Successful insurgents may also seek to have the corporation reimburse their expenses. The reimbursement of successful insurgents has been permitted if:

1) Approved by the shareholders, and

2) The dispute involved "policy" rather than "personalities." *Rosenfeld v. Fairchild Engine and Airplane Corp.*, 128 N.E.2d 291 (N.Y. 1955).

e. As a result the corporation ends up paying for the expenses of both sides if the insurgents are successful. Some judges have unsuccessfully agreed that insurgents' reimbursement should be prohibited.

f. Unsuccessful insurgents may perform a socially useful function, since proxy fights can be viewed as basically desirable phenomena that help to rid corporations of inefficient or ineffective management.

1) Not surprisingly, however, there appears to be no instance where management has voluntarily paid unsuccessful insurgents, except in connection with a settlement of the controversy that allowed incumbent management to retain control of the enterprise.

2) A proposal to require reimbursement of unsuccessful insurgents would have to be carefully structured to avoid possible abuse, particularly encouraging groundless proxy fights.

6.   DEFENSIVE TACTICS

Incumbent management faced with a serious proxy contest may use its control over corporate affairs in an attempt to defeat the insurgents. The validity of such tactics are judged by whether a reasonable business purpose exists for the corporate action independent of the effect on the proxy contest.

Example: A board of directors has authority to set the annual meeting date within certain parameters set forth in the bylaws. The board elects to move the meeting date forward as much as possible solely to make the successful solicitation of proxies by the insurgents more difficult. Such action is invalid because there is no proper business purpose and may be set aside. *Schnell v. Chris-Craft Indus. Inc.*, 285 A.2d 437 (Del. 1971).

Caveat: Not all cases agree with the *Schnell* holding. Cases holding that management may exercise powers granted to it without regard to the purpose of the action tend to be older cases.

C.   TENDER OFFERS AND OTHER TAKEOVER DEVICES

In the late 1960s, numerous cash tender and public exchange offers were largely based on the element of surprise, virtually blitzkrieg tactics. Since then developments in various areas have greatly modified the manner in which takeover bids are now pursued.

1.   **THE WILLIAMS ACT**
The Williams Act amends the Securities Exchange Act of 1934 and applies to tender offers for corporations with securities registered under section 12 of the 1934 Act. This Act requires:

a.   Disclosure of information by any person who makes a cash tender offer. Disclosure must include information as to the source of funds used in the offer, the purpose for which the offer is made, plans the aggressor may have if successful, and any contracts or understandings it has with, or with respect to, the target corporation.

b.   Disclosure of similar information is required by any person or group who acquires more than 5 per cent of the outstanding shares of any class of stock.

   1)   In *Rondeau v. Mosinee Paper Corp.*, 422 U.S. 49, 95 S.Ct. 2069 (1975) the Court held that an issuer could not use the failure to make this filing as a basis for enjoining the later voting of the stock.

   2)   Filing is required of a "group" that is formed with a view toward acquisition of control if the group's holdings exceed 5 per cent. *GAF Corp. v. Milstein*, 453 F.2d 709 (2d Cir. 1971).

c.   Similar information must be disclosed by:

   1)   Issuers making an offer for their own shares, or

   2)   Issuers in which a change of control is proposed through seriatim resignations of directors.

d.   Miscellaneous substantive restrictions are imposed on the mechanics of a cash tender offer, e. g., oversubscribed tender offers must be accepted pro rata rather than on a first-come-first-bought basis; tenders must be revocable except during limited time periods.

e.   Section 14(e) imposes a broad prohibition against the use of false, misleading or incomplete statements in connection with a tender offer.

   1)   Section 14(e) is patterned after rule 10b–5 and adopts the same standards of materiality, scienter, and disclosure. The Supreme Court has held that section 14(e), like rule 10b–5, only relates to nondisclosure or deception and does not affect unfair practices generally. *Schreiber v. Burlington Northern, Inc.*, ___ U.S. ___, 105 S.Ct. 2458 (1985).

Example: A plan to use the target's cash to pay for the target's shares must be disclosed. *General Host Corp. v. Triumph American, Inc.*, 359 F.Supp. 749 (S.D.N.Y. 1973). If disclosed, the plan does not violate section 14(e) even if the transaction constitutes waste or injures creditors.

2) In *Piper v. Chris-Craft Industries, Inc.*, 430 U.S. 1, 97 S.Ct. 926 (1977), the Court held that a defeated tender offeror did not have standing to sue for damages under this provision of the Williams Act. Injunctive relief may not be foreclosed by this decision.

3) Tendering shareholders have standing to seek injunctive relief and, probably, damages. *Lowenschuss v. Kane*, 520 F.2d 255 (2d Cir. 1975).

4) The Supreme Court in *Chris-Craft* specifically left open the question whether a nontendering shareholder might have standing to sue an offeror.

2. STATE ANTI-TAKEOVER STATUTES

Before 1982 virtually all states adopted statutes or administrative regulations to regulate tender offers affecting corporations with significant contacts with the state in question. In fact, these statutes were largely designed to protect such corporations from aggressors by imposing hearing requirements and fairness standards that would significantly delay or make impractical takeover attempts.

a. In *Edgar v. Mite Corporation*, 457 U.S. 624, 102 S.Ct. 2629 (1982) the Supreme Court held unconstitutional the Illinois Business Take-Over Act as preempted by the Williams Act and as involving unreasonable burdens on interstate commerce. Following this decision, most pre-1982 state statutes were either abandoned or held unconstitutional by lower courts.

b. New attempts by states to impose restrictions on tender offers are usually referred to as "post-Mite" statutes. They all build on the admitted power of states to regulate the internal affairs of domestic corporations, and may be classed into three broad categories.

1) Ohio type statutes establish shareholder approval for "control share acquisitions" that break through the 20 per cent, 33 per cent, and 50 per cent levels. A person seeking to acquire additional shares that break through the specific level must give notice to the corporation and the proposed transaction must be submitted to shareholders for approval. Shares owned by the acquiring person and by corporate management may not be counted in this vote.

Under the Ohio statute, the effect of a negative vote is that the transaction may not be completed; under similar statutes in Indiana and Minnesota, the transaction may be completed but the shares owned by the acquiring shareholder lose their voting power either indefinitely or for a specified period.

Caveat: At least two lower courts have held Ohio-type statutes unconstitutional under *Mite* principles.

2)   Pennsylvania type statutes provide that if a shareholder acquires more than 20 per cent of the voting shares of a corporation, other shareholders have the right to compel that shareholder to acquire their shares at a "fair value."   Also, a merger transaction between a 20+ per cent shareholder and the corporation must be approved by a majority of the shares excluding the vote of the 20+ per cent shareholder.   Finally, Pennsylvania broadens the duty of the directors to consider the position of employees and localities as well as shareholders in assessing decisions.

3)   New York type statutes provide that an "interested shareholder" (one that acquires more than 20 per cent of the voting shares) for a period of five years after the acquisition that causes the interest to exceed 20 per cent may not enter into "business combinations" with the corporation except with a majority vote of shareholders other than the interested shareholder or except on "best price" terms based on acquisitions within the previous five years.   "Business combinations" are defined to include merger and asset transactions, dissolutions, share reclassifications, and the like.

Caveat: All these statutes are applicable only to corporations that are incorporated in the state in question and also registered under section 12 of the Securities Exchange Act of 1934.

Caveat: The constitutionality of the Pennsylvania and New York type statutes is uncertain.   Many persons believe the mandatory buy-out feature of the Pennsylvania statute is of doubtful constitutionality and that the New York statute has the best chance of being upheld.

3.   SOPHISTICATED DEFENSIVE TACTICS

Defensive tactics that make takeover bids more difficult vary widely but clearly have increased in sophistication over time.   Such tactics include:

a.   Finding a more congenial suitor (a "white knight").

b.   Buying a business that increases the chances that the threatened takeover will give rise to anti-trust problems.

c.   Making it difficult for an offeror who acquires a majority of the voting shares to replace the board of directors.

d.   Instituting suit to enjoin the offer for violations of the Williams Act, the antitrust laws or on other grounds. E. g., *Corenco Corp. v. Schiavone & Sons, Inc.*, 488 F.2d 207 (2d Cir. 1973).

e.   Issuing or proposing to issue additional shares to friendly persons to make a takeover more difficult (a "lockup").

f.   Increasing the dividend or otherwise driving up the price of shares to make the takeover price unattractive.

g.   Amending the basic corporate documents to make a takeover by even a majority·shareholder more difficult ("porcupine provisions").

h.   Buying off the aggressor, *Cheff v. Mathes*, 199 A.2d 548 (Del. 1964).

i.   Buying up its own shares in the market to drive up the price. Advance disclosure of such purchases is required under rule 13e–1 under the Williams Act. See part XV, D, infra.

j.   Buying up shares pro rata excluding those of the offeror, *Unocal Corp. v. Mesa Petroleum Co.*, 493 A.2d 946 (Del. 1985).

k.   Creating new classes of stock that increase in rights if any person acquires more than a specified percentage of shares ("poison pills").

l.   Imposing restrictions in connection with the creation of debt that thwart attempted takeovers.

4.   ROLE OF ARBITRAGERS
When a take-over tender offer is made, the open market price for the shares increases dramatically close to the tender price. Persons owning shares thus have the choice of selling their shares in the open market at a discount or tendering their shares. Most shares sold on the open market are ultimately tendered because of the activities of "risk arbitragers."

a.   Risk arbitragers are speculators who purchase shares in the open market at prices below the tender offer price in order to tender them and profit by the difference between the two prices.

b.   In some tender offers, the volume of transactions effected by risk arbitragers has been very substantial.

c.   Risk arbitragers are the natural allies of aggessors since they profit only if the transaction is consummated.

5.   EXCHANGE OFFERS

An exchange offer involves the issuance of debt or equity securities by the aggressor to complete the acquisition of the target. Such an issuance is almost always subject to the registration and disclosure requirements of the Securities Act of 1933, which are at least as substantial as the disclosure requirements of the Williams Act.

6.   MISCELLANEOUS TAKEOVER TECHNIQUES

Because of the state anti-takeover statutes and the development of sophisticated defensive tactics, new techniques for takeovers are being devised.

a.   An issue often raised by these new devices is whether they constitute tender offers under the Williams Act.

Example: A simultaneous offer to purchase shares of the target corporation made to some 40 institutional and other investors by telephone in a single evening is a tender offer. *Wellman v. Dickinson*, 682 F.2d 355 (2d Cir. 1982).

Example: A "widespread solicitation of public shareholders in person, over the telephone and through the mails," by agents and employers is a tender offer and must be registered under the Williams Act. *Cattlemen's Investment Co. v. Fears*, 343 F.Supp. 1248 (W.D.Okl. 1972).

Example: A purchase of a single 30 per cent block of shares followed by an offer to purchase shares owned by all directors of the company plus purchases on the open market over an exchange is not a tender offer. *Nachman Corp. v. Halfred, Inc.*, Fed.Sec.L.Rep. (CCH) ¶ 94,455 (N.D.Ill. July 13, 1973), *Hanson Trust PLC v. SCM Corp.*, 774 F.2d 47 (2d Cir. 1985).

Example: Regular bids to purchase shares executed exclusively on the exchanges to acquire control are not a tender offer. *Kennecott Copper Corp. v. Curtiss-Wright Corp.*, 584 F.2d 1195 (2d Cir. 1978).

Example: A corporation withdraws a tender offer after a spirited contest. Minutes thereafter it offers to purchase shares from a limited number of risk arbitragers who had assembled large blocks of shares. This was held not to constitute a tender offer. *Hanson Trust PLC v. SCM Corp.*, 774 F.2d 47 (2d Cir. 1985).

7.   ECONOMIC ANALYSIS OF CASH TAKEOVER BIDS
There has been widespread discussion about the causes of and effects of takeover bids.

    a.   The economist views such transactions as improving the quality of management by weeding out inefficient managers and assuring that undervalued or underutilized assets are redeployed in a more efficient manner.

    b.   Economists and others have also argued that takeovers may provide "synergistic" benefits by combining complementary businesses.

    c.   A more skeptical explanation is that the trend represents "empire building" by managers who believe that various advantages arise from size:

        1)   Greater remuneration;

        2)   Greater prestige and psychic income;

        3)   Greater protection from takeovers; and

        4)   Enhanced market power.

    d.   It is possible that other explanations, e. g. tax advantages, may explain specific transactions.

8.   LITIGATION DEALING WITH DEFENSIVE TACTICS
Several cases have considered the validity of defensive tactics in different contexts. In the following decisions particular weight should be given to the Delaware decisions because of the importance of that state as the state of incorporation of publicly held corporations.

    a.   Two courts have applied New Jersey law to conclude that the board of directors may not adopt "poison pill" preferred stock plans that materially change the voting power of shareholders without approval of the shareholders, *Asarco, Incorporated v. Court*, 611 F.Supp. 468 (D.N.J. 1985); *Minstar Acq. Corp. v. AMF*, 621 F.Supp. 1252 (S.D.N.Y. 1985). The second case also invalidates a "scorched earth" plan under which the target corporation granted excessive amounts of compensation to high-level employees.

b. *Gearhart Industries, Inc. v. Smith International, Inc.*, 741 F.2d 707 (5th Cir. 1984), upheld a "poison pill" preferred (issued in the context of a takeover struggle) under the business judgment rule and Texas law.

c. *Unocal Corp. v. Mesa Petroleum Co.*, 493 A.2d 946 (Del. 1985) upheld an exchange offer of debt for stock that excluded the aggressor from participation on the theory that the business judgment rule protected management's conclusion that the aggressor's two-tier offer was "inadequate and coercive," and that extreme tactics were justified.

d. *Moran v. Household International, Inc.*, 500 A.2d 1346 (Del. 1985), upheld the adoption of a "poison pill" as a defensive tactic in advance of a specific takeover attempt. The court concluded that the poison pill did not prevent takeover attempts, and the management's response to a specific takeover attempt would be considered when the occasion arose.

e. *Revlon, Inc. v. MacAndrews & Forbes Holdings, Inc.*, 506 A.2d 173 (Del. 1986), held that a "lock up" agreement that favored one contestant in a takeover attempt over another was invalid and should be enjoined since the board of directors had resolved to sell the corporation and, upon making the decision, the board had an obligation to get the best possible price for shareholders and could not arbitrarily favor one contestant over another.

D. INTERNAL STRUGGLES FOR CONTROL

Internal struggles for control may take several different forms.

1. A pure "palace coup" in which lower level management personnel compel the resignation of the CEO and other senior management is relatively infrequent. Such a coup usually requires the assistance and encouragement of either an influential shareholder with substantial holdings usually not directly connected with incumbent management or a substantial faction on the board of directors.

2. Forced resignations of the CEO because of loss of confidence of the board of directors are much more common. This pattern often occurs in corporations with serious financial troubles. The decision to force such an issue may be precipitated by institutional investors or commercial or investment bankers who first sense the loss of confidence by the financial community; even after such problems are first discussed, many directors may find it difficult to agree to oust incumbent management which was responsible for their election to the board.

3. Where a single shareholder holds decisive voting control, his or her loss of confidence in incumbent management may itself cause a change in such management.

4. In a few instances both insurgent and incumbent factions have obtained substantial representation on the board of directors. A substantial period of infighting may then ensue which should ultimately be resolved by an election by shareholders. *Campbell v. Loew's, Inc.*, 134 A.2d 852 (Del.Ch. 1957). Until such ultimate resolution, however, internal fighting may erupt over the composition of the board, the stewardship of the incumbent management, the permissible actions of the insurgent faction, and other matters.

REVIEW QUESTIONS

XIII–1. In a successful proxy fight in which the insurgents triumph, who pays the expenses and costs?

XIII–2. The argument has been made that all proxy fight contestants should have their expenses reimbursed by the corporation. What is the basis of this argument and what is its weakness?

XIII–3. How are proxy contests regulated?

XIII–4. What is a tender offer and how are they regulated?

XIII–5. What is the "Williams Act"?

XIII–6. Why have states adopted statutes dealing with tender offers despite the existence of the Williams Act?

XIII–7. What role is played in takeover attempts by risk arbitragers?

XIII–8.   What are "porcupine provisions"?

XIII–9.   What is a "poison pill"?

XIII–10.   The decisions by the Supreme Court of Delaware on permissible defensive tactics in takeovers are hopelessly confused; the court wavers from one side to another.

True _____   False _____

XIII–11.   P is a dissident shareholder who is attempting to replace the management of corporation X. X's bylaws provide that the annual meeting shall be held on January 11 of each year. The board of directors in accordance with statutory provisions allowing the directors to change the date of the annual meeting have advanced the date to December 8 of the prior year. P brings an action against X Corporation for an injunction preventing the advancement of the meeting date. P contends that management has attempted to use the provisions of law and the corporate machinery to perpetuate itself in office and to obstruct the efforts of the dissident stockholder to undertake a proxy contest against management. These contentions are not disputed. Management contends that it has complied strictly with the provisions of state law in changing the date which is all that is required. Is P entitled to an injunction?

XIV

DUTIES OF DIRECTORS, OFFICERS AND SHAREHOLDERS

The duties of directors, officers, and shareholders to the corporation and to other interests within the corporation are each defined to some extent by their unique roles within the corporation. These duties are generally created by state law but the federal securities statutes also impose duties that are similar to, and partially overlap, state created duties.

Analysis

A. Duties in General
B. Duty of Care
C. Self-Dealing
D. Executive Compensation
E. Corporate Opportunities
F. Duties in Connection With Freeze Out Mergers
G. Miscellaneous Transactions Subject to the Fairness Test
H. Relationship of "Fairness" and "Business Judgment" Rules
I. State Statutory Liabilities

A. DUTIES IN GENERAL

The following is a brief description of the effects of the roles of directors, officers, and shareholders on the scope of their fiduciary duties to the corporation and to other interests within the corporation.

1. DIRECTORS

Directors have the broad responsibility of overseeing the management of the corporation. They occupy a unique position within the corporate structure, and owe both a duty of care and a high degree of fidelity and loyalty to the corporation. The relationship between director and corporation, in short, is a unique one.

    a.   The duties of directors are sometimes analogized to those of a trustee of a trust. However, directors of corporations are not strictly trustees, since they are not automatically liable for consequences of actions which exceed their powers. Further, the area of their discretion and judgment is considerably greater than that possessed by traditional trustees.
However, the directors' duties of fidelity and loyalty are essentially the same as a trustee's duties. *Guth v. Loft, Inc.*, 5 A.2d 503 (Del. 1939); *Litwin v. Allen*, 25 N.Y.S.2d 667 (Sup.Ct. 1940).

    b.   In most instances, directors owe duties to the corporation as a whole rather than to individual shareholders or to individual classes of shareholders. However, if a director deals with a shareholder directly, or if he acts in a way which injures a specific shareholder, he may become directly liable to that shareholder.

    c.   Directors are not full-time employees of the corporation and are not required to devote their efforts exclusively to the corporation. (Of course, a full-time employee may also be a director, but the role of director as such is not a full-time responsibility.)

2. OFFICERS AND AGENTS

The relationship between corporate officers and agents and the corporation depends to some extent on the position occupied by the officer or agent and the type of liabilities that are being imposed.

    a.   A full-time, high-level managing officer may owe substantially the same duties to the corporation as a director.

    b.   Officers or agents in subordinate or limited positions may owe a correspondingly lesser degree of duty, though even the lowest agent owes the principal certain minimum duties of care, skill, propriety in conduct, and loyalty in all matters connected with his agency.

c.   A distinction also may be made between full-time and part-time officers or agents in some contexts.

3.   SHAREHOLDERS

Since shareholders as such have no power to manage the business and affairs of the corporation and do not perform services for the corporation, their fiduciary relationship to the corporation differs from the relationship of a director or officer.

a.   Many cases state that a shareholder as such owes no fiduciary duty to his corporation.   Such statements, however, are too broad, since shareholders clearly owe a duty to their corporation or their fellow shareholders in some circumstances.

b.   Controlling shareholders owe duties to creditors, holders of senior securities and minority shareholders when they transfer control of the corporation to a third party.

c.   Minority shareholders do not have an open license to abuse or sell their voting power, or exercise it fraudulently.

d.   Shareholders are not subject to the same conflict-of-interest rules as directors.   For example, shareholders may usually vote their shares in favor of ratification of their own self-dealing transactions but a director should not participate in an analogous decision by the board.

e.   Several recent cases state that shareholders in a closely held corporation owe duties to other shareholders similar to the duties one partner owes to other partners.   See e.g. *Matter of T.J. Ronan Paint Corp.* [Doran], 469 N.Y.S.2d 931, 936 (App.Div. 1984); *Fender v. Prescott*, 476 N.Y.S.2d 128 (App.Div. 1984).

B.   DUTY OF CARE

A director may be liable to the corporation for losses incurred as a result of a failure to exercise proper care in performing his or her duties with respect to the corporation's affairs.

1.   GENERAL TESTS

RMBCA § 8.30 states that the standard test for directors' duty of care is that the duties must be discharged "(1) in good faith; (2) with the care an ordinarily prudent person in a like position would exercise under similar circumstances; and (3) in a manner he reasonably believes to be in the best interests of the corporation."   A similar test that is often quoted is the exercise of that degree of diligence, care and skill "which ordinarily prudent [person] would exercise under similar circumstances in their personal business affairs." See *Selheimer v. Manganese Corp. of America*, 224 A.2d 634 (Pa. 1966). A stricter test might discourage persons from becoming directors.

a.   Courts feel that they should not second-guess corporate managers with the benefit of hindsight. Honest business decisions made in good faith are universally held not actionable, even though the decision was mistaken or unfortunate. *Shlensky v. Wrigley*, 237 N.E.2d 776 (Ill.App. 1968) [decision not to play night games at Wrigley Field]; *Kamin v. American Express Co.*, 383 N.Y.S.2d 807 (S.Ct. 1976), aff'd on opinion below, 387 N.E.2d 993 [decision to pay dividend in property on which tax loss was available]. This is usually referred to as "the business judgment rule." If the decision is illegal, however, the business judgment rule may not be a shield. *Miller v. American Tel. & Tel. Co.*, 507 F.2d 759 (3d Cir. 1974).

b.   A related rule prevents the validity of the business decisions themselves (made by directors) from being questioned or set aside by a court. This principle is sometimes referred to as the "business judgment doctrine" to contrast it with the "rule" that protects directors from liability.

c.   Issues relating to dividend policies and distributions are often stated to be peculiarly appropriate for the application of the business judgment rule. *Kamin v. American Express Co.*, 383 N.Y.S.2d 807 (Sup.Ct. 1976).

d.   Historically, relatively few cases imposed liability upon directors for failure to comply with their duty of care. An early case imposing liability upon a bank director for unreasonable or imprudent actions is *Litwin v. Allen*, 25 N.Y.S.2d 667 (Sup.Ct. 1940), and several other early cases involving bank directors also imposed liability. More recently, several cases have imposed liability.

    1)   *Smith v. Van Gorkom*, 488 A.2d 858 (Del. 1985) imposed liability upon directors for accepting an outside offer for the purchase of the corporation without investigating whether a higher price might be obtained and without making an investigation into the value of the business.

    2)   *Francis v. United Jersey Bank*, 432 A.2d 814 (N.J. 1981), imposed liability on an elderly woman for misappropriations committed by her sons. The defendant had received financial statements showing the transactions but had made no attempt to prevent them. In this case, the defendant had received a small part of the misappropriated amounts personally; there is thus an element of self dealing in this case.

2.   **FAILURE TO DIRECT**
Sometimes the claim is made that a director should be liable for
mismanagement because he or she totally failed to direct.

   a.   The director may be aged, ill, resident of a distant state, or merely lazy
         or unduly trusting. He or she may feel that he was elected only as a
         figurehead or as an accommodation and was not intended to have any
         significant function.

         1)   This is generally not a defense: When a person agrees to be a
               director he accepts certain responsibilities and obligations, and if
               these are too burdensome, the proper course is to resign rather
               than fail to meet them.

         2)   The test of skill and prudence is based on an average person of
               reasonable intelligence and competence.

         3)   A director is not considered to be acting in good faith if he or she
               has or should have knowledge concerning the matter in question
               that would cause such reliance to be unwarranted.

               Example: A director who is an attorney does not object to a
                            transaction even though he knows it probably violates the
                            antitrust laws. His duty must be evaluated on the basis
                            of the legal knowledge he has as a lawyer; he may thus
                            be liable even though a non-lawyer director in the same
                            situation would not be.

   b.   *Barnes v. Andrews*, 298 F. 614 (S.D.N.Y. 1924), holds that a director who
         was negligent in failing to direct can be held liable only if the plaintiff
         shows a causal relationship between his failure and some specific loss.
         Allied Freightways, Inc. v. Cholfin, 91 N.E.2d 765 (Mass. 1950) holds
         that a housewife-director is not liable for losses suffered by a corporation
         as a result of her husband's defalcations because her negligence was not
         the "proximate cause" of the loss, it being doubtful that she could have
         prevented the loss in any event. If these holdings are correct liability
         will seldom be imposed on "directors who fail to direct."

   c.   Defendants in "failure to direct" cases may also rely on the principle that
         directors, in the absence of other information, may assume that managers
         and officers are honest.

   d.   Bank directors may owe a higher degree of due care than directors of
         ordinary business corporations. E. g., *Bates v. Dresser*, 251 U.S. 524, 40
         S.Ct. 247 (1920). On the other hand, there is dicta in other cases to the
         effect that bank directors should not be treated differently in this regard.

e.   In summary, only a few cases impose liability on non-bank directors for total failure to direct, and these usually also involve an element of self dealing.

3.   KNOWING AUTHORIZATION OF WRONGFUL ACT
Liability has sometimes been imposed where the director knowingly authorizes or participates in a wrongful act.

Example: Personal liability has been imposed on directors where they authorize the improper use of corporate funds, knowing that the use is not in furtherance of corporate affairs, or where they assent to the corporation's use of a financial statement to obtain credit when they know that it is false or fraudulent.

a.   Directors have been held liable for a tortious or unlawful act of the corporation if they personally participated in the act.

b.   Attempts to hold directors or officers personally liable for antitrust fines imposed on the corporation, or for bribes, improper payments or illegal campaign contributions made by the corporation, have generally been unsuccessful.   *Graham v. Allis-Chalmers Mfg. Co.*, 188 A.2d 125 (Del. 1963).

1)   There was evidence in some of these cases of the directors' or officers' personal involvement in the conduct or payments in question.

2)   A partial explanation is that potential liability in such cases may be enormous, running into the millions of dollars, and totally out of proportion to the wrongfulness of the directors' conduct.

3)   In some cases, particularly those involving campaign contributions or improper payments, it may have been felt that the corporation benefitted from the payments.

4)   In *Miller v. American Telephone & Telegraph Co.*, 507 F.2d 759 (3d Cir. 1974), the court upheld a shareholder's complaint against AT & T that that corporation had failed to try to collect a debt of $1,500,000 owed to the company by the Democratic National Committee for communications service provided during the 1968 Democratic Convention.   The decision was based in part on a statute prohibiting campaign contributions by corporations to political parties.

c.   Directors are not automatically liable if they approve an act that turns out to be ultra vires.

4. **DISMISSAL OF LITIGATION**

One of the most controversial applications of the business judgment rule today is whether a disinterested majority of the board of directors (or a disinterested committee of the board of directors) may determine that as a matter of business judgment a derivative suit brought by a shareholder should not be pursued since it is not in the best interests of the corporation.

    a.   The first decisions on this issue involved suits involving improper foreign payments or compensation matters and the courts initially accepted with little reservation the conclusion that dismissal of derivative litigation was no different than other questions resolved by disinterested directors as a matter of business judgment. *Gall v. Exxon Corp.*, 418 F.Supp. 508 (S.D.N.Y. 1976); *Auerbach v. Bennett*, 393 N.E.2d 994 (N.Y. 1979); *Burks v. Lasker*, 441 U.S. 471, 99 S.Ct. 1831 (1979).

    b.   A leading case, *Zapata, Inc. v. Maldonado*, 430 A.2d 779 (Del. 1981), takes the position that where a demand on directors is excused, a court should exercise its own independent "business judgment" to determine whether litigation should be dismissed over the objection of the plaintiff solely on the basis of the business judgment of directors.

    c.   A later case in Delaware, *Aronson v. Lewis*, 473 A.2d 805 (Del. 1984), made it clear that the *Maldonado* approach was only applicable in "demand unnecessary" or "demand futile" cases. The test for demand futility is two-fold: (1) whether on the basis of the particular facts alleged there is a reasonable doubt that the directors reflect the independence and disinterestedness necessary for application of the business judgment rule, and (2) whether the facts alleged with particularity, when taken as true, support a reasonable doubt that the challenged transaction was the product of a valid exercise of business judgment. Unless both conditions are met, the demand requirement must be met and the decision of the board or committee is entitled to the protections of the business judgment rule.

    d.   Other courts have accepted the principle of *Maldonado* without apparently restricting it to demand unnecessary cases. *Joy v. North*, 692 F.2d 880 (2d Cir. 1982) [Connecticut law], was the first case.

        1)   *Miller v. Register & Tribune Syndicate, Inc.*, 336 N.W.2d 709 (Iowa 1983), and *Alford v. Shaw*, 324 S.E.2d 878 (N.C.App. 1985) both hold that where a majority of the directors are named as defendants, the board may not establish a litigation committee with the power of the board to terminate derivative litigation. Rather, the board must apply to a court for the appointment of a trustee or receiver if it wishes to discontinue the litigation.

2)   The concern expressed in these cases is that even directors who are not themselves defendants in the litigation may have a "structural bias" in favor of the directors who are named as defendants. See Comment, The Propriety of Judicial Deference to Corporate Boards of Directors, 96 Harv.L.Rev. 1894 (1983).

Example: Exxon learns that over $50,000,000 of questionable payments have been made by an Italian subsidiary. A minority shareholder brings a derivative suit against persons who were directors when the payments were made; some defendants knew of the payments while others did not. A committee of uninvolved directors is formed to review the desirability of pursuing this litigation; the committee decides that it is in the best interests of the corporation not to pursue it and the corporation moves that it be dismissed. This decision must be accepted under the business judgment rule and the case should be dismissed. *Gall v. Exxon Corp.*, 418 F.Supp. 508 (S.D.N.Y. 1976).

Example: In the foregoing example, the plaintiff may be able to show that the committee was not a "disinterested" committee; if so, its conclusion would not be protected by the business judgment rule.

Example: If all the directors were involved in the payments so that a demand on the board of directors was excused, under *Zapata v. Maldonado* the court would exercise its own independent business judgment as to whether it is in Exxon's best interest to pursue the litigation.

5.   DUTIES IN CONNECTION WITH SALE OF THE CORPORATION
Delaware cases require that the board of directors, when it resolves to sell the corporation, make a preliminary inquiry into the value of the business and whether a higher price might be obtained before it enters into a contract to sell the corporation. *Smith v. Van Gorkom*, 488 A.2d 858 (Del. 1985). Further, if the board of directors of a target in a takeover struggle concludes that the business is to be sold, it thereafter has a duty to obtain the best price it can for the shareholders; it may not arbitrarily favor one contestant over another. *Revlon, Inc. v. MacAndrews & Forbes Holdings, Inc.*, 506 A.2d 173 (Del. 1986).

C.   SELF–DEALING

Self-dealing transactions, unlike due care issues, have produced a steady stream of litigation. In many such cases, personal liability has been imposed on directors. A number of states have adopted legislation dealing with this subject. See RMBCA § 8.31.

1.   DEFINITION

A self-dealing transaction is one between a director and his corporation.   Most such transactions are directly between director and corporation, but some may be indirect, e. g., transactions between a relative of the director and the corporation, between two corporations with a common director, or between a parent corporation and its partially-owned subsidiary.

RMBCA § 8.31 defines a "conflict of interest transaction" to be a "transaction with the corporation in which a director of the corporation has a direct or indirect interest."   An "indirect" interest in a transaction is defined to occur when "another entity in which [the director] has a material financial interest or in which he is a general partner" is a party to the transaction, or when another entity "of which he is a director, officer or trustee is a party to the transaction and the transaction is or should be considered by the board of directors of the corporation."

2.   THE DANGER OF SELF–DEALING TRANSACTIONS

The danger of self-dealing transactions between a corporation and a director is the risk that the corporation may be treated unfairly in such a transaction, since the director's selfish interest may outweigh his or her loyalty to the corporation.

a.   When such a transaction is questioned, the director must usually justify the propriety and fairness of the transaction; the burden of proof is thus shifted from the person questioning the transaction.

b.   The form the transaction takes is not significant.

> *Example:*   The same test is applicable to all of the following transactions: the sale of corporate property to a director, the sale of property to a director's spouse, the sale of property by a director to a corporation, a contract between the corporation and a director for the director to perform services such as selling stock or managing the business, and a loan by a director to his corporation.   [The test is discussed below.]

c.   The early common law took the position that because of the risk inherent in all self-dealing transactions, all such transactions were automatically voidable at the election of the corporation. *Stewart v. Lehigh Valley R. R. Co.*, 38 N.J.L. 505 (1875).   Such a rule has been abandoned since many self-dealing transactions are entirely fair and reasonable; indeed, in many situations directors may give their corporations terms that are more favorable than the corporation might obtain elsewhere. *Robotham v. Prudential Ins. Co. of America*, 53 A. 842 (N.J.Eq. 1903).

> *Example:*   Loans by directors to the corporation are often made when the corporation could not borrow elsewhere; such transactions should obviously be encouraged.

3.   THE MODERN TEST FOR SELF–DEALING TRANSACTIONS IN ABSENCE OF STATUTE

The test for self-dealing transactions developed by the courts in absence of statute combines procedural and substantive requirements essentially as follows:

a.   If the court feels the transaction to be *fair to the corporation*, it will probably be upheld. The burden of proving fairness requires full disclosure of the dual interest of the director.

b.   If the court feels that the transaction involves *fraud, undue overreaching* or *waste of corporate assets* it will definitely be set aside or the directors will otherwise be required to restore the status quo before the transaction.

c.   If the court feels that the transaction is not clearly fair to the corporation but does not involve fraud, overreaching or waste of corporate assets, the transaction will be upheld where the interested director can convincingly show that the transaction was approved (or ratified) by a disinterested majority of the board of directors without participation by the interested director, or by a majority of the shareholders after full disclosure of all relevant facts.

> *Example:*   A fair transaction is not ratified either by disinterested directors or by the shareholders. It may nevertheless not be set aside.

> *Example:*   All the directors are interested in a fair transaction; they ratify the transaction but shareholder ratification is not sought. It may not be set aside. *Wiberg v. Gulf Coast Land & Development Co.*, 360 S.W.2d 563 (Tex.Civ.App. 1962).

> *Caveat:*   Tests established by some authorities would require ratification or approval even for fair transactions. If this test is applied, the transactions in the above examples would be voidable.

> *Example:*   The director and majority shareholder misappropriates corporate funds for personal purposes. The disinterested directors approve the transaction. The transactions may nevertheless be set aside. There is a possibility that such a use of corporate funds could be justified as compensation if there is prior understanding as to the amount of such withdrawals over a period of time.

Example: In the same situation, the transaction is submitted to the shareholders and approved by 87 per cent of them. Since the transaction involves fraud or waste it may still be set aside on suit brought by a nonconsenting shareholder: the partial ratification is not binding on the other shareholders.

Example: In the same situation, the transaction is submitted to the shareholders and approved by all of them. The transaction may not be set aside by a shareholder; creditors or preferred shareholders may be able to set them aside if they can show injury to or fraud on creditors.

Example: A majority of disinterested directors approve a transaction consisting of the sale of land by the corporation to a director. The price is close to, but lower than, the corporation's asking price; the land had been on the market for a year at the asking price without any serious offers. The approval by the disinterested directors if preceded by full disclosure makes the transaction immune from attack by shareholders. In the absence of full disclosure the transaction is voidable. *State ex rel. Hayes Oyster Co. v. Keypoint Oyster Co.*, 391 P.2d 979 (Wash. 1964).

Example: A majority of directors approve a musical program for radio advertising unaware that the wife of the CEO will be one of the performing artists. The performer is competent and receives no special treatment or prominence. No duty has been breached. *Bayer v. Beran*, 49 N.Y.S.2d 2 (S.Ct. 1944).

d.   Two recurring issues relating to common law ratification are who may be considered disinterested for purposes of ratification, and what degree of specific knowledge or notice is required to constitute an effective ratification. There is a tendency in cases to relax these requirements in situations where the transaction appears to be fair and to stiffen them when the transaction seems questionable.

e.   Where a subsidiary corporation has minority shareholders, transactions between parent and subsidiary may injure the minority shareholders of the subsidiary. The basic test for such transactions is fairness to the subsidiary. *Case v. New York Central R.R. Co.*, 204 N.E.2d 643 (N.Y. 1965) [filing of consolidated return]. See also the discussion of "freezeout mergers" (Part F), "miscellaneous transactions subject to the fairness test" (Part G), and "relationship of 'fairness' and 'business judgment' rules" (Part H), infra.

4.   RATIFICATION BY SHAREHOLDERS
Ratification by shareholders of a transaction between a director and the corporation will sometimes validate the transaction.

    a.   At common law, interested directors may be able to vote their shares as shareholders in favor of the transaction. *North-West Trans. Co. v. Beatty*, 12 App.Cas. 589 (Eng. 1887); *Gambler v. Queens County Water Co.*, 25 N.E. 201 (N.Y. 1980).

    b.   A shareholder who is also a creditor may be able to vote his or her shares in favor of a transaction which benefits him or her as a creditor. *Allaun v. Consolidated Oil Co.*, 147 A. 257 (Del.Ch. 1929).

    c.   Not all self-dealing transactions may be ratified by majority vote. Transactions which involve fraud, undue overreaching, or waste of corporate assets (e. g., a director using corporate assets for personal purposes without paying for them) can only be ratified by a unanimous vote, and even then, may be attacked by representatives of creditors if the corporation becomes insolvent. *Schreiber v. Bryan*, 396 A.2d 512 (Del.Ch. 1978).

5.   STATUTORY TESTS FOR SELF–DEALING TRANSACTIONS
Statutes in many states address the issue of self-dealing transactions. Most such statutes, like RMBCA § 8.31, purport to exonerate self-dealing transactions from a rule of automatic voidability if the transaction is approved by disinterested directors, by the shareholders, or if the transaction is fair. Provisions of these statutes, however, vary widely.

    a.   These statutes are usually construed as simply removing a cloud from self-dealing transactions but not as validating unfair transactions or removing transactions from judicial scrutiny. *Fliegler v. Lawrence*, 361 A.2d 218 (Del. 1976). Claims that the transaction constituted waste, or involved fraud, ultra vires conduct, or were not properly approved are not affected by compliance with these statutes. Further, unfair or unreasonable transactions may not be validated under these statutes. *Remillard Brick Co. v. Remillard-Dandini Co.*, 241 P.2d 66 (Cal.App. 1952); *Kennerson v. Burbank Amusement Co.*, 260 P.2d 823 (Cal.App. 1953).

    b.   Compliance with these statutes generally require full disclosure of conflicting interests and the approval of transactions by disinterested directors or by shareholders. RMBCA § 8.31 excludes interested shareholders from approving conflict-of-interest transactions but most state statutes do not expressly do so.

6.   REMEDIES

Rescission is normally the proper remedy for a voidable transaction. In such a suit, the corporation must be prepared to return any consideration received by it in the transaction. Normally, it may not simultaneously retain the consideration and in effect seek to reduce the price by attacking the validity of the transaction.

> *Example:*   A director sells valuable real estate to her corporation in exchange for promissory notes and cash without fully disclosing her interest. The transaction is voidable. The corporation, however, simply refuses to make payments on the promissory notes, claiming that the price was too high. The corporation must either rescind (and return the land) or not rescind (and pay the stipulated price). It may not in effect renegotiate the transaction or have the court set a lower price for the land. *New York Trust Co. v. American Realty Co.,* 155 N.E. 102 (N.Y. 1926).

7.   INDIRECT TRANSACTIONS

Transactions between corporations with common directors may lend themselves to the same evil as self-dealing transactions between a director and his corporation, since the interest of a common director may be small in one corporation and large in the other.

   a.   The common law standard for evaluating transactions between corporations with common directors is simply one of manifest unfairness (or "entire fairness") to one corporation. *Globe Woolen Co. v. Utica Gas & Electric Co.,* 121 N.E. 378 (N.Y. 1918); *Chelrob, Inc. v. Barrett,* 57 N.E.2d 825 (N.Y. 1944); *Ewen v. Peoria & E. Ry. Co.,* 78 F.Supp. 312 (S.D.N.Y. 1948); *Shlensky v. South Parkway Building Corp.,* 166 N.E.2d 793 (Ill. 1960); *Case v. New York Central R. R. Co.,* 204 N.E.2d 643 (N.Y. 1965); *Chasin v. Gluck,* 282 A.2d 188 (Del.Ch. 1971).

   b.   The role of the common director in approving the transaction may also be relied upon in evaluating a transaction, e. g., *Puma v. Marriott,* 283 A.2d 693 (Del.Ch. 1971) but the test usually applied is an objective one of fairness, not a procedural test based on the degree of the common director's participation. The concern is that even "disinterested directors" may lack the needed objectivity in evaluating colleagues' conduct, particularly if the colleague may be responsible for their presence on the board.

8.   EXONERATORY PROVISIONS FOR SELF–DEALING TRANSACTIONS IN ARTICLES OF INCORPORATION

Provisions are sometimes placed in the articles of incorporation of a corporation which attempt to validate transactions between directors and the corporation which otherwise might be voidable under the above principles. These clauses are not construed literally, and will not validate fraudulent or manifestly unfair acts. *Abeles v. Adams Engineering Co., Inc.*, 173 A.2d 246 (N.J. 1961). Such clauses may, however,

a.   Permit an interested director to be counted in determining whether a quorum is present, and

b.   Exonerate transactions between corporation and director "from adverse inferences which might be drawn against them." *Everett v. Phillips*, 43 N.E.2d 18 (N.Y. 1942).

D. EXECUTIVE COMPENSATION

Directors of a corporation often serve as compensated corporate officers or agents. The establishment of the amount of compensation payable to a director involves a specific application of the principles relating to self-dealing. Even where the officer is not a director, the problem is often compounded because of considerations of friendship, mutual respect and, sometimes, mutual "back-scratching." Many corporations have created compensation committees composed of nonmanagement directors to review all compensation issues for highly compensated executives.

1.   TEST FOR EXCESSIVE COMPENSATION

Courts are reluctant to inquire into issues of executive compensation in publicly held corporations. In such corporations, the test for excessive compensation is whether the payments are so large as to constitute spoliation or waste. *Rogers v. Hill*, 289 U.S. 582, 53 S.Ct. 731 (1933).

Example: A bylaw duly approved by the shareholders provides that a stated percentage of the profits are set aside each year and paid as a bonus to specified executive officers. Twenty-five years later, the business of the corporation has increased many-fold; the profits payable to the executive officers under the bylaw are roughly ten times higher than the compensation payable by comparable corporations to comparable officers. The payments may be reduced by the court to a reasonable amount.

Example: A corporation creates a non-discriminatory pension plan for its employees, including its chief executive officer. Because of his nearness to retirement and large pension that he commands, over $10,000,000 of the initial payment of $14,000,000 is attributable to the inclusion of the CEO in the plan, an amount far in excess of reasonable compensation. The plan may be attacked by a shareholder as waste. *Fogelson v. American Woolen Co.*, 170 F.2d 660 (2d Cir. 1948).

Example: A chief executive of a corporation receives a salary of $4,000,000 per year. While large, this salary is not so out of line with modern executive compensation arrangements as to constitute waste.

2. COMPARISON WITH TESTS UNDER INTERNAL REVENUE CODE

In closely held corporations large salary payments are usually designed to limit the "double tax problem" of doing business in the corporate form. The IRS may disallow a deduction for unreasonable salaries (treating the excess as a dividend). The test in the tax cases is whether the compensation is for services and is reasonable. *Charles McCandless Tile Service v. United States,* 422 F.2d 1336 (Ct.Cl. 1970), *Herbert G. Hatt,* 28 T.C.M. 1194 (1969).

a. In the closely held corporation, excessive compensation paid a controlling shareholder may be recovered by the corporation (at the suit of a minority shareholder) if the compensation is unreasonable. *Fendelman v. Fenco Handbag Mfg. Co.,* 482 S.W.2d 461 (Mo. 1972). In this respect, an adverse tax determination is evidence of unreasonableness. *Wilderman v. Wilderman,* 315 A.2d 610 (Del.Ch. 1974).

b. In the publicly-held corporation, on the other hand, such a test for measuring excessiveness of compensation for fiduciary purposes has been rejected as being unworkable and involving courts in business decisions with respect to which they have little or no competence. *Heller v. Boylan,* 29 N.Y.S.2d 653 (Sup.Ct. 1941).

3. NEED FOR BENEFIT TO CORPORATION

The doctrine of consideration requires that services be given or promised in exchange for compensation. A post-death payment to the estate of a deceased employee or surviving spouse not made pursuant to a preexisting plan has sometimes been attacked on this ground. *Adams v. Smith,* 153 So.2d 221 (Ala. 1963); *Alexander v. Lindsay,* 152 So.2d 261 (La.App. 1963).

Caveat: The court usually can find some way to avoid this technical objection to the enforceability of a compensation arrangement if it wishes to do so. Regular pension or profit sharing plans, for example, are not subject to this objection because they are part of an overall plan of compensation entered into while services are being performed.

Example: A retiring employee agrees to be available for consultation after his retirement at the corporation's request in exchange for specified payments for life. The employee is never requested to consult. The payments are nevertheless supported by consideration. *Osborne v. Locke Steel Chain Co.,* 218 A.2d 526 (Conn. 1966).

4.   COMPENSATION BASED ON STOCK PERFORMANCE
Courts have generally upheld compensation arrangements based on the price or
value of shares.

   a.   Stock option and stock purchase plans may have special tax benefits.
        Such plans are generally upheld if approved by disinterested directors or
        by shareholders, and the benefits being conferred bear a reasonable
        relationship to the services being performed. *Beard v. Elster*, 160 A.2d
        731 (Del. 1960); *Eliasberg v. Standard Oil Co.*, 92 A.2d 862 (N.J.Super.
        Ch.Div. 1952).

   b.   A "phantom stock" plan provides compensation that is computed over a
        period of time as though the officer had owned a specified number of
        shares. Each year bookkeeping entries are made to reflect "dividends,"
        "stock splits" and similar transactions; when the employee retires or
        leaves the employment of the corporation, an additional amount equal to
        the hypothetical increase in market price of the hypothetical shares is paid
        to him or her. Such an arrangement is a legitimate form of
        compensation. *Lieberman v. Koppers Co., Inc.*, 149 A.2d 756 (Del.Ch.
        1959); *Berkwitz v. Humphrey*, 163 F.Supp. 78 (N.D.Ohio 1958).

   e.   Stock appreciation rights (SAR's) are bonus payments computed on the
        basis of growth of value of the corporation's shares. In recent years
        bonus payments based on the attainment of a predetermined goal (e. g.
        ten per cent increase in gross sales of the division) have become popular.
        These are referred to as performance unit payments (PUP's).

E.   CORPORATE OPPORTUNITIES

The corporate opportunity doctrine requires a corporate director to render to Caesar
at the best possible price that which is Caesar's.

1.   GENERAL TEST
     As a fiduciary, a director owes a duty to further the interest of the
     corporation and to give it the benefit of his uncorrupted business judgment.
     He may not take a secret profit in connection with corporate transactions,
     compete unfairly with the corporation, or take personally profitable business
     opportunities which belong to the corporation.

   a.   Very often the application of the doctrine of corporate opportunity to a
        specific situation ultimately comes down to a judicial evaluation of
        business ethics.

b. If the opportunity is not a "corporate opportunity" the director may take advantage of it personally for his or her own private gain and need not share it with the corporation or with other participants in the corporation.

2. WHEN IS AN OPPORTUNITY A "CORPORATE OPPORTUNITY?"

Several competing tests exist as to when an opportunity should be considered a corporate opportunity.

a. The test established by some modern cases combines a "line of business" test with the pervasive issue whether it is unfair for the director under the circumstances to take advantage personally of the opportunity. *Miller v. Miller*, 222 N.W.2d 71 (Minn. 1974). The "line of business" test compares the closeness of the opportunity to the types of business in which the corporation is engaged. The closer it is, the most likely it is to be a corporate opportunity.

b. An earlier test was that the opportunity must involve "property wherein the corporation has interest already existing or in which it has an expectancy growing out of an existing right." Many modern courts refer to this language. E. g., *Burg v. Horn*, 380 F.2d 897 (2d Cir. 1967); *Litwin v. Allen*, 25 N.Y.S.2d 667 (Sup.Ct. 1940). However, this is a narrower test of corporate opportunity than the line of business/fairness test and has been rejected by some courts. E. g., *Kerrigan v. Unity Sav. Ass'n*, 317 N.E.2d 39 (Ill. 1974).

c. A third test that has been adopted by some courts is that the opportunity must in some sense arise out of the line of the corporation's business as it is then conducted. This test has been categorized as "too broad." *Burg v. Horn*, 380 F.2d 897 (2d Cir. 1967).

d. Another influential test simply applies the test of fairness or "intrinsic fairness" to the transaction in question. *Schreiber v. Bryan*, 396 A.2d 512 (Del.Ch. 1978).

e. The ALI Corporate Governance Project defines a corporate opportunity for a principal senior executive or director who is a full-time employee as an opportunity that is reasonably closely related to the business in which the corporation is engaged; the test also includes opportunities offered to directors (inside or outside) or principal senior executives in the belief that they would be offered to the corporation or which arise out of the use of corporate information or property. *Klinicki v. Lundgren*, 695 P.2d 906 (Or. 1985) adopts the Project definition even though it is a tentative test subject to revision by the American Law Institute.

3. FACTORS CONSIDERED IN EVALUATING WHETHER AN OPPORTUNITY IS A CORPORATE OPPORTUNITY

A number of factors are considered in evaluating the director's decision to take advantage of an opportunity.

a. Whether there were prior negotiations with the corporation about the opportunity;

b. Whether the opportunity was offered to the corporation or to the director as an agent of the corporation;

c. Whether the director disclosed the opportunity to the corporation or took advantage of it secretly;

d. Whether the director learned of the opportunity by reason of his or her position with the corporation;

e. Whether the director used corporate facilities or property in taking advantage of the opportunity;

f. Whether as a result of taking advantage of the opportunity the director is competing with the corporation or thwarting corporate policy (*Zidell v. Zidell, Inc.*, 560 P.2d 1091 (Or. 1977));

g. Whether the director acquired at a discount claims against the corporation when the corporation could have done so (*Weissman v. A. Weissman, Inc.*, 97 A.2d 870 (Pa. 1953); *Manufacturers Trust Co. v. Becker*, 338 U.S. 304, 70 S.Ct. 127 (1949));

h. Whether the need of the corporation for the opportunity was substantial; and

i. Whether the director was involved in several ventures and the opportunity in question was not uniquely attributable to one such venture. (*Johnston v. Greene*, 121 A.2d 919 (Del. 1956)).

> *Example:* A corporation is planning to build a new plant at a specified location. An officer buys up a portion of the land on which the plant is to be built and resells it at a profit to the corporation without disclosing his identity. The officer must account to the corporation for his entire profit.

> *Example:* A corporation is in the boat building business and does not buy or sell used boats. The corporate president learns that a used boat is for sale at a favorable price. She buys the boat personally and resells it profitably. The used boat is not a

corporate opportunity and she need not account to the corporation for her profit.

Example: The president of a corporation operating a retail department store learns that a competitive store is for sale two blocks away. He secretly buys the competing store, and uses his knowledge of inventory control and relations with suppliers to make the new store more competitive. The new store is a corporate opportunity and the president must account for his profit.

Example: In the same situation, the corporation has previously decided not to expand into new locations in the community in question. The competing store is not a corporate opportunity but the president may be liable for conversion of trade secrets or unfair competition in the manner he improved the competitive nature of the store. *Lincoln Stores v. Grant*, 34 N.E.2d 704 (Mass. 1941).

4.   REJECTION OF CORPORATE OPPORTUNITY

Even if an opportunity is a corporate opportunity, directors are not precluded from taking advantage of it if the corporation elects not to take advantage of it or if the corporation is unable or incapable of taking advantage of it. *Zidell v. Zidell, Inc.*, 560 P.2d 1091 (Or. 1977).

a.   The corporation may voluntarily relinquish a corporate opportunity, though such a relinquishment is a self-dealing transaction and will be scrutinized by the courts on the basis of principles described earlier, see part XIV, C; *Johnston v. Greene*, 121 A.2d 919 (Del. 1956). A persuasive reason for the relinquishment helps to make it clear that the corporation voluntarily decided not to pursue the opportunity.

Example: The retail department store referred to above receives a purchase proposal from the competing store to purchase its business; the board of the department store reviews the proposal and decides that under the circumstances it would be unwise to expand the corporation's business. The opportunity is no longer a corporate opportunity and individual directors may thereafter take advantage of the opportunity if they do so fairly.

b.   Directors may take advantage of a corporate opportunity if the corporation is unable or incapable of taking advantage of the opportunity.

> *Example:*　A third person refuses to deal with the corporation but is willing to deal with one or more directors individually. The opportunity is not a corporate opportunity.

c.　Most courts permit directors to take advantage of a corporate opportunity if the corporation is financially unable to capitalize on the opportunity. *A. C. Petters Co. v. St. Cloud Enterprises, Inc.*, 222 N.W.2d 83 (Minn. 1974).

　　1)　The ALI Corporate Governance Project tentative draft does not recognize a defense of financial inability, and *Klinicki v. Lundgren*, 695 P.2d 906 (Or. 1985) accepts this position. Under this approach, before a director or officer may take advantage of an opportunity, he or she must make full disclosure to the corporation of the opportunity to the corporation and the corporation must have rejected it, or unreasonably failed to act on the proposal.

　　2)　The "financial inability" defense is often troublesome since it may tempt directors to refrain from exercising their strongest efforts on behalf of the corporation if they can thereafter take advantage personally of a profitable opportunity. *Irving Trust Co. v. Deutsch*, 73 F.2d 121 (2d Cir. 1934).

　　3)　A "rigid rule" prohibiting directors from taking advantage of a corporate opportunity on this ground seems overstrict since it is clear that a director cannot be compelled to lend funds to the corporation; under such a rule directors would have to forego the opportunity if they are unwilling to lend the necessary funds to the corporation.

　　4)　When courts permit a director to utilize a corporate opportunity on a theory of financial inability under these circumstances they require a convincing showing that the corporation indeed lacked the independent assets to take advantage of its opportunity.

5.　DIRECTOR'S COMPETITION WITH THE CORPORATION

Directors may engage in similar line of business in competition with the corporation's business where it is done in good faith and without injury to the corporation. A director is not a full-time employee and may utilize his or her time as the director sees fit.

a.　Many cases, however, have found a competing director guilty of a breach of fiduciary duty on any of several possible theories: conflict of interest, corporate opportunity, misappropriation of trade secrets or customer lists, or wrongful interference with contractual relationships. *Duane Jones Co. v. Burke*, 117 N.E.2d 237 (N.Y. 1954).

b. Tort concepts of unfair competition in this area are close to fiduciary duties.

c. Judicial notions of fairness or fair play seem dominant, and cases require a close appraisal of the fiduciary's conduct in light of ethical business practice. *Aero Drapery of Kentucky, Inc. v. Engdahl*, 507 S.W.2d 166 (Ky. 1974). See also the examples in 4. above.

F. DUTIES IN CONNECTION WITH FREEZE OUT MERGERS

In "freeze out" mergers, the plan of merger treats minority shareholders differently from majority shareholders: usually the minority are compelled to accept cash for their shares and the majority end up owning all the outstanding interests in the corporation. Cases agree that the validity of such transactions is based on a test of entire fairness and that compliance with statutory formalities alone is not sufficient. *Weinberger v. UOP, Inc.*, 457 A.2d 701 (Del. 1983).

a. *Singer v. Magnavox Co.*, 380 A.2d 969 (Del. 1977), combined a "business purpose" test along with the test of "entire fairness." The "business purpose" test adds little protection, however. For example, *Tanzer v. International Gen. Indus., Inc.*, 379 A.2d 1121 (Del. 1977), held that the business purpose requirement may be satisfied by considering the interests of the majority shareholder; a purpose of facilitating long term borrowing capacity of the majority shareholder was a valid business purpose.

b. *Weinberger v. UOP, Inc.*, 457 A.2d 701 (Del. 1983), overruled this aspect of *Singer* in Delaware, but other states may continue to require a "business purpose" test. See e. g. *Alpert v. 28 Williams Street Corp.*, 473 N.E.2d 19 (N.Y. 1984).

c. *Weinberger* states that the statutory right of dissent and appraisal (see RMBCA ch. 13) is normally the sole remedy for minority shareholders in freeze-out mergers. State statutes vary widely on the exclusivity of the appraisal remedy [RMBCA § 13.02(b) provides, for example, that the appraisal remedy is exclusive "unless the action is unlawful or fraudulent"]; *Alpert v. 28 Williams Street Corp.* holds that the RMBCA language does not limit minority shareholders to their appraisal remedy where the price or other terms are unfair to the minority shareholders.

d. *Weinberger* suggests that strong evidence of fairness of a transaction is approval, after full disclosure, by a majority of the minority shares being cashed out.

G. MISCELLANEOUS TRANSACTIONS SUBJECT TO THE FAIRNESS TEST

The fairness test is also applicable to a variety of transactions which defy precise categorization, but which may be lumped loosely under the title "fairness to minority shareholders." These situations may represent duties of controlling shareholders or of directors named by controlling shareholders.

Example: Preemptive rights are excluded; directors elected by a controlling shareholder cause the corporation to issue to the controlling shareholder new or treasury shares to cement her control. The shares are issued at a bargain price. The transaction is obviously unfair to minority shareholders and may be set aside.

Example: In the foregoing example, the price for the additional shares is fair but the purpose is to give the controlling shareholder enough shares to approve unusual corporate transactions. Since the transaction has no valid business purpose, the transaction should be set aside.

Example: Directors of a corporation know that inventory owned by the corporation has appreciated greatly in value over the value reflected on the books of the corporation. To obtain the greatest portion of this appreciation for itself, the directors elected by the majority shareholder cause the corporation to call a convertible participating preferred security. The corporation does not disclose the inventory appreciation and, as a result, most of the holders of the preferred security permit their holdings to be redeemed at $80.00 per share rather than converting them into common worth over $100.00 per share. This transaction violates a duty owed to the minority shareholders: in effect, the directors are required to treat fairly each class of stock and may not take actions which are designed to enhance the value of one class at the expense of another. *Zahn v. Transamerica Corp.*, 162 F.2d 36 (3d Cir. 1947).

Example: In the foregoing example, the directors' decision whether or not to call the preferred is not evaluated by a fairness test. Preferred shareholders who acquire shares that are subject to redemption should realize that decision may be based on a judgment as to what benefits the common shares. The directors must treat the preferred holders fairly only in the sense of not misleading them as to which option they should elect. *Speed v. Transamerica Corp.*, 235 F.2d 369 (3d Cir. 1956).

Example: In the preceding situation, before the preferred is called the directors elected by the common shareholders declare extra dividends on the common shares after making the required provision for the senior securities. The holders of senior securities cannot complain of the extra dividends paid to the common shareholders.

Example: The directors offer to repurchase shares owned by the father of the majority shareholder at a price of $600.00 per share. Previously, the corporation offered to repurchase shares of other minority shareholders at $300.00 per share. The transaction is voidable unless the other minority shareholders are also given an opportunity to sell shares to the corporation at the favorable price. *Donahue v. Rodd Electrotype Co.*, 328 N.E.2d 505 (Mass. 1975).

Example: A majority of the directors of a corporation have been named by the bank supplying most of the credit needed by the corporation to operate and the other directors have acquiesced in the prior credit transactions. The creditor demands a pledge of all the corporate assets as security for a further loan. This pledge does not require shareholder approval under state law. The minority shareholders should be advised of the demand and a failure to do so may make the transaction voidable. *Wright v. Heizer Corp.*, 560 F.2d 236 (7th Cir. 1977).

H. RELATIONSHIP OF "FAIRNESS" AND "BUSINESS JUDGMENT" RULES

The "business judgment rule" [see part XIV, B, 1, (a)] states that courts should accept the good faith exercise of discretion by directors in operating the company, and should not stigmatize as improper transactions that with hindsight turn out badly. This rule should not be applied to self-dealing transactions but to claims based on alleged mismanagement. The appropriate test for self-dealing transactions is "fairness" or "intrinsic fairness." [See part XIV, C, 3].

Example: The board of directors elects a manager and president who is highly recommended after reasonable investigation, but who turns out to be dishonest. The decision is protected by the business judgment rule since no element of self-dealing is involved.

Example: Suit is brought by a minority shareholder seeking a recovery in favor of the corporation against one or more officers or directors, e. g., for causing the corporation to make improper foreign bribes or other payments. The members of the board of directors who are not defendants or involved in the acts complained of are formed into a "Litigation Committee" to review the wisdom of the corporation's pursuing the suit. Cases holding the "business judgment rule" applicable to such issues are necessarily proceeding on the assumption that no self-dealing is involved, i. e., that the "Litigation Committee" is truly independent and not involved in the litigation.

Example: Plaintiffs are minority shareholders of a corporation which is 97 per cent owned by the parent corporation. They attack decisions (1) to pay large dividends by the subsidiary to ease the cash needs of the parent (but the plaintiffs received their proportionate share of the distributions) and (2) to cause the subsidiary not to pursue claims for breach of contract against the parent. The question of the excessive dividends should be evaluated by the "business judgment rule" since all shareholders are being treated proportionately. However, the refusal to enforce the contract claim should be judged on the basis of the "intrinsic fairness" test since it obviously involves self-dealing—the parent received something from the subsidiary "to the exclusion and detriment of the minority shareholders." *Sinclair Oil Corp. v. Levien*, 280 A.2d 717 (Del. 1971).

I. STATE STATUTORY LIABILITIES

State business corporation acts may impose personal liability on directors for transactions which violate specific statutory provisions. This liability is usually in addition to other liabilities, and usually is not dependent on bad faith.

1. ACTS FOR WHICH LIABILITY IS IMPOSED
While provisions vary from state to state, liability for the following actions are typical:

a. Paying dividends or making distributions in violation of the act or in violation of restrictions in the articles of incorporation. See RMBCA § 8.33. Liability is usually limited to the excess of the amount actually distributed over the amount which could have been distributed without violating the act or restriction.

b. Purchasing its own shares by a corporation in violation of the act. The liability is usually limited to the consideration paid for such shares which is in excess of the maximum amount which could have been paid without violating the statute.

c. Distributing assets to shareholders during the liquidation of the corporation without paying and discharging, or making adequate provision for the payment and discharge of, all known debts, obligations, and liabilities of the corporation.

d. Permitting the corporation to commence business before it has received the minimum required consideration for its shares. The liability is usually limited to the unpaid part of the minimum required capitalization and the liability terminates when the required consideration has actually been received.

e. Permitting the corporation to make a loan to an officer or director, or to make a loan secured by shares of the corporation when such transactions are prohibited. The liability is limited to the amount of the loan until it is repaid.

Caveat: Many of these liability provisions appear in older statutes that contain restrictive requirements that have been eliminated from more modern statutes. Most modern state statutes, like the RMBCA, do not contain minimum capital requirements for new corporations, do not prohibit loans secured by shares of the corporation, and have greatly relaxed older prohibitions against loans to officers and directors. See RMBCA §§ 8.32, 8.33. Where the restrictions have been eliminated, the reason for the liability provisions has been also.

2. DIRECTORS WHO ARE LIABLE

Business corporation acts usually provide that joint and several liability is imposed on all directors present at the meeting at which the action in violation of the statute is taken, unless a director's negative vote is duly entered in writing in the corporate records or the secretary is notified in writing by registered mail of his negative vote.

3. DEFENSES

Statutes imposing strict liability may relieve directors of liability if in the exercise of ordinary care, they

a.   Relied in good faith upon written financial statements of the corporation represented to be correct by appropriate corporate officials [RMBCA § 6.40(d)]; or

b.   Relied in good faith on book values in determining the amounts available for distribution; or

c.   Relied in good faith upon the written opinion of an attorney for the corporation [RMBCA § 8.30(b)].

4. PRACTICAL IMPORTANCE OF STATUTORY LIABILITY

There has been virtually no litigation over the scope of the statutory liabilities for unlawful distributions or the scope of the defenses described in this subsection.

REVIEW QUESTIONS

XIV–1.   What is meant by a "duty of care?"

XIV-2. What is meant by "the business judgment rule?" By the "business judgment doctrine"?

XIV-3. A director offers to sell his corporation a piece of land owned by a family trust at a questionable price. What standards are applicable to determine the validity of such a transaction?

XIV-4. What rule is applicable to determine the validity of a transaction between two corporations with common directors?

XIV-5. May the shareholders ratify a self dealing transaction that does not meet the standard of fairness?

XIV-6. Today many executives in publicly held corporations receive executive compensation of a million dollars or more per year. Is this self dealing? What is the standard for determining the validity of such very large compensation?

XIV-7. May executive compensation be tied directly to the performance of the stock in the stock market?

XIV-8. What is meant by the doctrine of "corporate opportunity"?

XIV-9. What is the test for determining when an opportunity is a corporate opportunity?

XIV–10.   May a director take advantage of a corporate opportunity if the corporation is unable or unwilling to do so?

XIV–11.   A corporation enters into a transaction with its subsidiary of which it owns 98 per cent of stock. Which standard should be applied to such a transaction, the business judgment rule or the fairness standard of self-dealing transactions?

XIV–12.   Corporation A owns 93 per cent of the outstanding shares of Corporation B. The remaining 7 per cent of the shares are held by 50 individuals. Corporation A desires to raise capital for itself by pledging certain liquid assets of Corporation B. May it do so?

XIV–13.   In the foregoing question, Corporation A determines that it should eliminate the minority shareholders of Corporation B before entering into the transaction in question. It therefore creates a new wholly owned corporation, Corporation C, and merges Corporation B into Corporation C. The merger agreement provides that the minority shareholders of Corporation B are to receive $60 per share in cash, a fair price, and that the transaction is to be approved only if a majority of the minority shareholders approve it. If the required approval is obtained, is the transaction valid? What remedy, if any, do minority shareholders have who are dissatisfied with the $60 price?

XIV–14.   A corporation has two classes of authorized shares: 1,000 preferred shares and 3,000 common shares. Outstanding are: (1) 1,000 noncumulative $100 par value preferred shares with full voting rights and a nonparticipating liquidation preference of $200 per share, redeemable at $105 per share, each share convertible into two common shares; and (2) 1,000 common shares without par value with full voting rights.

The corporation has net assets of $210,000, of which $105,000 is earned surplus. It is about to dissolve. What should the board of directors do in fairness to both classes? [This question and answer is drawn from Ballantine, Problems in Law 238 (5th Ed. 1975).]

XIV–15.   A is a large corporation with over 30,000 employees. The corporation and certain employees entered pleas of guilty to indictments charging violations of the federal anti-trust laws. Ds are directors of the corporation who were not charged with any violation of the anti-trust laws in the proceeding against the corporation. P brings an action on the corporation's behalf to hold Ds liable for the losses sustained by the corporation by reason of the violations of its employees. There is no evidence presented to the effect that Ds knew or had any knowledge that would have put them on notice that violations were occurring. Are Ds liable to the corporation?

XIV–16.   X corporation, a mining company, entered into a contract with M corporation, a smelting company, which provided that M should smelt all of X's ore for a period of 10 years at a specific price per ton of ore. The price agreed to be paid by X to M was 10% higher than the regular and customary price for smelting. A, B and C were directors of X corporation and also of M corporation. When this contract came up for approval before the boards of directors of the two corporations, the directors A, B and C, refrained from voting, but the contract was approved by the board of directors of X corporation because the directors other than A, B and C, were advised that A, B and C wanted such contract approved. The metal market was dropping when this contract was made and continued to drop thereafter. Usually the price of smelting drops with the market. The X corporation elected a new board of directors which made an investigation and found that the contract with M was causing the company to lose money. The new board voted to cancel the contract with M and brought suit for a declaratory judgment to determine that the cancellation was legal. M's defense is that the contract is valid because the directors who were common to both corporations, A, B and C, abstained from voting on the contract. Is the defense good?

XIV–17.   X corporation, in which D is the majority stockholder but not on the board of directors, is engaged in mining copper. D completely controlled the board of directors of X. As a result of being a stockholder in X corporation D learns that a vein of ore runs directly into B's mining property which adjoins X's property. An opportunity to buy B's mining property arises and without mentioning the opportunity to X corporation, D buys B's mines for $100,000 cash. T, a minority stockholder in X, sues D on behalf of the corporation to compel him to turn over to X at cost the mining property he purchased from B. D's defense is that B would sell his property only for cash and that at the time D bought the mines from B the X corporation was unable to raise more than $10,000 in cash. Is the defense good?

XV

DUTIES RELATING TO THE PURCHASE OR SALE OF SHARES

The common law relating to transactions in corporate shares by directors and officers (or by the corporation itself) has been largely overshadowed by the development of federal law, particularly rule 10b–5, discussed below. However, with the apparent decline of federal corporations law resulting from Supreme Court decisions (also described below), greater attention should be paid in the future to the state law in this area.

Analysis

A. *Transactions in Shares by an Officer or Director on the Basis of Inside Information*

B. *Purchase at a Discount of Claims Against the Corporation*

C. *Purchase or Sale of Shares in Competition With the Corporation*

D. *Purchase or Sale of Shares by a Corporation in a Struggle for Control*

E. *Rule 10b–5*

F. *Section 16(b) of the Securities Exchange Act*

G. *Sale of Controlling Shares*

A. TRANSACTIONS IN SHARES BY AN OFFICER OR DIRECTOR ON THE BASIS OF INSIDE INFORMATION

An officer or director of a corporation may obtain knowledge about corporate affairs which will affect the price or value of the corporate shares before it becomes known to the general public or to other shareholders. As a result, the director or officer may be tempted to make a personal profit either by purchasing or selling shares (depending on the nature of the information) without disclosing the information.

1.   STATE LAW RELATING TO INSIDER TRADING
The common law did not develop a simple test for handling inside trading. Some cases permitted such trading in the absence of fraud. *Goodwin v. Agassiz*, 186 N.E. 659 (Mass. 1933). However, liability might be imposed on several common law theories.

a.   Fraud or Misrepresentation.
If an affirmative misrepresentation was made normal fraud principles dictate that the defrauded person might rescind the transaction.

b.   Special Facts.
Where certain facts were of critical importance and peculiarly within the knowledge of the insider, some courts found a duty to disclose "special facts" without attempting to define which facts are "special." *Strong v. Repide*, 213 U.S. 419 (1909); *Taylor v. Wright*, 159 P.2d 980 (Cal.App. 1945). It may be that this was first considered as a species of fraud, but it quickly became a significantly easier burden to establish than fraud.

c.   Fiduciary Duty.
Kansas early adopted a stricter rule of fiduciary duty to protect all outsiders, *Hotchkiss v. Fischer*, 16 P.2d 531 (Kan. 1932), though the difference between these cases and the cases applying the "special facts" rule appears to be one of degree. Apparently, no other state has adopted this broad rule.

d.   Knowledge as a Corporate Asset: The Rule of *Diamond v. Oreamuno.*

1)   The broadest common law rule was articulated in *Diamond v. Oreamuno*, 248 N.E.2d 910 (N.Y. 1969) where the court permitted the corporation to recover gains made by insiders by selling securities on the basis of adverse inside information. Relying on analogies with the federal securities laws, the court in effect concluded that inside information was corporate property and the insider should not be permitted to profit from the use of that corporate property even though the corporation was not injured thereby. This view has not yet been accepted by any other state court and has been rejected by two courts. *Schein v. Chasen*, 313

So.2d 739 (Fla. 1975); *Freeman v. Decio*, 584 F.2d 186 (7th Cir. 1978) (Indiana law).

2) In *People v. Florentino*, 456 N.Y.S.2d 638 (N.Y.Crim.Ct. 1982), the court upheld a criminal proceeding against an attorney who, while representing issuers of securities in takeover attempts, purchased shares of target companies before the takeover was announced.

2. FEDERAL LAW RELATING TO INSIDER TRADING
Federal law has sharply circumscribed insider trading under rule 10b–5 promulgated by the Securities & Exchange Commission under section 10(b) of the Securities Exchange Act of 1934. See part XV, D, below.

B. PURCHASE AT A DISCOUNT OF CLAIMS AGAINST THE CORPORATION

A corporate officer or director may purchase claims against a solvent corporation at a discount though in some circumstances the opportunity to acquire a claim at a discount may itself be a corporate opportunity. *Weissman v. A. Weissman Inc.*, 97 A.2d 870 (Pa. 1953). Different principles, however, are applicable where the corporation is insolvent. Corporate directors should then attempt to settle or discharge claims against the corporation on the best possible terms from the corporation's standpoint in order to benefit other creditors and the shareholders rather than seeking to share personally in the distribution. However, claims validly bought at a discount when a corporation is solvent may share at face value in a subsequent distribution in insolvency or bankruptcy. *Manufacturers Trust Co. v. Becker*, 338 U.S. 304, 70 S.Ct. 127 (1949).

C. PURCHASE OR SALE OF SHARES IN COMPETITION WITH THE CORPORATION

In some circumstances an officer or director may attempt to sell personal stock in competition with the corporation's attempt to raise capital by selling stock. The opportunity to sell shares to a third person in this situation is usually a corporate opportunity and subject to attack by the corporation. *Brophy v. Cities Service Co.*, 70 A.2d 5 (Del.Ch. 1949) applies this principle to an insider who buys shares knowing that the corporation is planning to reacquire shares in the near future.

D. PURCHASE OR SALE OF SHARES BY A CORPORATION IN A STRUGGLE FOR CONTROL

If outsiders are seeking to wrest control of a publicly held corporation away from incumbent management, the incumbents may use the corporate assets in order to preserve their position.

1.   QUESTIONABLE TRANSACTIONS
Transactions that may involve the use of corporate assets to consolidate the position of incumbent management include the following:

a.   The corporation makes open market purchases of its own shares for ostensibly proper reasons; such transactions drive up the price and make a purchased takeover more difficult. *Bennett v. Propp*, 187 A.2d 405 (Del.Ch. 1962); *Herald Co. v. Seawell*, 472 F.2d 1081 (10th Cir. 1972).

b.   The corporation may buy out the insurgents at a premium price ostensibly to protect the corporation from "raiders." This is sometimes called "green mail". *Cheff v. Mathes*, 199 A.2d 548 (Del. 1964).

c.   Additional shares may be issued by the corporate management to themselves or to friendly persons ostensibly for proper purposes (a "lock up"). The effect of such a transaction is to make a purchased takeover more difficult because both the total number of outstanding shares and the number of shares controlled by management is increased.

>   ***Example:***   A publicly-held corporation, incorporated in Panama, is threatened with a takeover attempt. It issues two large blocks of its shares, one to a wholly-owned subsidiary, and the other to an Employee Stock Option Plan (ESOP), the trustees of which are directors of the corporation. Neither transaction is protected by the business judgment rule because of self-interest. In addition, circularly-owned shares (i. e. shares owned by a subsidiary of the issuing corporation) cannot usually be voted under American law (see RMBCA § 7.21(b)) and the court extended that ban to a Panamanian corporation whose principal business was in New York. The ESOP was viewed as "solely a tool of management self-perpetuation" without serving any legitimate corporate purpose. The grant of a preliminary injunction barring the voting of both blocks of shares was affirmed. *Norlin Corp. v. Rooney, Pace Inc.*, 744 F.2d 255 (2d Cir. 1984).

d.   A new class of shares may be created and issued to friendly persons; the articles may be amended to require approval of mergers by a majority of each class of shares. The effect may be to make any unwanted amalgamation of the corporation impossible.

e. A corporation is faced with a threatened "front-end-loaded tender offer" (an offer for 51 per cent of the outstanding shares for cash plus, if successful, an offer for the remaining 49 per cent at a lower price payable in subordinated debentures rather than cash). Such an offer tends to force shareholders to tender even though they may believe the offer is unattractive since in all events they do not want to have their shares purchased at the "back end" price. To avoid this threat, the corporation offers to purchase a portion of the shares owned by all shareholders *except the aggressor in the tender offer*. Under the circumstances of the threat faced by the corporation and its shareholders, this exclusion was an appropriate exercise of business judgment. *Unocal Corp. v. Mesa Petroleum Co.*, 493 A.2d 946 (Del. 1985).

Caveat: Shortly following the *Unocal* decision, the SEC proposed a new rule under the Williams Act that would have the effect of overruling that case.

2. APPLICABLE TEST
The general test of propriety adopted by the courts to evaluate all such transactions is one of underlying purpose: if the actions of the board were motivated by a sincere belief that the transaction is reasonable and necessary to maintain what the board believes to be the security and integrity of the corporation, the transaction is proper. If, on the other hand, the board or management acted solely or primarily because of the desire to perpetuate itself in office, the transaction is improper and may be invalidated. *Cheff v. Mathes*, 199 A.2d 548 (Del. 1964).

a. This test may be criticized on the ground that it is possible to dress up virtually every transaction with a "proper business purpose."

b. A number of cases have invalidated transactions of the various types described, so that in practice this test obviously does provide some protection against improper transactions.

3. APPLICATION OF FEDERAL LAW
Attempts to attack such transactions under rule 10b–5 appear to be foreclosed by the United States Supreme Court decisions in *Santa Fe Industries v. Green*, 430 U.S. 462, 97 S.Ct. 1292 (1977) [which limits rule 10b–5 to cases of deception rather than unfairness or breach of fiduciary duty] and *Schreiber v. Burlington Northern, Inc.*, __ U.S. __, 105 S.Ct. 2458 (1985) [extending the same limitation to suits under § 14(e) of the Williams Act]. On the other hand, some of the foregoing transactions might be subject to attack under other provisions of the Williams Act, which regulates cash tender offers and

prohibits issuance or repurchase of shares by target corporations in certain circumstances. See generally part XIII, C, supra.

E. RULE 10b–5

Rule 10b–5, promulgated by the Securities and Exchange Commission under section 10(b) of the Securities Exchange Act of 1934, is the source of most current principles relating to transactions in securities by officers, directors, and others. It reads as follows:

"It shall be unlawful for any person, directly or indirectly, by the use of any means or instrumentality of interstate commerce, or of the mails or of any facility of any national securities exchange,

(1) to employ any device, scheme, or artifice to defraud;

(2) to make any untrue statement of a material fact or to omit to state a material fact necessary in order to make the statements ade, in light of the circumstances under which they were made, not misleading, or

(3) to engage in any act, practice, or course of business which operates or would operate as a fraud or deceit upon any person,

in connection with the purchase or sale of any security."

1. **HISTORY OF THE RULE**
    Rule 10b–5 was originally promulgated for narrow reasons. However, its history has some of the attributes of a roller coaster: a dizzying growth until about 1975 followed by a sudden decline as the Supreme Court attempted to limit the growth of the jungle of case law.

    a. In analyzing rule 10b–5 cases it is important to note the date the case was decided.

    b. Despite the post-1975 decline rule 10b–5 is still widely cited and applied.

2. **RULE 10b–5 AS FEDERAL LAW**
    Rule 10b–5 is a federal regulation and claims arising under it are federal claims. This has both procedural and substantive implications when compared to the analogous state law.

    a. Even though it is a regulation adopted by the SEC, rule 10b–5 has the same force as a statute; its violation may be made the basis of a criminal prosecution or civil suit.

b. There is no need for diversity of citizenship.

c. Suit may be brought only in federal court; state courts do not have power to adjudicate rule 10b–5 claims.

d. State security for expenses statutes (see part XVIII, C) are not applicable.

e. The procedures in federal court may be simpler than in state courts and the discovery rights broader.

f. There is nationwide service of process in rule 10b–5 suits under section 27 of the Securities Exchange Act, and broad venue provisions. *Securities Investor Protection Corp. v. Vigman*, 764 F.2d 1309 (9th Cir. 1985).

g. The doctrine of pendent jurisdiction permits the joinder of both state and federal claims arising from the same transaction in a rule 10b–5 suit but a rule 10b–5 claim cannot be joined with a state cause of action in a state court.

h. The substantive principles developed under rule 10b–5 have probably been more favorable to plaintiffs than the correlative principles of state law.

  1) Many rule 10b–5 cases arise on motions to dismiss; courts are reluctant to close off plausible sounding allegations without a trial so that pro-plaintiff decisions are numerous.

  2) There are more rule 10b–5 precedents than state court precedents and hence "more law" on which to build one's case.

  3) There may be a feeling, perhaps unjustified, that federal judges are more sympathetic to minority shareholder complaints than state court judges.

i. A private cause of action is created by rule 10b–5 so that a person injured by a transaction that violates the rule may have direct recourse to the federal courts. *Kardon v. National Gypsum Co.*, 73 F.Supp. 798 (E.D.Pa. 1947), *supplemented* 83 F.Supp. 613 (E.D.Pa.).

j. Rule 10b–5 is applicable to any "security," including those issued by closely held as well as publicly held corporations. The so-called "sale of business" doctrine was rejected in *Landreth Timber Co. v. Landreth*, ___ U.S. ___, 105 S.Ct. 2297 (1985).

k. Rule 10b–5 is applicable to every transaction using the facilities of interstate commerce or the mails. A single intrastate telephone call has been held to involve the use of a facility of interstate commerce, thereby making applicable rule 10b–5.

3. LIMITING PRINCIPLES ON RULE 10b–5

United States Supreme Court decisions since 1975 have imposed significant substantive rules governing the scope of rule 10b–5:

a. *Ernst & Ernst v. Hochfelder*, 425 U.S. 185, 96 S.Ct. 1375 (1976). This case holds that a private plaintiff under rule 10b–5 must allege and prove "scienter," that is, "intentional wrongdoing" or a "mental state embracing intent to deceive, manipulate or defraud."

   1) The Court rejected several lower court holdings that mere "negligence" was sufficient.

   2) The Court reserved the issue whether in some circumstances recklessness might satisfy the scienter requirement. Later decisions by lower federal courts have almost unanimously held that "recklessness" or "severe recklessness" satisfies the scienter standard. *Broad v. Rockwell Int'l Corp.*, 642 F.2d 929 (5th Cir. 1981).

   3) The Court also reserved the question whether a lesser standard of conduct might satisfy rule 10b–5 in cases where injunctive relief was being sought by the SEC (as contrasted with suits brought by private plaintiffs). This issue was resolved against the SEC in *Aaron v. SEC*, 446 U.S. 680, 100 S.Ct. 1945 (1980), holding that scienter must be established in SEC injunctive suits also.

b. *Santa Fe Industries, Inc. v. Green*, 430 U.S. 462, 97 S.Ct. 1292 (1977). This case holds that rule 10b–5 is limited to situations involving deception. Unfair transactions (e. g., mergers) that are adequately disclosed cannot be attacked under rule 10b–5.

c. *Blue Chip Stamps v. Manor Drug Stores*, 421 U.S. 723, 95 S.Ct. 1917 (1975). This case holds that only persons who are purchasers or sellers of securities may bring suit as plaintiffs. This doctrine is based on the early decision in *Birnbaum v. Newport Steel Corp.*, 193 F.2d 461 (2d Cir. 1952) and is sometimes referred to as the "Birnbaum doctrine" or "Birnbaum rule." The opinion also contains strong dicta criticizing federal securities law litigation in general.

d. Claims may be made under rule 10b–5 even though under the same factual situation a claim might also be made under the more specific provisions of the Securities Act of 1933 or other sections of the Securities

Exchange Act of 1934. *Herman & MacLean v. Huddleston*, 459 U.S. 375, 103 S.Ct. 683 (1983).

4.   RULE 10b–5 AS AN ANTIFRAUD PROVISION

A private cause of action exists under rule 10b–5 on behalf of every person who buys or sells securities as a result of fraud or misrepresentation. Since the rule is applicable to both closely and publicly held shares and since it is triggered by the use of a facility of interstate commerce, rule 10b–5 is a far-reaching antifraud provision that is applicable to virtually all securities transactions.

Example: The president of a small Colorado corporation offers to purchase the shares owned by a Colorado shareholder on the basis of a misrepresentation or a failure to disclose "material" facts about the corporation. If the transaction involves a single telephone call, even from one floor in a Denver office building to another floor in the same building, the transaction is covered by rule 10b–5.

Example: A purchaser of all of the outstanding shares of a closely held corporation claims that she entered into the purchase because of false or misleading statements by the seller; the purchaser also claims that the seller had failed to state material facts as to the value of the corporation. A claim under rule 10b–5 is stated since shares of a closely held corporation are "securities" under the Securities Exchange Act of 1934. *Landreth Timber Co. v. Landreth*, ___ U.S. ___, 105 S.Ct. 2297 (1985). It is not relevant that the purchase involved a business that the purchaser planned to operate herself.

a.   Rule 10b–5 proscribes not only affirmative misrepresentations and half-truths but also failures to disclose "material facts;" thus mere silence may constitute a violation. *Speed v. Transamerica Corp.*, 99 F.Supp. 808 (D.Del.1951), *supplemented* 100 F.Supp. 461 (D.Del.).

b.   The test of what is "material" is whether a reasonable person would attach importance to the information in determining a course of action—in other words, if the information would, in reasonable and objective contemplation, effect the value of the securities, it should be considered "material." *SEC v. Texas Gulf Sulphur Co.*, 401 F.2d 833 (2d Cir. 1968); *TSC Industries, Inc. v. Northway, Inc.*, 426 U.S. 438, 96 S.Ct. 2126 (1976) [§ 14(a) case].

c.   If the misrepresentation relates to a publicly traded security, a purchaser or seller may be able to recover without establishing knowledge of or reliance on the misrepresentation. *Panzirer v. Wolf*, 663 F.2d 365 (2d

Cir. 1981) certiorari vacated on ground case is moot, 459 U.S. 1027 (1982); *Shores v. Sklar*, 647 F.2d 462 (5th Cir. 1981).

1) This principle is now generally referred to as the "fraud on the market theory." It has been referred to approvingly in law review commentary but has not been considered by the Supreme Court of the United States.

2) This principle is based on an earlier United States Supreme Court decision holding that in a case of a failure to disclose a material fact, proof of reliance on the failure to disclose may be inferred and need not be separately established. *Affiliated Ute Citizens v. United States*, 406 U.S. 128, 92 S.Ct. 1456 (1972).

3) This principle has also been extended to cases where a person invests in a newly issued security on the belief that an unlawfully issued security could not be marketed. *T.J. Ramey & Sons, Inc. v. Fort Cobb Irrigation Fuel Authority*, 717 F.2d 1330 (10th Cir. 1983), cert. denied 465 U.S. 1026, 104 S.Ct. 1285 (1984).

4) A false or misleading press release by the corporation may give rise to liability analogous to that imposed by the "fraud on the market theory."

d. A person having knowledge of "material facts" may avoid liability only by disclosing them to the other party to the proposed transaction. If disclosure is impractical, the person with material information must forego the transaction.

e. A transaction in violation of rule 10b–5 may be rescinded by the innocent party, or damages may be computed on the assumption that the contract had not been entered into.

5. RULE 10b–5 AS A PROHIBITION AGAINST INSIDER TRADING

The above principles are also applicable to transactions in shares of publicly held corporations effected anonymously over securities exchanges or through brokers. As a result, rule 10b–5 is also a broad prohibition against trading on the basis of insider information.

a. The basic principle that trading on inside information may violate rule 10b–5 was established in *In re Cady Roberts, Inc.*, 40 S.E.C. 907 (1961), and *S.E.C. v. Texas Gulf Sulphur Co.*, 401 F.2d 833 (2d Cir. 1968), cert. denied 394 U.S. 976, 89 S.Ct. 1454 (1969).

b. The Insider Trading Sanctions Act of 1984 legislatively recognizes this principle and imposes a potential penalty of up to three times the insider's profit for violations of the insider trading prohibitions. Other sanctions, including criminal prosecution for wilfull violations, also may be available.

c.   In anonymous transactions it is usually impractical for the person with material information to disclose the material facts. That is a corporate function.

1)   *SEC v. Texas Gulf Sulphur Co.*, supra, holds that officers, directors, and employees of an issuer who know of a material favorable development as a result of their position with the corporation violate rule 10b–5 if they purchase shares [or options to purchase ("calls")] on shares before the information is released.

   Example: The president of a corporation learns of an adverse corporate development. Before it is announced he sells his shares in the company. The president has violated rule 10b–5 irrespective of any violation of state law.

2)   *SEC v. Texas Gulf Sulphur Co.*, also holds that insiders must wait until the information has been reasonably disseminated to the investing public through wire services and the like before they may trade.

   Example: The corporate president holds a press conference to announce a major favorable development. Immediately after the press conference he calls his broker and places an order to buy shares. The president has violated rule 10b–5.

   Caveat: Several aspects of the holding in *SEC v. Texas Gulf Sulphur* have been affected by later holdings of the United States Supreme Court.

3)   The New York Stock Exchange has published guidelines as to when it is appropriate for an insider to purchase shares of his own corporation. These guidelines suggest periodic investment purchases (e. g., buying a few shares every month) or limiting transactions to brief periods after public information is released.

4)   A person may be able to recover from an insider who violates rule 10b–5 even though the plaintiff is not in privity with the defendant. The scope of liability in such cases is not fully settled.

   (i)   *Shapiro v. Merrill Lynch, Pierce, Fenner & Smith, Inc.*, 495 F.2d 228 (2d Cir. 1974) suggests that the insiders may be liable for all trading losses suffered by the general public when the insiders traded on the basis of inside information. This "draconian" approach appears to be based on an affirmative "duty to disclose" rather than a "duty of staying out of the market."

(ii) The Federal Securities Code would limit the recovery in such cases to the amount of the defendants' trading profits. At least one case accepts this suggestion under rule 10b–5. *Elkind v. Liggett & Myers, Inc.*, 635 F.2d 156 (2d Cir. 1980).

(iii) Other cases have basically refused to allow non-privity plaintiffs to maintain suit at all. *Fridrich v. Bradford*, 542 F.2d 307 (6th Cir. 1976).

b. Rule 10b–5 applies, literally, to "any person." As a result of two recent United States Supreme Court decisions, *Chiarella v. United States*, 445 U.S. 222, 100 S.Ct. 1108 (1980), and *Dirks v. SEC*, 463 U.S. 646, 103 S.Ct. 3255 (1983), however, this broad language should not be taken literally.

1) Rule 10b–5 clearly applies to prohibit insider trading by corporate officers, directors, and employees. *SEC v. Texas Gulf Sulphur Co.*, supra.

Example: A geologist employed by a mining company learns of a major ore strike before information is publicly announced. A purchase of shares before this information is publicly announced constitutes a violation of rule 10b–5.

2) A person who receives inside information from the issuer in connection with duties to the issuer—e.g. accountants, investment banking firms or law firms—may be "constructive insiders" and subject to the same rules as a corporate officer, director, or employee. *Dirks v. SEC*, 463 U.S. 646, n. 14, 103 S.Ct. 3255, n. 14 (1983).

Example: A brokerage firm obtains information about a corporation in connection with a contemplated debt financing before the information is generally available. The brokerage firm violates rule 10b–5 if it purchases (or sells) corporate securities before the information is released. *Shapiro v. Merrill Lynch, Pierce, Fenner & Smith, Inc.*, 495 F.2d 228 (2d Cir. 1974).

Example: To avoid inadvertent violations of rule 10b–5 in this connection brokerage firms attempt to maintain a firm internal separation between underwriting and sales activities. This internal separation is usually called a "Chinese wall."

3) *Chiarella v. United States*, involved a criminal prosecution of a printer employed by a legal printing firm who purchased shares on the basis of information obtained from the documents he had access to at his place of employment.

   (i)   The majority set aside the conviction on the ground that the defendant had not violated any duty to the general public or to the issuer by such transactions.

   (ii) The possibility that the conviction might be upheld on the theory that the employee violated a duty to his employer was strongly urged in a dissenting opinion but was not addressed by the majority since it was not raised below.

   (iii) Subsequent courts have accepted the suggestion that a violation of rule 10b–5 may be based on a breach of duty to a private employer. *United States v. Newman*, 664 F.2d 12 (2d Cir. 1981), cert. denied 464 U.S. 863, 104 S.Ct. 193 (1983); *S.E.C. v. Materia*, 745 F.2d 197 (2d Cir. 1984), cert. denied __ U.S. __, 105 S.Ct. 2112 (1985) [printing firm employee]; *United States v. Winans*, 612 F.Supp. 827 (S.D.N.Y. 1985) [Wall Street Journal editorial writer].

   (iv) Following *Chiarella*, the SEC adopted rule 14e–3, that makes it unlawful for a person who wrongfully obtains advance information about a tender to use that information in securities transactions. If valid, that rule would clearly cover the printer in *Chiarella*.

4) *SEC v. Texas Gulf Sulphur Co.* suggested that "tippees," i.e. persons who obtain material information before it is publicly released have an obligation not to trade on that information. In *Dirks v. S.E.C.*, 463 U.S. 646, 103 S.Ct. 3255 (1983), however, the Court held that such a person violates rule 10b–5 only if the tipper provided the information for the purpose of obtaining an improper benefit, and the tippee is aware of that purpose.

   Example: A corporate officer provides information to the writer of an industry newsletter in order to get a "reputational benefit." The writer violates rule 10b–5 if he trades on the basis of that information. *S.E.C. v. Gaspar*, 1985 Fed.Sec.L.Rep. (CCH) ¶ 92,004 (S.D.N.Y. April 16, 1985).

Example: The CEO of a publicly held corporation provides material inside information to his mistress, who trades on the basis of this information. The S.E.C. charged Paul Thayer, then Deputy Secretary of Defense, with a violation of rule 10b–5 on the basis of this "close personal relationship."

Example: While taking a sunbath on the bleachers at a high school track meet, the coach of the University of Oklahoma football team overhears a corporate officer explain to the officer's wife a corporate matter that involves material information. The court concluded that the officer was unaware of the football coach's presence, and there was no expectation of benefit. The football coach was a pure eavesdropper and his trading does not violate rule 10b–5. *S.E.C. v. Switzer*, 590 F.Supp. 756 (W.D.Okl. 1984).

5) A person who violates rule 10b–5 in a market transaction on the basis of a tip has violated the "disclose or abstain" principle. He or she may or may not be liable to persons who were active in the market without knowledge of the inside information.

    (i) A person who has received inside information from an aggressor and trades in shares of the target may not owe any duty to the shareholders of the target and may not be liable to them. *Walton v. Morgan Stanley & Co.*, 623 F.2d 796 (2d Cir. 1980); *Moss v. Morgan Stanley Inc.*, 719 F.2d 5 (2d Cir. 1983), cert. denied 465 U.S. 1025, 104 S.Ct. 1280 (1984).

    (ii) Where the person has obtained inside information from the issuer, an insider, or a "temporary insider," he or she may owe a duty to the shareholders of the issuer.

        (a) He may be liable for recission to the person who by chance was on the other side of the transaction.

        (b) More likely, however, a private class action will be brought by a person on behalf of all persons who traded during the period the defendant was trading before the information was released. See part 5.a.4), supra.

        (c) In any event he may be required to disgorge his profit to be recovered by the corporation and held as a fund for the benefit of injured members of the public. *SEC v. Texas Gulf Sulphur, Inc.*, 446 F.2d 1301 (2d Cir. 1971).

(A)   Presumably persons who actually entered into transactions with the insider will be limited to claims against this fund, thereby eliminating any risk of double liability.

(B)   If no injured persons appear, the corporation may keep the fund, thereby eliminating a financial incentive on the part of insiders or tippees to violate rule 10b–5.

c.   In 1984 Congress enacted the Insider Trading Sanctions Act which authorizes the SEC to recover up to treble damages for violations of the insider trading rules described above.

1)   By the enactment of this legislation, Congress reaffirmed the basic policy of enforcing sanctions against insider trading.

2)   In several proceedings since the enactment of this statute, the SEC has required persons violating the insider trading rules to repay double the profits obtained.

6.   RULE 10b–5 AS A PROTECTION AGAINST DECEPTION OF THE CORPORATION IN CONNECTION WITH THE ACQUISITION OR DISPOSITION OF SHARES

Rule 10b–5 is potentially applicable when a corporation issues or acquires its own shares since the phrase "purchase or sale" is broad enough to cover such transactions.

a.   If shares are issued or acquired by a corporation as a result of deception or a failure of some persons to disclose material facts to the corporation, the corporation may have a claim under rule 10b–5, and this claim may be asserted derivatively by a minority shareholder. *Drachman v. Harvey,* 453 F.2d 722 (2d Cir. 1971).

Example: Stock options granted to officers who knew of a major favorable development may be cancelled if the recipients do not advise the members of the option committee of the development. *SEC v. Texas Gulf Sulphur Co.,* 401 F.2d 833 (2d Cir. 1968).

b.   A rule 10b–5 violation also occurs if the corporation is fraudulently induced to issue shares for inadequate compensation even though such conduct also constitutes a violation of state-created fiduciary duties.

7. RULE 10b–5 AS A REGULATOR OF CORPORATE PUBLICITY

A corporation may violate rule 10b–5 if it issues a false or misleading press release and investors rely on this release in securities trading. *SEC v. Texas Gulf Sulphur Co.*, 401 F.2d 833 (2d Cir. 1968). This is a variation of the "fraud on the market" doctrine. See part XV, D.4(c), supra. An investment analyst may similarly violate rule 10b–5 if he has a financial interest in the securities he is discussing and fails to disclose it.

a.   While the *Birnbaum* rule requires that the plaintiff be a purchaser or seller of shares, there is no similar requirement for defendants: a person may violate rule 10b–5 even though he neither purchases nor sells a security.

b.   Scienter is required under *Hochfelder* and *Aaron* [see: part XV, D.3(a).] Pre-*Hochfelder* cases held that an evil intent or wrongful purpose was unnecessary.

Caveat: A misleading statement that was negligently prepared might be as injurious to a "free and open public market" for securities as a statement published with scienter, *SEC v. Texas Gulf Sulphur Co.*, 401 F.2d 833 (2d Cir. 1968), but these earlier cases are no longer valid.

c.   Individual shareholders who rely on a corporate press release that is misleading may recover damages from the corporation. *Mitchell v. Texas Gulf Sulphur Co.*, 446 F.2d 90 (10th Cir. 1971). A class action on behalf of all persons who purchased during the period of the misrepresentation may be permitted. *Blackie v. Barrack*, 524 F.2d 891 (9th Cir. 1975). Obviously, the potential liability to the corporation as a result of a false press release may be very substantial and the scope of this liability is still developing. See *Green v. Occidental Petroleum Corp.*, 541 F.2d 1335 (9th Cir. 1976), Sneed, J. concurring.

d.   The financial analyst who "touts" a stock without disclosing that he is financially interested in it also violates rule 10b–5. *Zweig v. Hearst Corp.*, 521 F.2d 1129 (9th Cir. 1975); 594 F.2d 1261 (9th Cir. 1979).

e.   Some cases have been reluctant to conclude that press releases issued by corporations have in fact been false or misleading, see e. g. *Greenfield v. Heublein, Inc.*, 742 F.2d 751 (3d Cir. 1984), or that a corporation had an affirmative duty to disclose a specific event before it issued a press release, see e. g. *State Teachers Retirement Board v. Fluor Corp.*, 654 F.2d 843 (2d Cir. 1981). These courts refer to the business judgment rule but there is also concern about the scope of potential liability if the opposite result were reached.

F. SECTION 16(b) OF THE SECURITIES EXCHANGE ACT

Section 16(b) of the Securities Exchange Act of 1934 is an *in terrorem* provision designed to prevent specified persons from trading in a corporation's securities on an in-and-out basis on the strength of inside information.

1.   SCOPE OF SECTION 16(b)

The scope of section 16(b) can best be described by contrasting it to rule 10b–5.

a.   Section 16(b) is applicable only to corporations registered under section 12 of the Securities Exchange Act—corporations (1) with securities traded on a national securities exchange or (2) with assets of more than $3,000,000 and more than 500 shareholders of record of any class of equity security. Rule 10b–5 is applicable to all corporations, registered and unregistered.

b.   Section 16(b) is only applicable to officers, directors and ten per cent shareholders of the issuer. Rule 10b–5 covers geologists, brokers, tippees and others.

   Caveat: Attribution rules apply to section 16(b) so that transactions in the name of spouses, relatives or nominees may be attributed to an officer, director, or ten per cent shareholder.

c.   Section 16(b) is applicable only to offsetting purchases and sales or sales and purchases of an equity security of the issuer within any six-month period. Rule 10b–5 may be violated by a single purchase or a single sale.

   Example: If there is a sale on January 1, section 16(b) is applicable if there is an offsetting purchase made at any time from six months before to six months after January 1. However, a purchase made six months plus one day after the sale cannot be matched under section 16(b).

d.   The sequence of section 16(b) transactions—that is sale-and-purchase or purchase-and-sale—or the fact that different certificates are involved in the two transactions, does not affect section 16(b) liability.

   Example: In the previous example, a sale made on the following May 1 will be matched with the January 1 purchase even though the shares actually sold on May 1 had been owned for five years.

e.   The words "purchase" and "sale" in section 16(b) are construed broadly. The test is not a dictionary one; rather, a transaction will be considered a "purchase" or a "sale" for purposes of section 16(b) if it is of a kind which can possibly lend itself to the speculation encompassed by section 16(b).

Example: A gift may be a sale, as may be a redemption, conversion or a simple exchange of shares pursuant to a merger or consolidation.

Example: The acquisition of a warrant may be a purchase.

f.   Section 16(b) creates an automatic liability; it is unnecessary to show actual use of inside information. In contrast, rule 10b–5 requires proof of scienter. A sale for entirely justifiable reasons—e. g., unexpected medical expenses—triggers section 16(b) if there has been an offsetting purchase within the previous six months.

g.   Profits are always payable to the corporation. In contrast, rule 10b–5 authorizes private damage recovery in many situations by buyers or sellers.

h.   "Profits" are computed so as to squeeze out all possible profit.

1)   The computation involves matching the highest sale price with the lowest purchase price, the next highest sale price with the next lowest purchase price, and so forth so long as a profit is shown; all loss transactions are ignored.

Example: A director buys 100 shares for $60.00 per share on January 10 (1/10) and sells them for $50.00 per share on January 19 (1/19). On April 5 (4/5) the same director buys 100 shares for $10.00. All purchases and sales take place within a six-month period. The highest sale price of $5,000 (1/19) is matched with the lowest purchase price of $1,000 (4/5) to produce a section 16(b) profit of $4,000. As a matter of common sense, most people would feel that these transactions were not profitable. *Gratz v. Claughton,* 187 F.2d 46 (2d Cir. 1951).

2)   The United States Supreme Court has never passed on this rather draconian measure of recovery.

Caveat: Where the exercise of an option is the "purchase" the SEC has long had a regulation that provides that the "purchase price" is not the option-exercise price (set years earlier) but the lowest market price within 6 months of the sale. *B. T. Babbitt, Inc. v. Lachner,* 332 F.2d 255 (2d Cir. 1964).

i.   Section 16(a) requires all transactions in shares by covered persons to be reported monthly to the SEC; the SEC publishes this information and it is therefore possible to locate section 16(b) violations from the public record.

j.   Even though all section 16(b) profits are recoverable by the corporation, corporations may be reluctant to enforce section 16(b) against its own officers, directors, and substantial shareholders. Section 16(b) recognizes that enforcement by private shareholders may be necessary. There is a significant amount of such litigation.

   1)   This litigation is basically champertous. Suits are brought solely for the award of attorneys' fees; the plaintiffs are nominal and have no interest in the outcome; violations are discovered by examining the published section 16(a) filings.

   2)   Such litigation is the principal enforcement device of section 16(b).

   3)   It is unlikely that any violation of section 16(b) escapes detection under these circumstances.

k.   The SEC has authority to exempt classes of transactions from section 16(b). While it has exercised this power in a number of instances, the exemptions tend to be narrowly drawn to cover specific situations.

   1)   Like rule 10b–5, the jurisdiction of section 16(b) suits is exclusively federal.

2.   APPLICATION OF SECTION 16(b) IN TAKEOVER SITUATIONS
The foregoing statement of principles gives little picture of the substantial volume and variety of section 16(b) litigation. The United States Supreme Court has struggled with the application of this section to takeover situations where an unsuccessful aggressor acquires over ten per cent of the target's shares and then sells that interest or has it "merged out" within six months thereafter. In the following decisions, inconsistent approaches and vigorous dissents are evident:

a.   *Reliance Elec. Co. v. Emerson Elec. Co.*, 404 U.S. 418, 92 S.Ct. 596 (1972), holds that a 13.2 per cent shareholder could dispose of its holding by first selling 3.2 per cent subject to section 16(b) and thereafter dispose of the balance free of section 16(b) since it was then less than a ten per cent shareholder.

b.   *Kern County Land Co. v. Occidental Petroleum Corp.*, 411 U.S. 582, 93 S.Ct. 1736 (1973) holds that a complex series of transactions including an "involuntary" merger and a voluntary option to sell securities were not "sales," and therefore not covered by section 16(b).

c.   In *Foremost-McKesson, Inc. v. Provident Securities Co.*, 423 U.S. 232, 96 S.Ct. 508 (1976), the Court finally "solved" the application of section 16(b) to the unsuccessful tender offeror by holding that the initial purchase that puts the aggressor over ten per cent was not a section 16(b) purchase.

3.   SECTION 16(b) AND TRADING PARTNERSHIPS

In *Blau v. Lehman*, 368 U.S. 403 (1962), a partner in Lehman Brothers was a director of the issuer. Unknown to him, Lehman Brothers engaged in purchases and sales of the issuer's stock (but never became a ten per cent holder). The Court held that the partnership might be considered a director only if the partnership "deputized" the partner to represent the partnership on issuer's board of directors. See *Feder v. Martin Marietta Corp.*, 406 F.2d 260 (2d Cir. 1969).

4.   SECTION 16(b) AND TRADING IN DIFFERENT CLASSES OF SECURITIES

The securities the purchase and sale of which are matched under section 16(b) must generally be of the same class. There is normally no meaningful basis for computing profits by matching a sale of common with a purchase of preferred. However, if the preferred is convertible into common and is trading at or close to the conversion price, matching may be permitted since the two securities are trading as economic equivalents.

Caveat: In *Gund v. First Florida Banks*, 726 F.2d 682 (11th Cir. 1984), the court matched sales of convertible debentures with purchases of common stock even though the two were not trading as market equivalents. The court computed "profits" by comparing the actual purchase price of the common stock with the highest price the common attained within six months before or after the debentures were sold.

5.   SECTION 16(b) IN PERSPECTIVE

It seems clear that people never knowingly violate section 16(b); most violations appear to be a result of ignorance rather than the actual misuse of inside information.

a.   Most inadvertent violations probably are a result of the failure to appreciate how broadly the words "purchase" and "sale" are construed.

b.   Despite its shortcomings and erratic imposition of liability, section 16(b) effectively eliminated the evil of in-and-out trading by pools composed in part of officers and directors that existed prior to 1934.

G. SALE OF CONTROLLING SHARES

When a controlling shareholder sells his or her interest to third persons, he or she is selling more than the property represented by his shares. Control of a going business in which other persons—minority shareholders, senior security holders, and unsecured creditors—may have a substantial interest is also being sold. A controlling shareholder has duties towards these interests.

1. CONTROL PREMIUMS
Shares owned by a controlling shareholder command a premium over other shares simply because they represent the power to control the business, to designate the corporate officers, and so forth.

    a.   This premium is usually referred to as the "control premium" and may be expressed as a per share differential or as an additional lump sum payment for the controlling shares. Shares which carry with them control of the corporation are often referred to as "control shares."

    b.   A "controlling" shareholder usually owns more than 50 per cent of the shares. However, a shareholder with less than 50 per cent of the outstanding shares may be a "controlling" shareholder if the remaining shares are widely held and fragmented.

    c.   Following the sale of initial shares, control of the board of directors is often transferred by the seriatim resignation of directors so that each vacancy is filled by the directors in office, either "new" or "old."

2. TESTS FOR SALE OF CONTROL
Many cases attest that generally a controlling shareholder may sell controlling shares for whatever price he or she can obtain; the virtually unanimous position of courts is that there is nothing inherently wrong in receiving a premium for control shares. *Zetlin v. Hansen Holdings, Inc.*, 397 N.E.2d 387 (N.Y. 1979); *Tryon v. Smith*, 229 P.2d 251 (Or. 1951); *McDaniel v. Painter*, 418 F.2d 545 (10th Cir. 1969). However, since the seller and buyer are not the only persons interested in a sale of control shares courts have imposed duties on the selling shareholder with respect to investigating the honesty of the purchaser.

    a.   A controlling shareholder who sells his shares to unscrupulous third persons who thereafter "loot" the corporation may be liable for the loss suffered by the corporation.

        1)   The controlling shareholder has a duty to make a reasonable investigation of potential purchasers and to refuse to transfer control to them unless the investigation reveals that they are honest, responsible persons. *Gerdes v. Reynolds*, 28 N.Y.S.2d 622

(Sup.Ct. 1941); *DeBaun v. First Western Bank and Trust Co.*, 120 Cal.Rptr. 354 (Cal.App. 1975).

> *Example:* Danger signs include, (1) an obviously excessive price for the shares willingly paid, (2) an unusual interest in the liquid and readily salable assets owned by the corporation, (3) insistence by the buyers on an immediate transfer of control, (4) insistence by the buyers that the liquid assets be made available immediately, (5) little interest by the purchasers in the operation of the corporation's business, and (6) the insistence that the purchase be handled with dispatch. *Swinney v. Keebler Co.*, 480 F.2d 573 (4th Cir. 1973) holds that on the facts of that case no duty to investigate arose even though with hindsight several of these factors existed.

2)   If the duty of reasonable investigation is not met, liability may be imposed on the sellers based on their negligence. Recovery will be based on the damage suffered, i. e., the amount looted by the purchasers rather than by the purchase price paid or the amount of the control premium. *DeBaun v. First Western Bank & Trust Co.*, 120 Cal.Rptr. 354 (Cal.App. 1975).

3)   In effect the sellers become the guarantors of the honesty of purchasers they do not fully investigate.

4)   Many looting cases involve investment companies that have liquid and readily salable assets but some cases involve regular business corporations.

> *Example:* Common shares of *X* Investment Company trade in the range of $1.00–$2.00 per share. An anonymous offer to buy the controlling shares at $3.00 per share is received through an intermediary. If the controlling shareholders accept this offer without investigation, they will be liable if the purchasers wrongfully convert the assets of *X* Investment Company to their own use.

b.   Outside of the looting cases, courts have not evolved consistent theories about the propriety of a controlling shareholder receiving a control premium.

1)   As indicated above, most cases allow the controlling shareholder to retain the control premium.

2)   Some cases have compelled the controlling shareholder to share the control premium with minority shareholders.

(i)   Some of these cases contain broad statements to the effect that a director owes a fiduciary duty to the corporation and to the minority shareholders. E. g., *Perlman v. Feldmann*, 219 F.2d 173 (2d Cir. 1955). Such statements are little more than make-weight since they do not explain when the premium may be recovered and when it may not.

(ii)   Some cases have permitted the recovery of a control premium on a theory of "corporate action" or usurpation of corporate opportunity.

Example: The purchaser first offers to buy the assets of the corporation at an attractive price; the controlling shareholder suggests that the transaction be recast in the form of a purchase of the controlling shares. The favorable sale opportunity is a corporate opportunity belonging to all the shareholders, rather than to the majority shareholder. The facts of *Perlman v. Feldmann* may be explained on this basis.

(iii)   Some cases have viewed the control premium as being for the sale of a corporate office rather than for the sale of stock. Since a sale of office is against public policy, the excess payment may be recovered by the corporation for the benefit of the minority shareholders. This argument proves too much since all sales of control stock at a premium may be analyzed in this fashion.

(iv)   A noncontrolling shareholder who is also a director has been held to be not subject to the same duties as a controlling shareholder. Treadway Companies, Inc. v. Care Corp., 638 F.2d 357 (2d Cir. 1980).

Example: A contract provides that part of the purchase price for the sale of control shares is payable only upon the immediate transfer of corporate office. A sale of office may be inferred from this contract provision.

Example: The selling shareholder holds 28.3 per cent of the shares of a publicly held corporation. The contract provides for a control premium and the seriatim resignation of directors to permit the immediate transfer of control. This agreement is not of itself against public policy. *Essex Universal Corp. v. Yates*, 305 F.2d 572 (2d Cir. 1962).

Example: The selling shareholders own three per cent of the outstanding shares. The sales agreement provides for a seriatim resignation of directors; and the price greatly exceeds the market value of the shares being sold. A sale of office may be inferred from these circumstances. *In re Caplan's Petition*, 246 N.Y.S.2d 913 (Sup.Ct. 1964).

(v) Some cases have imposed liability for a control premium on a theory of nondisclosure or misrepresentation.

Example: A controlling shareholder contracts to sell more shares than she owns, planning to purchase the additional shares from other shareholders; if she purchases the additional shares without disclosing the resale contract, she may be liable under rule 10b–5 or state law.

Example: A controlling shareholder contracts to sell his shares for $1,500 per share. The purchaser offers to buy minority shares at the same time at $300 per share. The controlling shareholder permits the $300 offer to be made without disclosing that he is receiving five times as much per share. The nondisclosure makes this transaction actionable and the minority shareholders may share in the control premium. *Brown v. Halbert*, 76 Cal.Rptr. 781 (Cal.App. 1969).

(vi) Some cases have imposed liability for the control premium on the basis of the extreme unfairness of the transaction. The leading case is *Jones v. H. F. Ahmanson & Co.*, 460 P.2d 464 (Cal. 1969) which perhaps goes furthest toward acceptance of the general theory that control premiums are inherently improper. The majority shareholders of a savings and loan association created a holding company and exchanged their shares for holding company shares. Minority shareholders in the association, however, were not permitted to exchange their shares for holding company shares. The holding company then made a public offering of its own shares and a public market was created for its shares. The minority shareholders of the association were, of course, excluded from this market since they were not permitted to exchange their S & L shares for holding company shares. This conduct violated the majority's fiduciary responsibility to treat the minority fairly. Further, recovery was based either on the appraised value of the "exchange shares" when the holding company was created or the value of such shares on the date litigation was commenced. This option gave the plaintiffs a risk-free election with the benefit of hindsight.

c.   Law review commentators in the 1950s and 1960s suggested that the best rule would be that all control premiums should be shared with all shareholders in every sale of control case. These commentators essentially argue that since shares of stock are fungible, the control premium represents the pure power to control which should be a corporate asset available to all shareholders. The cases, however, have not accepted this position.

d.   More recent commentators have argued that transactions based on a control premium are desirable since they permit transactions to occur that benefit not only the purchaser of control but also shareholders in the corporation. These arguments are based on economic analysis and are most strongly put forward by Professor Fischel and Judge Easterbrook.

e.   A form of control premium is also involved in cases such as *Honigman v. Green Giant Co.*, 309 F.2d 667 (8th Cir. 1962), where a class of voting shares agree to share the voting power with a larger class of nonvoting common in exchange for a larger "slice of the equity." Such transactions have been approved where the additional equity is not excessive, or to put it a different way, where the transaction seems fair.

f.   Where a control premium is recoverable, courts have permitted either the corporation or the minority shareholders to recover, depending on the theory adopted.

   1)   If the theory of recovery is looting, corporate opportunity, corporate action, or the sale of corporate office, logically only the corporation should recover and a suit by a shareholder should be considered exclusively derivative in nature.

   2)   If the theory is misrepresentation or violation of rule 10b–5, the minority shareholders should recover in their own right.

   3)   A corporate recovery indirectly enriches the purchaser of control who paid the premium. Because of this, *Perlman v. Feldmann* allowed the minority shareholders to recover directly even though the theory adopted in that case apparently was corporate

opportunity which would dictate solely a corporate recovery. See generally: part XVIII, G.

REVIEW QUESTIONS

XV–1. What is meant by "insider trading?"

XV–2. Are the rules relating to insider trading based on state or federal law?

XV–3. Isn't any transaction by an insider that is based on personal use of non-public information subject to attack on the theory that it involves the misuse of corporate assets?

XV–4. Is rule 10b–5 applicable only to publicly held corporations that are subject to registration under section 12 of the Securities Exchange Act of 1934?

XV–5. A Colorado corporation has three shareholders, all of whom reside in Denver. Its business is located in Denver and all of its sales are made to Denver residents. The majority shareholder defrauds minority shareholders by inducing them to sell shares on the basis of false representations. This transaction involves only Colorado law and not rule 10b–5.

   True _____   False _____

XV–6. What kinds of transactions are subject to rule 10b–5?

XV–7. What limiting factors have been applied to rule 10b–5?

XV–8. How does section 16(b) of the Securities Exchange Act differ from rule 10b–5?

XV–9. How are profits to be determined in a section 16(b) case?

XV–10. A person who owns a controlling interest in the shares of a corporation may sell those shares for any price that she can get.

True _____   False _____

XV–11. Why not adopt a rule that control is a corporate asset and that the profit from its sale must be divided among all shareholders?

XV–12. Dynamic, Inc. is a successful computer component manufacturer whose excellent engineering staff is developing a seemingly matchless production technique. Partially because of its engineering expertise, Dynamic, Inc.'s shares, which are registered under section 12(g) of the Securities Exchange Act of 1934 and actively traded over-the-counter, sell at about $180 per share. Ian Sider, director and vice president of Dynamic, Inc., learns at a board of directors' meeting that the cream of the engineering staff of Dynamic, Inc. is threatening to leave and establish their own computer operation. Rather than wait to see if the threat materializes, Sider calls his broker and directs the sale of his 10,000 shares of Dynamic, Inc. The shares are sold for $170 per share.

One week later the disgruntled engineering faction publicly announces its intention to leave. The shares of Dynamic, Inc. drop to $100 per share. Ben Taken, a new shareholder of Dynamic, Inc., who purchased one day prior to the public announcement for $175 per share, consults you as to possible recourse against Sider. What is your advice? [This question and answer is drawn from Ballantine, Problems in Law 239 (5th Ed. 1975).]

XV–13. Maggie M. is a paralegal with the law firm of Jones and Smith, a firm with a substantial corporate practice. She is asked to work on certain documents from which she infers that Apex Corporation is to announce the successful settlement of a major lawsuit. Maggie M. tells her boyfriend about what she has learned and together they purchase calls on Apex Corporation stock. Has Maggie M. violated Federal law?

XV–14.   In the situation described in question XV–14, would it make any difference if the information Maggie M. obtained related to a takeover bid by a client of Jones and Smith and Maggie M. bought stock in the target corporation?

XV–15.   Peter Jones is a vice president of Apex Corporation. His college roommate, John Smith, is a stock broker and old personal friend. Peter Jones tells Smith of the successful settlement of the law suit; Jones then purchases calls on Apex Corporation Stock. Has either Peter Jones or John Smith violated Federal law?

XV–16.   X corporation was a manufacturer of steel. Because of wartime conditions steel was in short supply and a grey market existed with respect to it although there were government controls on prices. D, the controlling shareholder of X, sold his stock to Y corporation at a premium over the price which non-control shares could command. Y was an end-user of steel and used its control of X to allocate steel to itself at the government prices. P, a minority shareholder of X, brings a derivative action on behalf of the corporation against D for breach of D's fiduciary duty. Is D liable to the corporation?

XVI

INDEMNIFICATION AND LIABILITY INSURANCE

"Indemnification" simply means the corporation reimburses a defendant who is a present or former corporate officer or director for expenses incurred in defending against an asserted claim or prosecution. If indemnification is allowed at all, it will normally cover legal fees and other expenses; in some instances it may also cover amounts paid in settlement, amounts needed to satisfy a judgment entered against defendant officers or directors, or even the amount of a criminal fine. Liability insurance for directors and officers (usually called "D & O insurance") against such risks is also commercially available to a limited extent.

Analysis

A. Indemnification and Public Policy
B. Scope of Indemnification Under Modern State Statutes
C. D & O Liability Insurance

A. INDEMNIFICATION AND PUBLIC POLICY

There are basic policy questions posed by indemnification.

1. POLICIES FAVORING INDEMNIFICATION
Policy justifications for indemnification of officers and directors include:

    a.   It encourages innocent directors to resist unjust charges;

    b.   It encourages responsible persons to accept the position of director; and

    c.   It discourages groundless shareholder litigation.

2. POLICY LIMITATIONS ON INDEMNIFICATION
There can be little objection to indemnification of expenses if a director is totally absolved of liability or misconduct. *In re E. C. Warner Co.*, 45 N.W.2d 388 (Minn. 1950). At the other extreme, indemnification against liabilities imposed on some kinds of wrongful acts clearly violates public policy. The policy issue raised is to sort out the situations where indemnification is proper and should be encouraged and situations where it is against public policy and should be prohibited.

> *Example:* Liability is imposed under section 16(b) of the Securities Exchange Act of 1934. Indemnification is not permitted since it would create circularity, and vitiate the policy underlying that section.

> *Example:* The defendant is found guilty of wrongful misconduct and is held liable to a third person in damages for such misconduct. In view of the finding that the defendant was guilty of wrongful conduct, neither indemnification of expenses nor against the judgments themselves should be permissible.

B. SCOPE OF INDEMNIFICATION UNDER MODERN STATE STATUTES

State statutes attempt to work out a compromise of these various competing considerations. Statutes on indemnification vary from skeletal authorization to elaborate procedural and substantive requirements, largely based on either the Delaware statute or on one of the more recent versions of the indemnification provisions of the Model Business Corporation Act: section 5 of the 1969 Model Act, section 5 as amended in 1979, or RMBCA §§ 8.50 thru 8.58.

> *Caveat:* The RMBCA provisions approved in 1984 are based directly on the 1979 amendments to section 5 of the MBCA, but are reorganized and broken down into nine different sections to simplify the structure. Experience with

the 1969 Model Act indicated that a number of problems were not adequately addressed by that statute. The Delaware statute is similar to the 1969 Model Act. Some state indemnification provisions are modeled after the 1960 version of the Model Act.

1. **INDEMNIFICATION WHEN THE DEFENDANT HAS BEEN SUCCESSFUL IN THE PROCEEDING**

Under most modern statutes a defendant is entitled to indemnification *as a matter of statutory right* if "he is wholly successful, on the merits or otherwise." RMBCA § 8.52.

Example: A defendant prevails because of the statute of limitations or because of pleading defects. Under these statutes, he is entitled to indemnification as a matter of right.

Example: In a criminal securities case, a defendant pleads *nolo contendere* on one count in a plea bargain that results in the dismissal of other counts. *Merritt-Chapman & Scott Corp. v. Wolfson*, 321 A.2d 138 (Del.Super. 1974) held that the defendant was entitled to indemnification for expenses with respect to the dismissed counts. It is doubtful if this was the intention of the statutory draftsmen, and the Revised Model Business Corporation Act reverses this result by requiring the defendant to be "wholly" successful on the merits or otherwise. RMBCA § 8.52.

a. The language "on the merits *or otherwise*" may result in some directors being entitled to indemnification even though they were successful because of a procedural defense that does not go to the merits of the claim against the director. In some of these instances, further investigation might show that the director had engaged in conduct that would have prevented indemnification if the procedural defense had not been available. The award of indemnification in this situation is justified on the ground that it is unreasonable to require the successful director to litigate the merits of his or her claim in order to establish a right to indemnification. It also is assumed that in most cases in which a nonsubstantive defense is established, e. g. the statute of limitations, that the director or officer also has a substantive defense that is never reached.

b. The California statute does not include the phrase "or otherwise," thereby limiting mandatory indemnification to cases where the director or officer establishes his innocence on the merits.

c. If a director is entitled to mandatory indemnification but the corporation refuses to make the required payment, the director may petition a court for an order compelling the payment of indemnification. RMBCA

§ 8.54(1). If such an order is entered, the director is entitled also to recover expenses incurred in obtaining the order.

2. PERMISSIVE INDEMNIFICATION

Under modern statutes, indemnification is permitted *as a matter of discretion but not as a matter of right* in a variety of situations upon certain findings being made as to the conduct of the person. Directors cannot compel corporations to grant indemnification for conduct falling within the category of permissive indemnification. *Tomash v. Midwest Technical Development Corp.*, 160 N.W.2d 273 (Minn. 1968). Permissive indemnification is authorized in the following situations:

a. Liabilities that may be indemnified against include "the obligation to pay a judgment, settlement, penalty, fine (including an excise tax assessed with respect to an employee benefit plan), or reasonable expenses incurred with respect to a proceeding." RMBCA § 8.50(4).

b. The test for whether indemnification is permitted depends on whether or not the conduct was in the person's "official capacity." See RMBCA § 8.50(5).

   1) For actions in the official capacity of a person, indemnification is permitted only if the person acted in good faith and can establish that he reasonably believed that his conduct was *in* the corporation's best interest. RMBCA § 8.51(a)(2)(i).

   2) For all other actions, indemnification is permitted only if the person acted in good faith and can establish that he reasonably believed that his conduct "was *at least not opposed to*" the corporation's best interest. RMBCA § 8.51(a)(2)(ii).

   3) In the case of a director, "official capacity" means "the office of director in a corporation." In the case of an individual other than a director, "official capacity" means the office in the corporation or the employment or agency relationship undertaken by that individual for or on behalf of the corporation. All relationships other than the foregoing do not involve actions in "official capacity."

      Example: A director serves at the request of the corporation as an officer of a trade association. That service is not in the official capacity of the director.

c. In the case of a criminal proceeding, the person, in addition to the tests of subpart b), must have had no reasonable cause to believe his or her conduct was unlawful. RMBCA § 8.51(a)(3).

d.   Even though an individual arguably meets these standards, indemnification is not permitted in two situations:

1)   In a suit or proceeding by or in the name of the corporation in which the person is adjudged liable to the corporation; and

2)   In a proceeding charging the receipt of an improper personal benefit in which the person is adjudged liable for receiving that personal benefit.

Example: A director is named as a defendant in a derivative suit brought in the name of the corporation claiming that the director improperly diverted a corporate opportunity to his own personal advantage. The director thereafter settles the case, agreeing to return the opportunity to the corporation but not admitting that he violated his duty to the corporation. The suit involves an action by the director in his "official capacity;" he is entitled to indemnification of his expenses in connection with the suit if he can establish that he acted in good faith and that his conduct was in the corporation's best interest. In no event is he entitled to indemnification for the amount paid over to the corporation in the settlement of the claim.

Example: The director in the foregoing example does not settle but litigates the matter to a conclusion. If he is "adjudged" liable to the corporation, he is not eligible for indemnification of his expenses. If he is successful "on the merits or otherwise" he is entitled as a matter of right to indemnification.

Example: A director is charged with violation of rule 10b–5 in connection with sales of shares on the open market allegedly on the basis of inside information. Sales of stock are not in the director's official capacity and the standard for eligibility for indemnification is that the director acted in good faith and that she reasonably believed that her conduct "was at least not opposed to" the corporation's best interests. If the director settles the case she is eligible to have both her expenses and the amount of the settlement indemnified by the corporation if it is determined that her conduct met this standard.

Example: In the foregoing case, if a court concludes that the sales violated rule 10b–5, the director has received an improper benefit and would not be eligible for indemnification without regard to her good faith and reasonable belief that her conduct was not opposed to the corporation's best interests. The director, however, may request court approval for indemnification under RMBCA § 8.54.

Example: The CEO of the corporation concludes that it is in the best interest of the corporation to pay a bribe in order to obtain a defense contract. After the contract is obtained, an investigation occurs and the CEO is prosecuted and indicted. Since he knew that his conduct was unlawful, he is not entitled to indemnification without regard to his good faith and the belief that the bribe was in the best interests of the corporation.

Example: A director is requested to serve as a trustee of an employee benefit plan. As a trustee, she votes in favor of a ruling that deprives certain striking employees of benefits under the plan. In this regard, she reasonably believes that her decision is in the interests of the participants and beneficiaries of the plan. If she is thereafter sued individually by employees who were denied benefits as a result of the ruling, both the director's expenses and any judgment entered against her may be indemnified by the corporation. See RMBCA § 8.51(b).

Caveat: RMBCA § 8.51(c) provides that the termination of a proceeding by judgment, order, settlement, plea of nolo contendere, or similar terminating event is not "of itself" determinative that the director did not meet the foregoing standards of conduct.

Caveat: In all cases where a person is not eligible for indemnification under the specific RMBCA provisions, the person may petition a court for a determination that the person "is fairly and reasonably entitled to indemnification in view of all the relevant circumstances" even though the specific requirements of the indemnification statute are not met. RMBCA § 8.54.

e. Many corporations, by bylaw provision, grant a contractual right of indemnification in all cases in which indemnification is permissive. Such a provision is valid. RMBCA § 8.58(a), Official Comment.

3. **"AUTHORIZATION" AND "DETERMINATION" OF INDEMNIFICATION**

RMBCA § 8.55 distinguishes between a "determination" of indemnification and an "authorization" of indemnification. A "determination" relates to the eligibility of the officer or director for indemnification while an "authorization" is a corporate judgment that an appropriate use of corporate resources is to pay the director or officer the amount so "determined."

a. A "determination" may be made:

1) By the board of directors by majority vote of a quorum consisting exclusively of directors who were not parties to the proceeding. RMBCA § 8.55(b)(1).

2) If a quorum cannot be obtained, by a majority vote of a committee designated by the board of directors that consists of two or more members who were not parties to the proceeding. In this selection process, directors who are parties to the proceeding may participate. RMBCA § 8.55(b)(2).

3) By the shareholders, but shares owned by or voted under the control of directors who are parties to the proceeding may not participate. RMBCA § 8.55(b)(4).

4) By special legal counsel. According to the Official Comment, such counsel "should normally be counsel having no prior professional relationship with those seeking indemnification, should be retained for the specific occasion, and should not be either inside counsel or regular outside counsel." Such counsel may be selected by:

a) The board of directors or a committee of the board meeting the requirements described in subparts 1) or 2) above.

b) If there are not sufficient disinterested directors to select the special legal counsel as described in part a), then the full board, by a majority vote of all directors, including those who are parties to the proceeding may select the special counsel. RMBCA § 8.55(b)(3).

b. "Authorization" of indemnification cannot be made by special legal counsel, but may be made by the directors or shareholders who may "determine" eligibility for indemnification under part a). If special legal counsel is employed, indemnification may be authorized by the persons or groups entitled to select the counsel. RMBCA § 8.55(c).

c. Issues relating to the reasonableness of expenses must also be resolved by the persons or groups "authorizing" indemnification and not by special legal counsel "determining" eligibility for indemnification.

4. COURT–APPROVED INDEMNIFICATION

RMBCA § 8.54(2) recognizes that a person ineligible for indemnification under the technical requirements of the statute may in some circumstances be fairly entitled to indemnification, and provides that a person otherwise not eligible for indemnification may petition a court (which may be either the court in which the proceeding occurred or another court) for a determination that the person is "fairly and reasonably" entitled to indemnification.

a. Court-approved indemnification is limited to the indemnification of reasonable expenses.

b. A corporation may avoid the obligation imposed by court-ordered indemnification by an appropriate provision in the articles of incorporation.

Example: A director is named as a defendant in a suit charging violation of the insider trading rules because of sales by the defendant of more than 100,000 shares of stock in a two-month period. After a trial, the court concludes that with respect to the sales of 99,800 shares, the director did not violate the insider trading rules since he did not have material inside information when the sales were made; with respect to the sale of 200 shares, however, the court concludes that a violation of rule 10b–5 occurred and orders the profits returned to the corporation. The latter holding renders the defendant director ineligible for indemnification under the statute; a court, however, might conclude that the director is fairly and equitably entitled to indemnification of his expenses since the violation of rule 10b–5 was minor in comparison to the essential vindication of the defendant on the bulk of the litigation.

5. ADVANCES FOR EXPENSES

RMBCA § 8.53 authorizes a corporation to pay or reimburse the expenses of a proceeding as they are incurred without waiting for a final determination that the person is eligible for indemnification. This provision recognizes that as a practical matter, adequate legal representation and adequate preparation of a defense often requires substantial payments of expenses before a final determination. If advances were not permitted less affluent officers and directors might be unable to finance their own defense. On the other hand, advances for expenses may lead to payments to defendants who are ultimately determined to be ineligible for indemnification.

a.   In the absence of specific statutory authorization of such advances, a court may not authorize them. *Gross v. Texas Plastics, Inc.,* 344 F.Supp. 564 (D.N.J. 1972), aff'd mem. 523 F.2d 1050 (3d Cir. 1975).

b.   A director seeking advance indemnification must furnish the corporation a written affirmation of the director's good faith belief that he or she meets the standard of conduct that permits indemnification, RMBCA § 8.53(a)(1), and a written undertaking to repay the advance if it is ultimately determined that the director did not meet the applicable standard of conduct. RMBCA § 8.53(a)(2).

   Caveat: The written undertaking must be unlimited and general, but need not be secured and may be accepted without regard to the financial ability of the defendant to make repayment. RMBCA § 8.53(b). The theory of this provision is that discrimination in this regard should not be based on the outside wealth of defendants.

c.   Before making a specific advance, a determination must be made that on the basis of the facts then known to those making the determination, indemnification is not precluded. RMBCA § 8.53(a)(3). This determination is to be made by the persons entitled to make indemnification determinations under RMBCA § 8.55, discussed above.

   Caveat: Advances for expenses are also subject to the authorization of indemnification by appropriate corporate officers. RMBCA § 8.53(c).

6. INDEMNIFICATION OF OFFICERS, EMPLOYEES AND AGENTS

The foregoing provisions relate specifically to directors. Different principles may be applicable to officers, employees and agents of a corporation, who may have broader rights of indemnification based on contract, specific corporate action, or general principles of agency. RMBCA § 8.56.

   Caveat: Indemnification under these broader principles are subject to limitations of public policy. In *Koster v. Warren,* 297 F.2d 418 (9th Cir. 1961), the court allowed indemnification of an officer and an employee, both of whom pleaded nolo contendere to an antitrust indictment at the request of the corporation. The court stated, however, that an agreement in advance to indemnify all employees convicted of antitrust violations would be against public policy.

a.   The indemnification of an officer, agent or employee who is not a director is not subject to the limiting principles applicable to indemnification of directors. However, the statute grants the corporation the same *discretionary* right to indemnify an officer, employee or agent of the corporation as it has to indemnify directors. RMBCA § 8.56(2).

b. An *officer* of the corporation (but *not* employees or agents generally) has the same right to *mandatory* indemnification as a director and also may apply for court-ordered indemnification to the same extent as a director. RMBCA § 8.56(1). The purpose of this provision is to assist officers but not to extend the duty to indemnify to lower level personnel within the corporation unless the corporation is willing to make the payments.

c. A *director* who is also an officer, agent or employee of the corporation is limited to the rights of directors under this chapter. The purpose of this limitation is to ensure that all directors are treated alike with respect to indemnification.

7. MODIFICATION OF STATUTORY INDEMNIFICATION POLICIES

Statutes based on the Delaware statute or on the 1969 Model Act generally provide that the indemnification statute is not exclusive and corporations may include broader indemnification provisions in their articles of incorporation or bylaws. RMBCA § 8.58(a) does not make the statute non-exclusive but rather provides that a contractual or voluntary provision relating to indemnification "is valid only if and to the extent the provision is consistent with this subchapter." The Official Comment to RMBCA § 8.58 states that the quoted language "is believed to be a more accurate description of the limited validity of nonstatutory indemnification provisions."

Example: A special provision provides that indemnification decisions shall be made by an outside committee consisting of law professors with no interest in the proceeding. That provision is valid.

Example: A corporation agrees to grant indemnification on a mandatory basis whenever it may do so on a voluntary basis. The provision is valid.

8. INDEMNIFICATION OF WITNESSES

RMBCA §§ 8.50–8.58 applies only when a director is made a "party" to a proceeding, i.e. "was, is, or is threatened to be made a named defendant or respondent in a proceeding." RMBCA § 8.50(6). On the other hand, RMBCA § 8.58(b) provides expressly that the chapter does not limit the power of a corporation to pay or reimburse the expenses of a director in connection with an appearance as a witness in a proceeding, assuming that the director is not a "party."

9. NOTIFICATION OF INDEMNIFICATION

RMBCA § 16.21(a) requires the corporation to notify shareholders of all indemnifications or advances of expenses to defendants in connection with suits brought by or in the name of the corporation. The notification must be in writing and must be given with or before the next annual notice of the meeting.

10. **INDEMNIFICATION IN FEDERAL PROCEEDINGS**
Indemnification of liabilities incurred under Federal statutes may raise additional questions of public policy.

    a.   The Securities and Exchange Commission has long taken the position that it is against public policy for a corporation to indemnify officers or directors against liabilities imposed by the Securities Act of 1933. Rule 460, 17 C.F.R. § 230.460 (1985), provides that acceleration of a registration statement may be denied unless a waiver of rights to indemnification is filed assuring that a claim to indemnification against 1933 Act liabilities will be submitted to a court for final determination.

    b.   Some cases indicate that indemnification is also more narrowly permitted against liabilities imposed by federal securities acts than under common law or state statutory provisions, *Globus v. Law Research Serv. Inc.*, 418 F.2d 1276 (2d Cir. 1969), *cert. denied* 397 U.S. 913, 90 S.Ct. 913 (1970), including indemnification against negligent conduct by officers or directors of investment companies. *S.E.C. v. Continental Growth Fund, Inc.*, 1964 Fed.Sec.L.Rep. (CCH) ¶ 91,437 (S.D.N.Y. Oct. 7, 1964). See also *Gould v. American-Hawaiian Steamship Co.*, 387 F.Supp. 163 (D.Del. 1974), vacated on other grounds 535 F.2d 761 (3d Cir. 1976).

C. D & O LIABILITY INSURANCE

"D & O" ["directors' and officers'"] insurance is a relatively new phenomenon. It provides useful but limited protection against costs and liabilities for negligence, for misconduct not involving dishonesty or knowing bad faith, and for false or misleading statements in disclosure documents. Most persons today would decline to serve as a director of a publicly held corporation unless protected by a D & O policy.

1. **INSURABLE RISKS**
Companies writing D & O liability insurance write policies that cover only insurable risks in the traditional sense. This limitation largely eliminates the public policy issues that may be raised by broad indemnification clauses.

    Example: Wrongful misconduct, dishonest acts, acts in bad faith with knowledge thereof, or violations of statutes such as section 16(b) are not insurable risks and are excluded from coverage.

2. **POLICY EXCLUSIONS**
D & O policies contain important exclusions from coverage.

a. There is an exclusion for failing to disclose contingent liabilities on the application for insurance. A misrepresentation or omission by the corporation may invalidate the D & O coverage for all officers and directors. *Bird v. Penn Central Co.*, 341 F.Supp. 291 (E.D.Pa. 1972).

b. There is an exclusion for transactions for personal profit or advantage.

3. POLICY COVERAGE AND PREMIUMS

D & O policies are purchased by the corporation for all its officers and directors. The cost of the premium is shared: a typical pattern is for the corporation to pay 90 per cent and the covered persons 10 per cent. This division in cost reflects the fact that D & O insurance largely protects against liabilities that fall within the corporation's obligation to indemnify officers and directors under statute or bylaw provisions.

4. STATE STATUTES

Many state statutes specifically authorize corporations to purchase D & O insurance. See RMBCA § 8.57. Where no statutory authorization exists, the power to purchase such insurance is usually thought to be implicit in the general corporate power to provide executive compensation. Corporate bylaws often specifically authorize the purchase of such insurance.

REVIEW QUESTIONS

XVI–1.   What does "indemnification" mean?

XVI–2.   Should not all indemnification be considered to be against public policy?

XVI–3.   Is it against public policy to indemnify a defendant who has been found guilty of improper conduct?

XVI–4.   What is "D & O insurance?"

XVI–5.   Is not D & O insurance against public policy?

XVII

INSPECTION OF BOOKS
AND RECORDS

Both shareholders and directors have the right to inspect corporate books and records in certain circumstances. However, the right of a director is considerably broader than the right of a shareholder and rests on an entirely different theoretical base.

Analysis

A.   INSPECTION BY DIRECTORS

A director is a manager of the corporation and owes certain duties to it and to all the shareholders. A director may be liable for negligent mismanagement if he or she does not adequately acquaint himself or herself with the business and affairs of the corporation. Some decisions state that the directors' right of inspection is therefore absolute and unqualified, *Pilat v. Broach Systems Inc.*, 260 A.2d 13 (N.J.Super.Law Div. 1969) but courts have sometimes denied inspection rights to directors where it was clear that the director was acting with manifestly improper motives and adequate information prepared by unbiased persons was available to the directors. The ALI Corporate Governance Project adopts the latter view.

B.   INSPECTION BY SHAREHOLDERS

The right of a shareholder to inspect books and records is narrower than the right of directors. A shareholder has a financial interest in the corporation and the common law recognizes a right to inspect books and records to protect this interest. However, the shareholder is not charged with management responsibility, is not subject to a broad fiduciary duty, and may have conflicting or inconsistent financial interests; as a result, a shareholder's right to inspect is limited to inspections for "proper purposes." Most litigation of this type by shareholders relates to inspecting a current list of shareholders.

1.   SOURCES OF THE SHAREHOLDERS' RIGHT OF INSPECTION
A shareholder may have either a common law or a statutory right of inspection. In some states shareholders may have both a common law and a statutory right, i. e. the statutory right supplements but does not supplant the common law right. A shareholder may also have rights of discovery if he or she is in litigation with the corporation and, to the extent the corporation is required to make disclosure to the public generally, shareholders also have the rights of members of the general public. In many states, shareholders also have a special statutory right to inspect a list of shareholders before or during a shareholder's meeting. RMBCA § 7.20. This subchapter deals only with general common law or statutory rights of inspection of a shareholder as such.

2.   THE SHAREHOLDERS' COMMON LAW RIGHT OF INSPECTION
The common law inspection right was available to any shareholder of record who established a proper purpose for examining the books and records of the corporation. It is a right of shareholders not subject to limitation by provisions in articles of incorporation. *State ex rel. Cochran v. Penn-Beaver Oil Co.*, 143 A. 257 (Del. 1926).

   a.   From the standpoint of the corporation, a shareholder's demand to inspect a shareholder's list or the corporation's books and records is viewed as a hostile and threatening act.

b.   The practice therefore developed of routinely denying all requests for common law inspection and compelling the shareholder to litigate in every case, relying on whatever pretext may be available for the denial, and putting the shareholder to his or her proof as to purpose.

3.   DEVELOPMENT OF THE STATUTORY RIGHT OF INSPECTION

In an effort to combat this attitude, the statutes of many states supplement the common law right of inspection with a statutory right of inspection which may include a "penalty" on corporate officers who arbitrarily refuse to permit proper examination of books and records. The 1969 Model Business Corporation Act contains a provision of this type.

a.   This type of statutory right of inspection is typically available to persons (a) who have been shareholders of record for at least six months prior to the demand or (b) who own at least five per cent of the outstanding shares of the corporation.

b.   This statutory right to inspect, like the common law right, also requires a showing of "proper purposes" for the inspection which must be stated in the shareholder's written demand. However, in the event a shareholder qualifies for the statutory right, the corporation has the burden of showing the plaintiff does not have a proper purpose.

c.   Under many statutes a corporate officer or agent who refuses to grant a statutory right of inspection is liable for a "penalty" equal to a specified per cent of the value of the shares owned by the shareholder or some other fixed amount.

1)   A corporation or officer may avoid imposition of the penalty only by showing reasonable grounds for the denial of inspection. These grounds may be set forth in the statute as defenses.

2)   As a practical matter, such penalty provisions are rarely enforced because the basic test of eligibility—a proper purpose—is a vague and uncertain one. While the potential of a substantial penalty may have had a healthful, *in terrorem* effect, there are few reported cases in which a penalty was successfully imposed.

4.   REVISED MODEL BUSINESS CORPORATION ACT INSPECTION RIGHT

RMBCA §§ 16.01 through 16.04 adopts a somewhat different approach toward enforcement of shareholders' inspection rights.

a.   Shareholders have an unrestricted right to inspect certain fundamental documents that the corporation must preserve at its principal office. RMBCA § 16.02(a). This right of inspection is absolute and not subject to a proper purpose limitation. The documents are listed in RMBCA § 16.01(e) and include:

1)   Articles or restated articles of incorporation;

2)   Bylaws;

3)   Resolutions creating classes or series of shares;

4)   Minutes of shareholders' meetings and records of action taken by consent of the shareholders for the past three years;

5)   Written communications to shareholders within the past three years, including financial statements required to be provided to shareholders (RMBCA §§ 16.20, 16.21);

6)   A list of the names and business addresses of directors and officers; and

7)   The corporation's most recent annual report (RMBCA § 16.22).

b.   RMBCA § 16.02(b) authorizes a shareholder to inspect and copy additional records only upon a showing of "proper purpose" and good faith, and upon providing a statement setting forth "with reasonable particularity his purpose and the records he desires to inspect." The records must be directly connected with that purpose. The records subject to this additional inspection right include:

1)   Excerpts from minutes of the board of directors, records of actions of committees of the board of directors, and minutes of shareholders meetings more than three years old (and therefore not available under a. above);

2)   Accounting records of the corporation; and

3)   The record of shareholders.

> **Caveat:** The classes of records available for inspection under RMBCA § 16.02 are narrower than the scope of inspection permitted by many courts under earlier statutes. Some courts, for example, have permitted inspection of correspondence or internal records that do not fall within any of the categories set forth in § 16.02.

> **Example:** Accounting records might be construed in an appropriate case to include receipts, vouchers, bills and other

documents evidencing the financial condition of the corporation.

> *Example:* Accounting records in an appropriate case might also be construed to include accounting records of a subsidiary or other venture controlled by the corporation.

c.   The rights of inspection set forth in RMBCA § 16.02 are expressly made nonexclusive of other inspection rights. RMBCA § 16.02(e). Further, they may not be restricted or eliminated by provisions in the articles of incorporation or bylaws. RMBCA § 16.02(d).

d.   The scope of the inspection right, including the right to have copies made by photographic, xerographic, or other means, is defined in RMBCA § 16.03. The corporation may impose a reasonable charge for making copies of records but may not limit the inspection right to the right to make longhand copies or notes with respect to the contents of the books and records. RMBCA § 16.03(b), (c). The shareholder is entitled to be accompanied by his attorney or accountant. RMBCA § 16.03(a).

> *Caveat:* Most earlier statutes are silent on many of the issues discussed in RMBCA § 16.03. Many, however, contemplate inspection by agent or attorney. Court decisions, further, tend to construe broadly the inspection rights of shareholders, once established, to include copying by machine, etc.

e.   A shareholder who is denied the right of inspection may seek a summary judicial order compelling the inspection. RMBCA § 16.04. Further, the court must order the corporation to pay the shareholder's costs in compelling inspection unless the corporation "proves that it refused inspection in good faith because it had a reasonable basis for doubt about the right of the shareholder to inspect the records demanded." RMBCA § 16.04(c). The Official Comment states that this language establishes a "partially objective standard, in that the corporation must be able to point to some objective basis for its doubt that the shareholder was acting in good faith or had a purpose that was proper."

> *Example:* The corporation learns that a shareholder demanding a right of inspection had improperly used information obtained from the corporation in the past and refuses to permit the inspection. If the shareholder establishes a good faith and proper purpose for this inspection, a court should order the inspection. The corporation, however, cannot be compelled to pay the shareholder's expenses in obtaining the order compelling the inspection since the corporation had a reasonable basis for

doubt because of the shareholder's prior misuse of corporate information.

Example: In the previous example, the court may impose restrictions on the use of information by the shareholder. RMBCA § 16.04(d). It may, for example, prohibit the shareholder from disclosing it to a competitor.

5. WHAT IS A "PROPER PURPOSE?"

The basic test of inspection by shareholders is a "proper purpose." If the common law right of inspection is involved, the shareholder must affirmatively show a proper purpose; if the shareholder qualifies for the statutory right of inspection, the corporation has the burden of establishing an absence of proper purpose and may be subject to penalty if it fails to do so after denying inspection.

a. A purpose is proper if it is directed toward obtaining information bearing upon or seeking to protect the shareholder's interest and that of other shareholders of the corporation. A shareholder may have a proper purpose even though he or she is unfriendly to management.

Example: A shareholder demands a list of shareholders in order to communicate with other shareholders about matters of corporate concern; e. g., to solicit proxies, to initiate a proxy contest, to publicize mismanagement, to discuss a derivative suit, to discuss proposals of management, or to form a protective committee. These are all proper purposes. *General Time Corp. v. Talley Indus., Inc.*, 240 A.2d 755 (Del.Ch. 1968).

Example: The mere fact that the shareholder making the request is a competitor of the corporation does not necessarily make his or her purpose improper though such a demand may raise suspicions.

Example: It is not a proper purpose to seek the list in order to communicate one's own personal social or political views to shareholders. *State ex rel. Pillsbury v. Honeywell, Inc.*, 191 N.W.2d 406 (Minn. 1971).

Example: Inspection is demanded to determine the worth of the shareholder's holdings. Such a purpose is proper.

Example: Inspection is demanded to seek reasons for a decline in profits and to communicate with other shareholders. Such purposes are proper.

> *Example:* A desire to obtain trade secrets for a competitor is not a proper purpose.

> *Example:* Probably idle curiosity is not a proper purpose, though it is a rare shareholder who cannot allege a more specific purpose that would be considered proper.

b. Obviously, substantial and difficult factual issues of predominant motive and intent underlie this determination. A careful coaching of a shareholder's testimony may lead to the conclusion that the purpose for inspection is proper, while an outspoken or unusually forthright shareholder may run into difficulty.

6. INSPECTION RIGHTS OF BENEFICIAL OWNERS

A person who is a beneficial owner of shares but not the record owner has a common law right of inspection. Whether or not a beneficial owner has a statutory right depends on the precise wording of the statute. Under the RMBCA, a beneficial owner of shares has a statutory right of inspection.

a. Under some state statutes, pledgees or judgment creditors have a statutory right to inspect.

b. Holders of voting trust certificates also have a statutory right to inspect under many state statutes.

C. MANDATORY RECORD KEEPING REQUIREMENTS

All state statutes require each corporation to maintain a record of its shareholders to determine entitlement to vote, to dividends, and so forth. In addition, many statutes require each corporation to keep certain minimum records, such as minutes of meetings, books and records of account, and so forth, set forth in the statute.

1. RECORD OF SHAREHOLDERS

The record of shareholders is often referred to as the "list of shareholders" or "shareholders' list." With the development of computerization, the record of shareholders may not be kept in traditional written form. RMBCA § 16.01(c) requires only that a corporation maintain "a record of its shareholders, in a form that permits preparation of a list of the names and addresses of all shareholders, in alphabetical order by class of shares showing the number and class of shares held by each."

a. When inspection of the record of shareholders is demanded, RMBCA § 16.03(d) permits the corporation to provide a list of shareholders compiled no earlier than the date of the demand.

b.   Many states require a voting list to be compiled immediately before the meeting (see: part VII, B). This is a different document that is automatically open to inspection for a limited period of time during or immediately before a meeting.

c.   The record of shareholders consists of the names of record owners only; it does not attempt to list beneficial owners.

d.   There has been a substantial volume of litigation over whether records of shareholders in publicly held corporations must be produced in connection with proxy fights and takeover attempts.

   1)   A list of names and addresses of numerous well-to-do shareholders is itself valuable, and may be salable to mail-solicitation firms. Some state statutes specifically provide that a record of shareholders need not be produced if the applicant has offered to sell or assisted another person in the sale or offering for sale of a shareholders list within the preceding five years.

   2)   A solicitation of shareholders asking them to join in a request for a copy of the record of shareholders (in order to meet the 5 per cent requirement of state law) is itself a solicitation under federal proxy rules, and requires filing with the SEC if more than ten such solicitations are made. *Studebaker Corp. v. Gittlin*, 360 F.2d 692 (2d Cir. 1966).

   3)   Litigation dealing with attempts to obtain the shareholder's list often involves the "proper purpose" test. See: part XVII, B, 3.

   4)   Courts probably tend to be more lenient in granting access to shareholders lists than to other books and records but the right is not unlimited.

e.   Federal proxy regulations give alternative access to the record of shareholders. Rule 14a–7 requires a corporation either to supply a copy of the record of shareholders or to mail solicitations to shareholders on behalf of a shareholder upon payment of the postage by that shareholder. The corporation will usually elect the latter alternative.

2.   MANDATORY AND DISCRETIONARY RECORDS

RMBCA § 16.01(a) requires every corporation to "keep" certain basic records, such as minutes of meetings and records of actions taken by directors and shareholders. RMBCA §§ 16.01(b) and (c) require every corporation to "maintain" "appropriate accounting records" and a record of shareholders. "Keep" is used in the sense of permanent historical records while "maintain" is used in the sense of current records. RMBCA § 16.01(e) also requires that specified records be kept at its principal office where they may be inspected by shareholders.   RMBCA § 16.02(a).

a.   Many state statutes have analogous statutory provisions, that vary widely from state to state.   Provisions relating to accounting records, in particular, vary widely.   The 1969 Model Act, for example, required corporations to keep "correct and complete books and records of account." MBCA (1969) § 52.

b.   RMBCA § 16.01(d) permits a corporation to "maintain" records in other than written form if they can be converted into written form within a reasonable time.   Many state statutes have analogous statutory provisions, that vary widely from state to state.

c.   Many state statutes also recognize that corporations may keep discretionary records of various types.

3.   MANDATORY FINANCIAL DISCLOSURE TO SHAREHOLDERS

RMBCA § 16.20 requires every corporation to furnish shareholders with annual financial statements, containing at a minimum an income statement, a balance sheet, and a statement of changes in shareholders' equity.   These statements do not need to be prepared by an accountant or by following GAAP or other accounting principles; if not prepared in accordance with GAAP, they must contain a description of the basis on which they were prepared and describe whether they were prepared in a manner consistent with the statements for the preceding year.

a.   An increasing number of states require some kind of mandatory financial disclosure to shareholders.   Some states require disclosure of franchise tax reports or other documents that provide basic financial information.

b.   Many states have no mandatory disclosure requirements for financial information.

4.   OTHER MANDATORY DISCLOSURE REQUIREMENTS

RMBCA § 16.21 requires disclosure to shareholders of transactions involving issuance of shares for promissory notes or promises of future services and indemnification transactions in proceedings in which the corporation is a party. RMBCA § 16.01(e)(7) also requires corporations to maintain a copy of its most recent annual report at its principal office where it is available for inspection by shareholders.

Many states require disclosure of various types of information, usually the annual report of the corporation but in some instances additional information as well.   There is great diversity of requirements in this regard.

REVIEW QUESTIONS

XVII–1. What is the test for determining the propriety of a shareholder's demand to inspect corporate records?

XVII–2. If the test is a "proper purpose", why are further restrictions on the right of inspection necessary?

XVII–3. What is the test for a director's right to inspect?

XVII–4. To what extent must a corporation provide routine information to all shareholders, such as financial reports and the like?

XVII–5. The shareholders of X corporation adopted a bylaw which required that all shareholders, as a condition precedent to a right to inspect the books of the corporation, give at least three months notice before the proposed inspection, and that the purpose of such inspection must be approved by the board of directors. The state corporation statute provides for a right of inspection but is silent on whether the right may be limited by the corporation. P, a shareholder of X, demanded the right to inspect the books of X within two weeks of the date of the demand and stated that his purpose for inspection was to determine whether there had been mismanagement, a purpose that is proper under applicable state law. The demand was refused by the directors under the above bylaw. P seeks a writ of mandamus to compel the officers and directors to permit his inspection of the books. Should the writ issue?

XVIII

SHAREHOLDER LITIGATION

The term shareholder litigation primarily refers to litigation brought by a shareholder in connection with his capacity or role as shareholder.

Analysis

A. "DIRECT," "DERIVATIVE," AND "CLASS" LITIGATION

The most basic distinction in shareholder litigation is between "direct" and "derivative" litigation, since different procedural rules apply to these categories. A third, overlapping, category deals with the concept of "class" litigation.

1. "DIRECT" DEFINED

A direct suit involves the enforcement by a shareholder of a claim based on injury to the shareholder directly as an owner of shares.

> *Example:* Suits to recover dividends, to examine corporate books and records, and to compel the registration of a securities transfer are all direct suits.

> *Example:* A suit to compel the payment of a dividend may be either direct, *Knapp v. Bankers Securities Corp.*, 230 F.2d 717 (3d Cir. 1956), or derivative, *Gordon v. Elliman*, 119 N.E.2d 331 (N.Y. 1954) (a case later overruled by statute).

2. "DERIVATIVE" DEFINED

A derivative suit is an action brought by one or more shareholders to remedy or prevent a wrong to the corporation as such rather than to the shareholders personally.

> *Example:* A suit brought to compel a director to restore property wrongfully taken from the corporation is a derivative claim.

a. In a derivative suit, the plaintiff shareholders do not sue on a cause of action belonging to themselves as individuals. They sue in a representative capacity on a cause of action that belongs to the corporation.

b. In a derivative suit, the real party in interest is the corporation. In effect, the shareholder is suing as a champion of his corporation.

c. For most procedural purposes, however, the corporation is treated as a defendant. *Koster v. Lumbermens Mut. Cas. Co.*, 330 U.S. 518, 67 S.Ct. 828 (1947).

3. RELATIONSHIP WITH "CLASS SUITS"

A class suit is typically a direct suit in which one or more shareholder plaintiffs purport to act as a representative of a class or classes of similarly situated shareholders, for injuries to the interests of the class as such.

a. A class suit is typically direct and not derivative since all shareholders of a particular class (or all shareholders) are claiming they were injured by an act which did not itself injure the corporation. *Green v. Wolf Corp.*, 406 F.2d 291 (2d Cir. 1968).

    b.   A derivative action, however, usually has some aspects of a class action since a shareholder, when suing to right a wrong done to the corporation, is also protecting the interest of all other shareholders.

4.   PRACTICAL APPLICATION OF DISTINCTIONS
Different procedural and substantive rules are applicable to direct and derivative claims. Unfortunately, however, the line between the two classes is sometimes hazy.

    a.   Anything that harms the corporation also harms the shareholder by reducing the value of his or her shares. However, a shareholder may not transmute a derivative claim into a direct one merely by alleging a direct reduction in value of his or her shares because of injury to the corporation. *Armstrong v. Frostie Co.*, 453 F.2d 914 (4th Cir. 1971).

        1)   Where an injury is done to the corporation each shareholder is made whole if the corporation recovers damages from the wrongdoer.

        2)   A derivative action brought in the corporation's name obviously avoids a multiplicity of suits by shareholders.

        3)   Damages recovered by the corporation derivatively are also available for the payment of the corporation's creditors while a direct recovery by shareholders might adversely affect creditors; a direct recovery for a derivative injury has a mandatory dividend feature.

    b.   In some situations a single claim may give rise to both a direct and a derivative claim, or careful pleading may affect the categorization.

        Example: A suit charging officers and directors with misapplication of corporate assets or other breaches of duty is derivative in character and recovery should inure exclusively to the corporation.

                  Thus a suit claiming a conspiracy to injure the business of a corporation was held to state a derivative claim even though it was alleged that the motive behind the conspiracy was to compel a shareholder to sell her shares at less than real value. *Green v. Victor Talking Machine Co.*, 24 F.2d 378 (2d Cir. 1928).

        Example: Suits to recover improperly paid dividends or to require a controlling shareholder to account for a premium received on the sale of shares have also been held to be derivative since the benefit inures to the corporation.

Example: A suit charging that it was improper for a majority shareholder to vote on a resolution authorizing the corporation to repurchase shares owned by the majority shareholder has been held to be direct—it prevents the dilution of the voting power of the complaining shareholder's shares.

Example: A conspiracy of the directors to use their powers to depress the market price of the shares so that they can buy them at less than fair value states a direct claim since such action does not injure the corporation as such.

Example: A suit claiming the corporation issued shares without honoring preemptive rights seems direct; however, it may also arguably be derivative if it is alleged in the same transaction that the corporation was induced to issue shares for inadequate consideration through fraud or a violation of federal securities law. *Shaw v. Empire Sav. & Loan Ass'n.*, 9 Cal.Rptr. 204 (Cal.App. 1960).

Example: A complaint charging that a plan of merger or reorganization was designed to dilute a shareholder's voting power states a direct claim. *Eisenberg v. Flying Tiger Line, Inc.*, 451 F.2d 267 (2d Cir. 1971).

B. DERIVATIVE SUITS IN FEDERAL COURTS

In recent years, the bulk of shareholder class and derivative litigation has been brought in the federal courts, usually under the federal securities laws, but also often on the basis of diversity of citizenship.

1. CLASSIFICATION OF PARTIES FOR DIVERSITY PURPOSES
For purposes of diversity in derivative suits, if it appears on the face of the pleadings and by the nature of the controversy that the corporation is antagonistic to the enforcement of the claim, the corporation is aligned as a defendant. *Smith v. Sperling*, 354 U.S. 91, 77 S.Ct. 1112 (1957).

2. PENDENT JURISDICTION
As federal corporation law developed, plaintiffs increasingly became able to state a cause of action under both federal and state law.

a. Suits involving such situations are usually brought in the federal courts since the concept of "pendent jurisdiction" permits the federal courts to determine both the federal and state claim in a single proceeding even in the absence of diversity of citizenship.

b.   State courts do not have jurisdiction over claims arising under the federal securities acts, and thus cannot adjudicate all claims for relief in a single proceeding.

c.   The preference for the federal forum also may be based on generous discovery rights, nationwide service of process under the federal securities acts, the avoidance of state security-for-expense statutes, and other procedural advantages.

d.   Substantive advantages that are sometimes cited—a belief that federal courts are more sympathetic to minority plaintiffs than state courts and the greater liberality of federal securities law—are doubtful, particularly in light of modern decisions of the United States Supreme Court.

C. PREREQUISITES FOR MAINTAINING DERIVATIVE SUITS

RMBCA § 7.40 is a recently revised state statutory provision dealing with the procedural requirements of derivative litigation.

The Federal Rules of Civil Procedure also contain carefully drawn and elaborate procedural requirements for derivative suits (rule 23.1) which are similar to RMBCA § 7.40 in most respects, though the underlying policies may differ. Many states have adopted similar statutes or rules in whole or in part. In diversity suits, state principles may be applied by federal courts under the *Erie* principle. *Hausman v. Buckley*, 299 F.2d 696 (2d Cir. 1962).

1.   DEMAND ON THE CORPORATION AND THE DIRECTORS
Generally, in a derivative suit, the plaintiff must allege and prove a good faith effort to first obtain redress from the corporation on the claim. RMBCA § 7.40(b).

a.   A demand on the directors may be a prerequisite to such a suit. *Ash v. International Business Machines, Inc.*, 353 F.2d 491 (3d Cir. 1965). RMBCA § 7.40 and rule 23.1 of the Federal Rules of Civil Procedure both require that a plaintiff must allege with particularity the efforts made to obtain redress from the directors, and if, if none, why such a demand on the directors was not made.

Example: An allegation that "the wrongdoers are in complete control and management of the corporation," may be a sufficient justification for not making a demand.

Example: A claim that the board participated in, authorized, and approved the challenged actions excuses the demand. *Barr v. Wackman,* 329 N.E.2d 180 (N.Y. 1975).

b.   In many derivative suits today no prior demand is made on directors, the plaintiff alleging circumstances that arguably makes a demand useless. Recent cases, however, have required more than *pro forma* allegations and have dismissed suits in which the reasons given for not making a demand are conclusionary. *In re Kauffman Mut. Fund Actions,* 479 F.2d 257 (1st Cir. 1973).

c.   This demand requirement is closely related to the issue whether the board may conclusively determine that in its business judgment, the litigation should not be pursued. See: part XIV, B, 3, d. *Zapata Corp v. Maldonado,* 430 A.2d 779 (Del. 1981); *Aronson v. Lewis,* 473 A.2d 805 (Del. 1984).

2. DEMAND UPON SHAREHOLDERS

RMBCA § 7.40 does not require a demand on shareholders.

The Federal Rules of Civil Procedure provide that if a demand on shareholders is not made, the plaintiff must show some adequate reason for not making the effort. Expense, or difficulty, may be justifiable reasons.

Example: An allegation that the wrongdoers own a majority of the shares and hence favorable shareholder action is unlikely is an adequate reason.

Example: An allegation that the number of shareholders is so large that it is unreasonable to require the plaintiff to incur the expense of what is essentially a proxy solicitation when there is little chance of success is an adequate reason.

Example: An allegation that the acts complained of cannot be ratified by the shareholders, so that action by the shareholders is useless has been held to be an adequate reason for not making a demand on shareholders. *Mayer v. Adams,* 141 A.2d 458 (Del. 1958). Essentially contra is *Claman v. Robertson,* 128 N.E.2d 429 (Ohio 1955).

a.   While some cases have required a demand on shareholders even when the cost would be substantial, many cases have held that such an act may be omitted on one ground or another. *Levitt v. Johnson,* 334 F.2d 815 (1st Cir. 1964).

b.   Massachusetts appears to have adopted the most stringent rule, requiring a demand in every case where a majority of shareholders are not wrongdoers. *Solomont & Sons Trust Inc. v. New England Theatres Operating Corp.*, 93 N.E.2d 241 (Mass. 1950); *Pomerantz v. Clark*, 101 F.Supp. 341 (D.Mass. 1951).

c. Other state courts that sometimes require a demand on shareholders have proceeded on a case-by-case basis, not requiring a demand when there are thousands of shareholders, and considering other factors such as the motives of the plaintiff, the number of shareholders joining in the action, and the proximity to the next shareholders' meeting.

d. If a demand is made on shareholders, and the shareholders reject the maintenance of the suit, the suit may nevertheless be brought by the minority shareholder. *Rogers v. American Can Co.*, 305 F.2d 297 (3d Cir. 1962).

3. CONTEMPORARY OWNERSHIP

RMBCA § 7.40(a) provides that a person may not commence a derivative suit "unless he was a shareholder of the corporation when the transaction complained of occurred or unless he became a shareholder through transfer by operation of law from one who was a shareholder at that time."

a. This is usually referred to as the "contemporary ownership rule."

b. Rule 23.1 of the Federal Rules of Civil Procedure has a similar requirement. In the federal courts the contemporaneous ownership rule was included primarily to prevent the collusive establishment of diversity of citizenship. *Hawes v. Oakland*, 104 U.S. (14 Otto) 450 (1882).

c. In RMBCA § 7.40 and analogous state statutes relating to derivative litigation, the contemporaneous ownership rule has been justified as necessary to prevent the "buying of a lawsuit."

1) Of course, if buying a lawsuit is the concern, the contemporaneous ownership requirement might be safely liberalized to allow suit by plaintiffs who discover the facts giving rise to the lawsuit only after becoming a shareholder. *Pollitz v. Gould*, 94 N.E. 1088 (N.Y. 1911). California has adopted this approach. Cal.Corp.Code § 800(b)(1).

2) Most state statutes, however, have not accepted this liberalizing principle. See *Goldie v. Yaker*, 432 P.2d 841 (N.M. 1967); *Jepsen v. Peterson*, 10 N.W.2d 749 (S.D. 1943).

3) It may be suggested that concern about abuses of shareholder litigation explains the reluctance to relax the contemporaneous ownership rule. On the other hand, where a suit seems reasonable, the "time of the transaction" has been construed flexibly to permit

suit to be maintained. *Maclary v. Pleasant Hills, Inc.*, 109 A.2d 830 (Del.Ch. 1954).

d. A principle related to the contemporaneous ownership rule prohibits a shareholder who purchases all or substantially all the shares of a corporation from a vendor at a fair price from having the corporation then bring suit against the vendor on grounds of prior corporate mismanagement. *Bangor Punta Operations, Inc. v. Bangor & Aroostook R. R. Co.*, 417 U.S. 703 (1974); *In re REA Express, Inc.*, 412 F.Supp. 1239 (E.D.Pa. 1976); *Courtland Manor, Inc. v. Leeds*, 347 A.2d 144 (Del.Ch. 1975); *Capitol Wine & Spirit Corp. v. Pokrass*, 98 N.Y.S.2d 291 (App.Div. 1950). This is an equitable principle which bars a suit by the corporation after the sale rather than simply barring a shareholder from serving as a plaintiff.

e. A shareholder plaintiff who sells or disposes of his or her shares during the pendency of derivative litigation loses the right to maintain or continue the suit. *Tenney v. Rosenthal*, 160 N.E.2d 463 (N.Y. 1959). A suit brought by a director is not abated, however, if the director is not reelected to the board of directors.

f. A shareholder plaintiff who is "cashed out" by a merger, receiving cash for his or her shares, may not continue the suit. *Lewis v. Anderson*, 477 A.2d 1040 (Del. 1984).

4. SECURITY FOR EXPENSES

Security-for-expenses statutes require certain plaintiff shareholders in derivative suits to give to the corporation "security for the reasonable expenses, including attorney's fees" which the corporation or other defendants may incur in connection with a derivative suit. These statutes also authorize the corporation or the individual defendants to recover their expenses from such security in some circumstances.

a. RMBCA § 7.40 does not contain a security-for-expenses statute even though earlier versions of the Model Act did. The Official Comment explains the decision to eliminate this requirement in part on the ground that "to the extent [the bond] was based on the size or value of the plaintiff's holdings rather than on the apparent good faith of his claim, [the requirement] was subject to criticism that it unreasonably discriminated against small shareholders."

1) RMBCA § 7.40(d) provides that the court, upon termination of a derivative suit, may require the plaintiff to pay "any defendant's reasonable expenses (including counsel fees) incurred in defending the proceeding if it finds that the proceeding was commenced without reasonable cause."

b.   Under statutes requiring security-for-expenses, the amount of the bond is fixed by the court in light of the expenses for which the corporation may be liable, including not only the direct expenses of the corporation, but also the expenses of other defendants for which the corporation may become liable by indemnification or otherwise.

1)   The amount of the required bond may be very substantial, running into the tens or hundreds of thousands of dollars. The security is usually in the form of a bond with sureties, though it also may be in the form of cash or marketable securities.

2)   Since the plaintiffs may be unable or unwilling to post a bond, this requirement often creates a major obstacle to the successful prosecution of a derivative suit.

Example: A decision that the securities-for-expenses statute is applicable and setting the amount of the bond at $75,000 may well be the decision that effectively terminates the litigation.

c.   Shareholder plaintiffs who are required to post security-for-expenses are defined in different ways in state statutes.

1)   In the older statutes (where the purpose to discourage derivative litigation is most manifest), the size of the plaintiff's holding is determinative.

(i)   A typical provision is that plaintiffs must post security-for-expenses unless their holdings are more than five per cent of the outstanding shares or exceed a specified market value, e. g., $25,000.   MBCA (1969) § 49.

(ii)   Intervening shareholder plaintiffs probably may have their shares counted toward meeting the statutory minima. *Sorin v. Shahmoon Indus. Inc.*, 220 N.Y.S.2d 760 (Sup.Ct. 1961). However, a solicitation of shareholders for this purpose may be deemed a proxy solicitation subject to the proxy solicitation rules adopted by the Securities Exchange Commission. *Studebaker Corporation v. Gettlin*, 360 F.2d 692 (2d Cir. 1966).

Caveat: A different rule is applicable in the Federal Courts in diversity cases where only plaintiffs who owned shares at the time of the wrong may serve as plaintiffs. *Kaufman v. Wolfson*, 136 F.Supp. 939 (S.D.N.Y. 1955).

(iii)   A corporation may not issue additional shares to reduce the plaintiff's holdings to less than 5 per cent and then seek security-for-expenses. *Roach v. Franchises Int'l, Inc.*, 300 N.Y.S.2d 630 (App.Div. 1969).

(iv)   The constitutionality of this type of statute was upheld in *Cohen v. Beneficial Indus. Loan Corp.*, 337 U.S. 541, 69 S.Ct. 1221 (1949).

2)   More modern statutes require security-for-expenses only upon a court finding that the suit was apparently brought without reasonable cause or seems patently without merit.

d.   Security-for-expenses statutes often do not define when the corporation may actually look to the security for reimbursement; rather, they usually state in effect that "[t]he corporation may have recourse to such security in such amount as the court thereafter determines."

1)   Under such statutes, courts usually allow reimbursement only if the plaintiff is unsuccessful and they conclude that the suit was brought without reasonable cause.

2)   Where reimbursement is allowed, an unsuccessful shareholder plaintiff posting security-for-expenses ends up paying the expenses of both sides of the litigation.

3)   If no security is posted and the case is dismissed, the plaintiff is not liable for the defendant's expenses in securing the dismissal. *Tyler v. Gas Consumers Ass'n*, 231 N.Y.S.2d 15 (Sup.Ct. 1962).

e.   Security-for-expenses statutes are applicable to suits in federal court based on state-created causes of action.

1)   This is a direct application of the *Erie* principle.

Example: A claim in federal court based solely on diversity of citizenship is subject to the security-for-expenses requirement.

2)   Security-for-expenses statutes are not applicable to suits in federal court based on violations of the federal securities acts.

Example: A suit is brought under rule 10b–5. The state security-for-expenses statute is not applicable.

> *Caveat:* If a state claim is brought in federal court in connection with a federal claim under the doctrine of pendent jurisdiction, it is subject to the security-for-expenses requirement.

f.   Security-for-expenses statutes are not applicable to *direct* class actions brought either in the federal or state courts. *Eisenberg v. Flying Tiger Line, Inc.*, 451 F.2d 267 (2d Cir. 1971); *Knapp v. Bankers Securities Corp.*, 230 F.2d 717 (3d Cir. 1956).

g.   The stated purpose of security-for-expenses statutes is to deter "strike" suits, that is, suits brought not to redress an injury to the corporation but in the hope of securing a settlement profitable to the plaintiff shareholders and their attorneys.

   1)   The older statutes do not distinguish between "strike" suits and bona fide shareholder suits but are applicable to all shareholder suits brought by small shareholders.

      (i)   Such statutes have the effect of making all such suits more difficult and reflect an antipathy toward shareholder derivative litigation.

      (ii) Such statutes also probably have the incidental effect of encouraging suits to be brought under the federal securities acts rather than state law.

   2)   More modern statutes, such as RMBCA § 7.40, impose security-for-expenses requirements only in connection with suits apparently brought without reasonable cause; these statutes are more directly addressed to the strike suit problem.

5.   VERIFICATION

Both RMBCA § 7.40 and rule 23.1 of the Federal Rules of Civil Procedure require that a derivative complaint must be "verified." A plaintiff shareholder may verify his complaint even though she may not understand all aspects of the transactions being complained of if serious fraud is charged and the plaintiff has reason to believe that serious misconduct occurred. *Surowitz v. Hilton Hotels Corp.*, 383 U.S. 363, 86 S.Ct. 845 (1966).

D.   DEFENSES IN DERIVATIVE SUITS

Defenses in derivative suits may be grouped into three broad classes.

1. FAILURE TO MEET UNIQUE PROCEDURAL REQUIREMENTS
A suit may be dismissed if there is a failure to comply with requirements which are peculiar to such suits.

Example: A failure to make a demand on the directors, or a failure to post security-for-expenses when required to do so, will result in the dismissal of the suit.

2. SUBSTANTIVE DEFENSES
A second class of defenses are those which would be available to third party defendants if the corporation had sued directly on the claim that is the underlying basis of the derivative suit.

Example: The action may be barred by the statute of limitations or statute of frauds. Such defenses usually may only be raised by the third party defendants, not the corporate defendant.

Example: A defense based on ratification of the transaction by directors or shareholders may be available if the transaction is voidable rather than void, or if it falls within the business judgment rule. Such defenses may arise from director or shareholder action after the claim is presented by the plaintiff, and usually may be raised by the corporate defendant as well as the individual defendants.

3. PLAINTIFF DISQUALIFICATION
A third class of defenses are those available against the specific plaintiff but which may not be available against other shareholder plaintiffs. Derivative suits basically involve two separate claims: first, the substantive claim by the corporation against a third person and second, the claim by the shareholder that he or she should be permitted to represent or champion the corporation. The defenses in this third class go to the latter issue.

Example: Laches may bar some shareholders but not others from acting as plaintiff.

Example: If the plaintiff actually participated in the wrongful transaction, or assented to it, he or she may be estopped from questioning the transaction. Shares owned by such a person are called "tainted shares" or "dirty stock" and even innocent transferees of such shares may be estopped from questioning the transaction.

E. MISCELLANEOUS PROCEDURAL PROBLEMS

The shareholder plaintiff and the corporate defendant both have unique roles in derivative litigation: the shareholder is a nominal plaintiff while the corporation is a nominal defendant but the real plaintiff. These unique roles lead to a variety of procedural issues.

1. NECESSARY PARTY
The corporation is a necessary party; without it the action cannot proceed. *Dean v. Kellogg*, 292 N.W. 704 (Mich. 1940).

2. COMBINATION OF CLAIMS
The power to mix personal and derivative claims in a single law suit is often restricted or prohibited.

   a.   The plaintiff shareholder may not combine individual or direct actions with a derivative action in the same suit, though many cases are more liberal.

   b.   The plaintiff shareholder may not be subject to personal counterclaims.

   c.   The defendant corporation may be limited in the defenses it may assert on behalf of its codefendants. *Otis & Co. v. Pennsylvania Ry. Co.*, 57 F.Supp. 680 (E.D.Pa. 1944).

3. MULTIPLE SUITS
Since a derivative suit has class as well as derivative aspects, multiple derivative suits may be filed by several different shareholders.

   a.   In the absence of other considerations, the suit first filed should proceed while later actions may be stayed, dismissed, or consolidated with the initial suit. *Schiff v. Metzner*, 331 F.2d 963 (2d Cir. 1964).

   b.   Counsel for the shareholder first bringing suit is usually permitted to control the litigation from the plaintiff's standpoint. The court, however, may designate an attorney for another shareholder as the principal counsel for plaintiffs.

   c.   Intervention by other shareholders is permitted and indeed may be encouraged if for some reason the representation of the original plaintiff shareholder may be considered questionable or inadequate.

4. THE ROLE OF COUNSEL
Even though the corporation is technically a defendant, its interest in the litigation is usually adverse to the interest of the other defendants.

   a.   Common counsel will therefore not be normally permitted to represent the defendant corporation as well as other defendants. *Cannon v. U. S. Acoustics Corp.*, 398 F.Supp. 209 (N.D.Ill. 1975); *Marco v. Dulles*, 169 F.Supp. 622 (S.D.N.Y. 1959). Such multiple representation may be permitted only if it is clear that there is no possible conflict. *Seifert v. Dumatic Industries, Inc.*, 197 A.2d 454 (Pa. 1964).

b. The attorney-client privilege between corporation and counsel may not be available at the whim of current management, who may be the real defendants in the suit. *Garner v. Wolfinbarger*, 430 F.2d 1093 (5th Cir. 1970).

c. An attorney involved in an investigation of wrongdoing for a client may be disqualified to serve later as a derivative plaintiff based on that wrongdoing. *Richardson v. Hamilton Int'l Corp.*, 469 F.2d 1382 (3d Cir. 1972); *Cannon v. U. S. Acoustics Corp.*, 398 F.Supp. 209 (N.D.Ill. 1975).

d. Corporations must appear through counsel. They cannot appear *in proper person* or be represented by a lay officer. *Union Sav. Ass'n v. Home Owners Aid, Inc.*, 262 N.E.2d 558 (Ohio 1970).

5. JURY TRIALS

Derivative suits are equitable in nature, a categorization which may be significant in resolving procedural questions. In *Ross v. Bernhard*, 396 U.S. 531 (1970), the United States Supreme Court held that a right to jury trial may exist in derivative suits brought in federal courts where the issue is of a "legal" (as contrasted with an "equitable") nature.

6. MERGER OF CORPORATE DEFENDANT

If the independent existence of the corporate defendant disappears by merger or similar transaction during the pendency of the suit, the suit will be dismissed unless the surviving entity is added as a party defendant. *Niesz v. Gorsuch*, 295 F.2d 909 (9th Cir. 1961).

a. Statutes may provide for the continuation of litigation against the surviving entity.

b. Shareholders of the new or surviving entity may be able to sue that entity derivatively on the same claim.

c. In the case of a "cash out" merger in which the plaintiff shareholder receives cash and ceases to be a shareholder, the plaintiff may no longer maintain the suit.

7. COLLATERAL ESTOPPEL

Defendants in a derivative suit may be prohibited from relitigating issues as to violations of securities acts resolved adversely to them in a prior proceeding brought by the SEC or other governmental agency. *Rachel v. Hill*, 435 F.2d 59 (5th Cir. 1970).

F. SETTLEMENT OF DERIVATIVE SUITS

Historically, the secret settlement of shareholders' suits was a serious evil. The settling shareholder often received substantial sums which in fact were payments to ignore a corporate wrong. Suits brought solely for their settlement value are usually called "strike suits."

1.   JUDICIAL APPROVAL
The problem of secret or corrupt settlements has now been largely resolved by bringing the process of settlement of derivative or class suits under judicial control.

   a.   Such suits may not be dismissed or compromised without the approval of the court.

   b.   Notice of the proposed dismissal or compromise must be given to shareholders or members in such manner as the court directs.

2.   DISCRETIONARY REVIEW OF PROPOSED SETTLEMENTS
In exercising discretion to review proposed settlements, courts consider whether the proposed settlement is reasonable, fair and adequate. *Saylor v. Bastedo*, 594 F.Supp. 371 (S.D.N.Y. 1984); *Lewis v. Newman*, 59 F.R.D. 525 (S.D.N.Y. 1973); *Perrine v. Pennroad Corp.*, 47 A.2d 479 (Del. 1946); *Shlensky v. Dorsey*, 574 F.2d 131 (3d Cir. 1978). Among the factors considered are:

   a.   The size of the potential recovery and the size of the suggested settlement.

   b.   The probability of ultimate success.

   c.   The complexity, expense and likely duration of the litigation.

   d.   The financial position of the defendants.

3.   NOTICE AND HEARING ON SETTLEMENT
Shareholders are entitled to notice of, and may appear at the hearing on, a proposed settlement and object to its terms.

4.   DERIVATIVE PURSUIT OF SECRET SETTLEMENT
Courts have held that where a secret settlement has led to a payment to a derivative plaintiff, other shareholders may bring a derivative suit in the name of the corporation against the settling shareholder to recover the payment. *Clarke v. Greenberg*, 71 N.E.2d 443 (N.Y. 1947). Basically for this reason, it has been held that a corporation may settle a claim that is involved in derivative litigation without prior court approval. *Wolf v. Barkes*, 348 F.2d 994 (2d Cir. 1965).

5.   **RES JUDICATA EFFECT OF SETTLEMENT**
See the discussion in part H below.

G.   RECOVERY IN DERIVATIVE SUITS

A recovery in a derivative suit is usually payable to the corporation rather than to individual shareholders on a pro rata basis or to the plaintiff.

1.   **JUSTIFICATION OF RULE**
This principle normally protects fully the interest of shareholders and creditors alike, and does not involve the court in making a business judgment as to whether corporate funds should be distributed as a kind of dividend to some or all of the shareholders.

2.   **EXCEPTION WHERE WRONGDOERS ARE MAJOR SHAREHOLDERS**
If an individual wrongdoer who is required to satisfy the judgment obtained in the derivative suit is also a significant shareholder, a corporate recovery permits that defendant to share indirectly in, and, if a controlling shareholder, to control the use of, the recovery.

   a.   In a few instances, courts have been persuaded to grant shareholders a pro rata recovery in this type of situation in order to limit the recovery to "innocent" shareholders or to prevent the "guilty" shareholder from "benefitting from his own wrong."

      Example: In *Perlman v. Feldmann,* 219 F.2d 173 (2d Cir. 1955) a control premium paid to a former controlling shareholder was held to be recoverable and payable to the nonselling shareholders pro rata on the theory that it was improper for the persons presently in control (who had paid the control premium to the defendants) to share in the recovery.

   b.   Such cases are a minority view. *Keenan v. Eshleman,* 2 A.2d 904 (Del. 1938); *Norte & Co. v. Huffines,* 416 F.2d 1189 (2d Cir. 1969). A pro rata recovery to "innocent" shareholders often gives rise to serious logical, practical and conceptual problems.

      Example: In the *Perlman* case, consider the situation if the persons presently in control of the corporation (who paid a control premium to Feldmann) themselves resell for another control premium. Can they argue that the noncontrol shareholders, having already been compensated for the absence of control by sharing in Feldmann's premium, cannot complain of the second sale?

Example: The controlling block in *Perlman* that was sold for a premium constituted 35 per cent of the outstanding shares. The noncontrol block that shared in Feldmann's premium was the remaining 65 per cent that was widely fragmented. If, however, the 65 per cent is combined or organized it may become the control block. Does it have any responsibility to return the "control premium" it previously received as noncontrolling shares?

3.   OTHER RELIEF

In appropriate cases plaintiffs may obtain affirmative relief, e. g. dissolution, *White v. Perkins*, 189 S.E.2d 315 (Va. 1972), or the appointment of a receiver, *Robinson v. Thompson*, 466 S.W.2d 626 (Tex.Civ.App. 1971).

H.   RES JUDICATA

The res judicata effect of the termination of a derivative suit depends on the manner of or basis for the termination.

1.   FINAL JUDGMENT ON THE MERITS

A final judgment on the merits is res judicata and binding on all other shareholders, including any who were original parties to the suit but thereafter withdrew.

Caveat: This assumes that the plaintiff shareholder was an adequate representative of the class of shareholders.

2.   SETTLEMENTS

A court-approved settlement ordinarily has the same effect as a final judgment on the merits. *Berger v. Dyson*, 111 F.Supp. 533 (D.R.I. 1953), though problems may arise as to whether shareholders are bound if they were not notified of the proposed settlement; *Manufacturers Mut. Fire Ins. Co. v. Hopson*, 25 N.Y.S.2d 502 (Sup.Ct. 1940); *Shlensky v. Dorsey*, 574 F.2d 131 (3d Cir. 1978); or if it is claimed that the settlement was based on culpable nondisclosure of relevant evidence or collusion between plaintiff's and defendant's counsel; *Alleghany Corp. v. Kirby*, 333 F.2d 327 (2d Cir. 1964).

3.   DISMISSAL OF SUIT

The res judicata effect of a dismissal of a derivative suit depends on the reason for the dismissal.

a.   A voluntary dismissal, or a dismissal because the plaintiff shareholder does not qualify as a proper plaintiff is "without prejudice" and does not bind the class.

Example: A dismissal for failure to post security for expenses does not bind the class.

Example: A dismissal for failure to respond to interrogatories does not bind the class. *Papilsky v. Berndt*, 466 F.2d 251 (2d Cir. 1972).

b. In some situations, the court may order that notice be given to all other shareholders before a derivative action is dismissed voluntarily. Such action may then be continued by intervening shareholders, or if none appear, the action may be dismissed "with prejudice."

c. A dismissal on the merits—that the complaint does not state a claim or on motion for summary judgment—may be binding upon the class.

I. PLAINTIFF'S EXPENSES

If the plaintiff is successful, he will usually be awarded his expenses, including attorney's fees. Such a recovery is justified in equity as encouraging meritorious shareholders' suits.

1. CREATION OF A FUND
Usually, the plaintiff's expenses will be paid out of the funds obtained by the corporation as a result of the suit.

2. NON–FUND CASES
Expenses of the plaintiff may also be ordered to be reimbursed by the corporation even where the corporation receives no money as a result of the litigation so long as the result of the suit was of "some benefit" or "substantial benefit" to the corporation. *Bosch v. Meeker Co-op. Light & Power Ass'n*, 101 N.W.2d 423 (Minn. 1960); *Fletcher v. A. J. Industries, Inc.*, 72 Cal.Rptr. 146 (Cal.App. 1968).

Example: Expenses may be awarded in a suit which results only in an injunction against the officers and directors of a corporation engaging in improper conduct.

a. A payment of the plaintiff's expenses by the corporation does not compel the "losing party" to pay the other's expenses since both the corporation and the plaintiff are winning parties.

3. AMOUNT OF PLAINTIFF'S ATTORNEY'S FEES
The size of the attorney's fee to be awarded successful plaintiff's counsel depends on a variety of factors: the nature and character of the litigation, the skill required, the amount of work actually performed, the size of the recovery,

the nature of the harm prevented, and other factors. The size of the fee is determined or approved by the court and is a question of fact on which evidence may be taken.

Example: A fee of $200,000 in a suit leading to a $1,025,000 settlement was upheld.

REVIEW QUESTIONS

XVIII–1. What is the difference betweeen "direct" and "derivative" litigation?

XVIII–2. Is there a clear distinction between direct and derivative litigation?

XVIII–3. What is a "class" suit?

XVIII–4. Is a derivative suit a class suit?

XVIII–5. In a derivative suit, is the corporation classed as a plaintiff or a defendant?

XVIII–6. To what extent are federal courts involved in derivative litigation?

XVIII–7. What is the "contemporaneous ownership" requirement and what is its justification in federal and state courts?

XVIII–8. What are the procedural prerequisities for maintaining a derivative suit?

XVIII–9.   Why is derivative litigation often treated with mistrust?

XVIII–10.   What are the policy considerations underlying a state legislative decision whether or not to eliminate the security-for-expenses statute?

XVIII–11.   What are the consequences of a decision that a derivative plaintiff must comply with the security-for-expenses statute?

XVIII–12.   Is the state security-for-expenses statute applicable in the federal courts?

XVIII–13.   Is the security-for-expenses statute applicable to direct and class litigation?

XVIII–14.   Is a final decision in a derivative suit *res judicata* and binding on all shareholders?

XVIII–15.   Are any limitations placed on the power of a plaintiff to accept a settlement offer in a derivative suit?

XVIII–16.   What is a "strike suit" and how are such suits handled under modern practice?

XVIII–17.   May a plaintiff who is successful in a derivative suit recover attorneys fees and other expenses even if the corporation does not receive any money from the suit?

XVIII–18.   Is there any situation in which a derivative suit recovery is paid directly to the shareholders?

XVIII–19.   Ps are shareholders in X corporation which is incorporated in State A. They have brought a derivative action on behalf of X in the courts of State B against X's majority shareholder, a director of X, and another corporation also owned by X's majority shareholder. Ps claim that the majority shareholder has looted X by a series of transactions with the other corporation and that X is entitled to an accounting. Ps have obtained service of process on all defendants except X. The defendants have moved to dismiss Ps' petition on the ground that the court lacked jurisdiction of X, an essential party. Ps claim that if the suit may not be maintained in personam it may be brought as an action in rem in that the cause of action is property of X within the state. Are the defendants who were served entitled to dismissal?

XVIII–20.   P brought an action against the directors of D corporation on D's behalf for breach of fiduciary duties. The court found the directors liable in an amount of $4,355,595, in that they had appropriated an opportunity of D to purchase shares in another corporation. The defendant directors contend the award of damages should be limited to those who were shareholders at the time of the share transaction. Are the defendants correct in their contention?

XIX

ORGANIC CHANGES

Organic or fundamental changes in corporations may be broadly classified by type: amendments to articles of incorporations, statutory mergers or consolidations, non-statutory amalgamations, sales of substantially all assets, and dissolutions. The rules about these changes depend to some extent on the type of change involved and each is discussed below.

Analysis

A. Amendments of Articles
B. Statutory Mergers and Consolidations
C. Sales of Substantially All Assets
D. Nonstatutory Amalgamations
E. Recapitalizations
F. "Going Private"
G. Leveraged Buyouts
H. Rights of Dissent and Appraisal
I. Voluntary Dissolution

A.   AMENDMENTS OF ARTICLES

Under modern statutes, articles of incorporation may be freely amended.   RMBCA § 10.01.   Some early cases adopted a view of "vested rights" in specific provisions, which in effect required unanimous agreement to amend;   these early cases have been largely reversed by statute.   *Cowan v. Salt Lake Hardware Co.*, 221 P.2d 625 (Utah 1950).

Caveat: The argument that such rights are "vested" is basically a constitutional argument.   *Dartmouth College v. Woodward*, 17 U.S. (4 Wheat.) 518 (1819) did impose restraints on the power of the state to adopt a statute that amended previously issued articles of incorporation.   However, the court also recognized that states might avoid this problem by enacting a "reservation" of power to amend statutes applicable to all corporations created thereafter.   All states have done so and hence the issues discussed in this section are not constitutional issues for modern corporations.   *Dentel v. Fidelity Sav. & Loan Ass'n*, 539 P.2d 649 (Or. 1975).   Constitutional arguments, however, continue to be made in these cases, and in a few instances (mostly from the nineteenth century) courts have found a constitutional obstacle by construing the reservation power very narrowly.

1.   MANDATORY REQUIREMENTS

Amended articles may contain only such provisions as may be lawfully contained in original articles of incorporation at the time of the amendment.   If a change is made in shares or rights of shareholders, or an exchange, reclassification or cancellation of shares or rights is to be made, the amendments must specifically set forth the provisions necessary to effect such change, exchange, reclassification, or cancellation.   Under the Revised Model Business Corporation Act these implementing provisions may appear in the articles of amendment rather than in the amendments themselves.   RMBCA § 10.06(3).

2.   PROCEDURAL REQUIREMENTS

Since under modern statutes no shareholder has a vested right in any specific provision in articles of incorporation, the exercise of the broad power of amendment contained in a business corporation act may adversely affect the holders of one or more classes of securities to the advantage of holders of another class of securities.   The protections against such changes are procedural:

a.   The principal protection against abuse, in most states, lies in the provision that requires an amendment that is burdensome to a single class of shares in a specified way to be approved by a separate vote of that class of shares.

1) RMBCA § 10.04(a) lists nine types of amendments that give rise to such a vote:

a) Amendments that increase or decrease the aggregate number of shares of that class;

b) Amendments that effect an exchange or reclassification of shares of the class into shares of another class;

c) Amendments that exchange or reclassify shares of another class into shares of the class;

d) Amendments that change the designation, rights, preferences, or limitations of all or part of the shares of that class;

e) Amendments that change the shares of all or part of the class into a different number of shares of the same class;

f) Amendments that create a new class with rights or preferences relating to distributions or dissolution that are superior to or equal with the class;

g) Amendments that increase the rights, preferences or number of shares of a class that have superior or equal rights with the class;

h) Amendments that affect the preemptive rights of the class of shares; and

i) Amendments that cancel or otherwise affect rights of the class to distributions that have accumulated but have not paid.

2) In the Revised Model Business Corporation Act the right to vote by classes is referred to as "voting by voting groups." See RMBCA §§ 10.02, 10.03, 10.04, 7.25, 7.26, 1.40(26). In most older statutes it is described as "class voting" or "voting by class."

3) The basic idea is that if a specified percentage of the class adversely affected is willing to accept an amendment of the type set forth in part 1) above, it should be approved (though dissenting members of the class may have a right of dissent and appraisal). These statutes are generally construed to further the objective of requiring voting by voting groups on all amendments that are uniquely burdensome to the voting group as such. *Levin v. Mississippi River Fuel Corp.*, 386 U.S. 162, 87 S.Ct. 927 (1967).

4)   Most statutes extend the right to vote by class only to classes of shares and not to series within a class, even though differences between series may be as great as differences between classes. RMBCA § 10.04(b) and (c) in general terms extends the right to vote by voting groups to series that are affected in different ways but states that if an amendment affects two or more series in essentially the same way, the two series are to be combined as a single voting group on the amendment.

5)   Under the RMBCA, amendments that give rise to dissenters' rights must be approved by a majority of all the outstanding shares of each voting group entitled to vote separately on the amendment. Classes of shares entitled to vote generally on the amendment but not as separate voting groups all vote together. RMBCA § 10.03(e).

    a)   If an amendment does not create dissenters' rights, under the RMBCA the amendment is approved by a simple majority of the voting shares present at a meeting at which a quorum is present.

        Example: A corporation has outstanding one class of voting common shares with 200 shares outstanding, and one class of nonvoting preferred shares, with 100 shares outstanding. The board of directors proposes amendments to the articles of incorporation that would increase the size of the board of directors from 3 to 5 members, change the name of the corporation from ABC Corporation to Oomph Corporation, and grant all directors the right to be indemnified to the extent the corporation is lawfully permitted to do so. None of these changes require class voting; all may be approved by a simple majority of the common shares present at a meeting at which a quorum is present. If 120 shares are present at a meeting of common shareholders, the amendments are approved by the affirmative vote of 61 or more shares.

        Example: In the foregoing example, if the preferred shares were also voting shares, the same principles would control. The preferred and common would vote together; the quorum required would be 150 or more shares of the outstanding voting shares, and the vote needed would be a simple majority of that quorum.

Example: In the foregoing example, the proposed amendment would reduce the preferential dividend right of the preferred shares from $5.00 per year to $4.90 per year. In this situation, the preferred is entitled to vote as a separate voting group whether or not it is entitled to vote generally under the articles of incorporation. To be approved, the amendment must be approved by 51 votes of the preferred shares and by a simple majority of the common shares at a meeting of the common shareholders at which a quorum is present. If the preferred were also entitled to vote generally under the articles of incorporation, the amendment would have to be approved by the same 51 votes of the preferred shares (counted separately) and by a simple majority of the combined common and preferred shares at a meeting at which a quorum is present. In this situation the votes of the preferred shares are in effect counted in two different elections, first, in the separate voting group vote of the preferred, and second, in the vote of the voting shares entitled to vote on the amendment by the articles of incorporation.

Example: In the foregoing example, the class of preferred shares consists of three series, each with different preferential dividend rights. A proposed amendment would reduce the rate of dividend applicable to the Series A preferred and would change the dividend right of the Series B shares from cumulative to noncumulative. The Series C preferred's dividend right would not be affected. Since the Series A and Series B are affected in different ways, each would constitute a separate voting group and would have to approve the amendment separately. The Series C preferred is not entitled to vote as a separate voting group; if nonvoting under the articles of incorporation, that series could not vote at all on the amendment.

Example: If the proposed amendment would change the dividend right of both the Series B and Series C preferred from cumulative to noncumulative, the Series B and Series C would be affected in essentially the same way and would be entitled to vote only as a single vote group on the amendment.

The Series A would continue to be entitled to vote as a separate voting group. If these series of shares were separate classes of shares (rather than series), the Class A, Class B and Class C would each be entitled to vote as separate voting groups.

b)   State statutes relating to approval of amendments vary widely. Many require a ²/₃ds vote of all outstanding shares, both voting and nonvoting, rather than a majority vote for all amendments. Many require only a majority vote of all outstanding voting shares but do not distinguish between amendments that create dissenters' rights and amendments that do not. Some do not grant dissenters' rights for amendments but provide that the right to vote separately by class (or voting group) is the sole protection against injurious amendments.

c)   Under the RMBCA, directors must approve amendments before they are presented to shareholders for approval. RMBCA § 10.03. The board of directors must also recommend approval of the amendment, and may condition the submission on terms it desires, e. g., that the amendment be approved by each class of shares, voting as separate voting groups, or by a specified percentage of the outstanding shares.

d)   The RMBCA also permits the board of directors to amend articles of incorporation without shareholder approval in connection with specified minor amendments.

3.   REMNANTS OF THE VESTED RIGHTS THEORY

The theory that certain rights are "vested" rights that cannot be eliminated over the objection of any owner of shares by an amendment to the articles of incorporation continues to have limited vitality in some states.

a.   One issue on which the theory is most likely to be applied is the status of arrearages of cumulative dividends on preferred stock.

b.   In lieu of the vested rights theory some courts have evolved a broad equitable principle that majority shareholders and directors must act in a fair way toward the corporation and minority shareholders.

1)   This principle may provide entry into the courtroom for minority shareholders who claim that an amendment serves no purpose other than injuring minority shareholders. *Dentel v. Fidelity Sav. & Loan Ass'n*, 539 P.2d 649 (Or. 1975).

2) The test may be phrased as "good faith" or "reasonableness" or "business purpose."

c. A transaction that runs afoul of the vested rights theory as an amendment to the articles may sometimes be valid if it is structured as a merger transaction. *Bove v. Community Hotel Corp. of Newport, R. I.,* 249 A.2d 89 (R.I. 1969). Often an amendment may be structured as a merger of a corporation into its newly created and wholly owned subsidiary.

d. If there is a failure to provide accurate and complete information about the effect of a proposed amendment, the amendment may also be attacked under federal or state law. See part XII, F.

B. STATUTORY MERGERS AND CONSOLIDATIONS

Business corporation statutes specifically refer to and authorize certain kinds of corporate amalgamations. Alternative nonstatutory transactions may achieve the same economic result. Business corporation acts usually authorize the following type of transactions: (1) the "merger" of one domestic corporation into another domestic corporation; (2) the "consolidation" of two domestic corporations into a new domestic corporation; (3) the "merger" of a subsidiary of a domestic corporation into that corporation; (4) the "merger" or "consolidation" of a domestic corporation and a foreign corporation; and (5) a share exchange.

1. DEFINITIONS

a. Technically a "merger" of corporation A into corporation B means that corporation B survives and corporation A disappears while in a "consolidation" of corporation A and corporation B, both corporation A and corporation B disappear and a new corporation C is created.

1) These statutory methods of amalgamations are often simply described as "statutory mergers" to distinguish them from nonstatutory asset-purchase and stock-purchase transactions described immediately below.

2) The Revised Model Business Corporation Act does not include the concept of a "consolidation". The Introductory Comment to Chapter 11 states that this concept is obsolete, since it is nearly always advantageous for one of the parties to the transaction to be the surviving corporation, and if not, a new entity may always be created and the other entities merged into it.

3)   The Internal Revenue Code describes a statutory merger or consolidation as a class "A" reorganization.

4)   In a merger between a domestic and a foreign corporation, the surviving corporation may be the foreign corporation if it complies with minimal statutory requirements. See RMBCA § 11.07.

b.   In a "share exchange" all shareholders of a class of shares are obligated to exchange their shares for the consideration specified in the plan of share exchange. A plan of share exchange must be approved by essentially the same procedure that is applicable to a merger.

2.   PROCEDURES

Business corporation acts require statutory-recognized amalgamations to be approved by the board of directors and by a specific percentage of the shareholders of each corporation. The RMBCA requires a majority of all the outstanding shares entitled to vote on the transaction.

a.   A plan of merger must be approved by the board of directors and recommended to the shareholders. The board of directors may condition the plan on such terms as it deems desirable, e. g. that the plan be approved by one or more classes of shares voting as separate voting groups or that no more than a specified number of shareholders elect the right of dissent and appraisal.

b.   The traditional percentage was two-thirds of all outstanding shares, both voting and nonvoting, but many states permit such transactions by a simple majority vote of all outstanding voting shares. In some states with a two-thirds voting requirement other transactions that have the same economic effect as a merger may require only a majority vote.

> *Caveat:*   The vote required for approval of a merger under the RMBCA is a majority of all the outstanding voting shares. Amendments of articles of incorporation may be approved by a significantly less onerous requirement if the amendment does not give rise to the right of dissent and appraisal: approval by a majority of the voting shares present at a meeting at which a quorum is present. If an amendment gives rise to dissenters' rights, the same vote is required for approval as is required for all mergers.

c.   Shareholders have the right of dissent and appraisal if the plan of merger must be approved by the shareholders. However, only shareholders that have the right to vote have the right of dissent and appraisal. RMBCA § 13.02(a)(1).

d. Shareholders have the right to vote by separate voting groups if the plan of merger contains provisions that would create a right to vote by separate voting group if they were contained in articles of incorporation. RMBCA § 11.03(f)(1). Thus, a class of nonvoting shares may be entitled to vote on a merger if the plan of merger affects their rights in any of the ways set forth in RMBCA § 10.04(a); minority holders of that class of shares will have the right of dissent and appraisal pursuant to section 13.02(a)(1) even though the shares are made nonvoting by the articles of incorporation.

e. If the directors of the two corporations are not acting at arms length, e. g., in the case when one corporation owns enough shares of the other to name the board, the merger is a form of self-dealing and may be judicially reviewed for fairness. (*Weinberger v. UOP, Inc.*, 457 A.2d 701 (Del. 1983); *Singer v. Magnavox Co.*, 380 A.2d 969 (Del. 1977); *Sterling v. Mayflower Hotel Corp.*, 93 A.2d 107 (Del. 1952); *Abelow v. Midstates Oil Corp.*, 189 A.2d 675 (Del. 1963); *Smith v. Good Music Station, Inc.*, 129 A.2d 242 (Del.Ch. 1957). The same standard is applicable to mergers of investment companies subject to the Federal Investment Company Act of 1940. *E. I. du Pont de Nemours & Co. v. Collins*, 432 U.S. 46, 97 S.Ct. 2229 (1977).

3. TRIANGULAR MERGERS, CASH MERGERS AND SUBSIDIARY–PARENT MERGERS
Statutory mergers traditionally contemplated that all shareholders in disappearing corporations would receive shares in the surviving corporation in exchange for their shares in the disappearing corporation or corporations.

a. This restrictive view created problems for "triangular mergers" in which the acquiring corporation formed a wholly owned subsidiary into which the acquired corporation was merged with the shareholders of the acquired corporation receiving shares of the acquiring corporation rather than shares of the subsidiary into which the acquired corporation was merged.

1) In such transactions the parent corporation was typically a publicly held corporation with a market for its shares while the subsidiary was created solely for the purpose of the particular transaction.

2) In order to validate triangular mergers, the merger statutes of many states were amended to provide expressly that some parties to the merger might receive "shares, obligations or other securities of the surviving *or any other corporation or into cash or other property in whole or in part*". RMBCA § 11.01(b)(3).

b.   The power to compel some parties to accept cash or property for shares
led to the "cash merger" in which certain shareholders are lawfully
frozen out of the continuing enterprise through a statutory merger.

> ***Example:*** A corporation merges into its own subsidiary with the majority
> shareholders receiving stock in the subsidiary while other
> shareholders are compelled to accept a specified amount of
> cash for their shares. This transaction is expressly
> contemplated by modern corporation statutes.

1)   A cash merger is often used as part of a two-step acquisition of all
the outstanding shares of an unwilling target corporation:

   (i)   A majority of the outstanding shares of the target are obtained
   by open market purchase or tender offer.

   (ii) The target is merged into the aggressor (or a subsidiary of the
   aggressor) through a cash merger in which the remaining
   shareholders of the target are compelled to accept cash.
   Typically the cash received in the merger is the same as
   originally paid in the tender offer.

   > ***Caveat:*** In the takeover device known as a "front end loaded"
   > tender offer, an offer is made for a majority of the
   > stock at a favorable price. The offeror also
   > announces that if the offer is successful it will
   > require the balance of the shares in a "cash merger"
   > or "back end merger." The price to be paid in the
   > "back end" or "mop-up" merger is announced in
   > advance as being lower than the original cash offer
   > and is also often payable in securities rather than in
   > cash. This device tends to cause shareholders to
   > tender for fear of being "left behind."

2)   A cash merger is a very flexible device. It may be used to effect a
recapitalization, to "freeze out" an unwanted minority shareholder,
or to force out public shareholders in a "going private" transaction.

c.   Special statutes authorizing the merger of a partially-owned subsidiary
into a parent permit transactions similar to cash mergers. See RMBCA
§ 11.04.

1)   A merger of the subsidiary into the parent is an "up stream"
merger. A merger of the parent into the subsidiary is a "down
stream" merger.

2)   RMBCA § 11.04 permits a parent corporation that owns 90 percent or more of the outstanding shares of each class of the subsidiary corporation to merge the subsidiary into the parent without a shareholders' vote of either corporation and with the shareholders of the subsidiary are to receive a specified amount of cash; they also have the right to dissent and receive the appraised value of shares.

  (i)   This procedure is usually called a "short form merger."

  (ii)   The theoretical basis for omitting the vote of the subsidiary's shareholders is that the minority shareholders of the subsidiary are unable to block the merger.

  (iii) The theoretical basis for omitting the vote of the parent's shareholders is that the merger does not materially affect their rights which already include a 90 percent interest in the subsidiary. The merger thus causes a relatively slight increase in the parent's interest in the subsidiary.

  (iv)   The practical justification for short form merger statutes is that they avoid the cost of proxy solicitations and meetings of publicly held parent corporations.

  (v)   The short form merger procedure creates no appraisal rights on the part of dissenting shareholders of the parent but does create a special appraisal procedure for the minority shareholders of the subsidiary. RMBCA § 13.02(b)(2).

d. The development of cash mergers, short form mergers, and related practices raise the question whether all such transactions are valid so long as the formal statutory procedural requirements are complied with.

1)   One argument is that courts should not judge motive or subjective fairness, and should be satisfied if the procedures and minority protection devices required by statute are made available.

2)   The case law has developed in the opposite direction.

  (i)   Several cases have held that cash mergers and related practices must meet two tests under state law: a "business purpose" test and an "intrinsic" or "entire" fairness test. *Singer v. Magnavox Co.*, 380 A.2d 969 (Del. 1977); *Gabhart v. Gabhart*, 370 N.E.2d 345 (Ind. 1977). "Freeze out" mergers designed solely to eliminate an unwanted shareholder may be particularly subject to attack under these cases. In *Weinberger v. UOP, Inc.*, 457 A.2d 701 (Del. 1983), however, the Delaware Supreme

Court concluded that the "business purpose" test did not provide any additional meaningful protection, and substituted an increased emphasis on the "entire fairness" of the transaction, including full disclosure of all elements relating to fairness, and a liberalized appraisal remedy for the shareholder.

> ***Example:*** In a transaction with a reasonable business purpose, a majority of the independent shareholders approve a cash merger transaction. This approval is persuasive evidence of the fairness of the transaction. *Schulwolf v. Cerro Corp.*, 380 N.Y.S.2d 957 (Sup.Ct. 1976).

> ***Caveat:*** Despite *Weinberger*, courts in other states may continue to apply a business purpose test to these transactions. See e. g. Alpert v. 28 Williams Street Corp., 63 N.Y.2d 557, 473 N.E.2d 19 (1984).

(ii)   Similar principles apply to short form mergers of subsidiary corporations into parent corporations. *Roland Int'l Corp. v. Najjar*, 407 A.2d 1032 (Del. 1979).

(iii)   In *Santa Fe Indus., Inc. v. Green*, 430 U.S. 462, 97 S.Ct. 1292 (1977), the Supreme Court held that the essence of a rule 10b–5 violation was nondisclosure or misrepresentation of material facts and that unfair cash mergers and related transactions could not be attacked under federal law unless there was nondisclosure.

(iv)   As a result of *Santa Fe*, judicial controls over the cash mergers and related transactions now appear to be solely a matter of state law. *Cole v. Shenley Indus., Inc.*, 563 F.2d 35 (2d Cir. 1977). Cases have held, however, that nondisclosure in connection with such transactions may continue to give rise to a rule 10b–5 claim despite *Santa Fe*. *Goldberg v. Meridor*, 567 F.2d 209 (2d Cir. 1977) *cert. denied* 434 U.S. 1069, 98 S.Ct. 1249 (1978); *Healey v. Catalyst Recovery of Pennsylvania, Inc.*, 616 F.2d 641 (3d Cir. 1980).

4.   REVERSE TRIANGULAR MERGERS AND SHARE EXCHANGES

In some instances, it is important to assure that the continued existence of the acquired corporation is preserved. Such transactions were first achieved through reverse triangular mergers; in a few states mandatory share exchanges permit these transactions in a simpler and more direct fashion.

a.   Retention of the separate existence of the acquired corporation is important where that corporation is organized under a special statute under which incorporation is difficult (e. g., banks, insurance companies) or where the corporation has government or other contracts that do not permit assignment.

b.   Such a result may be obtained through the cumbersome process of a "reverse triangular merger": the formation of a new subsidiary of the acquiring or holding company, followed by a merger of that subsidiary into the corporation to be acquired in which securities of the subsidiary's parent are exchanged for securities of the corporation to be acquired.

c.   A compulsory share exchange authorized by RMBCA § 11.02 is a direct, simple, and straightforward procedure to accomplish the same end. Several states have adopted this procedure.

    1)   A compulsory share exchange requires approval of the board of directors of the corporation whose shares are to be acquired and submission of the proposed share exchange to the shareholders of the class of shares being acquired.

    2)   If a majority of the shares being acquired approve the transaction, it is binding on all holders of the class, majority and minority alike.

    3)   Shareholders of the class of shares being acquired objecting to the share exchange are entitled to the statutory right of dissent and appraisal, thereby obtaining cash for their shares. RMBCA § 13.02(a)(2).

C.   SALES OF SUBSTANTIALLY ALL ASSETS

A sale, lease, exchange or other disposition of all, or substantially all, the property and assets of a corporation, not in the usual and regular course of business, must under the statutes of most states be submitted to and approved by the shareholders as an organic change. See RMBCA § 12.02.

1.   SALES IN ORDINARY COURSE OF BUSINESS
    If the sale is in the ordinary course of business (which is conceivable but not likely), shareholder approval usually is not required. RMBCA § 12.01(a)(1).

a.   Many states consider a pledge, mortgage, or deed of trust covering all the assets of the corporation to secure a debt to be in the ordinary course of business. RMBCA § 12.01(a)(2).

b. RMBCA § 12.01(a)(3) adds a third class of case: where a corporation spins substantially all of its assets off to a corporation whose shares are wholly owned by the corporation. The purpose of this clause is to reverse the result reached in *Campbell v. Vose*, 515 F.2d 256 (10th Cir.1975). The Official Comment notes that RMBCA § 12.01(a)(3) should not be permitted to be "used as a device to avoid a vote of shareholders by a multiple-step transaction."

c. "Substantially all" assets of a corporation are sold even if the corporation retains some small amount of property as a pretext. *Stiles v. Aluminum Products Co.*, 86 N.E.2d 887 (Ill.App.1949).

d. The official comment to RMBCA § 12.01 states that the phrase "all or substantially all" should be read "to mean what it literally says.   *   *   *   The phrase 'substantially all' is synonymous with 'nearly all' and was added merely to make it clear that the statutory requirements could not be avoided by retention of some minimal or nominal residue of the original assets. A sale of all the corporate assets other than cash or cash equivalents is normally the sale of 'all or substantially all' of the corporation's property. A sale of several distinct manufacturing lines while retaining one or more lines is normally not a sale of 'all or substantially all' even though the lines being sold are substantial and include a significant fraction of the corporation's former business. If the lines retained are viewed only as a temporary operation or as a pretext to avoid the 'all or substantially all' requirements, however, the statutory requirements of Chapter 12 must be complied with."

Example: Under this definition a sale of a plant but retention of operating assets (e. g. machinery and equipment), accounts receivable, good will, and the like, which permits the operation of the same business at another location is not the sale of "all or substantially all" of the corporation's property.

Caveat: Several decisions adopt a narrower view of the scope of the phrase "all or substantially all." These cases tend to view the test as whether the change of business activity is sufficiently important as to require shareholder approval. *Gimbel v. Signal Companies, Inc.*, 316 A.2d 599 (Del.Ch. 1974), aff'd per curiam 316 A.2d 619 (Del. 1974); *but see Murphy v. Washington American League Base Ball Club, Inc.*, 293 F.2d 522 (D.C.Cir. 1961).

2. APPRAISAL RIGHTS

In most states, shareholders have a statutory right of dissent and appraisal in connection with transactions involving the disposition of substantially all the assets of the corporation not in the ordinary course of business.

D. NONSTATUTORY AMALGAMATIONS

A statutory merger or share exchange is only one of several alternative ways of effecting a corporate acquisition or creating an amalgamated corporation out of formerly independent operations.

1.   TYPES OF TRANSACTIONS
The Internal Revenue Service classification of transactions is widely used.

a.   A class "A" reorganization (in the IRC terminology) is a statutory merger or share exchange.

b.   A class "B" reorganization (in the IRC terminology) occurs when one corporation purchases all or most of the outstanding shares of the other corporation in voluntary transactions, thereby making the acquired corporation a subsidiary of the acquiring corporation. Thereafter, the parent may liquidate or merge the acquired corporation, perhaps using the short form merger procedure discussed above. This transaction often is referred to as a "stock purchase" or "stock acquisition" transaction.

   1)   The purchase price for the shares may be paid in cash, debt, stock, other property, or in a combination of forms.

   2)   In a stock acquisition, the acquiring corporation may have to deal with a fairly large number of sellers, i. e., each shareholder of the acquired corporation.

   3)   The acquired business remains liable for undisclosed or unknown liabilities, such as income tax deficiencies of prior years.

c.   A class "C" reorganization (in the IRC terminology) occurs when one corporation purchases the assets of another corporation. This transaction is often referred to as an "asset purchase" or "asset acquisition" transaction.

   1)   The purchase may include all or virtually all of the assets of the acquired corporation, or it may include only the assets used in one line of business. If the former, compliance with the sale of business provisions described above will usually be necessary.

   2)   The purchase price for the assets may be paid in cash, debt, stock, other property, or in a combination of forms.

3) After the transaction is completed, the acquired corporation retains its separate existence with assets consisting of the proceeds of the sale, usually cash or stock.

(i) Such a corporation may continue in existence operating thereafter as a holding or investment corporation.

(ii) More commonly, however, such a corporation will thereafter liquidate after making provision for liabilities not assumed by the purchaser, distributing the proceeds of the sale to its shareholders.

2.   SELECTION OF FORM OF TRANSACTION

The same basic economic result can be reached by casting a transaction in the form of a statutory merger (a Class A reorganization) a Class B reorganization, or a Class C reorganization.   The question as to which form a particular transaction should take is a complex one, involving a variety of tax and nontax considerations.

a. There is nothing inherently unlawful in structuring a transaction in one form rather than another. *Hariton v. Arco Electronics*, 188 A.2d 123 (Del. 1963).

b. Often the parties to a specific transaction may have different views on this question, one preferring an asset purchase, the other a stock purchase or statutory merger. These views may be based on tax or business factors and generally the controlling shareholders may shape the transaction in light of their own interests. *Grace v. Grace Nat'l Bank of New York*, 465 F.2d 1068 (2d Cir. 1972).

c. Because of the similar economic effect no matter which form is followed, there is a possibility that the selection of a particular form to achieve some goal may not succeed. A court may reject form, "look at substance," and recast the transaction into a different form. This is the "de facto merger" doctrine. *Applestein v. United Bd. & Carton Corp.*, 159 A.2d 146 (N.J.Super.Ch.Div. 1960).

Example: In Pennsylvania, dissenting shareholders have appraisal rights in a statutory merger. A transaction is cast as an asset transaction where the "selling" corporation sells assets, receives shares of the acquiring corporation and thereafter dissolves and distributes the shares to its shareholders. The "selling" corporation is larger that the "acquiring" corporation and, after the transaction is completed, the "selling" corporation dominates the combined operation. In *Farris v. Glen Alden Corp.*, 143 A.2d 25 (Pa. 1958) the court held that this transaction was the economic equivalent of a statutory merger and appraisal rights had to be granted.

Caveat: Several cases are contra to *Farris* and academic writing is critical of the case. *Hariton v. Arco Electronics, Inc.*, 188 A.2d 123 (Del. 1963); *Orzeck v. Englehart*, 195 A.2d 375 (Del. 1963). The Pennsylvania statutes were later amended in an effort to reverse the result in *Farris*. *See Terry v. Penn Central Corp.*, 668 F.2d 188 (3d Cir. 1981).

Example: A manufacturing corporation sells its assets to a large publicly held corporation for cash or stock, distributes the proceeds and liquidates. The acquiring corporation expressly does not assume the liabilities of the manufacturing corporation, but continues the same business using the same plant, same work force, and the same corporate or trade name. Four years later a product liability suit is filed for personal injuries caused by a defective product sold by the old manufacturing company. Despite the express disclaimer of the assumption of liabilities, several cases have held the publicly held corporation liable on the products liability claim on the basis of the de facto merger doctrine. *Knapp v. North American Rockwell Corp.*, 506 F.2d 361 (3d Cir. 1974)

Example: Two corporations develop close working relationships so that one assumes most risks, responsibilities, and profits. However, there is no pooling of assets and liabilities. There is no de facto merger even though many of the economic attributes of a merger have been attained. *Good v. Lackawanna Leather Co.*, 233 A.2d 201 (N.J.Super.Ch.Div. 1967).

E. RECAPITALIZATIONS

A recapitalization is simply a restructuring of the capital structure of the corporation to improve the ability to attract capital.

1. ECONOMICS OF TRANSACTIONS
The classic example of a corporation that benefits from a recapitalization is the corporation with many years of arrearages in cumulative preferred dividends.

a. Directors elected by common shareholders are unwilling to exhaust cash resources by paying off the arrearages.

b. No one is willing to invest fresh capital in the form of new stock so long as the arrearages remain as a restriction on future distributions.

    c.   In a recapitalization, most holders of the preferred with arrearages may be willing to exchange the preferred for common, giving up the arrearages, since they are receiving no dividends on the preferred and the corporation is unlikely to pay them anything unless it is recapitalized.

2. FORM OF TRANSACTION

Recapitalizations usually take one of two forms:

    a.   An amendment to the articles of incorporation.

    b.   A merger into a wholly owned subsidiary or similar transaction that has the same economic effect.

3. VALIDITY OF TRANSACTIONS

These transactions are not subject to a frontal attack on the ground they impair vested rights. *McNulty v. W. & J. Sloane*, 54 N.Y.S.2d 253 (Sup.Ct. 1945). However, established standards for evaluating such transactions have been created.

    a.   There may be different procedural rules applicable to these transactions depending on how they are structured and the precise language of the applicable state statute. In light of the objective need for a recapitalization in many cases, courts have usually allowed the transaction to be cast in a form in which it is likely to succeed. *Bove v. Community Hotel Corp. of Newport, R.I.*, 249 A.2d 89 (R.I. 1969).

    b.   One protection to shareholders often applicable in such transactions is the right to vote by separate voting group. See part XIX, 2.a.

    c.   A shareholder objecting to the recapitalization also may have the right of dissent and appraisal under the statute.

    d.   Some courts have tested the validity of such transactions on a test of fraud, or "unfairness so great as to constitute fraud," *Porges v. Vadsco Sales Corp.*, 32 A.2d 148 (Del.Ch. 1943); *Barrett v. Denver Tramway Corp.*, 53 F.Supp. 198 (D.Del. 1944).

    e.   Finally, some courts have construed narrowly the amendment and reservation of power sections of the business corporation act to invalidate transactions deemed by the court to be of questionable fairness. *Bowman v. Armour & Co.*, 160 N.E.2d 753 (Ill. 1959). Most courts, however, have rejected arguments that in effect would restore the "vested rights" theory. *Langfelder v. Universal Laboratories, Inc.*, 163 F.2d 804 (3d Cir. 1947).

F. "GOING PRIVATE"

The term "going private" refers to transactions that were popular several years ago entered into by a publicly held corporation to force out the public shareholders. The transaction had the effect of returning one hundred per cent of the shareholdings to the control group, thereby eliminating reporting and other requirements under the securities acts. A related type of transaction, the "leveraged buyout" is considered in the following section.

1.   ECONOMICS OF TRANSACTION
Most corporations considering a traditional going private transaction "went public" by selling shares publicly at a time when market conditions were favorable. Typically only a minority interest was sold to the public. The going private transaction is likely to occur some years later when the stock prices are depressed. There is also a saving in not having to comply with the requirements applicable to publicly held corporations.

Example: Power Mate sold shares publicly in 1968 at $5.00 per share. In 1975 the controlling shareholders proposed a going private transaction at a time when the market price was under $2.00 per share and the price offered the public shareholders was $2.00 per share. This transaction was enjoined. *Berkowitz v. Power Mate Corp.*, 342 A.2d 566 (N.J. 1975).

2.   FORM OF GOING PRIVATE TRANSACTIONS
The form of a going private transaction may be a cash merger of the publicly held corporation into a corporation wholly owned by the control group. It also may take the form of a "reverse" stock split with mandatory purchase of fractional shares for cash. The ratio is then set high enough that every public shareholder's holding will become a fractional share.

3.   REGULATION OF GOING PRIVATE TRANSACTIONS
Regulation of such transactions may be under state law or the SEC regulations under the Williams Act.

a.   The principles set forth by the Delaware Supreme Court in *Singer* or *Weinberger* (See part XIX, B) of "entire fairness" would appear to apply to such transactions.

b.   In 1979 the SEC adopted rules 13e–3 and 13e–4 to assure full disclosure of the transaction; disclosure must include a statement as to the belief of the issuer whether the transaction is fair or unfair to the public shareholders and a discussion "in reasonable detail" of the material factors upon which the belief is based.

c.   As a result of *Santa Fe Industries v. Green,* it is clear that going private transactions cannot be attacked under rule 10b–5 if there is full disclosure.

G.   LEVERAGED BUYOUTS

A leveraged buyout (LBO) is a transaction by which an outside entity (that is not itself a publicly held corporation) acquires all the outstanding shares of a publicly held corporation.   Initial purchase of a majority of the outstanding shares may be by tender offer followed by a mop-up merger of the balance.   The outside entity includes investors, speculators, and incumbent management, though much of the financing may be from "junk bonds" or other borrowings.   After the LBO is completed, the corporation is no longer publicly owned.

1.   CHARACTERISTICS
The following characteristics are typical of modern LBOs:

a.   A LBO differs from a going private transaction primarily in that outside investors rather than incumbent management acquire the predominant equity ownership of the company.   However, incumbent management often participates in a LBO and its interest is usually increased significantly as a result of the transaction.

b.   An LBO saves the cost of compliance with the securities acts.

c.   An LBO may improve the incentives to management for risk taking and profitable operation since their proportional interest in the company is greater and they are free from restrictions applicable to publicly held corporations and the threat of litigation that public shareholders present.

d.   It appears likely, however, that the predominant reason for the success of LBO transactions is the tax savings arising from the transaction.   In effect, the tax savings improves the cash flow of the business and permits it to cover the greatly increased indebtedness arising from the LBO.   Nevertheless, the success of many LBO transactions is far from assured.

H.   RIGHTS OF DISSENT AND APPRAISAL

State statutes give shareholders the right to dissent from certain types of transactions and to obtain the appraised value of their shares through a judicial proceeding.   See RMBCA §§ 13.01 through 13.31.

1. **SCOPE OF RIGHT**

The appraisal right is a creature of statute and available only when the statute specifically so provides. It may also be lost if the statutory procedures are not precisely followed, in which case the dissenting shareholder must go along with the objectionable transaction. See e. g. RMBCA §§ 13.21(b), 13.23(c), 13.28(b). However, the corporation has a duty to provide correct information as to the procedures to be followed. *Gibbons v. Schenley Indus., Inc.*, 339 A.2d 460 (Del.Ch. 1975). See RMBCA §§ 13.20(b), 13.22(a), 13.25(b).

a. The appraisal right extends only to transactions described in the statute. RMBCA § 13.02 extends the right of the following types of transactions:

    1) Plans of merger in which the shareholder has the right to vote on the plan, RMBCA § 13.02(a)(1)(i);

    2) Short form merger of subsidiary into parent (shareholders of subsidiary only), RMBCA § 13.02(a)(1)(ii);

    3) Plans of share exchange, if the shareholder owns shares in the corporation whose shares are being acquired and the shareholder is entitled to vote on the transaction, RMBCA § 13.02(a)(2);

    4) Sales of substantially all corporate assets if the shareholder is entitled to vote on the sale, RMBCA § 13.02(a)(3);

    5) Amendments of articles of incorporation "that materially and adversely affect( )" the rights of shareholders in any of five specified ways, RMBCA § 13.02(a)(4); and

    6) Transactions on which the articles of incorporation, bylaws or a resolution of directors specify that dissenters' rights are to be provided, RMBCA § 13.02(a)(5).

        Caveat: Not all state statutes provide dissenters' rights in all the categories. Several states, for example, do not provide dissenters' rights in connection with amendments to the articles of incorporation. Some states also provide dissenters' rights in additional classes of cases.

b. The statutes of a number of states provide that the statutory dissent and appraisal procedure is the exclusive remedy for dissenting shareholders. RMBCA § 13.02(b) provides the remedy is exclusive "unless the action is unlawful or fraudulent" with respect to the shareholders.

1)   Despite such language, several courts have allowed direct attacks on unfair transactions (or transactions without business purpose) that gave rise to an appraisal right.

2)   Other courts have accepted such statutory language at face value and limit a dissenting shareholder to his appraisal right, at least in the absence of fraud. *Matteson v. Ziebarth*, 242 P.2d 1025 (Wash. 1952).

c.   Some states do not grant appraisal rights in connection with shares that are traded on a securities market (or held by a specified number of shareholders) on the theory that the existence of a liquid market on which the shares may be sold provides a reasonable alternative to the appraisal procedure. RMBCA does not contain such an exception.

2. PROCEDURE FOR APPRAISAL

Most state statutes provide an elaborate procedure for establishing the right to an appraisal and fixing the price. See RMBCA §§ 13.20 through 13.28.

a.   A notice of meeting to shareholders at which the transaction is considered must state that dissenters' rights may arise from the transaction. RMBCA § 13.20(a).

b.   A written notice of intent to demand payment must be filed by the dissenting shareholder before the vote of shareholders is taken on the proposed action. RMBCA § 13.21(a).

c.   Following approval, each shareholder filing a notice of intent to dissent must be sent a "dissenters' notice" by the corporation (RMBCA § 13.22(a)) and must thereafter file a demand for payments. RMBCA § 13.23.

1)   Because appraisal claims may constitute serious cash drains, it is not uncommon in merger and other agreements to provide an "out" for the parties if an excessive number of dissents are filed.

2)   Following the affirmative vote on the proposal, shareholders who file demands for payment have the status of creditor rather than shareholder. *Lichtman v. Recognition Equipment, Inc.*, 295 A.2d 771 (Del.Ch. 1972).

3)   To reflect the creditor status of such shareholders, the statutes of many states require dissenting shareholders to submit their certificates with the demand for payment. The corporation notes that the shares have been submitted for appraisal on the certificate and returns them to the shareholders. Under the Revised Model

Business Corporation Act the certificates are retained by the corporation in the expectation that payment will be made promptly.

d.   Most statutes provide that the price is to be set through a two-stage process.

1)   The first stage involves negotiation between the shareholder and the corporation.

2)   If negotiation fails, a court proceeding to establish the appraised price follows.

3)   In the procedure set forth in the Revised Model Business Corporation Act, the corporation must estimate the fair value of the shares and pay to each dissenter that amount immediately. If the dissenting shareholder is dissatisfied with this payment, he or she must submit an estimate of the fair value of his shares. If the shareholder and the corporation cannot agree as to the additional value, the shareholder or the corporation may obtain a judicial appraisal of the value of the shares.

Caveat: Most states do not require that the corporation make immediate payment of the amount it estimates to be the fair value of the shares but all payments are deferred until after the completion of the judicial appraisal procedure. The result is that no payment at all may be received for several years after the transaction; this long delay is one of the unattractive features of the traditional appraisal procedure from the standpoint of shareholders contemplating dissent.

Caveat: The right to receive immediate payment under the Revised Model Business Corporation Act opens up the possibility that a shareholder may be tempted to speculate on the availability of the dissenters' remedy. RMBCA attempts to prevent such speculation by requiring (1) that a shareholder must dissent with respect to all the shares held (an exception is made for record owners where the beneficial ownership is held by more than one person), RMBCA § 13.03, and (2) that a corporation may refuse to make immediate payment to a shareholder who acquires shares after the public announcement of the transaction, RMBCA § 13.27. Such a shareholder is entitled to payment only upon the completion of the appraisal proceeding.

e. The "fair value" of shares is to be fixed as of a time immediately before the transaction in question occurs, but no account is to be taken of the impact of the transaction on the value of the shares. (RMBCA § 13.01(3)). Appraisal may consider various factors:

1) The market value of the stock.

2) The earnings potential of the stock.

3) The net asset value or liquidation value of the stock.

> *Example:* In a case in which the market for the stock consisted of only a few transactions, these factors were weighed: market value—10%, earnings value—40%, net asset value—50%. *Piemonte v. New Boston Garden Corp.*, 387 N.E.2d 1145 (Mass. 1979).

4) The Revised Model Business Corporation Act allows consideration of the "appreciation or depreciation in anticipation of the corporate action" if that is equitable. RMBCA § 13.01(3).

> *Example:* In a close corporation there may be no market price for shares but a price may be "reconstructed" if there are a limited number of sales. *Brown v. Hedahl's-Q B & R, Inc.*, 185 N.W.2d 249 (N.D. 1971); *Application of Delaware Racing Ass'n*, 213 A.2d 203 (Del. 1965).

> *Example:* Earnings value may be based on a capitalized value for average earnings over a recent prior period, such as five years. *Francis I. duPont & Co. v. Universal City Studios, Inc.*, 312 A.2d 344 (Del.Ch. 1973).

> *Caveat:* There is no assurance under these tests that the court-determined price will be equal to or more than the price earlier offered voluntarily. *Gibbons v. Schenley Indus., Inc.*, 339 A.2d 460 (Del.Ch. 1975) (acquirers of stock offered $53.33 per share; appraisers valued at $43.87; court concluded actual value was $33.86 per share).

5) In *Weinberger v. UOP, Inc.*, 457 A.2d 701 (Del. 1983), the Delaware Supreme Court abandoned the "Delaware block" approach of assigning weights to asset value, market value, and earnings potential, and adopted a more flexible approach that permitted use of more modern valuation techniques that are acceptable in the financial community.

f. RMBCA § 13.30 authorizes all appraisal proceedings to be resolved in a single proceeding in a single court. RMBCA § 13.31 authorizes the court to assess costs, including attorneys' fees, against either the corporation or the dissenting shareholders:

1) Costs may be assessed against the corporation if it "did not substantially comply" with chapter 13;

2) Costs may be assessed against the dissenting shareholders if they "acted arbitrarily, vexatiously, or not in good faith" with respect to the rights granted them by chapter 13.

3. EVALUATION OF APPRAISAL REMEDY

The appraisal remedy has a superficial appeal and plausibility. However, from the dissenting shareholder's point of view it is traditionally not an attractive remedy, and much litigation seeks to avoid remitting the shareholder to that remedy. The RMBCA attempts to alleviate many of these traditional disadvantages. From the shareholders' standpoint there are several disadvantages:

a. The process involves potentially long delays while the price is established.

b. Litigation over the value of shares is viewed as expensive and unrewarding.

c. The corporation is an active participant in the judicial proceeding and seeks to establish the lowest possible valuation. The corporation has extensive knowledge about its own affairs and virtually unlimited resources to litigate the issue.

I. VOLUNTARY DISSOLUTION

Most state statutes have several dissolution provisions designed for different situations.

1. DISSOLUTION BEFORE COMMENCEMENT OF BUSINESS

Streamlined provisions permit dissolution before commencement of business by the incorporators or initial directors filing a simple notice of dissolution. RMBCA § 14.01.

2. DISSOLUTION BY UNANIMOUS CONSENT OF SHAREHOLDERS

Dissolution is permitted in many states at any time with the unanimous consent of the shareholders if suitable provision is made for creditors. This provision is widely used by closely held corporations. RMBCA does not contain a special provision to this effect; though shareholders may act by unanimous consent, action by directors is also required.

3.   REGULAR DISSOLUTION

Where other dissolution provisions are not applicable, a corporation may dissolve upon approval of the board of directors and vote of a majority (or some other specified percentage) of the shareholders. See RMBCA § 14.02. In this regard, dissolution is similar to other organic changes by the corporation.

4.   NOTICE OF INTENT TO DISSOLVE

Some states require the filing of a notice of intent to dissolve, followed by a period in which the business and affairs of the corporation are wound up, followed by the filing of final articles of dissolution. The 1969 Model Business Corporation Act followed the 2-step procedure. In other states, only articles of dissolution are filed. The Revised Model Business Corporation Act, § 14.03 follows this procedure.

5.   DISSOLUTION PROCEDURES

Notice of the impending dissolution must be given to creditors. RMBCA §§ 14.06, 14.07. Final dissolution occurs only after all franchise and other tax obligations have been fully satisfied.

Example: An Illinois corporation qualifies to transact business in New Jersey. It later dissolves under Illinois law but takes no steps to withdraw from New Jersey even though that state provides a procedure for withdrawal of dissolved corporations. The corporation remains liable to suit in New Jersey until it follows the required New Jersey procedure. *Dr. Hess & Clark, Inc. v. Metalsalts Corp.*, 119 F.Supp. 427 (D.N.J. 1954).

a.   State statutes usually provide that the existence of a corporation continues after dissolution for a stated period so that the corporation may be sued on pre-dissolution claims. RMBCA § 14.07.

b.   For obvious reasons, there is no statutory right of appraisal in connection with a voluntary dissolution.

6.   EQUITABLE LIMITATIONS ON DISSOLUTION

Equitable limitations on the power to dissolve have sometimes been imposed in situations where a voluntary liquidation is unfair to minority shareholders or is a "freeze out" of such shareholders. Standards, however, are elusive.

a.   Where the business prognosis is bad and the corporation is losing money immediate dissolution is reasonable, since the majority should not be required to wait until the corporation is insolvent and their investment lost. However, dissolution in such circumstances may involve the sale of assets at grossly inadequate prices.

b. Cases have arisen where dissolution is part of a broader scheme to eliminate some shareholders from sharing in the future profits of a good business.

1) The business may be turned over to a new corporation which is owned by some but not all of the original owners. *Lebold v. Inland Steel Co.*, 125 F.2d 369 (7th Cir. 1941).

2) Were such transactions broadly sanctioned, a minority could be ejected from a successful venture through the process of dissolution rather than a cash merger. The tests developed in the cash merger cases may have potential applicability in such dissolutions as well.

REVIEW QUESTIONS

XIX–1. An amendment to articles of incorporation may be freely made so long as it does not eliminate vested rights.

True ——————   False ——————

XIX–2. What is the difference between a merger and a consolidation? Why does the Revised Model Business Corporation Act fail to recognize "consolidations"?

XIX–3. How does a "cash merger" differ from an ordinary merger?

XIX–4. What is a "short form merger"?

XIX–5. What are the alphabetical references to reorganizations, "A", "B", "C", and so forth?

XIX–6.   What is the relationship between statutory and non-statutory methods of combining two corporations?

XIX–7.   What is a "de facto merger"?

XIX–8.   What are "appraisal rights"?

XIX–9.   May a corporation sell substantially all its assets without the approval of shareholders?

XIX–10.   What are "going private" transactions and what legal requirements are applicable to them?

XIX–11.   What is a "leveraged buyout"?

XIX–12.   If a person has a right of dissent and appraisal he is fully protected and has no reason to complain about the treatment of his interest in the corporation.

True _____   False _____

XIX–13.   D corporation has a provision in its articles of incorporation providing for cumulative voting for directors. The corporation law of D's state of incorporation does not require that shareholders be afforded cumulative voting. In addition the state statute gives the corporation the right to amend, alter or repeal any provisions in the articles of incorporation. D has sent a notice to its shareholders of a meeting at which a resolution to amend its articles of incorporation to eliminate the provision for cumulative voting will be considered. P is a minority shareholder who has enough shares to elect one director voting cumulatively but will be unable to do so if the cumulative voting provision is eliminated. P brings an action to restrain D from amending its article of incorporation by eliminating the cumulative voting provisions. Is P entitled to an injunction?

XIX–14.   P is the owner of 40% of the stock in D corporation which operates the Grey Sox Baseball Team in Fun City, under a league franchise. D's directors have approved the removal of the franchise to another location. P brings an action to enjoin the club's move. He contends that D's directors have agreed to dispose of subtantially all D's assets outside the ordinary course of business and that such a transaction is valid only if it complies with the state corporation act that requires the owners of ⅔rds of the common stock to consent to the transfer. Is P entitled to an injunction?

XIX–15.   P is a preferred shareholder in D corporation, a corporation of State Y. There are accumulated unpaid dividends on P's stock of $1,800 per share. D has adopted a plan of merger wherein it plans to merge with its wholly-owned subsidiary DD. Under the plan of merger P's preferred stock would be converted into one share of new preferred and 5 shares of new common. Under the laws of State Y a shareholder who objects to a merger is entitled to dissent and have the fair value of his or her shares paid to him in money but this remedy is not exclusive. P however brings an action to enjoin the merger on the ground that the merger is unfair to the preferred shareholders since they lose all their accumulated unpaid dividends. May P obtain an injunction?

APPENDIX A

GLOSSARY

A

accounts payable are amounts owed by a business on open account to creditors for goods and services. Analysts look at the relationship between accounts payable and total purchases as an indication of sound day-to-day financial management.

accounts receivable are amounts owing to a business for merchandise or services sold on open account. See liquidity.

adoption is a contract principle by which a person agrees to assume a contract previously made for his or her benefit. An adoption speaks only from the time such person agrees, in contrast to a "ratification" which relates back to the time the original contract was made. In corporation law, the concept is applied when a newly formed corporation accepts a preincorporation contract made for its benefit by a promoter. See: part III, B.

affiliate is a corporation that is related to another corporation by shareholdings or other means of control. It includes not only a parent or a subsidiary but also corporations that are under common control.

aggressor corporation is a corporation that attempts to obtain control of a publicly held corporation, often by a direct cash tender or public exchange offer to shareholders, but also possibly by way of merger, which requires agreement or assent of the target's management.

air pocket is a market phenomena where shares fall sharply, usually in the wake of negative news such as unexpected poor earnings. Shareholders rush to sell and few buyers can be found: as a result, the price plunges dramatically, i. e., like an airplane hitting an air pocket.

amortization is an accounting procedure that gradually reduces the cost or value of a limited life or intangible asset through periodic charges against income. For fixed assets amortization is called "depreciation", and for wasting assets (natural resources) it is "depletion". The periodic charges are usually treated as a current expense for purposes of determining income.

amotion is the common law procedure by which a director may be removed for cause by the shareholders.

annuity is a contractual obligation to make certain payments in the future. An annuity may be purchased from insurance or similar companies for a fixed payment. Life insurance premiums or retirement proceeds are often converted upon their maturity into annuities for the life of one or more persons. An annuity may be for a definite period or for the life or lives of one or more persons. In a fixed annuity the periodic amount depends solely on the amount originally invested. In a variable annuity, the periodic amount of the future payments varies with the value of the investments in the account.

antidilution provisions appear in convertible securities to guarantee that the conversion privilege is not affected by share reclassifications, share splits, share dividends, or similar transactions that may increase the number of outstanding shares without increasing the corporate capital.

appraisal is a limited statutory right granted to minority shareholders who object to certain fundamental transactions such as mergers. In an appraisal proceeding a court determines the appraised value of their shares and the corporation pays such appraised value to the shareholder in cash. The Revised Model Business Corporation Act uses the term "dissenters' rights to obtain payment for their shares" to describe this right. An appraisal right exists only to the extent specifically provided by statute. See: part XIX, G.

arbitragers are market investors who take off-setting positions in the same or similar securities in order to profit from small price variations. An arbitrager, for example, may buy shares on the Pacific Coast Exchange and simultaneously sell the same shares on the New York Stock Exchange if any price discrepancy occurs between the quotations in the two markets. By taking advantage of momentary disparities in prices between markets, arbitragers perform the economic function of making those markets more efficient.

arbs is a slang term for arbitragers.

articles of incorporation is the name customarily given to the document that is filed in order to form a corporation. Under various state statutes, this document may be called the "certificate of incorporation," "charter," "articles of association," or other similar name.

asked price. See: bid and asked.

authorized shares are the shares described in the articles of incorporation which a corporation may issue. Modern corporate practice recommends authorization of more shares than it is currently planned to issue. See: part V, B, 3.

B

back-end-load. See: load.

basis in tax law is roughly the equivalent of the amount invested in property by the taxpayer. To compute gain or loss on the sale or exchange of property, the basis of property is generally subtracted from the amount realized from the sale or exchange.

bear is a slang term for a speculator who believes securities prices are going to decline. A pessimist is "bearish." Contrast: bull.

beneficial holders of securities are persons who have the equitable or legal title to shares but who have not registered the shares in their names on the records of the corporation. See also: record owner.

bid and asked are terms that deal with price quotations for securities or commodities. "Bid" is the highest price a prospective buyer is prepared to pay at a particular time for a trading unit; "asked" is the lowest price a prospective seller of the same unit is prepared to accept. Together, the two prices constitute a quotation; the difference between the two prices is the "spread". Although bid and asked prices are common to all securities trading, "bid and asked" usually refers to securities traded "over the counter" and to commodities and commodities futures trading. See also: spread; over the counter.

block is a large quantity of securities involved in a single trade. As a general guide, block trades involve 10,000 or more shares or bonds with a total face amount in excess of $200,000.

blockage is a price phenomenon: a large block of shares may be more difficult to market than a smaller block, particularly if the market is thin. The discount at which a large block sells below the price of a smaller block is blockage. Blockage is generally a phenomenon of shares which do not represent the controlling interest in a corporation. Compare: control premium.

blue chip shares are common shares of nationally known companies that have a long record of profit growth and dividend payment and reputations for quality management, products, and services. Blue chip shares typically are relatively high priced and low yielding, and are viewed as conservative investments.

blue sky laws are state statutes that regulate the sale of securities to the public. Most blue sky laws require the registration of new issues of securities with a state agency that reviews selling documents for accuracy and completeness. Blue sky laws also often regulate securities brokers and salesmen.

bond discount. See: discount.

bonds are long term debt instruments secured by a lien on some or all the corporate property. Typically a bond is payable to bearer and inter-est coupons representing annual or semi-annual payments of interest are attached (to be "clipped" periodically and submitted for payment). Bondholders in effect have an IOU from the issuer; they are viewed as creditors and not as owners of the enterprise. The word bond is sometimes used more broadly to refer also to unsecured debt instruments, i. e., debentures. Income bonds are hybrid instruments that take the form of a bond, but the interest obligation is limited or tied to the corporate earnings for the year. Participating bonds are another type of hybrid instruments that take the form of a typical debt instrument but the interest obligation is not fixed so that holders are entitled to receive additional amounts from excess earnings or from excess distributions, depending on the terms of the participating bond.

bonus shares are par value shares issued without consideration, usually in connection with the issuance of preferred or senior securities, or debt instruments. Bonus shares are considered a species of watered shares and may impose a liability on the recipient equal to the amount of par value. See: part V, B, 7.

book value is the "value" of shares determined on the basis of the books of the corporation. Using the corporation's latest balance sheet, the liabilities are subtracted from assets, an appropriate amount is deducted to reflect the interest of the senior securities (preferred shares) and what remains is divided by the number of outstanding shares to obtain the book value of a share. Book value is widely used as an estimate of value, particularly of closely held shares, but has certain limitations: it is based on accounting conventions, may not reflect unrealized appreciation or depreciation of assets, and does not take into account future prospects of the business.

broker in a securities transaction, means a person who acts as an agent for a buyer or seller, or an intermediary between a buyer and seller, usually charging a commission. A broker who specializes in shares, bonds, commodities or options must be registered with the exchange where the specific securities are traded. A broker should be distinguished from a securities dealer who, unlike the broker, is in the business of buying or selling for his own account. See: dealer; underwriting.

bull is a slang term for a speculator who believes securities prices are going to increase. An optimist is "bullish." Contrast: bear.

buyout is the purchase of a controlling percentage of a company's shares. A buyout often involves all of the company's outstanding shares. A buyout can be accomplished through negotiation, through a tender offer, or through a merger.

bylaws are the formal rules of internal governance adopted by a corporation. Bylaws define the rights and obligations of various officers, persons or groups within the corporate structure and provide rules for routine matters such as calling meetings and the like. Most state corporation statutes contemplate that every corporation will adopt bylaws. See generally: part II.

C

call for redemption. See: redemption.

calls are options to buy securities at a stated price for a stated period. Many calls or call options to purchase shares of companies listed on the New York Stock Exchange are themselves publicly traded. Calls also are written on a variety of indexes, foreign currencies, and other securities. The person who commits himself or herself to sell the security upon the request of the call holder is referred to as the call writer; the act of making the purchase of the securities pursuant to the call option is referred to as exercise of the option. See also: puts; stock index future; index options.

capital gain for income tax purposes, is the difference between a capital asset's basis and the selling price when the difference is positive.

capital loss for income tax purposes, is the amount by which the proceeds from the sale of a capital asset are less than the basis of the asset.

capital stock is another phrase for common shares, often used when the corporation has only one class of shares outstanding.

capital surplus. In the old Model Business Corporation Act nomenclature, capital surplus is an equity or capital account which reflects the capital contributed for shares not allocated to stated capital: the excess of issuance price over the par value of issued shares or the consideration paid for no par shares allocated specifically to capital surplus. See: part V, B, 5. Capital surplus may be distributed to shareholders under certain circumstances or used for purchase or redemption of shares more readily than stated capital. See: part V, G.

capitalization is an imprecise term that usually refers to the amounts received by a corporation for the issuance of its shares. However, it may also be used to refer to the proceeds of loans to a corporation made by its shareholders (which may be in lieu of capital contributions) or even to capital raised by the issuance of long term bonds or debentures to third persons. Depending on the context, it may also refer to accumulated earnings not withdrawn from the corporation.

cash flow refers to an analysis of the movement of cash through a venture as contrasted with the earnings of the venture. For example, a mandatory debt repayment is taken into account in a cash flow analysis even though such a repayment does not reduce earnings. See: negative cash flow.

cash merger is a merger transaction in which certain shareholders or interests in a corporation are required to accept cash for their shares while other shareholders receive shares in the continuing enterprise. Modern statutes generally authorize cash mergers, though courts test such mergers on the basis of fairness and, in some states, business purpose. See: part XIX, B, 3.

cash tender offer is a technique by which an aggressor corporation seeks to obtain control of a target corporation by making a public purchase offer for a specified fraction (usually a majority) of the target corporation's shares.

CEO stands for "chief executive officer" of a publicly held corporation. *CEO* is a preferred and useful designation because official titles of such persons vary widely from corporation to corporation.

certificate of incorporation in most states is the document prepared by the Secretary of State that evidences the acceptance of articles of incorporation and the commencement of the corporate existence. In some states the certificate of incorporation is the name given to the document filed with the Secretary of State, i. e., the articles of incorporation. The Revised Model Business Corporation Act has eliminated certificates of incorporation, requiring only a fee receipt.

charter may mean (i) the document filed with the Secretary of State, i. e., the articles of incorporation, or (ii) the grant by the State of the privilege of conducting business with limited liability. Charter is often used in a colloquial sense to refer to the basic constitutive documents of the corporation.

churning is the slang term for the unethical practice of convincing a customer to trade unnecessarily. Churning increases the broker's commissions, and usually leaves the client worse off or no better off than before. Churning is illegal under SEC and exchange rules, but is often difficult to prove.

close corporations or **closely held corporations** are corporations with relatively few shareholders and no regular markets for their shares. There is no litmus test for when a corporation should be considered closely held and the definition may in part depend on the

substantive context in which it arises. In addition to the small number of shareholders and lack of public market, close corporations usually have made no public offering of shares and the shares themselves are usually subject to restrictions on transfer. Close and closely held are synonymous in this context.

closely held. See: close corporation.

closing sale. See: last sale.

commercial paper is a generic term for short-term obligations usually with maturities ranging from 2 to 270 days, issued by banks, corporations, and other borrowers to investors with temporarily idle cash. Such instruments are unsecured and usually sold at a discount from face value, although some are interest-bearing.

commission in a securities transaction, is the fee paid to a broker for executing a trade. The commission is usually based on the number of shares traded or the dollar amount of the trade.

common shareholders are holders of common shares, the ultimate owners of the residual interest of a corporation. See: common shares.

common shares represent the residual ownership interests in the corporation. Holders of common shares select directors to manage the enterprise, are entitled to dividends out of the earnings of the enterprise declared by the directors, and are entitled to a per share distribution of whatever assets remain upon dissolution after satisfying or making provisions for creditors and holders of senior securities.

consolidation is an amalgamation of two corporations pursuant to statutory provision in which both of the corporations disappear and a new corporation is formed. The Revised Model Business Corporation Act eliminates the consolidation as a distinct type of corporate amalgamation. See: part XIX, B, 1. Compare: merger.

control of a corporation by a person normally means that the person has power to vote a majority of the outstanding shares. However, control may be reflected in a significantly smaller block if the remaining shares are scattered in small, disorganized holdings.

control person in securities law is a person who is deemed to be in a control relationship with the issuer. Sales of securities by control persons are subject to many of the requirements applicable to the sale of securities directly by the issuer.

control premium refers to the pricing phenomenon by which shares that carry the power to control a corporation are more valuable per share than the shares that do not carry a power of control. See: part XV, G, 1. The control premium is often computed not on a per share basis but on the aggregate increase in value of the "control block" over the going market or other price of shares which are not part of the "control block."

conversion securities are the securities into which convertible securities may be converted. See: convertible securities.

convertible securities are usually preferred shares or debentures. The conversion privilege consists of the right of exchanging the convertible securities, at the option of their holder, for a designated number of shares of another class, usually common shares, called the conversion securities. The ratio between the convertible and conversion securities is fixed at the time the convertible securities are issued, and is usually protected against dilution.

co-promoters. See: promoters.

corporate opportunity is a fiduciary concept which limits the power of officers, directors and employees to take personal advantage of opportunities that belong to the corporation. See: part XIV, E.

corporation by estoppel is a doctrine which prevents a third person from holding an "officer," "director," or "shareholder" of a nonexistent corporation personally liable on an obligation entered into in the name of the nonexistent corporation on the theory that the third person relied on the existence of the corporation and is now "estopped" from denying that the corporation existed. See: part III, B, 2.

crown jewel option is a strategy used by the target company under which it conveys to a third party some of its valuable property. The purposes of the crown jewel option are to deprive an aggressor of the opportunity to acquire the target's valuable property and to induce the third party to make a bid for the target in response to a possible takeover.

cumulative dividends on preferred shares carry over from one year to the next if a preference dividend is omitted. An omitted cumulative dividend must be made up in a later year before any dividend may be paid on the common shares in that later year. However, cumulative dividends are not debts of the corporation but merely a right to priority in future discretionary distributions.

cumulative to the extent earned dividends on preferred shares are cumulative dividends that are limited in any one year to the available earnings of the corporation in that year.

cumulative voting is a method of voting that allows substantial minority shareholders to obtain representation on the board of directors. When voting cumulatively, a shareholder may cast all his available votes in an election in favor of a single candidate. See: part VII, C.

current ratio is calculated by dividing current assets by current liabilities. It shows a company's ability to pay its current obligations from current assets. For the most part, a company that has a small inventory and readily collectible accounts receivable can operate safely with a lower current ratio than a company whose cash flow is less dependable. See also: quick ratio.

current yield in the case of a bond, is the ratio between market price of the bond and the coupon rate, taking no account of any discount on premium paid by the purchaser.

D

D & O insurance refers to directors' and officers' liability insurance. Such insurance, which is widely available commercially, insures such persons against claims based on negligence, failure to disclose, and to a limited extent, other defalcations. Such insurance provides coverage against expenses and to a limited extent fines, judgments and amounts paid in settlement. See: part XVI, B.

deadlock in a closely held corporation arises when a control structure permits one or more factions of shareholders to block corporate action if they disagree with some aspect of corporate policy. A deadlock often arises with respect to the election of directors, e. g., by an equal division of shares between two factions, but may also arise at the level of the board of directors itself.

dealer is a person who trades in securities for his own account. Compare: broker.

debentures are long term unsecured debt instruments. Typically a debenture is payable to bearer and interest coupons representing annual or semiannual payments of interest are attached. See: bonds.

deep rock doctrine is a principle in bankruptcy law by which unfair or inequitable claims presented by controlling shareholders of bankrupt corporations may be subordinated to claims of general or trade creditors. The doctrine received its name from the corporate name of the subsidiary involved in the leading case articulating the doctrine. See: part IV, F, 3.

de facto corporation at common law is a partially formed corporation that provides a shield

against personal liability of shareholders for corporate obligations; such a corporation may be attacked only by the state. See: part III, B, 2.

de facto merger is a transaction that has the economic effect of a statutory merger but is cast in the form of an acquisition of assets or an acquisition of voting stock and is treated by a court as if it were a statutory merger. See: reorganization; part XIX, D.

deflation occurs when there is a general decline in the prices of goods and services. Generally, the economic effects of deflation are the opposite of those produced by inflation, with two notable exceptions: (1) prices that increase with inflation do not necessarily decrease with deflation—a traditional example is union wage rates; (2) while inflation may or may not stimulate output and employment, marked deflation tends to cause unemployment to rise and output thereafter to fall.

de jure corporation at common law is a corporation that is sufficiently formed to be recognized as a corporation for all purposes. A de jure corporation may exist even though some minor statutory requirements have not been fully complied with. See: part III, B, 2.

delectus personae is a Latin phrase used in partnership law to describe the power each partner possesses to accept or reject proposed new members of the firm.

depletion. See: amortization.

depreciation. See: amortization.

depression is a sharp decline in aggregate business activity that persists over an extended period of time.

deregistration of an issuer occurs when the number of securities holders of an issuer registered under section 12 of the Securities Exchange Act of 1934 has declined to the point where registration is no longer required. See: registered corporation.

derivative suit is a suit brought by a shareholder in the name of a corporation to correct a wrong done to the corporation. See: part XVIII.

dilution of outstanding shares results from the issuance of additional shares. The dilution may be of voting power if shares are not issued proportionately to the holdings of existing shareholders, or it may be financial, if shares are issued disproportionately and the price at which the new shares are issued is less than the market or book value of the outstanding shares prior to the issuance of the new shares. See: part V, F. See also: antidilution provisions.

directory requirements are minor statutory requirements. At common law, a de jure corporation may be created despite the failure to comply with directory requirements relating to its formation. Important statutory requirements are called mandatory requirements. See: part III, B.

discount is a general term for the issuance of a security at less than the face amount or stated amount of the security. Issuance of a bond or debenture at a discount increases the effective interest rate on such a security if it is held to maturity since the face amount is paid at maturity.

discount shares are par value shares issued for cash less than par value. Discount shares are considered a species of watered shares and may impose a liability on the recipient equal to the difference between the par value and the cash for which such shares were issued. See: part V, B, 5.

dissension in a closely held corporation refers to personal quarrels or disputes between shareholders that may make business relations unpleasant and interfere with the successful operation of the business. Dissension, however, may occur without causing a deadlock or adversely affecting the corporation's business.

dissenters' right. See: appraisal.

distribution is a payment to shareholders by a corporation. If out of present or past earnings it is a dividend. The word distribution is sometimes accompanied by a word describing the source or purpose of the payment, e. g., Distribution of Capital Surplus, or Liquidating Distribution.

dividend is a payment to shareholders from or out of current or past earnings. The word dividend is sometimes used more broadly to refer to any payment to shareholders though a more appropriate term for payments out of capital is distribution.

double taxation refers to the structure of taxation under the Internal Revenue Code of 1954 which subjects income earned by a corporation to an income tax at the corporate level and a second tax at the shareholder level if the same income is distributed to shareholders in the form of dividends.

down stream merger is the merger of a parent corporation into its subsidiary.

E

earnings per share is a firm's net income divided by the number of shares held by shareholders. Earnings per share is a key statistic in evaluating a share's outlook.

earnings yield. See: price-earnings ratio.

equity or **equity interest** are financial terms that refer in general to the extent of an ownership interest in a venture. In this context, equity refers not to a legal concept but to the financial definition that an owner's equity in a business is equal to the business's assets minus its liabilities.

equity financing is raising money by the sale of common shares or preferred shares. Equity financing is most popular when securities prices are high so that the most capital can be raised with the issuance of the smallest number of shares.

equity security is a security that represents an interest in the equity of a business. See: equity. Equity securities are usually considered to be common and preferred shares.

ESOP is an acronym for employee stock ownership plan. Such plans acquire shares of the employer for the benefit of employees usually through contributions of the employer to the plan. The purpose of such plans is to acquire ownership of shares of the employer corporation for the benefit of employees. This is usually accomplished through contributions of the employee to the plan.

ex dividend refers to the date on which a purchaser of publicly traded shares is not entitled to receive a dividend that has been declared and the seller of such shares is entitled to retain the dividend. The ex dividend date is a matter of agreement or of convention to be established by the securities exchange. On the first day shares are traded without the right to receive a dividend, the price will decline by approximately the amount of the dividend; such shares are often referred to as "trading ex dividend."

ex rights refers to the date on which a purchaser of publicly traded shares is not entitled to receive rights that have been declared on the shares. Compare: ex dividend.

F

face value is the value of a bond, note, mortgage, or other security, as given on the certificate or instrument, payable upon maturity of the instrument. The face value is also the amount on which interest or coupon payments are calculated. Thus, a 10% bond with a face value of $1000 pays bondholders $100 per year. Face value is also often referred to as the par value or nominal value of the instrument.

fixed annuity. See: annuity.

float is the supply of securities in street name that comprises the source of most securities

delivered by speculators to complete their transactions. The term float may also be used to mean the delay in processing transactions by banks and others which may permit the interest-free use of funds for brief periods.

forced conversion refers to a conversion of a convertible security that follows a call for redemption at a time when the value of the conversion security into which it may be converted is greater than the amount that will be received if the holder permits the security to be redeemed. Normally, a holder of a convertible redeemable security has a period of time after the call for redemption to determine whether or not to exercise the conversion privilege.

freeze-out refers to a process, usually in a closely held corporation, by which minority shareholders are prevented from receiving any direct or indirect financial return from the corporation in an effort to persuade them to liquidate their investment in the corporation on terms favorable to the controlling shareholders. See: part XIX, B.

freeze-out merger. See: cash merger.

futures contract is an agreement to buy or sell on a stipulated future date a specific amount of a commodity or a financial instrument at a particular price. The price is established between buyer and seller on the floor of a commodity exchange at the time of the agreement. A futures contract obligates the buyer to purchase the underlying commodity and the seller to sell it. Futures contracts rarely lead to the delivery of the commodity, since both investors usually "net out" their position before the delivery date by buying or selling an offsetting agreement.

futures index. See: stock future index.

G

general partners are unlimitedly liable for the debts of the partnership. General partner is usually used in contrast with limited partner in a limited partnership, but general partner is also sometimes used to refer to any partner in a general partnership.

going private refers to a transaction in which public shareholders of a publicly held corporation are compelled to accept cash for their shares while the business is continued to be owned by officers, directors, or large shareholders. A going private transaction may involve a merger of the publicly held corporation into a subsidiary in a cash merger. See: part XIX, F.

going public refers to the first public distribution of securities by an issuer pursuant to registration under the securities acts. If a corporation has been in business for several years, the initial registration by which the corporation goes public is apt to be difficult and expensive.

going short refers to selling a stock or commodity that the seller does not have. An investor who goes short borrows stock from his or her broker, planning to purchase replacement shares at a lower price. If successful, the investor keeps the difference as profit. See also: selling short.

golden parachute is a slang term for a lucrative contract given to a top executive of a company. The contract usually provides additional benefits in case the company is taken over and the executive is either forced to leave the target company or voluntarily leaves it. A golden parachute might include generous severance pay, stock options, or a bonus payable the executive's employment at the company ends.

gray knight is a slang term for a bidder in a takeover attempt who, without solicitation from the target, tries to take advantage of the resistance of the target.

greenmail is a slang term that refers to a payment by the target to a potential aggressor to buy back acquired shares at a premium over

market. The acquirer in exchange agrees not to pursue its takeover bid.

growth fund is a mutual fund that invests in growth stocks with the goal of providing capital appreciation for the fund's shareholders. Growth funds tend to be more volatile than mutual funds that invest in more conservative income or money market instruments. They tend to rise faster than conservative funds in bull (advancing) markets and to drop more sharply in bear (falling) markets. See: mutual fund.

H

hedging is a strategy used to offset investment risk. A perfect hedge is one that eliminates all possibility of future gain or loss. A shareholder worried about a possible decline in price of an important security in his portfolio, for example, may hedge his or her holdings by buying a put option on the stock or selling a call option. See: puts; calls.

holding company is a corporation that owns a majority of the shares of one or more other corporations. Usually a holding company is not engaged in any business other than the ownership of such majority shares. See: investment companies.

hybrid securities are securities that have some of the attributes of both debt securities and equity securities.

I

income bond. See: bonds.

income fund is a mutual fund that has an investment goal of maximizing current income for the benefit of investors who value income over growth. Income funds often invest in bonds or high-dividend shares or may write call options on shares in their portfolios.

incorporators are the person or persons who execute the articles of incorporation. See: part II, D. In modern statutes only a single incorporator is required, the role of the incorporator is largely limited to the act of execution of the articles of incorporation, and restrictions on who may serve as incorporators have largely been eliminated.

indemnification refers to the practice by which corporations pay expenses of officers or directors who are named as defendants in litigation relating to corporate affairs. In some instances corporations may indemnify officers and directors for fines, judgments, or amounts paid in settlement as well as expenses. See: part XVI. Broad indemnification rights may raise issues of public policy; on the other hand, it may be difficult or impossible to persuade persons to serve as directors in the absence of indemnification.

indenture is the contract which defines the rights of holders of bonds or debentures as against the corporation. Typically, the contract is entered into between the corporation and an indenture trustee whose responsibility is to protect the bondholders. The indenture often constitutes a mortgage on specified corporate property to secure the bonds.

index is a statistical composite that measures the ups and downs of prices of shares, bonds, or commodities. Some well-known indexes are the Dow Jones Industrial Index, the New York Stock Exchange Index, the American Stock Exchange Index, Standard & Poor's Index, and the Value Line Index.

index fund is a mutual fund whose portfolio is designed to match the performance of a broad-based index such as Standard & Poor's Index and whose performance therefore mirrors the market as reflected by the index.

index options are calls or puts on share indexes. These options are publicly traded. Index options may be broad-based covering a wide range of companies and industries, or narrow-based covering shares in only a single industry or sector of the economy. Index options allow investors to trade in a particular market or industry group without purchasing options on individual shares.

inflation is an increase in general price levels of goods and services. Inflation occurs when spending increases more rapidly than the supply of goods on the market—in other words, too much money chasing too few goods. See also: deflation.

in pari delicto is a common law principle that usually is referred to as the "unclean hands" doctrine. The principle limits a person intending to engage in wrongful conduct from suing another wrongdoer when things do not work out as expected.

inside directors are directors of a publicly held corporation who hold executive positions with management. See: part XI, A.

insider is a term of uncertain scope that refers to persons having some relationship to an issuer, and whose securities trading on the basis of nonpublic information may be a violation of law. Insider is broader than inside director. See: insider trading. See also: part XV, A.

insider trading refers to transactions in shares of publicly held corporations by persons with inside or advance information on which the trading is based. Usually the trader himself is an insider with an employment or other relation of trust and confidence with the corporation.

insolvency may refer to either equity insolvency or insolvency in the bankruptcy sense. Equity insolvency means that the business is unable to pay its debts as they mature while bankruptcy insolvency means that the aggregate liabilities of the business exceeds its assets. Since it is not uncommon for a business to be unable to meet its debts as they mature yet have assets that exceed in value its liabilities, or vice versa, it is often important to specify in which sense the term insolvency is being used.

institutional investors are large investors, such as mutual funds, pension funds, insurance companies, and others who largely invest other people's money. See: part XI, B, 3. Since World War II, institutional investors have accounted for an increasing portion of all public securities trading.

interlocking directors are persons who serve simultaneously on the boards of directors of two or more corporations that have dealings with each other. Federal antitrust law prohibits interlocking directors of competing businesses; such directors may also create problems involving fiduciary duties.

in the tank is a slang expression meaning market prices are dropping rapidly. Stock market observers may say, "the market is in the tank" after a day in which stock prices fell.

intra vires means acts within the powers or stated purposes of a corporation. Intra vires is the opposite of ultra vires.

investment bankers are commercial organizations involved in the business of handling the distribution of new issues of securities. See: underwriters. An investment banker may also provide other investment and advisory services to corporations.

investment club is a cooperative effort usually by small shareholders to pool their funds. An investment club gives these investors the opportunity to share in a portfolio that offers a greater diversification and, hopefully, a better return on their money than they could get individually.

investment companies are corporations that are engaged in the business of investing in securities of other businesses. The most common kind of investment company is the mutual fund. An investment company differs from a holding company in that the latter seeks control of the ventures in which it invests while an investment company seeks the investment for its own sake and normally diversifies its investments. Investment companies are subdi-

vided into "open end" and "closed end" companies. An "open end" company stands ready at all times to redeem its securities at net asset value and to issue new shares to investors on demand; such an investment company is usually known as a mutual fund. An investment company that has a fixed capitalization and neither issues new shares or redeems outstanding shares on request is called a "closed end" company.

issued shares are shares a corporation has actually issued and has not cancelled. Issued shares should be contrasted with authorized shares. Issued shares that have been reacquired by the corporation are called treasury shares. The Revised Model Business Corporation Act and the statutes of several states have eliminated the concept of treasury shares.

J

joint venture is a limited purpose partnership largely governed by the rules applicable to partnerships. In an earlier day, many states permitted corporations to participate in joint ventures but treated as ultra vires an attempt by a corporation to become a partner in a general partnership.

junior securities are issues of debt or equity that are subordinate in claim to other issues in terms of dividends, interest, principal, security or payments upon dissolution. See also: preferred share; senior security; subordinated.

K

kicker is an added feature of a debt or preferred share obligation, usually designed to enhance marketability by offering the chance of equity participation. The conversion feature of a convertible bond is a "kicker". Kickers are also sometimes called sweeteners.

L

last sale is the most recent trade in a particular security. It may be, but usually is not, the final transaction in a trading session which is called the closing sale. The last sale is the point of reference for two SEC rules relating to short sales: (1) on a national exchange, no short sale may be made below the price of the last regular sale; (2) no short sale may be made at the same price as the last sale unless the last sale was at a price higher than the preceding different price. See: short sale.

leverage refers to the advantages that may accrue to a business through the use of debt obtained from third persons in lieu of contributed capital. Such debt improves the earnings allocable to contributed capital if the business earns more on each dollar invested than the interest cost of borrowing funds. See: part V, D.

leveraged buyout (or "LBO") is a transaction by which an outside entity that is not publicly held acquires all the shares of a public corporation. In a leveraged buyout the incumbent management usually has a financial and participatory interest in the outside entity. See: part XIX, G.

limit order or **limit price** is an order to buy or sell a security at a specific price or better that is not the market price. The trade will be executed only within the price restrictions of the order.

limited partner. See: limited partnership and general partner.

limited partnership is a partnership consisting of one or more limited partners (whose liability for partnership debts is limited to the amount originally invested) and one or more general partners (whose liability for partnership debts is unlimited). To create a limited partnership a certificate must be filed with a state official, and even if a certificate is filed a limited partner may lose the shield of limited liability by actively participating in the management of the business.

liquidating dividend is a distribution of assets in the form of a dividend from a corporation

that is reducing capital or going out of business. Such a payment may arise, for example, when management decides to sell off certain company assets and distribute the proceeds to the shareholders. Such a distribution may not be from current or retained earnings.

liquidity refers to the market characteristic of a security or commodity with enough units outstanding and traded to allow large transactions to occur without a substantial variation in price. Most shares traded at the New York Stock Exchange have liquidity. Institutional investors usually prefer liquid investments since their trading activity have less influence on the market price than if they traded in less liquid securities.

listed security is a security that is publicly traded on a securities exchange. For a security to be listed the issuing corporation must meet the requirements established by the exchange and, in most exchanges, sign a listing agreement with the exchange.

load is the sales charge paid by an investor who buys shares in a mutual fund that imposes such a charge. Loads are usually charged when fund shares are purchased; a charge for withdrawing shares from a fund is called a "back-end-load". Back-end-loads are not used widely. See: mutual funds; investment company; no-load fund.

load fund is a mutual fund that adds a sales charge to the net asset value when the security is purchased from a brokerage firm. Such funds may be stock, bond, or commodity funds. The stated advantage of a load fund is that the salesperson explains the fund to the customer, and advises him when it is appropriate to sell the fund, or increase the investment in the fund. See load; no-load fund.

locked market is a highly competitive market with numerous identical bid and ask prices for a security. The appearance of more buyers and sellers "unlocks" the market.

lockup is a slang term that refers to the setting aside of securities for purchase by friendly interests in order to defeat or make more difficult a takeover attempt.

lollipop strategy is an anti-take-over measure designed to avert a possible take-over. In the event any person or group acquires a specified percentage of shares, the target company gives the other shareholders a "lollipop", e. g., the right to exchange their shares for notes and/or preferred shares valued above current market prices or the right to sell the shares back to the firm at a premium over market. A lollipop raises the cost of share acquisitions, hopefully deterring the take-over bid. See also: poison pill; white knight; shark repellent.

long position is the net ownership position of a speculator in a specific security. A speculator is "long" if he owns a positive number of shares; he is "short" if he has sold borrowed shares in a number greater than the number he owns. Long position is often used with reference to the investor's ownership position with a brokerage firm.

M

make a market is the maintenance of bid and asked prices by a single broker or dealer in a given security. The market maker stands ready to buy or sell round lots at any time. The term market maker is used in connection with the over-the-counter market. A dealer who makes a market over a long period is said to "maintain" a market.

mandatory requirements are substantive statutory requirements which must be substantially complied with if a de jure corporation is to be formed. See: part III, B.

margin is the amount a purchaser of a security must deposit with a broker if the purchaser wishes to borrow from the broker part of the purchase price on the collateral of the shares. If the margin requirement is fifty per cent, for example, a speculator purchasing $10,000 of securities would have to deposit $5,000 in cash

and could thereafter borrow the remaining $5,000 from the broker at the market rate of interest for such transactions. A margin transaction increases the leverage of the transaction. See: margin call and margin requirement.

margin account is a brokerage account that permits customers to buy securities on margin.

margin call occurs when the market price of securities purchased on margin declines so that the investor must increase the amount deposited with the broker to maintain the minimum required margin. In the preceding example, if the market value of the securities purchased for $10,000 declines to $9,000, the purchaser must deposit $500 with his broker to keep the account open [$10,000 debt secured by $4,500 of securities requires $5,500 in deposits].

margin requirement is the percentage of the purchase price that must be deposited with a broker to purchase a security on margin. The margin requirement is set or adjusted by the Federal Reserve Board.

maturity date is the date on which the principal amount of a note, draft, acceptance, bond, or other debt instrument becomes due and payable.

member firm is a brokerage firm that has at least one membership on a major stock exchange, even though, by exchange rules, the membership may be in the name of an employee and not in the name of the firm itself. Such a firm enjoys the rights and privileges of membership.

merger is an amalgamation of two corporations pursuant to statutory provision in which one of the corporations survives and the other disappears. Compare: consolidation.

missing the market refers to a broker who negligently fails to execute a transaction on terms favorable to a customer. If the order is subsequently executed at a price demonstrably less favorable, the broker, as the customer's agent, may be required to make good the loss.

money market fund is an open-end mutual fund that invests in commercial paper, banker's acceptances, repurchase agreements, government securities, and similar cash-equivalent securities. A money market fund pays money market rates of interest. Many money market funds permit investors to switch their money from one money market fund to another within a "family" of funds and back again without charge.

mutual fund is a publicly held open end investment company that usually invests only in readily marketable securities. See: investment company. An "open end" investment company stands ready at all times to redeem its shares at net asset value. A mutual fund thus provides the advantages of complete liquidity, diversification of investment, and skilled investment advice for the small investor. A mutual fund that sells its shares for a premium over net asset value charges a front end load; a mutual fund that does not charge such a premium is called a no-load fund. See: load.

N

naked option is an option for which the buyer or seller has no underlying security position. A writer of a naked call option does not own a long position in the shares on which the call has been written. Similarly, the writer of a naked put option does not have a short position in the shares on which the put has been written. Naked options are risky investment strategies, although potentially very rewarding. See also: long position.

NASDAQ is an acronym for "National Association of Securities Dealers Automated Quotations" and is the principal recording device for transactions on the over-the-counter market.

negative cash flow refers to a situation where the cash needs of a business exceed its cash intake. Short periods of negative cash flow

create no problem for most businesses; longer periods of negative cash flow may require additional capital investment if the business is to avoid insolvency in the equity sense. See: insolvency.

net worth is the amount by which assets exceed liabilities.

net yield is the rate of return on a security net of out-of-pocket costs associated with its purchase, such as commissions or markups.

new issue is a security being offered to the public for the first time. The distribution of new issues is usually subject to SEC rules. New issues may be initial public offerings by previously private companies or additional securities offered by public companies. See also: primary market; secondary market.

nifty fifty is a slang term that refers to the 50 stocks most favored by institutions. The membership of this group changes from time to time, although companies that continue to produce consistent earnings growth over a long time tend to remain institutional favorites.

nimble dividends are dividends paid out of current earnings at a time when there is a deficit in earned surplus (or other financial account from which dividends may be paid). Some state statutes do not permit nimble dividends; these statutes require current earnings to be applied against prior deficits rather than being used to pay a current dividend.

no-load fund is a mutual fund that imposes no sales charges (load) on purchases of its shares. See: load; load fund; mutual fund.

nominal yield is the annual income received from a fixed-income security divided by the par or face value of the security. It is stated as a percentage figure.

nominee registration is a form of securities registration widely used by institutional investors to avoid onerous requirements of establishing the right of registration by a fiduciary. See: part XI, B, 4.

noncallable preferred shares or bonds are securities that cannot be redeemed at the option of the issuer. See: callable securities.

noncumulative voting or **straight voting** limits a shareholder to voting no more than the number of shares he owns for a single candidate. Compare: cumulative voting. In noncumulative voting, a majority shareholder will elect the entire board of directors. See: part VII, C.

nonvoting common shares are shares that expressly have no power to vote. Such shares may be created in most states; in some states, however, nonvoting shares may be entitled to vote as a class on certain proposed changes adversely affecting that class as such.

no par shares are shares which are stated to have no par value. See: part V, B, 4. Such shares are issued for the consideration designated by the board of directors; such consideration is allocated to stated capital unless the directors or shareholders determine to allocate a portion to capital surplus. As a result, in many respects no par shares do not differ significantly from par value shares.

novation is a contract principle by which a third person takes over the rights and duties of a party to a contract, such party thereby being released from obligations under the contract. In the law of corporations, the concept may be applied to the release of a promoter who is personally liable on a preincorporation contract when the corporation is formed and adopts the contract. See: part III, B, 1. A novation requires the consent of the other party to the contract, but that consent may be implied from the circumstances.

O

odd lots are units of securities less than the standard trading unit or round lot. In market trading, a purchase or sale of less than 100

shares is considered an odd lot transaction, although inactive shares often are traded in round lots of 10 shares. See also: round lot.

OPM (other people's money) is a slang term for the use of borrowed funds by individuals or companies to increase the return on invested capital. See also: leverage.

organizational expenses are the costs of organizing a corporation, including filing fees, attorneys' fees, and related expenses. Organizational expenses may also include the cost of raising the initial capital through the distribution of securities. Under the Internal Revenue Code of 1954, organizational expenses may be capitalized and written off against income over a five-year period.

out of the money describes an option with no current value since the price at which the option may be exercised is above the market price (in the case of a call) or below it (in the case of a put).

outside directors are directors of publicly held corporations who do not hold executive positions with management. Outside directors, however, may include investment bankers, attorneys, or others who provide advice or services to incumbent management and thus have financial ties with management.

over-the-counter refers to the broad securities market consisting of brokers who purchase or sell securities by computer hook-up or telephone rather than through the facilities of a securities exchange. At one time completely unorganized, the over-the-counter market is now relatively organized with computerized quotation and transaction reporting services.

P

pac man is a slang term for a strategy by which a target company threatens to take over the aggressor and begins buying its shares. The "pac man" strategy is named after a popular video game, in which each character that does not swallow its opponents is itself consumed. See also: takeover; tender offer.

par value or **stated value** of shares is an arbitrary or nominal value assigned to each such share. At one time par value represented the selling or issuance price of shares, but in modern corporate practice, par value has little significance and serves only a limited role. Shares issued for less than par value are usually referred to as watered shares. The Revised Model Business Corporation Act and the statutes have eliminated the concept of par value. See: part V, B.

participating bonds. See: bonds.

participating preferred shares are preferred shares that, in addition to paying a stipulated dividend, give the holder the right to participate with the common shareholder in additional distributions of earnings, if declared, under specified conditions.

pegging is stabilizing the price of a security, commodity, or currency by intervening systematically in a market.

pendent jurisdiction is a principle applied in federal courts that allows state created causes of action arising out of the same transaction to be joined with a federal cause of action even if diversity of citizenship is not present.

phantom stock plan is an employee benefit plan in which benefits are determined by reference to the performance of the corporation's common shares. For example, a person receiving benefits based on 1,000 "phantom shares" will have credited to his account each year an amount equal to the dividends declared on 1,000 shares; the number of "phantom shares" will be increased by share dividends or splits actually declared on real shares; on his death or retirement the person will receive a credit equal to the difference between the market price of the "phantom shares" in his account on the date of death or retirement (or a related date) and the market price of the "phantom

shares" in his account on the date he was awarded the rights.

plow back is the reinvestment of a company's earnings in the business rather than paying those profits to shareholders as dividends.

poison pill is a tactic by a takeover-target company to make its shares less attractive to an acquirer. For instance, a firm may issue a new series of preferred shares that gives shareholders the right to compel their redemption at a premium price after a takeover. A poison pill raises the cost of an acquisition, hopefully deterring a takeover bid. See also: lollipop tactic; shark repellent; white knight.

pooling agreement is a contractual arrangement among shareholders relating to the voting of their shares. So long as such agreement is limited to voting as shareholders, it is enforceable. See: part VII, E.

porcupine provisions are defensive provisions in articles of incorporation or bylaws designed to make unwanted takeover attempts impossible or impractical without the consent of the target's management.

portfolio theory or **portfolio management theory** is a theory that analyzes investment decisions by a rational investor. Portfolio theory considers both the kind and the amount of expected risk and return. Essential to portfolio theory are its quantification of the relationship between risk and return and the assumption that investors must be compensated for assuming risk.

preemptive rights give an existing shareholder the opportunity to purchase or subscribe for a proportionate part of a new issue of shares before it is offered to other persons. Its purpose is to protect shareholders from dilution of value and control when new shares are issued. In modern statutes, preemptive rights may be limited or denied. See: part V, F, 1.

preferred shares are shares that have preferential rights to dividends or to amounts distributable on liquidation, or to both, ahead of common shareholders. Preferred shares are usually entitled only to receive specified limited amounts as dividends or on liquidation. If preferred shares are entitled to share in excess distributions with common shareholders on some defined basis, they are participating preferred shares. Participating preferred shares may also be called class A common, or some similar designation to reflect its open-ended rights.

preferred shareholders are beneficial holders of preferred shares.

preferred shareholders' contract refers to the provisions of the articles of incorporation, the bylaws, or the resolution of the board of directors, creating and defining the rights of holders of the preferred shares in question. Preferred shareholders have only very limited statutory or common law rights outside of the preferred shareholders' contract. However, even provisions creating and defining the rights of holders of preferred shares may usually be amended without the consent of each individual holder of preferred shares. The major protection provided by statute against onerous amendments is the right of preferred shareholders to vote as a separate voting group on such changes. See: part XIX, A.

preincorporation subscription. See: subscription.

premium is a general term for the issuance of a security at a price greater than the face amount or stated amount of the security. Issuance of a bond or debenture at a premium reduces the effective interest rate on such a security since only the face amount is paid at maturity.

price-earnings ratio is the ratio of earnings per share to current stock price. Also known as earnings yield, it is used in comparing the relative attractiveness of investments in stocks, bonds, and money market instruments.

primary market is the market for new issues of securities sold by the issuers to raise capital. A market is "primary" if the proceeds go to the issuer of the securities sold. See also: secondary market.

private placement of securities is the sale of securities to sophisticated investors without registration under federal or state securities acts under the private offering exemption or under Regulation D.

promoters are persons who develop or take the initiative in founding or organizing a business venture. Where more than one promoter is involved in a venture, they are usually described as co-promoters.

prospectus is a document furnished to a prospective purchaser of a security that describes the security being purchased, the issuer, and the investment or risk characteristics of the security. SEC regulations require a prospectus meeting specified requirements to be provided to each prospective purchaser of registered public offerings of securities.

proxy is a person authorized to vote someone else's shares. Depending on the context, proxy may refer to the grant of authority itself, the document granting the authority, or the person granted the power to vote the shares.

proxy solicitation machinery is a phrase commonly used to describe the phenomenon that incumbent management of a publicly held corporation may usually produce large majorities of shareholder votes on any issue it desires. This power is based in part on the ability of incumbent management to use corporate funds to communicate at will with the shareholders and partially on the ability to represent their views as the views of "management." See: part XI, A.

proxy statement is the document that must accompany a solicitation of proxies under SEC regulations. The purpose of the proxy statement is to provide shareholders with the appropriate information to permit an intelligent decision.

public exchange offer is a technique by which an aggressor corporation seeks to obtain control over a target corporation by offering to exchange a package of its securities for the target corporation's voting shares. Usually, a specified number of target corporation shares must be presented for exchange before it will take place.

public offering involves the sale of securities by an issuer or a person controlling the issuer to members of the public. Generally, any offering that is not exempt under Regulation D or the private offering exemption of the Securities Act of 1933 and/or similar exemptions under state blue sky laws is considered a public offering. Normally registration of a public offering under those statutes is required though in some instances other exemptions from registration may be available.

publicly held corporation is a corporation with shares held by numerous persons. For a fuller discussion of the problem of definition see: part I, A. Typically, a publicly held corporation is registered under section 12 of the Securities Exchange Act of 1934, though such registration is not an essential attribute of being publicly held. See: part V, E. Shares of publicly held corporations are usually traded either on a securities exchange or over-the-counter.

purchase fund is the provision in some preferred share contracts and bond indentures requiring the issuer to use its best efforts to purchase a specified number of the preferred shares or bonds annually at a price not exceeding par or face value. Unlike sinking fund provisions (which require that a certain number of bonds be retired annually) purchase funds require only that an offer to the purchaser be made at the specified price; if no securities are tendered, none are retired.

puts are options to sell securities at a stated price for a stated period. If the price declines, a holder of a put may purchase the shares at the lower market price and "put" the shares to the put writer at the contract price. Puts on some New York Stock Exchange securities are publicly traded but more securities have call options written than put options. See: calls.

Q

qualified stock option is an option to purchase shares awarded to an employee of the corporation under terms that qualify the option for special tax treatment under the Internal Revenue Code.

qualifying share is a share of common stock owned by a person in order to qualify as a director of the issuing corporation in a corporation that requires directors to be shareholders.

quick ratio is calculated by dividing cash, marketable securities, and accounts receivable by current liabilities. Inventories are excluded in the calculation of the quick ratio in order to focus on the firm's more liquid assets, whose values are relatively certain. The quick ratio helps answer the question "If sales stopped, could this firm meet its current obligations with the readily convertible assets on hand?"

quo warranto is a common law writ designed to test whether a person exercising power is legally entitled to do so. In the law of corporations, quo warranto may be used to test whether a corporation was validly organized or whether it has power to engage in the business in which it is involved.

quoted price in the securities market, is the price at which the last sale and purchase of a particular security or commodity took place.

R

radar alert is a slang term for the monitoring of trading patterns in a corporation's shares by senior managers in an effort to uncover unusual buying activity that might signal a takeover attempt.

raider is an individual or corporation who attempts to take control of a target corporation by buying a controlling interest in its stock and installing new management. Raiders who accumulate 5% or more of the outstanding shares in the target company must publicly report their purchases under the Williams Act.

recapitalization is a restructuring of the capital of the corporation through amendment of the articles of incorporation or a merger with a subsidiary or parent corporation. Recapitalizations often involve the elimination of unpaid cumulated preferred dividends, but may also involve reduction or elimination of par value, the creation of new classes of senior securities, or similar transactions.

record date is the date on which the identity of shareholders entitled to vote, to receive dividends, or to receive notice is ascertained. See generally: part V, B.

record owner of shares is the person in whose name shares are registered on the records of the corporation. A record owner is treated as the owner of the shares by the corporation whether or not the beneficial owner of the shares.

redemption means the reacquisition of a security by the issuer pursuant to a provision in the security that specifies the terms on which the reacquisition may take place. A security is called for redemption when the issuer notifies the holder that the redemption privilege has been exercised. Typically, a holder of a security that has been called for redemption will have a limited period thereafter to decide whether or not to exercise a conversion right, if one exists.

reduction surplus is a term used in a few states with par value statutes to refer to the surplus created by a reduction of stated capital. In many states, such surplus is treated simply as capital surplus. See: part V, A.

registered corporation is a publicly held corporation which has registered under section 12

of the Securities Exchange Act of 1934. See: part XII for a discussion of the requirements of section 12 and the obligations imposed on a corporation registering under that section. Section 12 may apply to issuers other than corporations. The registration of an issuer under this section of the 1934 Act should be contrasted with the registration of an issue under the Securities Act of 1933.

registration of securities under the Securities Act of 1933 permits the public sale of such securities in interstate commerce or the use of the mails. That registration should be distinguished from the registration of corporations under the Securities Exchange Act of 1934.

registration statement is the document that must be filed to permit registration of securities under the Securities Act of 1933. A major component of the registration statement is the prospectus that is to be supplied prospective purchasers of the securities.

reorganization is a general term describing corporate amalgamations or readjustments. The classification of the Internal Revenue Code is widely used in general corporate literature. A Class A reorganization is a statutory merger or consolidation (i. e., pursuant to the business corporation act of a specific state). A Class B reorganization is a transaction by which one corporation exchanges its voting shares for the voting shares of another corporation. A Class C reorganization is a transaction in which one corporation exchanges its voting shares for the property and assets of another corporation. A Class D reorganization is a "spin off" of assets by one corporation to a new corporation; a Class E reorganization is a recapitalization; a Class F reorganization is a "mere change of identity, form, or place of organization, however effected." A Class G reorganization is a "transfer by a corporation of all or part of its assets to another corporation in a title 11 or similar case".

retained earnings are net profits accumulated by a corporation after payment of dividends.

Retained earnings are also called "undistributed profits" or "earned surplus".

return on equity is calculated by dividing common stock equity (net worth as shown on the books of the corporation) at the beginning of an accounting period into net income for the period after payment of preferred stock dividends but before payment of common stock dividends. Return on equity indicates the amount earned on each dollar of invested capital: it is expressed as a percentage and is a guide to common shareholders as to how effectively their money is being employed.

reverse stock split is a stock split in which shares are aggregated so that there are fewer shares outstanding after the split than before. Reverse stock splits often create fractional shares and may be used as a device to go private.

reverse triangular merger. See triangular merger.

rights are short term options to purchase shares from an issuer at a fixed price. Rights are often issued as a substitute for a dividend or as a "sweetener" in connection with the issuance of senior or debt securities. Rights are often publicly traded. Compare: warrants.

risk arbitrage is a strategy employed in takeover situations in which shares of a corporation that is about to be taken over are bought, while shares of the acquiring corporation that are to be exchanged are sold short or on a when-issued basis.

risk averse is the term referring to the assumption involved in portfolio theory that, given the same return and different risk alternatives, a rational investor will seek the security offering the least risk. In other words, portfolio theory assumes that the higher the degree of risk, the greater the return that a rational investor will demand. See: portfolio theory.

round lot is the standard trading unit of securities. On most securities exchanges a round lot is 100 shares.

running ahead is a slang term for the illegal practice of buying or selling a security for a broker's personal account before placing a similar order for a customer.

S

scrip is issued in lieu of fractional shares in connection with a stock dividend. Scrip merely represents the right to receive a portion of a share; scrip is readily transferable so that it is possible to acquire scrip from several sources and assemble the right to obtain the issuance of a full additional share.

saturday night special is a surprise tender offer which expires in one week. Designed to capitalize on panic and haste, such an offer may be made Friday afternoon to take advantage of the fact that markets and most offices are closed on Saturday and Sunday. Saturday night specials have been effectively prohibited by regulations under the Williams Act.

secondary market consists of the securities exchanges and over-the-counter markets where securities are bought and sold after their original issue (which took place in the primary market). Proceeds of secondary market sales accrue to selling investors not to the company that originally issued the securities. See also: primary market.

securities is a general term that covers not only traditional securities such as shares of stock, bonds, and debentures, but also a variety of interests that have the characteristics of securities, i. e., that involve an investment with the return primarily or exclusively dependent on the efforts of a person other than the investor.

securities exchanges are markets for the purchase and sale of traditional securities at which brokers for purchasers and sellers may effect transactions. The best known and largest securities exchange is the New York Stock Exchange.

security-for-expenses statutes require certain plaintiffs in a derivative suit to post a bond with sureties from which corporate or other defendants may be reimbursed for their expenses if they prevail. Designed as a protection against strike suits, security-for-expenses statutes have been widely criticized as being illogical and unnecessary. The Revised Model Business Corporation Act does not impose a security-for-expenses requirement.

seed money refers to a venture capitalist's initial contribution toward the financing or capital requirements of a new business. Seed money frequently takes the form of a subordinated loan or an investment in convertible bonds or convertible preferred shares. Seed money provides the basis for additional capitalization to accommodate growth.

seller's market is a description of a market in which there is more demand for a security or product than there is available supply. Prices rise in a seller's market.

sell out refers to the liquidation of a margin account by a broker after a margin call fails to produce additional equity capital.

senior security is a debt security or preferred share that has a claim prior to that of junior obligations or common shares on a corporation's assets and earnings. See: junior security.

series of preferred shares are subclasses of preferred shares with differing dividend rates, redemption prices, rights on dissolution, conversion rights and the like. The term of a series of preferred shares may be established by the directors so that a corporation periodically engaged in preferred shares financing may readily shape its preferred shares offering to market conditions through the use of series of preferred shares. Under the Revised Model Business Corporation Act, the board of directors may establish the terms of either a "class" or a "series". See: part V, C.

settlement date is the date upon which an executed order must be settled by the buyer paying for the securities with cash and by the seller delivering the securities sold.

share repurchase plan is a program by which a corporation buys back its own shares in the open market. It is usually done when the corporation believes its shares are undervalued by the market.

shareholders or **stockholders** are the persons who own shares of stock of the corporation. Such shares may be either common shares or preferred shares. The Revised Model Business Corporation Act and modern usage generally tends to prefer "shareholder" to "stockholder" but the latter word is deeply engrained in common usage.

shark repellent is a slang term that refers to measures undertaken by a corporation to discourage unwanted takeover attempts. At one time it also referred to state tender offer statutes. See also: lollipop tactics; poison pill; white knight. See: part XI, B, 3.

shark watcher is a slang term for firms specializing in the early detection of takeover activity. Such a firm, whose primary business is often the solicitation of proxies for client corporations, monitors trading patterns in a client's stock and attempts to determine the identity of parties accumulating shares.

short form merger is a merger of a largely or wholly owned subsidiary into a parent through a stream-lined procedure permitted under the Revised Model Business Corporation Act and statutes of many states. See: part XIX, B, 3.

short sale is a sale of a security or commodity futures contract not owned by the seller. The security to be sold is borrowed from a broker and the short seller anticipates replacing the borrowed security at a lower price at a later time. A short sale permits an investor: (1) to take advantage of an anticipated decline in the price or (2) to protect a profit in a long position against an anticipated price decline.

short sale against the box is a short sale where the speculator owns enough shares of the security involved to cover the borrowed securities, if necessary. The "box" referred to is the hypothetical safe deposit box in which the certificates are kept. A short sale against the box is not as risky as a short sale.

show stopper. See: smoking gun.

sinking fund refers to an obligation sometimes imposed pursuant to the issuance of debt securities by which the issuer is required each year to set aside a certain amount to enable the issuer to retire the securities when they mature. A sinking fund may be allowed to accumulate or may be used each year to redeem a portion of the outstanding debt securities.

sleeping beauty is a slang term that refers to a potential takeover target that has not yet been approached by an aggressor. Such a company usually has one or more attractive features from the standpoint of an aggressor, such as a large amount of cash or undervalued real estate or other assets.

smoking gun is a mistake by an aggressor that may be used by the target in a takeover attempt to gain additional time. A smoking gun that is so serious that the entire takeover attempt must be cancelled is called a show stopper.

spin-off is a form of corporate divestiture that results in a subsidiary or division of a corporation becoming an independent company.

split is a proportional change in the number of shares owned by every shareholder. Other things being equal, a stock split does not affect the aggregate market value of the shares. Stock splits differ from a share dividend in degree; typically in a share dividend no adjustment is made in the dividend rate per share

while such an adjustment is usually made in a stock split. There are other technical differences in the handling of stock splits and share dividends under the statutes of most states. See also reverse stock split.

spread in futures trading, is the difference between delivery months in the same or different markets. Spread, in fixed-income securities, is the difference between yields on securities of the same quality but different maturities or the difference between yields on securities of the same maturity but different quality.

squeeze-outs are techniques by which a minority interest in a corporation is eliminated or reduced. Squeeze-outs may occur in a variety of contexts, e. g., in a "going private" transaction in which minority shareholders are compelled to accept cash for their shares (see: part XIX, B, 3), or the issuance of new shares to existing shareholders in which minority shareholders are given the unpleasant choice of having their proportionate interest in the corporation reduced significantly or of investing a large amount of additional or new capital over which they have no control and for which they receive little or no return. Many squeeze-outs involve the use of cash mergers. Squeeze-out is often used synonymously with freeze-out.

staggered board is a classified board of directors in which a fraction of the board is elected each year. In staggered boards members serve two or three years, depending on whether the board is classified into two or three groups.

stated capital in the old Model Business Corporation Act nomenclature represented the basic capital of the corporation. Technically, it consisted of the sum of the par values of all issued shares plus the consideration for no par shares to the extent not transferred to capital surplus plus other amounts that may be transferred from other accounts. Distributions generally may not be made from stated capital. See: part V, B.

stated value. See: par value.

sticky deal is a slang term that refers to a new issue of securities that the underwriter fears will be difficult to sell.

stock dividend is a proportional distribution of shares without payment of consideration to existing shareholders. A stock dividend is often viewed as a substitute for a cash dividend, and shareholders may sell a stock dividend without realizing that they are diluting their ownership interest in the corporation.

stock index future is a security that combines features of traditional commodity futures trading and securities trading. It is a commitment to purchase a hypothetical bundle of securities at a specified future date at a price fixed at the time of the purchase or sale. See also index options.

stock split is a proportional change in the number of shares owned by every shareholder. It differs from a stock dividend in degree; however, typically in a stock dividend no adjustment is made in the dividend rate per share while such an adjustment is usually made in a stock split. There are other technical differences in the handling of stock splits and stock dividends under the statutes of most states. Stock splits usually result in an increase in the number of outstanding shares; see: reverse stock split.

stockholders. See: shareholders.

stop order is the order to a securities broker to buy or sell at the market price once a security reaches a specified price.

straddle is a strategy consisting of the combination of an equal number of put options and call options on the same underlying share, index, or commodity future. A straddle is a type of hedge.

straight voting. See: noncumulative voting.

street name refers to the common practice of registering publicly traded securities in the name of one or more brokerage firms with offices on Wall Street. Such certificates are endorsed in blank and are essentially bearer certificates transferred between brokerage firms. See: part XI, B.

strike suits is a slang term for derivative litigation instituted for its nuisance value or to obtain a favorable settlement.

subchapter S refers to a tax option under the Internal Revenue Code of 1954 which permits certain closely held corporations to be taxed in a manner similar to that applicable to partnerships. Under Subchapter S corporate income is taxable directly to shareholders whether or not actually distributed to them. Subchapter S was designed to eliminate the double taxation problem; however, the provisions of Subchapter S are complex and create unique problems not present in the tax treatment of partnerships.

subordinated. See: junior security.

subscribers are persons who agree to invest in the corporation by purchasing shares of stock. See: part III. Subscribers usually commit themselves to invest by entering into contracts defining the extent and terms of their commitment; at common law subscribers usually executed "subscriptions" or "subscription agreements." Modern contracts for the purchase of corporate shares from the issuer usually use the phrase "agree to purchase and subscribe for . . . ."

subscription is an offer to buy a specified number of theretofore unissued shares of a corporation. See: part III. If the corporation is not yet in existence, a subscription is known as a preincorporation subscription, which is enforceable by the corporation after it has been formed and is irrevocable despite the absence of consideration or the usual elements of a contract.

subsidiary is a corporation that is at least majority owned, and may be wholly owned, by another corporation.

surplus is a general term in corporate accounting that usually refers to either the excess of assets over liabilities or that amount further reduced by the stated capital represented by issued shares. Surplus has a more definite meaning when combined with a descriptive adjective from par value statutes, e. g., earned surplus, capital surplus or reduction surplus.

swap is the exchange of one security for another. A swap may be executed to change the maturities of a bond portfolio or the quality of the issues in a share or bond portfolio, or because investment objectives have shifted.

sweetener. See: kicker.

T

tainted shares are shares owned by a person who is disqualified for some reason from serving as a plaintiff in a derivative action. The shares are "tainted" since for policy reasons a good faith transferee of such shares will also be disqualified from serving as a plaintiff.

takeover attempt or **takeover bid** are generic terms to decribe an attempt by an outside corporation or group, usually called the aggressor or "insurgent" to wrest control away from incumbent management. The object of a takeover attempt is usually referred to as the target. A takeover attempt may involve purchase of shares, a tender offer, a sale of assets or a proposal that the target merge voluntarily into the aggressor.

target corporation is a corporation the control of which is sought by an aggressor corporation.

tender offer is a public invitation by an aggressor that shareholders of a target corporation tender their shares for purchase by the aggressor at a stated price. Tender offers are regulated by the Williams Act that amended the Securities Exchange Act of 1934. A creeping tender offer is a series of private acquisitions in the market place and may or may not be classed as a tender offer for regulatory purposes.

thin corporation is a corporation with an excessive amount of debt in its capitalization. A thin corporation is primarily a tax concept. See: part V, D.

thin market refers to a market for publicly traded securities in which the number of transactions and/or the number of securities offered for sale or purchase at any one time are relatively few. In a thin market a single substantial purchase or sale order may cause a significant price movement. A thin market is nevertheless a market, so that the phrase is not ordinarily used in connection with closely held shares for which there is no regular market at all.

three piece suitor is a slang term for an acquisition performed in three stages: (1) the purchase of a substantial number of shares, (2) a tender offer for the remaining shares, and (3) a squeeze-out merger to pick up the balance. See: Freund & Easton, The Three-Piece Suitor: An Alternative Approach To Negotiated Corporate Acquisitions, 34 Bus.Law 1969 (1979). See also: tender offer; squeeze-out.

tip is information passed by one person (a "tipper") to another (a "tippee") as a basis for a decision to buy or sell a security. Such information is presumed to be of material value and not available to the general public. The SEC prohibits trading on the basis of such information by insiders. See part XIV, C, 5. See also: insider; insider trading.

tout is a slang term referring to aggressive promotion of a particular security, usually by a corporate spokesman, public relations firm, broker, or analyst with an interest in promoting the shares. Touting is unethical if it misleads investors.

transfer agent is an organization, usually a bank, that handles transfers of shares for a publicly held corporation. Generally, a transfer agent assures that certificates submitted for transfer are properly endorsed and that there is appropriate documentation of the right to transfer. The transfer agent issues new certificates and oversees the cancellation of the old ones. Transfer agents also usually maintain the record of shareholders for the corporation and mail dividend checks.

treasury shares are shares that were once issued and outstanding but which have been reacquired by the corporation and "held in its treasury." Treasury shares are economically indistinguishable from authorized but unissued shares but historically have been treated as having an intermediate status. Many of the complexities created by treasury shares revolve around accounting concepts. The Revised Model Business Corporation Act and the statutes of several states have eliminated the concept of treasury shares, reacquired shares automatically having the status of authorized but unissued shares. See generally: part V.

triangular merger is a method of amalgamation of two corporations by which the disappearing corporation is merged into a subsidiary of the surviving corporation and the shareholders of the disappearing corporation receive shares of the surviving corporation. See: part XIX, B, 3. In a reverse triangular merger the subsidiary is merged into the disappearing corporation so that it becomes a wholly owned subsidiary of the surviving corporation.

trust indenture. See: indenture.

U

ultra vires is the common law doctrine relating to the effect of corporate acts that exceed the powers or the stated purposes of a corporation. See: part II, M. The modern view generally validates all corporate acts even though they may be ultra vires.

underwriters are persons who buy shares with a view toward their further distribution. Used almost exclusively in connection with the public distribution of securities, an underwriter may be either a commercial enterprise engaged in the distribution of securities (an investment banker), or a person who simply buys securities without an investment intent and with a "view" toward further distribution.

undigested securities are newly issued shares and bonds that remain undistributed because there is insufficient public demand at the offer price. See also: underwriting.

up stream merger is a merger of a subsidiary corporation into its parent.

V

variable annuity. See: annuity; fixed annuity.

venture capital is funding for new companies or others embarking on new or turnaround ventures that entails some investment risk but offers the potential for above average future profits. Venture capital is often provided by firms that specialize in financing new ventures with capital supplied by investors interested in speculative or high risk investments.

voting group is a term defined in the Revised Model Business Corporation Act to describe the right of shares of different classes to vote separately on fundamental corporate changes that adversely affect the rights or privileges of that class. The scope of the right to vote by voting groups is defined by statute. The right is of particular value to classes of shares with limited or no voting rights under the articles of incorporation. Most older state statutes use the terms "class voting" or "voting by class" to refer essentially to the same concept.

voting trust is a formal arrangement by which record title to shares is transferred to trustees who are entitled to exercise the power to vote the shares. Usually, all other incidents of ownership, such as the right to receive dividends, are retained by the beneficial owners of the shares. See: voting trust certificates. See: part VII, F.

voting trust certificates are certificates issued by voting trustees to the beneficial holders of shares held by the voting trust. Such certificates may be as readily transferable as the underlying shares, carrying with them all the incidents of ownership of the underlying shares except the power to vote.

W

warrants are a type of option to purchase shares issued by a corporation. Warrants are typically long period options, are freely transferable, and if the underlying shares are listed on a securities exchange, are also publicly traded. The price of warrants of publicly held corporations will obviously be a function of the market price of the shares and the option price specified in the warrants. See also: rights.

wash sale is the offsetting purchase and sale of a single security either simultaneously or within a short period of time. It may be done by a single investor or (where manipulation is involved) by two or more parties conspiring to create an artificial market activity in order to profit from a rise in the security's price. The entering of numerous offsetting transactions is sometimes called "painting the tape".

watered shares are par value shares issued for property which has been overvalued and is not worth the aggregate par value of the issued shares. Watered shares is often used as a generic term to describe all shares issued for less than par value—including discount and bonus shares. The issuance of watered shares may impose a liability on the recipient equal to the amount of the shortfall from par value. See: part V, B, 5.

white knight is a friendly suitor: a potential acquirer usually sought out by the target of an unfriendly takeover to rescue it from the unwanted bidder's takeover. See also: lollipop tactic; poison pill; shark repellent.

white squire is a slang term for a corporation that assists a takeover target by acquiring a large block of the target's stock, thereby making an unwanted takeover bid more difficult. The danger with the white squire strategy is that the squire may thereafter seek to take control of the target.

window dressing is a slang term for trading activity near the end of a quarter or fiscal year that is designed to "dress up" the performance of a portfolio. More generally, it is an accounting gimmick designed to make a financial statement appear more favorable than it actually is.

working capital is a measure of a corporation's liquidity and ability to discharge its liabilities as they arise. Working capital is the difference between current assets and current liabilities as shown on the corporation's balance sheet.

APPENDIX B

ANSWERS TO QUESTIONS

PART I

I–1.   *False.* While the corporate entity theory is useful and correctly answers most questions, it is only a partial explanation of the concept of a corporation.

I–2.   *False.* While a corporation involves elements of contracts, there are also mandatory noncontractual aspects. The economists' "nexus of contracts" approach is also a useful analytic device but not a complete explanation of the modern corporation.

I–3.   *Largely false.* The law treats a wholly owned corporation as a separate entity for many purposes. A wholly owned corporation is a separate taxable entity; it may enter into contracts with its shareholders, and so forth.

I–4.   *False.* The state grant of corporate authority is itself subject to constitutional restrictions. Further, Supreme Court decisions have granted a corporation many (though not all) of the constitutional rights possessed by an individual.

I–5.   *Largely true.* The articles of incorporation are often viewed as the contract which defines the rights of the various classes of shares in the corporation. Most case law dealing with rights of preferred shareholders involve construction of the specific articles of incorporation. Statutes, however, give some minimum rights to preferred shareholders independent of their "contract."

I–6.   *False.* The law of the state of incorporation controls most of the internal relationships within the corporation, but both federal law and the laws of other states regulate corporate conduct generally. Federal law has also superseded law in some areas of internal corporate governance.

I–7.   See part I. D. The number of shareholders is the most obvious difference. However, from an economic standpoint the most important difference is that a market exists for the shares of a publicly held corporation but no market exists for closely held shares, which may be unsalable except to other persons interested in the corporation.

PART II

II–1.   *False.* Most local businesses should incorporate locally rather than in a distant state. Publicly held corporations that do business in every state often incorporate in Delaware.

II–2.   *False.* Under most state statutes incorporation is simple and inexpensive. Over the years most states have attempted to make the process even simpler and less expensive.

II–3.   *True.* The role of incorporator today has no substantive significance.

II–4.   *False.* Articles of incorporation may contain any provisions relating to the corporation's affairs or governance that the draftsman elects to include in the articles. The articles generally may not contradict express provisions of the applicable corporation statute.

II–5.   The most common reason is that articles of incorporation are more difficult to amend than bylaws. A second reason is the belief that important restrictions or limitations should be made a matter of public record.

II–6.   *False.* In the absence of fraud or unfair competition a corporation may use an assumed name as freely as an individual. Compliance with "assumed name" statutes may be required.

II–7.   See part II. F. 2, and 3.

II–8. **Probably never.** Even in a limited venture, perpetual duration creates no problem and may avoid later difficulties.

II–9. **False.** In most states a corporation may be formed for the purpose of "engaging in any lawful business." Such a corporation is not restricted by the articles of incorporation in the businesses in which it may engage. The RMBCA does not require any statement of purpose (unless a purpose narrower than "any lawful business" is desired).

II–10. **False.** While a broad clause minimizes the risk of ultra vires, participants in a corporation may sometimes wish to have their corporation restricted as to its activities. Also regulatory statutes may sometimes require narrower or qualified purposes clauses.

II–11. The purpose of these requirements is to make sure that the corporation has a place where it may be found for service of process, tax notices, and the like.

II–12. **Generally no.** The only exception is if the statutory list of powers in a particular state does not clearly cover some action that the corporation may wish to engage in.

II–13. Beyond the purposes or powers of a corporation.

II–14. The common law of ultra vires was erratic and sometimes led to injustice. The modern view is that a corporation should have essentially the same powers as an individual to engage in profit making conduct, and a person unaware of a restriction on a corporation should not be bound by the restriction.

II–15. The statutes limiting the scope of the doctrine, broad purposes clauses in articles of incorporation, and the broadening of the statutory list of powers of the corporation.

II–16. Adoption of bylaws, sale of stock and election of officers are the most important. Other steps include preparation of minutes, opening of bank account, and so forth.

II–17. The most likely consequence is that participants will be held personally liable for corporate obligations on a piercing the corporate veil theory. However, many cases have not imposed liability in this situation.

II–18. The principal question is whether the two lawyers should form a professional corporation. A professional corporation to practice law (which may be formed under the laws of all jurisdictions) would offer more advantages than those enjoyed by the two lawyers under their present method of operation. The two lawyers might enjoy these corporate advantages: (1) continuity of life; (2) centralization of management; (3) limited liability; and (4) free transferability of interests.

Continuity of life means little in this situation, since the lawyers each have their own clientele, and when one leaves the firm, unless it adds more lawyers, those clients will probably retain other counsel, although the wills drafted by the estates lawyer might provide some basis for continuity.

In the corporate form, managerial responsibility can be conferred on one or the other lawyer, as spelled out in the articles of incorporation or more likely in the bylaws implemented by a shareholder agreement.

So far as limited liability is concerned, depending on the language of the statute, each might be able to achieve limited liability except for any negligent or wrongful act or conduct personally committed or committed by any person under that lawyer's direct supervision and control while rendering professional services on behalf of the corporation. Of course, the corporation would be liable vicariously for the tort of any employee of the corporation acting within the scope of employment.

In some states, a shareholder in a professional corporation may also be liable for malpractice by co-shareholders but not for liabilities, e. g. for rent, that are not related to the practice of a profession.

Free transferability, a normal corporate characteristic, means little in a professional corporation, since transfers of shares may be made only to eligible professional persons. The professional corporation statute itself imposes share transfer restrictions which can be implemented, within the statutory limitations, by first-option or buy-sell provisions.

The extra formalities and expenses in forming and operating as a corporation would be of little significance. The two lawyers themselves can attend to the legal matters involved.

Another advantage of incorporation would be to achieve the federal income tax advantages available to corporate employees, which the two attorneys would become. The major advantage today is the provision of tax-free benefits such as group hospitalization, group life insurance and similar employee benefits also with pre-tax dollars.

A concomitant tax disadvantage would be double taxation. This can be minimized at the corporate level by maximizing corporate deductions in the form of salaries, which would have to be "reasonable." Opportunities for deductions for interest and rents, including the rental of the premises or other property owned by the lawyers are possible but do not seem to be very substantial here. Double taxation could also be minimized at the shareholder level by not distributing dividends to the two lawyer-shareholders. Of course, improper accumulation of earnings should be avoided, but accumulations up to $250,000 are permissible regardless of the reasonable needs of the business.

Family share ownership by nonprofessionals is not possible in a professional corporation. For the same reason, estate planning cannot be facilitated in a professional corporation.

Corporateness will be recognized for federal income tax purposes only if the two lawyers' manner of operations is changed substantially. Corporate formalities, procedures, bookkeeping, and the like, should be observed to insure that the Internal Revenue Service does not reallocate the corporate income to the two lawyers.

Even in a corporation malpractice insurance to protect not only the professional and personal assets of the wrong-doing lawyer but also the firm assets in which both lawyers have an interest would be desirable.

In some jurisdictions, the corporate name would be subject to the limitations on partnership names of law firms and also would have to end with the abbreviation "Professional Corporation" or the abbreviation "P. C."

PART III

III–1. *False.* An incorporator performs the symbolic role of signing articles of incorporation. A promoter is the organizer of a business.

III–2. *Uncertain.* Most such promoters have been held personally liable in the litigated cases but theories exist that would excuse him. See also question III–11.

III–3. *Uncertain.* While many courts might find a novation in these circumstances, many courts have refused to do so, holding both the corporation and the promoter liable on the obligations.

III–4. The de facto cases involve transactions entered into in the name of the corporation before it has formed. Promoters' cases typically involve situations where both parties know, and the contract recites, that no corporation has been formed.

III–5.   *Uncertain.* While earlier versions of the Model Act attempted to do so, most courts continued to apply common law concepts despite the statute. As a result, the Revised Model Business Corporation Act (1984) does not directly address the de facto corporation doctrine; it simply provides that persons who act as or on behalf of a putative corporation "knowing" that articles of incorporation have not been filed are liable on obligations so created.

III–6.   A corporation by estoppel analysis accepts the argument that persons who deal with a "corporation" are estopped from thereafter claiming the individuals are personally liable. The problem with this reasoning is that it completely misapplies the concept of estoppel; the person being estopped is not the one making the representation but the one relying on the representation.

III–7.   *False.* A corporation assumes only the promoters' contracts it elects to assume.

III–8.   *True.* Promoters have fiduciary duties to each other.

III–9.   *Uncertain.* If the corporation represents subsequent investors who were unaware of the transactions, the answer is "true." If the investors knew of the transaction they cannot compel the corporation to sue since they presumably adjusted the purchase price to take into account the known transaction.

III–10.   *Usually False.* While some courts have treated subscriptions as contracts between subscribers, the most common view is that they are mere offers since no corporation is in existence and therefore a bilateral contract cannot exist between the subscriber and the corporation.

III–11.   *Yes.* Whether or not a promoter will be personally liable in acting for a proposed corporation depends on the construction of the contract. The promoter here may (1) take on behalf of the proposed corporation an offer from the other, which being accepted by the corporation after incorporation becomes a contract; (2) enter into a contract initially binding the promoter with the clear understanding that if the corporation is formed it will be substituted and the promoter will be relieved of further responsibility (a "novation"); or (3) bind himself so that both he and the corporation are thereafter liable but seek indemnity from the corporation. Where, as here, the contract calls for some performance before the corporation is organized it is a strong indication that the promoter is intended to be personally liable on the contract. Nothing in the contract authorized D to substitute the corporation as the sole responsible party; therefore D, as well as the corporation, is personally liable on the contract. [See O'Rorke v. Geary, 207 Pa. 240, 56 A. 541 (1903).]

III–12.   *Yes.*   Although a corporation is not liable on a contract made by its promoter for its benefit unless it takes some affirmative act to adopt such contract, it is not necessary that the adoption be express. It may be inferred from the acts of the corporation after incorporation. Here the court can imply that XYZ adopted the contract by reason of the failure to object by shareholders and directors and the actions of the corporation after incorporation. [See McArthur v. Times Printing Co., 48 Minn. 319, 51 N.W.2d 216 (1892).]

PART IV

IV–1.   The PCV cases all deal with correctly and fully formed corporations. The issue is, should the shield of limited liability be ignored under the circumstances despite the complete formation of the corporation?

IV–2.   *False.*   Motive, by itself, is not a ground for PCV.

IV–3.   *False.*   In contract cases, inadequate capital, by itself, is not sufficient reason to PCV. There must be some additional abuse of the corporate form.

IV–4.   *Probably false.*   Most courts will impose *tort* liability on shareholders on PCV theory if the original capital was inadequate in light of expected business needs.

IV–5.   *Probably true.*   Failure to follow corporate formalities and intermingling of corporate assets are classic reasons for PCV. Usually, personal liability is imposed on the shareholder even though no harm resulted from the shareholder's conduct.

IV–6.   *False.*   So long as "hats" are properly labeled, a subsidiary and parent may share the same officers and directors without becoming liable for each other's debts.

IV–7.   *True.*   Relatively small amounts of intermingling of parent and subsidiary affairs will give rise to PCV.

IV–8.   *False.*   The use of corporations to defeat or further governmental policy in this way depends on an analysis of the goals of the governmental policy. Several cases have permitted persons to qualify for social security benefits in this fashion.

IV–9.   *No.* A holding or parent company has a separate corporate existence and is treated separately from the subsidiary in the absence of circumstances justifying disregard of the corporate entity. The participation of A corporation in the affairs of S did not amount to a domination of the day-to-day business decisions of S even though A corporation had the opportunity to exercise control. Consequently, jurisdiction over A corporation cannot be established by reason of its stock ownership of S. [See Quarles v. Fuqua Indus., Inc., 504 F.2d 1358 (10th Cir. 1974).]

IV–10.   *Yes.* This case is a good illustration of an unsuccessful attempt of the use of corporate process to avoid personal responsibility. The corporation never had any equity capital despite the dangerous nature of the business. There was confusion and intermingling of personal and corporate finances. Formalities were not followed. The case involves a tort not a contract. For all these reasons—but principally the lack of capital in a tort case—the court should hold the shareholder personally liable. [See Dixie Coal Mining & Mfg. Co. v. Williams, 221 Ala. 331, 128 So. 799 (1930).]

PART V

V–1.   There are four major sources: the sale of shares, loans from shareholders, loans from third persons, and internally generated funds from operations.

V–2.   Little. Par value today provides a floor on the price of shares. Whether or not this is an advantage is questionable. It also establishes the amount to be allocated to stated capital and capital surplus when a corporation is originally capitalized. With the virtually universal use of nominal par values, it is probably fair to say that par value serves little practical purpose today. Indeed, it may be misleading since it appears to protect creditors against distributions to shareholders but in fact provides little or no protection to creditors. See Question V–12.

V–3.   No par shares do not solve all problems because they are tied in with the concept of par value. The artificial problems created by par value therefore also appear in a corporation that uses no par shares.

V–4.   *False.* While watered stock liability may easily be avoided by proper planning, the issuance of shares with high par values today may well give rise to classic watered stock liability.

V–5.   The RMBCA abolishes par value except as a voluntary planning device as a matter of contract. It is contemplated that relatively few corporations will voluntarily elect a par value. Assignment of par value to shares also may be important where statutes compute taxes on the basis of par values.

V–6. Preferred stock has preferences either in connection with the payment of dividends or in distributions on liquidation. Preferred stock usually is nonparticipating, that is, it is entitled to a fixed distribution and no more.

V–7. A bond is a secured long term debt instrument while a debenture is an unsecured long term debt instrument. The word "bond" is often used as a generic term to describe both bonds and debentures.

V–8. *False.* In periods of inflation, debt financing becomes even more attractive since money borrowed will be repaid in the future using inflated dollars. Of course, as inflation continues, interest rates tend to rise to offset this phenomenon.

V–9. *False.* The Federal Securities Act exemption for private offerings is not controlled by the number of offers. Thus an offer to a relatively small number of offerees who need the protection of the Act may require registration under the Securities Act of 1933. In contrast, most state security statutes (blue sky laws) contain numerical exemptions for offers to a small number of persons but even these exemptions are usually lost if there is a public offer or a public advertisement.

V–10. Preemptive rights are the rights of existing shareholders to purchase their proportionate share of new issues of securities by the corporation.

V–11. *False.* Even in the absence of preemptive rights, there is a broad fiduciary duty applicable to directors that prohibit the issuance of shares at prices that unreasonably dilute the interests of outstanding shareholders or of shares at reasonable prices if issued for improper purposes, such as to influence control of the corporation.

V–12. When a corporation repurchases its own shares, it distributes assets equal to the purchase price to the shareholder from whom the shares are being purchased. However, the shares of a corporation are not an asset of the corporation in any real sense. One cannot own shares of oneself. Shares of a corporation that were formerly outstanding are no more an asset of a corporation than are authorized but unissued shares.

This can be seen graphically by the accounting treatment for repurchased shares: the purchase price of the shares while an offsetting reduction is made in the "equity" portion of the right hand side of the balance sheet.

V–13.   *True.* It is generally recognized that modern corporation statutes are so liberal that capital may be freely distributed to its shareholders under the statutes. If a creditor wishes to assure a minimum capital is preserved so that its loan will be repaid, it must impose that restriction by agreement. See Question V–2.

V–14.   *False.* A share distribution is purely a paper transaction that does not reduce the real assets available to the corporation or increase the proportionate interest of any shareholder. In contrast, a cash dividend reduces the funds available to the corporation. If a shareholder receives a share dividend and sells the dividend (in order to obtain the cash) that shareholder's proportionate interest in the corporation is being reduced by a small fraction.

V–15.   The legality of the dividend last year out of current profits of that year even though there was an accumulated deficit in earned surplus depends on whether or not the state of incorporation has a "nimble dividend" statute. A "nimble" dividend is one paid out of current earnings before those earnings are applied against the deficit in earned surplus from other years. If the state does have such a statute, the dividend was lawful because Commerce was not insolvent at the time of the dividend.

           If the state of incorporation does not have a "nimble dividend" statute the dividend was unlawful unless the current earnings were large enough both to wipe out the earlier deficit in earned surplus and to cover the dividend.

           If the dividend is unlawful, the directors are jointly and severally liable to the corporation for the benefit of its creditors or shareholders. Directors who fail to dissent from the action are also liable. The directors are entitled to contribution from other directors who concurred in the action. Moreover, shareholders who received the dividend with knowledge that it was unlawful are also liable for their pro rata share of the dividend.

           In some states, Commerce, Inc. might be able to treat the distribution as a distribution of capital rather than a dividend.

           If Commerce, Inc. were incorporated in a state that has adopted the RMBCA, the distribution would be lawful if the dividend was made at the time when Commerce was solvent in both an equity and a balance sheet sense. The Revised Act completely eliminates the concept of earned surplus and, as a result, of nimble dividends as well.

V–16.   *Yes.* The stock was par-value stock and the property which was transferred to the corporation as consideration for the stock was worth only $100,000 and cannot constitute full payment for the shares issued with a par value of $250,000. Thus, the shareholder remains liable at the suit of a creditor or his representative. Two theories on which to base B's continued liability are (1) if there is no statute, expressly making B liable to pay at least the par value for newly issued shares, then B impliedly agreed to pay the par value of the shares upon their being issued to her; and (2) if there is a statute imposing such liability on B, then the provisions of the statute make B liable. This debt is a corporate asset which can be enforced by a creditor of the corporation.

If the valuation of $250,000 is made non-fraudulently B has a possible argument, under many state statutes, that that valuation is conclusive and cannot be attacked by R.

V–17.   *Yes.* The shareholders may not use corporate assets to repurchase their shares and thus repay themselves their investment if to do so would leave the corporation without sufficient funds to pay its creditors. If, however, a corporation has sufficient assets to pay its creditors in full and also pay the purchase price of the stock it may enter into an agreement to purchase the shares. Instead of paying cash therefor, the corporation should be able to issue notes for all or part of the purchase price, in which case the stockholder becomes a creditor of the corporation rather than a shareholder. In any subsequent insolvency proceeding the former shareholder is entitled to share equally with other creditors. Here, the purchase of shares was effected at a time when the corporation was solvent and subsequent insolvency does not affect the validity of the transaction.

[Several early cases agree with this rationale but several others did not and subordinated the claim of P in the above situation. Section 6.40 of the Revised Model Business Corporation Act accepts the rationale set forth above and permits P to share in the assets on a parity with other creditors.]

V–18.   *Yes.* Whether or not to declare a dividend is usually within the sound discretion and business judgment of the board of directors. With the exercise of such discretion the courts will not interfere, *except* when there is a clear case of abuse of discretion, bad faith or dishonesty. There is an implied obligation on the part of the board of directors and managers of the corporation to exercise good faith and reasonable business judgment in distributing profits to the shareholders. Of course, sound discretion dictates that there shall be kept in reserve enough money with which to carry on the corporate business, make replacements of worn out machinery, pay taxes, pay insurance, and provide for unforeseen losses and expenses. But here there is a surplus built up over a period of 10 years which is four times the capital, a continued annual profit, a continuing prosperity, and not a single dividend in the entire 10 year period. With $2,000,000 cash on hand and the corporation in such condition as these facts disclose, there is a clear abuse of discretion on the part of the board in not declaring a dividend. [*Dodge v. Ford Motor Co.*, 204 Mich. 459, 170 N.W. 668 (1919); *Gottfried v. Gottfried*, 73 N.Y.S.2d 692 (Sup.Ct.1947).]

PART VI

VI–1. These phrases refer to the statutory requirements that there be a board of directors and officers, that they be selected in a certain way, that they be invested with specific authority, and so forth. The statutory scheme is most realistic in corporations of a middle size and complexity.

VI–2. *False.* While the requirements of directors and officers make little sense when applied to such a closely held corporation, it is important to recognize that in the absence of statutory authorization, two shareholders who run a business as a partnership may well end up personally liable for the corporation's obligations. Also, control agreements that violate the statutory scheme may be unenforceable.

VI–3. The traditional view is that C should lose on the theory that a corporation must have a board of directors and that neither the incorporators nor the shareholders of a corporation may render such board completely impotent, sterile or helpless, a board devoid of power. The quoted provision in the articles of incorporation arguably does just that. It provides that the board of directors shall have no power to bind the corporation without the unanimous consent of the shareholders. This arguably renders the board wholly impotent and without any power to act if a unanimous vote of the shareholders cannot be obtained. Therefore, the provision providing that the board of directors of X corporation has no power to act without the unanimous consent of the shareholders, may be wholly void, and the board of directors of X corporation can act as though it did not exist.

More modern courts might recognize such a provision on the ground that the requirement was accepted unanimously and does not hurt anyone. *Galler v. Galler.* Also, several states have adopted close corporation statutes that would permit this kind of arrangement; as a result the chances of enforcing this agreement are significantly higher than they were twenty or more years ago. [See *Zion v. Kurtz.*]

PART VII

VII–1.   Under most statutes, a quorum must consist of a majority of the outstanding shares while a majority of the shares present at a meeting at which a quorum is present is necessary to adopt a resolution. As a result, in the absence of specific provision by the corporation, one half of one half, or approximately one quarter, of the outstanding shares, may adopt an ordinary resolution at a shareholder's meeting. The Revised Model Business Act changes the rule as to approval of actions by requiring that the affirmative votes exceed the negative votes. This is designed to treat abstentions as neutral.

VII–2.   The common law view was one vote per share but most state statutes today authorize a corporation to create a class of shares with multiple or fractional votes per share. Virtually all states also permit nonvoting common shares. However, the statutes of a specific state must be consulted before such a question can be answered definitively.

VII–3.   Record ownership refers to the status of the ownership of shares as shown on the books and records of the corporation. Beneficial ownership refers to the person who actually owns the shares. That person may or may not be the record owner. The corporation generally treats the record owner as the sole owner of shares without any consideration of who the beneficial owner may be. A beneficial owner should have the shares transferred to his or her name as record owner if unhappy about the powers of the record owner.

VII–4.   The corporation must set record dates for these actions in order to establish clearly, as between transferor and transferee of shares, who is entitled to vote or who is entitled to the dividend.

VII–5.   *True.* The effect of cumulative voting is to permit a large minority bloc of shares to obtain representation on the board. The size of the minimum bloc necessary to obtain representation may be determined mathematically from a relatively simple formula.

VII–6.   *Sometimes true.* However, such voting is more commonly known as straight voting.

VII–7.   Since proxies are revocable, the latest one revokes earlier ones. In this situation, A's shares will be voted for the insurgents.

VII–8.   *False.* A proxy appointment is irrevocable only if it is "coupled with an interest" in the underlying shares or in the corporation.

VII–9.   A pooling agreement is a simple contract between shareholders to vote shares in a certain way while a voting trust involves a transfer of the shares to trustees so that the trustees have the legal right to vote.

VII–10.   In a closely held corporation share transfer restrictions may: (1) assure each shareholder that he will have a voice in who else participates in the corporation, (2) provide a way for shareholders desiring to withdraw to liquidate their interests in the corporation in a systematic fashion, and (3) establish the value of the shares for estate tax purposes. While these advantages may not be assured in every case, they are the typical reasons for share transfer restrictions in closely held corporations.

VII–11.   *Yes.* Share transfer restrictions are most commonly used in publicly held corporations to preserve the availability of securities act exemptions that are dependent on the shares not being reoffered or resold publicly.

VII–12.   At issue are the validity of the removal of directors and of the merger.

The notice of the special meeting specified only consideration of a proposed merger. Therefore, the removal of the directors should not have been considered because specific reference to proposed removals of directors must appear in the notice of meeting. RMBCA § 8.08(d) provides that only matters related to those specified in the notice of meeting ordinarily may be entertained at a special meeting.

Under § 8.08 of the Revised Model Business Corporation Act, a director may be removed with or without cause by a vote of the holders of a majority of the shares then entitled to vote at an election of directors at a meeting called expressly for that purpose. When Gative and Servative were elected, their tenure as directors was subject to the statutory power of removal. However, because the meeting was not expressly called for removing directors, the purported removal is invalid and the two directors should be reinstated.

The effect of this invalid action on the status of the merger is not so easily resolvable. The substituted directors, Berl and Stamp, exercised their functions under at least color of office and arguably can be considered de facto directors, whose actions as directors are not subject to collateral attack. The action of the board during their tenure may thus be binding on the corporation. Also, an agreement of merger has been entered into with a presumably innocent party who has no notice of the infirmity of the action taken by the directors. It is likely that the merger could not be set aside.

The corporation may also argue that there was no causal relationship between the merger and the defective removal of directors if the votes of Berl and Stamp were not necessary for approval of the merger. This argument increases the likelihood that the merger could not be set aside.

VII–13.   *Yes.* As to proposal 1, even though the shareholders do not have power to effect a change in the officers of a corporation such power being reserved to the board of directors, they may express their opinion to the board of directors on the matter. As to proposal 2, shareholders have the inherent power to remove directors for cause. See *Auer v. Dressel,* 306 N.Y. 427, 118 N.E.2d 590 (1954).

PART VIII

VIII–1.   *False.* Unlike shareholders, directors may not vote by proxy. The reason for this rule is tied up in the common law view that directors may only act at a meeting.

VIII–2.   *False.* There are many statements in early cases to this effect. However, a number of cases recognized informal ratification or estoppel as binding the board without a formal meeting. Statutes today also authorize directors to act by unanimous written consent without a meeting.

PART IX

IX–1.   *No.* This lay view of the president does not reflect the legal relationship. In a corporation the directors, not the president, have the principal power of decision-making. Of course, a president need not own any specific number of shares, and many corporate presidents do not have significant share holdings. However, many corporate presidents in fact exercise a great deal of power, either by virtue of their office, as a member of the board of directors, or as a shareholder.

IX–2.   *False.* The period of the officer's employment contract and the term of the office are independent. If a board grants an officer a contract for a period longer than the term of the office and a subsequent board refuses to elect the officer to that office, the corporation has breached the employment contract.

IX–3.   *No.* Although in general there is a presumption that the president of a corporation has authority to institute litigation and engage counsel, absent a provision in the bylaws to the contrary, any actual or implied authority which M had to do so was terminated when a majority of the board of directors refused to sanction it. The fact that the directors were deadlocked or that the directors who voted against the suit were interested in the transaction does not affect the result. Other remedies exist to solve a deadlock—involuntary dissolution, receivership, or appointment of provisional directors, or a derivative suit by a shareholder of P corporation against P corporation's directors.

IX–4.   *No.* The president of a corporation is an agent for the corporation. In any given situation whether the president acted within the scope of that agency is a question of fact for the jury. The president's authority may be derived from: (a) certain powers implied by virtue of the office which allow the president to perform the acts necessary for the convenient management of the day-to-day business of the corporation, (b) express grants of power found in statutes, the corporate charter and bylaws and resolutions of the board of directors, and (c) powers which arise by reason of a course of conduct of both the president and the corporation showing that the president had acted on similar matters in the past, and that the corporation had acquiesced in, approved and ratified such former actions. The charge to the jury that was held to be appropriate was: "If you find from the evidence that the president . . . was not acting within the usual scope of his office and that he had not in the past acted alone in the signing of contracts and that the defendant company had never recognized any acts of the president alone or had not held him out as qualified to transact singly and alone all business dealings for the company, then your verdict must be for the defendant, for I say to you it is only upon these principles, upon the proven facts of the case that the act of the president could bind the corporation. If, however, you find . . . that the president was acting within the usual scope of his employment or that he had on prior occasions entered into contracts and bound the corporation which recognized and approved such acts and held him out as authorized to deal with the company's affairs, then your verdict may be for the plaintiff . . . ." See *Joseph Greenspon's Sons Iron and Steel Co. v. Pecos Valley Gas Co.*, 34 Del. 567, 156 A. 350 (1931). [To avoid questions of this nature it is customary to require the President to supply a certified copy of an express resolution of the board of directors authorizing the execution of the transaction.]

PART X

X–1.   *Partially true.* While not true as a matter of common law, as a result of decisions in the last ten or fifteen years, substantial fiduciary duties have been imposed on shareholders of closely held corporations. While these duties are often imposed on majority shareholders who are also directors of the corporation, several decisions recognize that shareholders in a corporation have somewhat the same relationship to each other that partners have in a partnership.

X–2.   *False.* A deadlock situation may be created by high quorum or high voting requirements as well as by an even division of voting power.

X–3.   While dissolution is the traditional remedy for the deadlocked corporation, other possible solutions exist. By advance planning a buy-sell arrangement or arbitration may avoid a deadlock. Many state close corporation statutes also provide for provisional directors, custodians, or temporary receiverships designed to attempt to solve deadlock problems. Several state statutes also provide for a buyout at an appraised price rather than involuntary dissolution.

X–4.   *False.* The evidence to date indicates that these statutes have not been widely used. It is probable, however, that a properly drafted statute would be a useful planning device in closely held corporations and therefore that widespread enactment of such statutes would be desirable.

PART XI

XI–1.   The "Wall Street Option" is a slang phrase to describe the option of a dissatisfied shareholder to sell his or her shares on the open market. This option is available in the publicly held corporation but of course is not generally available in closely held corporations.

XI–2.   A question such as this should be answered carefully since it can be answered at different levels. Formally, the shareholders select the directors. However, in most publicly held corporations, the shareholders in fact ratify the decision made earlier as to who should be on the management slate of directors. In a real sense, the persons who put together the management slate determine who the directors of a publicly held corporation are to be. And this usually means the incumbent management.

XI–3.   *False.* All recent studies indicate that the professional management, not the board of directors, establishes the broad business policies of the corporation. The role of directors is more one of oversight than of direction.

XI–4.   *Generally false.* While the board of directors ratifies the selection of the chief executive officer, and in some situations may actually make or actively participate in his selection, the more normal pattern is for the outgoing chief executive officer to have the predominant voice in selecting a successor. Answers to broad questions like this must be qualified by the possibility that a substantial block of shares owned by a single person may affect the locus of power within the corporation.

XI–5.   "Street name" refers to the registration of securities in the name of brokerage firms with offices on Wall Street in New York City. Such certificates are endorsed in blank and transferred merely by delivery. Such "street name certificates" are the normal method by which the routine transfer of shares sold on the securities exchanges is effected. Most street name certificates are transferred between brokerage firms. At any one time, a fairly large percentage (20 per cent or more) of a publicly traded corporation's outstanding securities may be held in street name.

XI–6.   Institutional investors include investment companies, mutual funds, pension funds, insurance companies, and bank trust accounts.

XI–7.   Institutional investors traditionally support management on the theory that they simply are acting as investors. In a few instances, however, institutional investors have supported insurgent bids. There has also been increasing institutional investor opposition to certain "shark repellant" provisions proposed by management.

PART XII

XII–1.   *False.* For a variety of reasons, including history, the law of proxy regulation in publicly held corporations arises under section 14 of the Securities Exchange Act of 1934, and, most importantly, the SEC regulations issued thereunder.

XII–2.   Corporations (1) with a class of security that is traded on a national securities exchange, and (2) with $3,000,000 (proposed to be increased to $5,000,000) of assets and a class of shares owned by more than 500 shareholders of record, are subject to the federal proxy regulation. These are the requirements for registration under section 12 of the 1934 Act and SEC regulations.

XII–3.   The constitutional bases of federal proxy regulation is the power over interstate commerce and the mails. Proxy regulation has been in effect since 1934 and its constitutional validity is beyond question.

XII–4.   The SEC proxy regulations require both proxy statements and annual reports to be distributed to shareholders by all registered companies even though they do not actually solicit proxies. In the absence of federal requirements, most states do not require the transmission of any information to shareholders.

XII–5. *Yes.* Rule 14a–9 forbids false and misleading statements in proxy statements. The early case of *J. I. Case v. Borak* held that a private cause of action is created for violations of this rule. Even though private causes of action have been largely restricted by the United States Supreme Court in recent years, it appears unlikely that *J. I. Case v. Borak* will be overruled.

XII–6. The requirement of materiality was emphasized by the United States Supreme Court in *TSC Industries v. Northway*, which defined "materiality" as a fact that *would* influence an investor in making a decision.

XII–7. *Yes.* Under *Mills v. Electric Auto-Lite Co.*

XII–8. *No.* The SEC proxy regulations require certain shareholder proposals to be included in proxy solicitation statements even though the corporation is opposed to them.

XII–9. This regulation is viewed as a method of calling management's attention to shareholder concerns. Many corporate officers have stated that they pay considerable attention to shareholder proposals that receive a vote of five or ten per cent of the outstanding shares, even though management has the power as a practical matter to cause all such proposals to be defeated. Recent academic commentary has sought to cast doubt on this justification.

XII–10. The SEC proxy rules do not apply to the solicitation of Hideaway's shareholders since it has no securities registered under the 1934 Act. However, if the proxies are materially misleading, causes of action exist not only under state law but also under rule 10b–5. The questions therefore presented are the lawfulness and fairness of the merger under state law and SEC rule 10b–5; the claims against Expansion or the surviving corporation and against the former controlling shareholders and former management of Hideaway. Also, a question is raised about Case's standing to attack the transaction since he is a dissenting shareholder of the merged corporation pursuing his appraisal remedy.

Federal courts have exclusive jurisdiction over rule 10b–5 actions and can award full relief as to state law claims and corporate matters such as the unwinding of the merger. If the merger had not been consummated, the federal court could have issued an injunction restraining the merger pending a determination of Case's allegations.

The proxy statements seem to be clearly misleading in their failure to disclose the financial history of Expansion. This omission would appear to satisfy the conventional "deception" standard of "fraud" required by rule 10b–5 and the requirement of scienter of *Hochfelder*. (See part XV).

There would also appear to be a substantial prospect of attack under state law. See part XIX. Recent decisions of state courts, particularly in Delaware, have adopted the rule of "entire fairness" for merger transactions. The nondisclosure by Hideaway's management of the commitments it received might well be sufficient to invalidate a merger whose terms are unfair under state law.

While it is possible to unwind a merger, practical difficulties develop if any substantial period has elapsed since the transaction, primarily because of the existence of subsequent innocent shareholders of the surviving corporation. Thus, damages are a plausible remedy in these circumstances. The measure of damages might be difficult to determine here. The defendants would contend that the Hideaway shareholders received Expansion shares of equivalent value. Case would apparently argue against such valuation and that an independent appraisal would be necessary to determine the true value of the Expansion shares. If it can be demonstrated that the true value was below that represented in the merger discussions and proxy solicitations, then a basis for recovery could be established.

Case may bring an individual action to recover his damages or a class action seeking to recover the damages suffered by himself and those similarly situated, at least to the extent of any profits realized by Expansion and others who breached their duties to minority shareholders. Presumably the profits of the Expansion shareholders at the time of the merger are equivalent to the damages of the Hideaway shareholders but not all of the former were involved in the wrongdoing and a large proportion of the latter were wrongdoers—suggesting that any recovery of profits should be limited pro tanto to the damages suffered by innocent Hideaway shareholders.

Case may face a further defense directed to his standing to sue. Case is presently pursuing a statutory right of dissent and appraisal. See part XIX. This is a remedy available to shareholders dissenting from extraordinary corporate changes and basically involves a proceeding to enable the dissenters to receive the fair value of their shares as if the change had not occurred. Some state appraisal statutes provide an exclusive remedy, precluding attack on the merger on the grounds of unfairness. Other states, either expressly or by court construction, permit a minority shareholder to sue in equity despite the availability of the legal appraisal remedy. RMBCA § 13.02(b) makes the statutory remedy exclusive "unless the action is unlawful or fraudulent." The fact that Case has dissented and is pursuing an appraisal remedy raises unresolved questions under state law as to standing to sue. Arguably in the federal courts at least with respect to federal question issues Case's standing to sue under rule 10b–5 would not be precluded by the vagaries of the appraisal provision of the corporate statute of the state of incorporation of Hideaway, since the enforcement of federal law should be uniform throughout the United States.

Of course, to the extent that Case receives an award in the appraisal proceeding his claim in any action he brings should at least be reduced pro tanto.

PART XIII

XIII–1.   In a successful proxy fight it is likely that the corporation will end up paying both the management's unsuccessful defense costs plus the insurgent's costs. This is a result of the general view that the corporation may be asked legitimately to pay proxy contest expenses in policy disputes.

XIII–2.   The argument basically is that proxy fights are a device for eliminating inefficient management and that making proxy fights easier will tend to keep management on its toes. The difficulty is that an unlimited right to reimbursement from the corporation would encourage proxy struggles in which there was little chance of success. Such fights could carry a high cost to the corporation.

XIII–3.   Proxy contests are largely regulated by SEC regulations. These regulations impose a truth in campaigning requirement. There is virtually no state law of proxy contests.

XIII–4.   A tender offer (or "cash tender offer," as it is often called) is a public offer by an aggressor to purchase shares of the target corporation. Often the offer is for 50+%, but it may be for more or less, depending on the circumstances, including the aggressor's current holdings of the target's securities. In recent years most struggles for control have been in the form of cash tender offer or merger proposal rather than by proxy fight. They are partially regulated by the Williams Act, though aspects of them are also regulated by state law, particularly the validity of defensive tactics.

XIII–5.   The Williams Act is a federal statute enacted in 1970 to regulate cash tender offers. Technically, the Williams Act is an amendment to the

Securities Exchange Act of 1934. The Williams Act is essentially neutral legislation, establishing ground rules and disclosure requirements for cash tender offers but not designed to make such attempts easier or more difficult.

XIII–6.   State statutes relating to tender offers were enacted to make successful tender offers more difficult. Unlike the Williams Act, they were largely designed to protect local, incumbent management. The Supreme Court decision in *Edgar v. Mite Corporation* invalidated most such legislation in 1982; since then several states have adopted new regulatory techniques based on the power of the state to regulate the internal affairs of domestic corporations. The validity of these "post-Mite" statutes is an open question.

XIII–7.   Arbitragers are speculators or investors who take offsetting positions in a single security selling at price differentials. In connection with cash tender offers, an arbitrager may purchase the shares of the target corporation at any price up to the cash tender offer price and submit their shares for tender to take advantage of the price differential. They may also sell short or on a "when issued" basis the aggressor's securities. In most takeovers, a very large percentage of the shares traded in the securities market after the announcement of a takeover attempt are purchased or sold by arbitragers.

XIII–8.   "Porcupine provisions" is a slang term for defensive provisions in articles of incorporation adopted by potential target corporations to make takeovers more difficult. A typical porcupine provision requires a greater than majority vote for approval of mergers or other transactions that are opposed by the target's board of directors.

XIII–9.   A poison pill is a new class or series of shares that increases in value or rights when an aggressor obtains a specified percentage of shares. A number of varieties of poison pills have been developed.

XIII–10.   *False.* In a series of decisions in the mid-1980s the Supreme Court of Delaware has created a set of rules as to when the business judgment rule may be relied upon by incumbent management in fighting an unwanted takeover. There is a clear logic to these cases: a board of directors may adopt a "poison pill" in advance of a takeover contest (at least if the pill does not foreclose all possible takeover attempts); when faced with a takeover contest, management may adopt strenuous defensive tactics if it believes the offer is coercive or unfair. On the other hand, if the decision has been made to sell the company, the role of the board of directors changes and it is obligated to obtain the best price it can for its shareholders; it may not continue to use defensive tactics to favor one bidder over another.

XIII–11.   *Yes.* There are equitable limitations to provisions governing the operation of a corporation. Here the management of X attempted to use the law to perpetuate itself in office and to obstruct the legitimate efforts of shareholders in their attempt to obtain new management. "Inequitable action does not become permissible simply because it is legally possible." [*Schnell v. Chris-Craft Indus., Inc.*, 285 A.2d 437 (Del. 1971).]

PART XIV

XIV–1.   The "duty of care" requires directors to exercise a minimum degree of skill and attention toward corporate affairs. While liability has been imposed for failure to meet this duty in only a few cases, it is nevertheless one of the fundamental duties owed by directors to corporations. Breaches of this duty may be argued in cases involving knowing authorization of wrongful acts by directors or to a lesser extent in cases of a failure to pay any attention to corporate affairs. Directors who are elderly or infirm must meet a minimum standard of care applicable to everyone. However, a director with specialized knowledge, e. g., an attorney, must use due care in light of that specialized knowledge.

XIV–2.   The "business judgment rule" is a common law doctrine related to the duty of care that immunizes directors from liability for costly decisions if they use good faith judgment in making the decision. As a result, a decision made in good faith that turns out unfavorably to the corporation may not be used as a basis for a claim against the directors making the decision. The business judgment rule has been applied in recent years to authorize the dismissal of derivative suits brought against a corporation by disinterested directors deciding that it would not be in the best interests of the corporation to pursue the litigation. This aspect of the business judgment rule was the subject of the decisions of the Supreme Court of Delaware in *Zapata v. Maldonado, Inc.* and *Aronson v. Lewis*. The "business judgment doctrine" makes the business decision itself (as contrasted with the liability of the directors) immune from judicial review.

XIV–3.   Such a transaction is known as "self-dealing." The common law test for the validity of a self-dealing transaction is whether the transaction is fair and whether the director's interest has been fully disclosed. The burden of establishing fairness may be placed on the director, who should not participate in the corporate decision whether or not to enter into the transaction.

XIV–4.   Such a transaction is an indirect self-dealing transaction and is also judged by a standard of fairness.

XIV–5.   The general view is that shareholders may not ratify a transaction which is fraudulent, oppressive, or overreaching. It is possible that a nonfraudulent transaction that is not valid under the fairness test, may be validated if it is approved by the disinterested vote of the shareholders. At the very least, such a vote will shift the burden of proof to those seeking to avoid the transaction. California may give more far-reaching effect to shareholder ratification.

XIV–6.   The test for executive compensation is that such compensation is valid unless it is so large as to constitute spoliation or waste. Such compensation is not generally viewed by the same standards as self-dealing transactions. As a practical matter, most corporations arrange to have compensation arrangements approved by outside, nonmanagement directors, and information about executive compensation levels is widely available, thereby providing a yardstick.

XIV–7.   Such arrangements which often take the form of stock options or stock appreciation rights are valid. The corporation, of course, must receive consideration for this additional compensation but a plan announced in advance should meet this requirement.

XIV–8.   "Corporate opportunity" is a fiduciary duty that directors and officers owe to the corporation to give the corporation profitable business opportunities to which the corporation has a reasonable claim.

XIV–9.   No single test has been generally accepted. The more traditional view is that an opportunity is a corporate opportunity only if it is something in which the corporation has an "interest or expectancy." Modern formulations of the corporate opportunity doctrine emphasize the fairness or unfairness of allowing an officer or director to take advantage of the opportunity and the degree to which the opportunity arises out of the corporation's business.

XIV–10.   *Yes.* If the corporation, for example, decides not to take advantage of the opportunity after full consideration, the director may do so. The burden, however, is in the director to establish the underlying premise.

XIV–11.   Either standard may be applied depending on the nature of the transaction. If the transaction involves a contract or other arrangement between the parent and the subsidiary, the fairness test will be applied. If the parent's action does not discriminate against the minority shareholders in the subsidiary, the business judgment rule will generally be applicable. For example, a dividend paid by the subsidiary to all shareholders will be judged by the business judgment rule not the fairness standard.

XIV–12. The transaction is a self dealing transaction since Corporation A is receiving something not received by all shareholders of Corporation B. Since the transaction is also not intrinsically fair, it is voidable upon the suit of the minority shareholders.

XIV–13. This is a freeze-out merger, and must meet the requirements of *Weinberger:* full disclosure and intrinsic fairness. In some states, a business purpose requirement may also be imposed. Assuming there was full disclosure, the requirements of *Weinberger* appear to be met; the need to raise additional capital by Corporation A may also be a valid business purpose in states with that requirement. Approval by a majority of the minority is also evidence of the fairness of the transaction. Thus, assuming that there was full disclosure the transaction is valid. Dissatisfied shareholders nevertheless have the right of statutory dissent and appraisal (Chapter 13 of the RMBCA).

XIV–14. The directors can: (1) propose dissolution, subject to shareholder approval; or (2) first redeem the preferred shares, without the necessity of shareholder approval, in which case the preferred shareholders prior to the redemption date could convert each of their preferred shares into common shares. The corporation may then dissolve.

Since there are 1,000 outstanding shares of each class and all shares have equal voting rights, the directors are elected by the combined votes of the two classes. The facts do not indicate the respective shareholdings of the several directors.

The directors are under fiduciary duties, not only to do what is in the best interests of the corporation, but to be fair to the shareholders of both classes. The transaction should carry the earmarks of an arm's length bargain especially if the directors have any conflicting interests because of their ownership of shares of one or the other of the classes or their representing or being under the domination of the holders of a particular class. This means that they should do what a disinterested board of directors would do in exercising their independent judgment under like circumstances. Normally this would permit the redemption of the preferred before the dissolution of the corporation with full disclosure of the surplus.

There are two alternatives.

If the corporation were dissolved without redemption of the preferred, the preferred shareholders would receive their liquidation preferences of

$200 per share or a total of $200,000 ($200 × 1,000 shares), leaving $10 for each common share ($10,000 ÷ 1,000 shares). Voluntary or nonjudicial dissolution generally would require approval by the holders of a majority or more of all the outstanding shares, depending on the applicable corporate statutory requirements.

If the preferred shares were redeemed (which would require only board of directors action), the preferred shareholders would receive the redemption price of $105 per share or a total of $105,000; there would then be available $105 for each common share ($105,000 ÷ 1,000 shares). However, each preferred share is convertible into two common shares, which conversion privilege ordinarily would terminate on the redemption notice sent to the preferred shareholders of the intended dissolution. The economics should cause the preferred shareholders to convert since, upon conversion, each would have two new common shares for each converted preferred share. If all convert, the former preferred shareholders would hold 2,000 or two-thirds of the then 3,000 outstanding common shares, and each former preferred shareholder would receive $70 for each new common share or $140 for each old preferred share or a total of $140,000 ($210,000 ÷ ²/₃). Each old common shareholder would also receive $70 for each of his shares or a total of $70,000 ($70 × 1,000 shares).

This problem is patterned after Zahn v. Transamerica Corp., 235 F.2d 369 (3d Cir. 1956).

XIV–15.   *No.* Directors of a corporation are not generally liable for losses suffered by the corporation by reason of its employees' violations of law. In managing the corporate affairs a director is required to use the amount of care which ordinary careful and prudent men would use in similar circumstances. Whether or not they have failed to exercise proper care depends upon the circumstances. Here the directors had no duty to put into effect a system of supervision until such time as something occurs to put them on notice that something is wrong. Until that time they are entitled to rely on the honesty and integrity of their employees. The size of the enterprise and its wide geographical distribution made it necessary that directors confine their oversight to broad policy matters, which they did, relying on reports, summaries and records which they were entitled to do. [*Graham v. Allis-Chalmers Mfg. Co.*, 41 Del.Ch. 78, 188 A.2d 125 (Sup.Ct.1963).]

XIV–16.   *No.* The contract should be cancelled. This contract was made between two corporations having an interlocking directorship, the directors, A, B and C, being common to the boards of both companies. In such case the two corporations may contract with each other and the contracts made are valid and enforceable if the contract is fair to both

companies. If it is not fair to one corporation that one may avoid it.
It is immaterial whether the common directors vote or refrain from
voting on the approval of the contract. The fact that this contract
provided that X corporation should pay M 10% more for smelting ore
than was the usual and customary price for such service, and the
additional fact that the contract was to continue for 10 years without
providing for any change in the price when the price of metals dropped
made the contract unfair to X corporation and therefore gave it a right
to cancel the contract. [*Globe Woolen Co. v. Utica Gas & Elec. Co.*,
224 N.Y. 483, 121 N.E. 378 (1918).]

XIV–17.   Possibly, if D can persuasively establish that X in fact totally lacked
the ability to finance the purchase. The opportunity was a corporate
opportunity. D, as the majority stockholder in X corporation and
person in complete control of the board of directors of X corporation,
occupied a fiduciary relationship to X corporation and owed to it a duty
of good faith and loyalty in the exercise of such power, exactly as
though he had been a director of X corporation. Hence, when D
learned of the value of B's properties and that it could be purchased
and that it would be advantageous to X corporation to own it, D had a
duty to give X corporation the first opportunity to buy that property
for its own purposes. D violated his fiduciary duty in not letting X
know of that opportunity. However, assume that such duty had been
performed by D. The performance would have been a futile gesture
for the reason that X was wholly incapable financially to take
advantage of the opportunity. D's duty to X did not require him to
lend money to X so that X could buy the property of B. And, D did
not have to sit by and let the opportunity pass because X could not
realize upon it. He could buy for himself as he did and for his own
personal benefit. [See *Zeckendorf v. Steinfeld*, 12 Ariz. 245, 100 P. 784
(1909).] Not all modern cases agree with this analysis; the ALI
Corporate Governance Project also would not accept a defense of
financial inability under these circumstances.

NOTE—In this case, the majority stockholder had a fiduciary duty by
virtue of his control of the board of directors. In the more typical
cases problems of corporate opportunity arise with respect to corporate
officers and directors.

PART XV

XV–1.   "Insider trading" refers to transactions by a corporate director or
officer in the shares of the corporation on the basis of information that
is not publicly available. Insider trading may also refer to trading by

other persons on the basis of nonpublic information. Insider trading is entirely a phenomenon of publicly held corporations.

XV–2.   ***Both.*** The early principles were based on state law notions of fraud or deception, and later expanded to a "special facts" doctrine that required disclosure of special facts. Most modern principles of insider trading are based on rule 10b–5 promulgated under the Securities Exchange Act of 1934.

XV–3.   Such an argument has been accepted by the New York Court of Appeals in *Diamond v. Oreamuno.* This view, however, has not been adopted by any other court. In *Chiarella* and *Dirks*, the United States Supreme Court required that the use of the information constitutes a breach of duty.

XV–4.   ***No.*** Rule 10b–5 applies to transactions in "any security" involving the use of any facility of interstate commerce. Thus it is applicable to closely held corporations as well as publicly held corporations.

XV–5.   ***False.*** If a single telephone call or use of the mails is made in connection with this fraudulent sale, the defrauded shareholder may sue under rule 10b–5 in Federal court.

XV–6.   Rule 10b–5 is a very broad anti-fraud statute triggered by any purchase or sale of a corporate security through the facilities of interstate commerce. Rule 10b–5 has been applied to insider trading, to fraudulent transactions between shareholders in a closely held corporation (see Question XV–5), to false press releases issued by corporations which influence the price of a security, to issuance of shares by a corporation at an inadequate price, to a sale of all the stock of a closely held corporation, and to other transactions as well.

XV–7.   Since 1975, the U.S. Supreme Court has decided three cases which have imposed significant limitations on rule 10b–5. First, *Manor v. Blue Chip Stamps* determined that the plaintiff in a rule 10b–5 case must be a purchaser or seller of shares. Second, *Hochfelder* held that a plaintiff must establish scienter as a critical element of a 10b–5 claim. Third, *Santa Fe Industries v. Green* held that rule 10b–5 only applied to misrepresentation, fraud or deceit, and not mere unfairness. Thus, the mere fact that a transaction is unfair does not create a rule 10b–5 liability so long as that unfairness is fully disclosed. These three cases do not affect the "core case" applications of rule 10b–5 to insider trading, fraud in sales of shares, and so forth.

XV–8.   Both of these principles deal with insider trading. However the application of the two is entirely different, though to some extent overlapping. Section 16(b) deals only with offsetting transactions within a six-month period by an officer, director, or 10 per cent shareholder of a corporation that is registered under section 12 of the Securities and Exchange Act of 1934. Rule 10b–5 has none of these limitations. A second major difference is that liability under section 16(b) is automatic and not dependent on the actual profiting from the use of inside information in the transaction. Rule 10b–5 requires the proof of scienter and the establishment of the wrongful use of information.

XV–9.   The theory under which profits are computed on "in-and-out" transactions under section 16(b) is to "squeeze out" all possible profit. To this end the highest sales price is matched against the lowest purchase price within a six-month period; the next highest purchase price is matched with the next lowest; all such transactions are sequentially matched until no profit remains. All losses in this comparison are ignored.

XV–10.   *True within limits.* A shareholder may generally sell her shares for whatever price she can negotiate and if they carry a "control premium" she may keep it. However, the law recognizes that a controlling shareholder has certain duties by reason of her unique position with respect to the corporation. This duty is owed to minority shareholders, preferred shareholders, and creditors who are essentially defenseless. The duty essentially is to make a good faith investigation of possible purchasers in order to avoid selling the shares to a person who may thereafter loot the corporation to the detriment of minority shareholders, preferred shareholders, and creditors. In addition there may be situations where a sale of control breaches other fiduciary duties of a majority shareholder.

XV–11.   The law has not adopted this view even though it has been strongly contended for in several cases. This may be a legislative rather than a judicial issue. In addition, there is a fear that an "all or nothing" approach may prevent desirable transactions from occurring as argued by economists of the "Chicago School".

XV–12.   The issues are the liability under state and federal law of Sider, an officer and director with insider information, for selling his shares and Taken's standing to assert such liability.

(a) *State law.* While the shares in question were registered under the Securities Exchange Act of 1934, the sale by Sider was over-the-counter or impersonal, and without any misrepresentation. Although there was a failure to disclose inside information, Taken was not a shareholder at the time of the nondisclosure. Because the transaction was anonymous and Taken was not a shareholder and thus was owed no fiduciary duty by Sider, the traditional common-law "special facts" and minority rules requiring disclosure by insiders of inside information in a person-to-person transaction to shareholders probably are not helpful.

However, *Diamond v. Oreamuno*, renewed the importance of state insider-trading law. In *Diamond*, the inside information was deemed to be a corporate asset. Any profit gained by corporate personnel through use of this asset was held to belong to the corporation. Therefore, under a *Diamond* approach, Sider would be liable to Dynamic, Inc. for the difference between what the shares were actually sold for and what they would have sold for had the information been public. This claim could be asserted directly by the corporation or derivatively by a shareholder or anyone else with standing to sue. Taken might not be able to maintain a derivative action because of the contemporaneous-share-ownership requirement of Federal Rule of Civil Procedure 23.1 since he was not a shareholder at the time of the transaction unless it can be shown that the wrong was a continuing one. This would be difficult since Taken bought his shares several days after Sider sold his shares.

(b) *Federal law.* The more likely basis of recovery is under rule 10b–5, creating a federal remedy for inside trading. Under rule 10b–5, the use of the mails or a facility of interstate commerce (such as the intrastate use of the telephone system) are the sole jurisdictional requirements; the shares do not have to be listed on an exchange or publicly traded (though the shares of Dynamic, Inc. were). Since Sider is an officer of Dynamic, Inc., his transactions constituted a violation of rule 10b–5 under *Chiarella* and *Dirks*.

An implied private right of action under rule 10b–5 has been found by the courts. Sider has clearly failed to state material information, which, had it been made public, would certainly have dissuaded Taken to buy at the then market price. Moreover, Sider knowingly failed to disclose, satisfying the scienter requirement of *Hochfelder*. While there is no privity between Sider and Taken, several cases have held that the defendant need not have purchased or sold his shares at all and have thus apparently eliminated any doubts that privity is a necessary element.

Sider should thus be liable to the extent of his profits. Presumably other new shareholders are in the same situation as Taken. If each were allowed to recover his full damages, Sider's liability might well be in excess of his profits. The Second Circuit has followed the suggestion of the Federal Securities Code in this regard and limited Sider's liability to the amount of his trading profits. One way of resolving this problem would be for Taken to bring a class action to recover Sider's profits on behalf of all those who innocently purchased shares during the one week prior to the public announcement. By analogy, a corporate fund composed of the profits of insiders and their tippees was created in *SEC v. Texas Gulf Sulphur Co.*

XV–13.   *Yes.* Maggie M. is guilty of insider trading in violation of rule 10b–5. The law firm of Jones and Smith is a temporary insider, so that the information obtained by Maggie M. is inside information. She may have breached a duty to the client in using the information to profit personally; even if not, she breached a duty to her employer, Jones and Smith, and this breach of a duty may be used to find a violation of rule 10b–5.

XV–14.   The only difference that the use of inside information about a takeover bid makes is that the conduct violates an explicit SEC rule, rule 14e–3, prohibiting such use of inside information.

XV–15.   Under the *Dirks* case, trading by the "tippee" in a case such as this is unlawful only if Jones made an improper use of inside information when he divulged it to Smith. This in turn depends on whether Jones obtained a personal benefit from divulging the transaction; an intention to allow Smith to make a profit on the information seems to be the only motive for disclosing the information, and hence it is probable that both Jones and Smith violated rule 10b–5 in this transaction.

XV–16.   *Yes.* This case can be analyzed in a number of ways to reach the result that D breached his fiduciary obligation to the corporation. A controlling shareholder may usually sell a control block of shares for any price he or she can get; however, in disposing of control shares the shareholder owes a fiduciary duty to the corporation and to the minority shareholders not to injure them in so doing. It can be argued that: (a) D's sale of shares was an usurpation of the corporation's business opportunity to use the demand for steel to its advantage in attracting financing and new customers to its business, (b) the sale of the shares at a premium was really an usurpation by D of the grey market premium for steel which was an asset of the corporation, or (c) D's premium on the sale of his shares was actually the sale of control which is a corporate asset which belongs to all shareholders collectively. The best approach is probably (a) or (b) above. The shareholder has breached a duty to the corporation and is liable to account to it for the control premium received by him for the sale of shares. [*Perlman v. Feldmann*, 219 F.2d 173 (2d Cir. 1955).]

PART XVI

XVI–1.   Indemnification permits the corporation to reimburse expenses incurred by officers or directors arising from litigation over their actions as officers or directors. In some instances it also permits payment of judgments, fines, or amounts paid in settlement of such litigation.

XVI–2.   Indemnification is not against public policy if the defendant is absolved of liability or acted in good faith and without engaging knowingly in wrongful conduct. The underlying reason for permitting indemnification is the concern that persons might refuse to serve as directors if they always had to bear the cost of defending against groundless litigation out of their own pockets.

XVI–3.   *Certainly in most cases.* Modern indemnification statutes, however, permit indemnification with court approval and in some cases, such as where the defendant settles or successfully prevails on a procedural defense, where it is possible that the defendant actually engaged in improper conduct.

XVI–4.   "D & O Insurance" refers to directors and officers liability insurance. It is commercially available insurance for some of the liabilities discussed above.

XVI–5.   *No.* D & O insurance only covers insurable risks. Most if not all cases of wrongful conduct are not insurable and are expressly excluded from coverage by policy exclusions.

PART XVII

XVII–1.   The basic test is that the shareholder's purpose must be a proper one.

XVII–2.   It is relatively easy to allege a proper purpose. Additional restrictions are appropriate to prevent "fishing expeditions" and to prevent misuse of valuable corporate information.

XVII–3.   A director has a broader right to inspect than a shareholder since directors have management responsibilities. The right of a director is often stated to be absolute; in fact some courts have limited it if the possibility of misuse of the information is high. The Corporate Governance Project adopts a limited right.

XVII–4.   The traditional view was that no information had to be disclosed. A number of state statutes have been amended in recent years to require some such disclosure, and the trend toward mandatory disclosure appears to be increasing. The RMBCA requires financial and other disclosure. If a corporation is subject to the registration requirements of section 12 of the Securities Exchange Act of 1934, it is subject to the disclosure requirements of the Federal proxy regulations.

XVII–5.   *Yes.* The bylaw is invalid. First, a requirement that three months notice must be given before an inspection of books is permitted is unreasonable. If the books would disclose mismanagement at the time of the notice, the three months thereafter would permit the management to "cook" the books to reflect a proper state of affairs or condition. Also, the two weeks notice given by P would seem to be reasonable. Second, to permit the directors of the corporation to determine on a subjective basis whether or not a purpose of inspection by a shareholder was proper, would nullify the right of inspection in the very cases where inspection would be necessary, that is, when the books would disclose mismanagement on the part of the directors, the persons who could shut off inspection. The restrictions on the right to inspect the books must be limited to time, place and proper purpose, and cannot in substance deny the right or make it exercisable only at the whim of the directors. [*State ex rel. Healy v. Superior Oil Corp.*, 40 Del. 460, 13 A.2d 453 (1940).]

PART XVIII

XVIII–1.   "Direct" litigation is a claim brought by a shareholder for injury as a shareholder; a derivative claim is a claim brought by a shareholder on behalf of the corporation for injury to the corporation which indirectly injures all shareholders.

XVIII–2.   *No.* Some claims may be phrased either as direct and derivative, and there is some judicial disagreement over whether certain types of claims, e. g., suits to compel a declaration of a dividend, should be classified as direct or derivative.

XVIII–3.   A class suit is brought by a member of the class on behalf of the class as a whole. A typical class suit is a direct suit.

XVIII–4.   A derivative suit is a class suit to the extent the plaintiff shareholder serves as a representative of the class of all possible plaintiffs.

XVIII–5.   As a defendant, though in fact it is an involuntary plaintiff.

XVIII–6.   The jurisdiction of the federal courts is not affected by the derivative-direct distinction. A suit brought under the Federal securities acts may be direct or derivative and in either event may or must be brought in

Federal court. A direct or derivative claim based on state law may be brought in Federal court if there is diversity of citizenship or on the theory of pendent jurisdiction.

XVIII–7.   The "contemporaneous ownership" requirement requires the plaintiff to be a shareholder at the time the cause of action arose. In the federal courts it was originally imposed to avoid the collusive creation of diversity jurisdiction. In the state courts it is justified in part because of dislike of derivative litigation and in part to avoid the purchase and sale of lawsuits.

XVIII–8.   In addition to the contemporaneous ownership requirement (see Question XVIII–7), the plaintiff must make a demand on the corporation and its directors, and (in some states) on its shareholders, or show why such demands should be dispensed with. In addition, a plaintiff may have to comply with the state security-for-expenses statute, which may require the posting of a bond. The RMBCA requires a demand on directors (unless excused) but does not require a demand on shareholders or the posting of security-for-expenses.

XVIII–9.   It is widely believed by members of the corporate bar that much derivative litigation is instituted without reasonable cause for the benefit of plaintiffs' attorneys, not for the corporation, or its shareholders.

XVIII–10.   The purpose of security-for-expenses statutes is to prevent strike suits by plaintiffs with nominal interests in the litigation which itself is often without substantive merit. The statute makes it more difficult for small plaintiffs to maintain derivative suits without regard to whether the underlying suit has merit. These statutes are illogical in the sense that they tend to bar meritorious as well as groundless suits. Modern statutes such as RMBCA § 6.40 eliminate these statutes on this ground but substitute other devices in an effort to close off meritless litigation, e. g. by authorizing the court to require a security bond when it feels that the suit is without merit or to impose all litigation costs on the plaintiff if the suit is ultimately found to be without merit.

XVIII–11.   In most states, the effect is two-fold: (1) the plaintiff is compelled to post a bond to secure the defendants' expenses, and (2) if the defendants are successful, the plaintiff may be required to pay their expenses. The proceeds of the bond may be used for this purpose.

XVIII–12.   This statute is "substantive" under the *Erie* doctrine, and therefore is applicable in derivative litigation based on diversity of citizenship and pendent jurisdiction. It is not applicable to claims arising under the Federal securities acts.

XVIII–13.   In most states, no.

XVIII–14.   It depends on the basis of the decision. If it is on the merits it is *res judicata* and binding on all shareholders. If it is based on a defect in the plaintiff's standing to maintain the suit, such as failing to make demand or complying with the security-for-expenses statute, it is not *res judicata* and other shareholders may refile the same suit.

XVIII–15.   In most states, a proposed settlement must be judicially approved before the suit may be dismissed. This is designed to prevent secret settlements.

XVIII–16.   A "strike suit" is a slang term for suits brought solely for their settlement value. The major device now used to prevent such suits is the judicial review of proposed settlements.

XVIII–17.   *Yes.* The test for plaintiffs' expenses is whether the suit yields a substantial benefit to the corporation, not whether it recovers cash, or tangible property.

XVIII–18.   There are a few such cases where the current management were found to be wrongdoers who should not have the use of the proceeds. A distribution directly to shareholders has some of the attributes of a partial or compelled dividend and as a result has not been widely required.

XVIII–19.   *Yes.* In a shareholders' derivative suit any recovery runs in favor of the corporation because it is "in the right of", or on behalf of the corporation that shareholders sue. If the defendants are held liable it must be to the corporation and not to the shareholders. The decree also must protect the defendants against any further suit by the corporation. This cannot be done unless the corporation is a party to the action. Hence X is an indispensable party to the action and if it cannot be served with process the action must be dismissed. Although the practice is to name the beneficiary corporation as a party defendant, in substance it is a party plaintiff; the flexibility of equity allows an affirmative judgment to be entered in favor of one defendant against another. Since X has not been served with process, it is not within the jurisdiction of the court and the action must be dismissed. [*Dean v. Kellogg*, 294 Mich. 200, 292 N.W. 704 (1940).]

XVIII–20.   *No.* In a shareholders' derivative action brought for the benefit of the corporation for damages caused by a breach of fiduciary duties to the corporation, the corporation is entitled to receive the entire amount of the damages suffered by it. The identity of the shareholders at the time is not a matter of proof in the action. It is the corporation as an entity which has been harmed and to whom the damages are to be rendered. [*Norte & Co. v. Huffines*, 416 F.2d 1189 (2d Cir. 1969).]

A few courts have permitted the shareholders to recover individually in a derivative suit on the theory that the persons now in control of the corporation should not be permitted to control the proceeds of the recovery since they participated in the wrongful conduct. Certainly, however, the *defendants* should not be able to restrict their recovery on this theory.

PART XIX

XIX–1.   *False.* Amendments are permitted without limitation since in most states there are no vested rights in modern corporation law. Shareholders are protected from adverse amendments by class voting (referred to as "voting by voting groups" in the RMBCA), and by the right of dissent and appraisal.

XIX–2.   In a merger one of the two combining corporations survive, in a consolidation both combining corporations disappear into a third, new corporation.

The Revised Model Business Corporation Act eliminates the concept of consolidations because they are not used in practice. It is usually advantageous for tax or other reasons for one of the present entities to be the survivor; if not, it is customary to create a new entity and merge the other entities into it.

XIX–3.   In an ordinary merger, the shareholders of the disappearing corporation receive shares in the continuing entity. In a cash merger, some of them receive cash or other property rather than shares of the surviving corporation.

XIX–4.   A "short form merger" is a merger of a subsidiary into a parent corporation subject to special statutory procedural rules applicable to this type of amalgamation. See RMBCA § 11.04.

XIX–5.   The Internal Revenue Code uses the alphabetical designations for certain types of amalgamations. This terminology is so useful that it has spread beyond the tax area. The principal designations are:

a. Class A—statutory merger;

b. Class B—an acquisition of the stock of the acquired corporation;

c. Class C—an acquisition of the assets of the acquired corporation.

XIX–6. They are often functional equivalents that may have different legal and tax implications.

XIX–7. A "de facto merger" is a nonstatutory amalgamation of two corporations that a court concludes is (a) the functional equivalent of a statutory merger and (b) participants should be accorded the rights they would have had in a statutory merger.

XIX–8. "Appraisal rights" (or "dissenters' rights," as they are called in the RMBCA) allow a dissenting shareholder to obtain the value of his or her shares in a judicial proceeding rather than go along with the merger or other transaction that gave rise to the appraisal right.

XIX–9. In most states, shareholder approval is required if the sale is not in the ordinary course of business.

XIX–10. A "going private" transaction involves the elimination of the public shareholders of a corporation through a cash merger or similar transaction. Such a transaction is widely believed to be susceptible of unfairness; the only special legal requirements are imposed by the SEC which requires a statement by management as to their opinion of the fairness of the transaction.

XIX–11. A "leveraged buyout" is a transaction by which an outside group acquires all the shares or assets of a public corporation. Usually incumbent management participates in the outside group and thereafter continues to manage the business. Most of the purchase price is in the form of debt (often "junk bonds"). The economic advantage of these transactions is a matter of controversy, though tax benefits appear to be a major attraction of such transactions.

XIX–12. *False.* Because of the cost of a judicial proceeding, the long delays, and the formidable litigation power of large corporations intent on keeping the appraised value as low as possible, dissenters' rights are often viewed as an unattractive remedy.

XIX–13. *No.* Since the state statute does not provide for mandatory cumulative voting, the shareholders may properly abandon the system without unanimous consent. Although the right to vote cumulatively is a valuable one, the corporation law that allows amendment of the articles is a part of P's contract with the corporation and he or she may not complain if the action is taken in the proper form with the requisite majority. [*Maddock v. Vorclone Corp.*, 17 Del.Ch. 39, 147 A. 255 (1929).]

XIX–14. *No.* The transfer of the franchise to another city is not a sale of all or substantially all the corporation's assets. The franchise remains an asset of the corporation with all of its rights and privileges intact. The corporation will continue to operate with substantially the same assets. [*Murphy v. Washington American League Base Ball Club, Inc.*, 293 F.2d 522 (D.C.Cir. 1961).]

XIX–15. *No.* A merger of a corporation with its wholly-owned subsidiary may eliminate preferred shareholders' rights to accumulated dividends if the terms of the merger agreement are fair and equitable in the circumstances. State law allows but does not require a shareholder objecting to the terms of a merger to obtain the value of his shares. Dissenting shareholders are thus not put to an election by the statute of State Y. While "the exercise of the statutory right of merger is always subject to nullification for fraud," here P has alleged only that the allocation between the old preferred and common shareholders is so unfair that it amounts to fraud. P has alleged no misrepresentation, concealment or deception. "When fraud of this nature is charged, the unfairness must be of such character and must be so clearly demonstrated as to impel the conclusion that it emanates from acts of bad faith or a reckless indifference to the rights of others interested, rather than from an honest error of judgment." [*Porges v. Vadsco Sales Corp.*, 27 Del.Ch. 127, 32 A.2d 148 (1943); *Barrett v. Denver Tramway Corp.*, 53 F.Supp. 198 (D.Del. 1944); *Bove v. Community Hotel Corp.*, 105 R.I. 36, 249 A.2d 89 (1969).]

APPENDIX C

TEXT CORRELATION CHART

Topic in Outline		Hamilton Corpora- tions (3rd Ed.) (1986)	Henn Corporations (2d Ed.) (1986)	Jennings and Buxbaum Corporations (5th Ed.) (1979)	Vagts Basic Corporation Law (3d Ed.) (1988)	Cary and Eisenberg Corporations (6th Ed.) (1988)
I.	Corporation Law in General	128–155	1–48	70–93	1–17	91–97
II.	Formation of Corporation	156–182	81–117 137–154	93–101 110–136	76–79	97–108
III.	Preincorporation Transactions	182–218	118–136 155–175	101–110	98–100	108–115 130–151
IV.	Piercing the Corporate Veil	219–250	176–227	141–153 976–1009	79–98	151–191
V.	Financing the Corporation	251–377	228–264	768–846 893–976	131–195 637–684	1399–1601 1294–1398
VI.	The Statutory Scheme of Management of Control	378–419 514–518	265–383	153–200		197–248
VII.	Shareholders' Meetings, Voting and Control Agreements	419–472	282–331 610–627	230–247, 261–287 334–417	362–402	241–248 339–378 402–414
VIII.	Directors	543–570 472–479	332–365 528–530	200–230	196–208	206–228
IX.	Officers	479–492	366–383 521–528	136–141	287–361	228–241
X.	Management of the Closely Held Corporation	378–518	587–670	334–441	751–798	339–470

Topic in Outline	Hamilton Corporations (3rd Ed.) (1986)	Henn Corporations (2d Ed.) (1986)	Jennings and Buxbaum Corporations (5th Ed.) (1979)	Vagts Basic Corporation Law (3rd Ed.) (1988)	Cary and Eisenberg Corporations (6th Ed.) (1988)
XI. Management in the Publicly Held Corporation	519–570	671–743			192–196
XII. Proxy Regulation	571–622	285–317 698–721	287–334	403–443	270–313
XIII. Proxy Fights, Tender Offers and Other Contests for Control	776–858	924–973	290–308 111–1157	704–750	314–328 1204–1268
XIV. Fiduciary Duties of Directors, Officers and Shareholders	633–775	384–520	441–618	209–286 443–455	471–655 690–719
XV. Duties Relating to the Purchase or Sale of Shares	859–1073	464–470	543–598	536–636 744–829	720–927
XVI. Indemnification and Liability Insurance	1115–1128	1114–1138	746–768	526–535	1030–1047
XVII. Inspection of Books and Records	623–632	321–330	247–261		249–264
XVIII. Shareholder Litigation	1074–1115	974–1113	618–746	455–535	928–1087
XIX. Organic Changes	1129–1144	830–923	1009–1108	684–703	1088–1203 1268–1293

Topic in Outline	Frey, Choper, Leech, Morris: Cases and Materials on Corporations (2nd Ed.) (1977)	Henn & Alexander Law of Corporations (3rd Ed.) (1983)	Hamilton Law of Corporations (Nutshell) (2d Ed.) (1987)	Solomon, Schwartz & Bauman Corporations (2d Ed.) (1988)
I. Corporations Law in General	1–25	36–47; 125–138 144–152	1–14	1–8 9–32 33–53
II. Formation of Corporation	25–33	163–201; 266–310 316–324; 467–486	29–59	128–167
III. Preincorporation Transactions	33–49, 77–105	236–264	60–80	134–144
IV. Piercing the Corporate Veil	49–77	344–375	81–99	238–269
V. Financing the Corporation	781–835, 1013–1143	376–463	100–153	168–237 447–501
VI. The Statutory Scheme of Management Control	105–397	486–492; 550–555 562–564	154–174	270–272
VII. Shareholders' Meetings, Voting and Control Agreements	397–507 519–540	487–550	175–216	296–319
VIII. Directors	105–133	551–585	217–231	289–296
IX. Officers	105–133	586–610	232–248	272–289
X. Management of the Closely Held Corporation	519–653	694–783	249–266	342–446

Topic in Outline		Frey, Choper, Leech, Morris: Cases and Materials on Corporations (2nd Ed.) (1977)	Henn & Alexander Law of Corporations (3rd Ed.) (1983)	Hamilton Law of Corporations (Nutshell) (2nd Ed.) (1987)	Solomon, Schwartz & Bauman Corporations (2d Ed.) (1988)	
XI.	Management in the Publicly Held Corporation	105–397	785–867	267–301	1313–1381	20–21
XII.	Proxy Regulation	427–507	518–528; 743; 781	280–291	502–590	13
XIII.	Proxy Fights, Tender Offers and Other Contests for Control	427–507	818–821; 847–849 966–967	291–301	996–1167	18
XIV.	Fiduciary Duties of Directors, Officers and Shareholders	147–241	625–628; 644–663 724–725	302–368	591–746	14
XV.	Duties Relating to the Purchase or Sale of Shares	856–1013	644–651 823–836	338–361 656–690	1168–1312	19
XVI.	Indemnification and Liability Insurance	767–781	1144–1146	361–367	908–925	16
XVII.	Inspection of Books and Records	133–147	536–546; 578–581	369–379	319–326	10
XVIII.	Shareholder Litigation	653–781	1020–1146	405–420	809–939	16
XIX.	Organic Changes	1143–1281	973–1018	421–440	940–995	17

APPENDIX D

COMPREHENSIVE EXAM

Time Allowed: Three Hours.

INSTRUCTIONS

1. This examination consists of five questions to be answered in three hours. The questions will be weighted in accordance with the approximate times set forth for each question. The total times add up to two hours and forty-five minutes; the remaining fifteen minutes may be used as you see fit. Subparts of questions will be weighted in accordance with the percentages set forth within the questions.

2. Unless otherwise specified, you are to assume that each corporation is a corporation incorporated under the Revised Model Business Corporation Act, and that all relevant action takes place within a state that has adopted the Revised Model Business Corporation Act and Uniform Partnership Act in their entirety. You may assume that the state has adopted either the Uniform Limited Partnership Act (1916) or the Revised Uniform Limited Partnership Act (1976).

    Please note that in question II you are to assume that the jurisdiction has adopted certain statutory provisions based on earlier versions of the Model Business Corporation Act set forth below.

3. Be sure to answer the specific questions that are asked.

500

4. If you feel additional facts are necessary to resolve an issue, please specify what additional facts you believe to be necessary and why they are significant.

5. Quality, not quantity, is desired. Think through your answer before you begin to write.

6. Write legibly.

7. In connection with Question II, you should assume that the state in question has adopted the following statutory provisions:

MODEL BUSINESS CORPORATION ACT (1969)

§ 15. Authorized Shares. Each corporation shall have power to create and issue the number of shares stated in its articles of incorporation. Such shares may be divided into one or more classes, any or all of which classes may consist of shares with par value or shares without par value, with such designations, preferences, limitations, and relative rights as shall be stated in the articles of incorporation. The articles of incorporation may limit or deny the voting rights of or provide special voting rights for the shares of any class to the extent not inconsistent with the provisions of this Act. * * *

§ 18. Consideration for Shares. Shares having a par value may be issued for such consideration expressed in dollars, not less than the par value thereof, as shall be fixed from time to time by the board of directors.

Shares without par value may be issued for such consideration expressed in dollars as may be fixed from time to time by the board of directors * * *.

§ 19. Payment for Shares. The consideration for the issuance of shares may be paid, in whole or in part, in cash, in other property, tangible or intangible, or in labor or services actually performed for the corporation. When payment of the consideration for which shares are to be issued shall have been received by the corporation, such shares shall be deemed to be fully paid and non-assessable.

Neither promissory notes nor future services shall constitute payment or part payment for the issuance of shares of a corporation.

In the absence of fraud in the transaction, the judgment of the board of directors or the shareholders, as the case may be, as to the value of the consideration received for shares shall be conclusive.

§ 21. Determination of Amount of Stated Capital. In case of the issuance by a corporation of shares having a par value, the consideration received therefor shall constitute stated capital to the extent of the par value of such shares, and the excess, if any, of such consideration shall constitute capital surplus.

In case of the issuance by a corporation of shares without par value, the entire consideration received therefor shall constitute stated capital unless the corporation shall determine as provided in this section that only a part thereof shall be stated capital. Within a period of sixty days after the issuance of any shares without par value, the board of directors may allocate to capital surplus any portion of the consideration received for the issuance of such shares. No such allocation shall be made of any portion of the consideration received for shares without par value having a preference in the assets of the corporation in the event of involuntary liquidation except the amount, if any, of such consideration in excess of such preference. * * *

§ 22. Expenses of Organization, Reorganization and Financing. The reasonable charges and expenses of organization or reorganization of a corporation, and the reasonable expenses of and compensation for the sale or underwriting of its shares, may be paid or allowed by such corporation out of the consideration received by it in payment for its shares without thereby rendering such shares not fully paid or assessable.

§ 25. Liability of Subscribers and Shareholders. A holder of or subscriber to shares of a corporation shall be under no obligation to the corporation or its creditors with respect to such shares other than the obligation to pay to the corporation the full consideration for which such shares were issued or to be issued. * * *

I. (30 minutes)

On February 1, 1984, Dennison Corporation (Dennison) owned 554,000 shares of common stock of General Baking Company, a large publicly held company. Dennison's block constituted about 33% of General Baking's common stock and gave Dennison effective control of General Baking. The president and seven of the twelve directors of General Baking were persons designated by Dennison.

Early in February, Goldfield Company approached Dennison with an offer to purchase the General Baking shares owned by Dennison. Negotiations followed and on March 10, 1984 an agreement was entered into by which Dennison agreed to sell 655,000 shares of General Baking to Goldfield at $12.50 per share. During the period February–March the market price of General Baking was in the $8.00–$10.00 range. Under this agreement Dennison committed itself to sell 101,000 more shares of General Baking than it owned. Beginning the next day, Dennison began lining up additional shareholders to sell their shares in General Baking. It privately communicated the offer to selected shareholders, including shareholders with whom Dennison had banking or business connections and with whom Dennison desired to curry favor. Ultimately, sixteen such shareholders agreed to sell an aggregate of 101,000 additional shares to Goldfield at $12.00 per share. Among these sellers were Dennison's investment banker, its insurance company, and several individuals. The 655,000 shares were sold to Goldfield on March 19 and the transaction was publicly announced on March 20.

Ferr is a shareholder of General Baking who was unaware of the Dennison-Goldfield transaction. On the morning of March 19, he sold his General Baking shares on the open market at the then current price of $8.75. Does he have a claim against anyone as a result of the Dennison-Goldfield transaction announced the next day? Would his position be better off or worse off if he had not sold his shares on March 19 but retained them until suit was filed?

II.   (60 minutes)

You are practicing law in the community of Clear Lake. Your client is Peter Smith, a successful general physician in Clear Lake. Smith has been highly successful in practice; he is now in his late 50s and has increasingly devoted his attention to a variety of business matters, in which he has enjoyed a considerable degree of financial success, rather than to the practice of medicine.

Peter Smith asks you to represent him in connection with a new venture to operate a lumber yard and hardware store in Clear Lake on a tract of land owned by Robert Realtor. There is presently no similar facility in Clear Lake. The participants in the venture, and their contemplated contributions, are described as follows in a memorandum prepared by Allen Alert, a promoter of the venture and a person known not to have substantial financial resources:

Proposed Alert Lumber Yard and Hardware Store Venture

Contributor	Form of contribution	Interest in Venture
Allen Alert	Promoter; Yard & store manager; 3 year minimim contract	30% of stock plus $36,000 salary per year
Peter Smith	$200,000 cash or ½ as surety	50% of stock
Robert Realtor	Ten year lease on yard; venture to have option to purchase at appraised value at end of lease	20% of stock; annual rental at commercial rate to be negotiated

A. [25 percent] You are advised by Alert that his economic projections indicate that it will take the lumber yard at least eighteen months to break even because of advertising and other start-up costs. Neither Smith nor Realtor are willing to assume any personal liability for the obligations of the lumber yard (over and above their commitments set forth in the original plan) and wish it to be made clear that their sole financial responsibilities are as described in the original proposal. You are asked whether the venture should be in the form of a corporation or a partnership. What choices are there? What form should be selected and why?

B. [75 percent] It has been decided to form a corporation. Upon your advice Smith insists that he must have the power (a) to name a majority of the board of directors in the event Alert and Realtor disagree with him, and (b) to buy out Alert's interest in the corporation and cancel his employment contract at any time Smith feels it desirable to do so during the first three years of the venture for a total payment of $36,000. Alert and Realtor reluctantly agree to these conditions.

The state you practice in has the traditional par value provisions set forth in the instructions to this examination. Plan the capitalization of the new corporation in light of all the corporate and tax goals set forth or implicit in the foregoing questions, I and IIA. The plan you set forth should include the class or classes of shares to be created, the number of shares of each class to be authorized, the number of shares of each class to be issued, the consideration for the shares, when they are to be issued, any tax elections, and any other pertinent provisions in articles of incorporation, bylaws, or agreements necessary to allow the participants in the lumber yard venture to enjoy the fruits of this venture as contemplated.

III. (15 minutes)

Articles of incorporation have been filed for the lumber yard venture. By chance you look through a weekly newsletter put out by the Clear Lake Board of Realtors and discover that Robert Realtor has placed an advertisement offering to sell to his fellow realtors all or a portion of his shares in the contemplated lumber yard and hardware store at a price to be negotiated. The closing of the transactions relating to the lumber yard is set for next week. Does the placing of this advertisement create any problems for the closing?

IV. (30 minutes)

International Paint Company is a publicly held Delaware corporation. It has offices in forty states, including Texas. Its sales are over $1,000,000,000 per year. It has major manufacturing and distribution centers for its products in New York City, New Orleans, and San Francisco. In 1975 engineers employed by International Paint Company developed a family of new industrial coatings. These coatings were suitable for use on oil and gas pipelines and other commercial uses where protection against corrosion was of primary importance. Because International Paint Company had no prior experience dealing specifically with these industries, it decided to create a wholly owned subsidiary, International Paint Company of California, to develop this business. All rights to the new coatings were assigned to the California subsidiary, which was initially capitalized by International Paint Company at $100,000,000. The California Company built a new plant in Pomona, California, to manufacture the coatings, and proceeded to market them on a world-wide scale. Unlike International Paint Company's other products, the industrial coatings manufactured and sold by the California subsidiary are sold directly to contractors and other ultimate end users and shipped directly from the California plant. The California subsidiary is operated entirely independently of the parent company in all financial and marketing respects; it has enjoyed a profitable operation each year after 1977. One of the most popular items in its line of industrial coatings is known as "Inter-Trop Red 50."

The California subsidiary, with the knowledge of International Paint, markets its industrial coatings under a variety of labels, all of which prominently use the name, "International Paint Company" or "International Paint Company, Inc." without the addition of "of California". This practice was originally adopted because of the belief of the executives of the California subsidiary that the use of the well known name "International Paint Company" might improve the willingness of industrial users to try the new coatings. The earliest labels contain the statement, "Offices in New York, New Orleans, and San Francisco," because it was believed that the subsidiary might use the parent's distribution system. Newer labels contain the notation "Manufactured by International Paint Company of California, Pomona, California."

Alfred Nelson was injured in 1978 when he inhaled toxic fumes while painting over a weld at a construction site in west Texas. At the time he was injured, Nelson was using "Inter-Trop Red 50." The label on the can Nelson was using was of the earlier type: it carried the name "International Paint Company, Inc.," and listed addresses for the company in New York, New Orleans, and San Francisco. Also present on the label was the trademark, "International Paint Company." There was no reference to the California subsidiary.

Nelson obtained workmen's compensation payments from his employer. The workmen's compensation system prohibits an employee from suing his employer for job-related injuries but does not prevent an employee from suing a negligent third person. Four days before the statute of limitations expired on Nelson's possible claim against third parties, he filed suit against "International Paint Company, Inc." in federal district court in Texas on the basis of diversity of citizenship. Service was made on an employee of the parent corporation at its Texas office. After determining that the coating was in fact manufactured and sold by its California subsidiary, International Paint Company moves for summary judgment on the ground that it was not responsible for the claimed injury. You represent Nelson. What theories might you set forth in opposition to the motion for summary judgment, and what are the chances of their success?   See *Nelson v. International Paint Co., Inc.*, 734 F.2d 1084 (5th Cir.1984).

V.   (30 minutes)

Oscar Wyatt, Jr. is the founder, chairman of the board of directors and chief executive officer of Coastal Corporation (Coastal), a publicly held corporation engaged in the business of exploring, producing and processing oil and gas and other resources.   WJS Shipping Company (WJS) is a partnership in which Carl Wyatt, Oscar's twenty-five year old son, owns a controlling interest.

In April, 1978, Coastal purchased an oil tanker, "Coastal Kansas," from a third person.   About a year later, the Coast Guard found that the tanker was not seaworthy.   In March, 1980, Coastal entered into a sale and leaseback agreement for the tanker with WJS.   WJS purchased the tanker for $1,000,000 in cash and agreed to make the necessary repairs, originally estimated at $9,000,000 but actually costing $10,000,000.   According to the leaseback, Coastal agreed to lease back the tanker for ten years for $1,970,000 per year.   Oscar Wyatt did not participate in the negotiation of this sale and leaseback arrangement on behalf of Coastal; Carl Wyatt represented WJS in the negotiations, and was known to be the CEO's son by the Coastal employees involved in the negotiation.

The sale and leaseback arrangement was first presented to the executive committee of Coastal and then to the board of directors of Coastal for final approval.   The executive committee consisted of five directors, all of whom were employees of Coastal; Oscar Wyatt was its chairman but did not attend the meeting of the executive committee at which the proposed sale and leaseback was discussed.   The committee concluded unanimously that the terms of the sale and leaseback were fair, that the transaction was a desirable one for Coastal, and recommended its approval.   The recommendation of the Executive Committee was presented by its vice chairman to the full board of directors; Oscar Wyatt was present during the presentation of this transaction, but did not comment on it and abstained from the vote.   The board approved the transaction upon the recommendation of the Executive Committee unanimously and without discussion.

A shareholder of Coastal brings a derivative suit against Coastal and Oscar Wyatt claiming that the transaction with WJS should be set aside.   What legal standards are applicable to the evaluation of this transaction?   May the corporation successfully move for summary judgment on the ground that the transaction was lawfully approved and is valid on its face?

END OF EXAM

APPENDIX E

TABLE OF CASES

†